Victorious Wives

*The Disguised Heroine in
19th-Century Malay Syair*

Victorious Wives

The Disguised Heroine in 19th-Century Malay Syair

Mulaika Hijjas

NUS PRESS
SINGAPORE

THE MALAYSIAN BRANCH OF
THE ROYAL ASIATIC SOCIETY

© 2011 Mulaika Hijjas

Published by:

NUS Press
National University of Singapore
AS3-01-02, 3 Arts Link
Singapore 117569
Fax: (65) 6774-0652
E-mail: nusbooks@nus.edu.sg
Website: http://www.nus.edu.sg/nuspress

and

Malaysian Branch of the Royal Asiatic Society
4B (2nd floor) Jalan Kemuja, off Jalan Bangsar
59000 Kuala Lumpur
Malaysia
Tel: 603-2283-5345
Fax: 603-2282-2458
Website: http://www.mbras.org.my

ISBN 978-9971-69-526-2 (Paper)

ISBN 978-967-9948-49-3 (Paper)

All rights reserved. This book, or parts thereof, may not be reproduced in any form or by any means, electronic or mechanical, including photocopying, recording or any information storage and retrieval system now known or to be invented, without written permission from the Publisher.

National Library Board, Singapore Cataloguing-in-Publication Data

Hijjas, Mulaika.
 Victorious wives : the disguised heroine in 19th-century Malay syair / Mulaika Hijjas. – Singapore : NUS Press, c2010.
 p. cm.
 Includes bibliographical references and index.
 ISBN-13 : 978-9971-69-526-2 (pbk.)

 1. Malay poetry – 19th century – History and criticism. 2. Women in literature. I. Title.

PL5136
899.2810093522 -- dc22   OCN607857791

Perpustakaan Negara Malaysia Cataloguing-in-Publication Data

Mulaika Hijjas
 Victorious wives : the disguised heroine in 19th-century Malay syair / Mulaika Hijjas.
 Includes index
 Bibliography: p. 304-316
 ISBN 978-967-9948-49-3
 1. Malay poetry – 19th century – History and criticism. 2. Women in literature. I. Title.
 899.2309

Typeset by: International Typesetters Pte Ltd
Printed by: Vinlin Press Sdn Bhd

To my parents, Angela and Hijjas

Contents

Abbreviations		ix
Acknowledgements		xi
Introduction	Romantic *Syair* in 19th-Century Riau	1
Chapter 1	Not Just Fryers of Bananas and Sweet Potatoes: Women in the Malay Literary Community	29
Chapter 2	The Best Ones Make You Cry: Genre, Gender and Catharsis	48
Chapter 3	Ruling Passions: The Control of Emotion in *Syair Siti Zuhrah* and *Syair Sultan Yahya*	75
Chapter 4	From Battlefield to Bedroom: War and Marriage in *Syair Siti Zubaidah* and *Syair Sultan Abdul Muluk*	109
Chapter 5	Calculating Women, Foolish Men: Reason in *Syair Siti Dhawiyyah* and *Syair Saudagar Bodoh*	142
Conclusion	The Heritage of the Disguised Heroine *Syair*	170
Appendix I	Women Authors and Copyists	181
Appendix II	List of Manuscripts	183
Appendix III	Extracts and Translations	187

Notes	276
Bibliography	304
Index	316

Abbreviations

Titles of the primary texts are abbreviated in the notes as follows:

SDh: *Syair Siti Dhawiyyah*
SSAM: *Syair Sultan Abdul Muluk*
SSB: *Syair Saudagar Bodoh*
SSY: *Syair Sultan Yahya*
SSZub: *Syair Siti Zubaidah*
SSZuh: *Syair Siti Zuhrah*

Other abbreviations used are as follows:

Bijdragen: *Bijdragen tot de Taal-, Land- en Volkenkunde*
BL: British Library
BN: Bibliothèque Nationale de France
DBP: Dewan Bahasa dan Pustaka
IMW: *Indonesia and the Malay World*
JMBRAS: *Journal of the Malaysian Branch of the Royal Asiatic Society*
JSBRAS: *Journal of the Straits Branch of the Royal Asiatic Society*
KITLV: Koninklijk Instituut voor Taal-, Land- en Volkenkunde
PNM: Perpustakaan Negara Malaysia
PNRI: Perpustakaan Nasional Republik Indonesia
RIMA: *Review of Malaysian and Indonesian Affairs*
UBL: Universiteitsbibliotheek Leiden

Acknowledgements

The support of the School of Oriental and African Studies, which granted me a Research Student Fellowship, and of Universities UK, for the Overseas Research Student Award, enabled me to carry out the research and writing that led to my PhD, and ultimately, this book. The British Academy's Postdoctoral Research Fellowship is allowing me to take my research further.

I benefited from the kind assistance of librarians at SOAS, the British Library, the Bibliothèque Nationale de France, the University of Leiden Library, and the National Library of Indonesia.

I am grateful to NUS Press for giving me the opportunity to publish my work, and to Paul Kratoska and Eunice Low for their assistance and patience. The comments of my examiners, Peter Riddell and Ulrich Kratz, and of the Press' two anonymous reviewers have been invaluable in improving the manuscript.

A version of Chapter 1 was published in the *Journal of Southeast Asian Studies* 41, 1 (February 2010), and I am grateful to the journal's editors for permission to reproduce sections of that article here.

I am indebted to Vladimir Braginsky for his great generosity with his time and wealth of knowledge. I also received much appreciated help and encouragement from Annabel Gallop, Pauline Khng, Rachel Harrison, Ben Murtagh, Din Sani and Justin Watkins.

May Jurilla, Sutanuka Ghosh and Sarah Hicks provided much needed comradeship through the long haul of the dissertation.

Finally, special thanks are due to my parents, my sister Bilqis, and to Vaughan Pilikian.

Hutang emas boleh dibayar, hutang budi dibawa mati.

Mulaika Hijjas
London, England
July 2010

Introduction

Romantic *Syair* in 19th-Century Riau

A group of women are gathered in a room, seated on mats on the plank floor, babies and children asleep on their laps, empty cups and plates pushed aside, and a single flaring oil lamp sending its twist of smoke up to the ceiling and a faltering light onto the pages of a manuscript. One woman is bent over the text, her voice rising and falling according to a measured cadence as she recites the words, and the only other sounds are those of the night insects outside the house. It is the crux of the story: the young prince — languidly graceful, beautiful to men and women alike, all-conquering in war — has defeated his infidel enemies and liberated from their clutches another less fortunate royal scion. The two stand face to face, the erstwhile captive full of gratitude and admiration for his rescuer, the radiant exemplar of all manly virtues. And yet there is something uncanny in the figure of this valiant knight, something familiar that the newly freed prince cannot quite identify. A pearl-like tear rolls down the burnished golden cheek of the hero, answered by the unrestrained weeping of the women gathered in the dim room who know, as the rescued prince does not, that his saviour is none other than his long-lost wife in disguise.

The scene in which the heroine disguised as a man rescues her husband but remains unrecognised by him is at the heart of some of the most popular Malay literary works of the 19th century. The scene of *syair* recitation described above must have taken place on countless evenings in homes across the Malay world.[1] The *syair* is a narrative verse form of rhyming quatrains that was especially prominent in Malay literature in the 19th century. While there are a plethora of kinds of *syair* treating a great diversity of topics, a small but significant group of texts featured a female protagonist who puts on masculine disguise in order to rescue a male relative, most commonly her husband. These may be termed the disguised heroine *syair*, and include *Syair Sultan Abdul Muluk*, *Syair Siti Zubaidah* and *Syair Sultan Yahya*, three of the most frequently republished titles of the boom years of Malay lithographic printing.[2] These texts, together with the best-selling didactic work *Syair Siti Dhawiyyah* and the less well-known *Syair Saudagar Bodoh* and *Syair Siti Zuhrah*, are the subject of this book. Five of these *syair* feature the disguised heroine plot, and several are known to have been composed by women, a rarity in a literary tradition where the relatively few texts by named authors are almost all attributed to men. Moreover, since these *syair* were primarily intended for female audiences, they provide a rare insight into the lives of 19th-century Malay women, especially those at the court of the Yamtuan Muda of Riau on the tiny island of Penyengat, the probable home of all six texts. The singular role of women in these *syair* — as authors, audience and protagonists — has been repeatedly noted by scholars, from the Dutch manuscript collector, H.C. Klinkert, in 1861, to the leading Malaysian expert on Riau literature, Abu Hassan Sham, in 1993.[3] Several of these works, especially *Syair Siti Zubaidah* and *Syair Sultan Abdul Muluk*, were well known into the 20th century, as *bangsawan* theatrical productions and even as films. Yet these *syair* have never been discussed as a distinctive corpus of women's literature from the Malay world, as this book sets out to do.

The disguised heroine *syair* are popular romances that were widely read and read for pleasure. While they could and often did contain elements of social or religious instruction, the transmission of such didactic messages was not the primary intent of texts such as these. Indeed, as we shall see, the messages covertly transmitted by the disguised heroine *syair* tend to challenge the roles for women set out in explicitly didactic or religious texts of the period. *Syair Siti Dhawiyyah* is one such didactic work, disguised as a romance, partaking of many of the same literary conventions as the disguised heroine *syair* and providing an illuminating comparison. Romantic *syair* meet Northrop Frye's tongue-in-cheek but apt definition of popular literature as "what people read without guidance from their betters".⁴ Romantic *syair* and *hikayat* were often read against the express guidance of readers' "betters": guardians of religion and arbiters of morals frequently disparaged such reading matter.⁵ These *syair* conjure not the world as it is or as it should be but an alternative realm of the imagination, and as such, they were condemned by thinkers and avidly consumed by audiences of their time. Of course, the relatively low literacy levels of the 19th-century Malay world meant that these *syair* would not have circulated as widely as oral stories or other forms of folk culture.⁶ For every literate reciter of a manuscript, however, there may have been many more illiterate auditors, swelling the numbers of those who enjoyed these texts. What is more, as soon as lithographic reproduction made the texts easily and cheaply available, romantic *syair* were taken up by far greater audiences. These lithographed versions did not differ in form or content from their manuscript predecessors, suggesting a continuity of literary tastes across historical time, geographical space and social classes.

In spite of the popularity of these *syair* — both in terms of the numbers of extant manuscripts and lithographs, and in terms of their demotic content — they have been little studied. Scholarship on the literature of the Malay chirographic tradition has focused on those works deemed to be of historical or political significance, or of outstanding literary merit. The Riau romantic *syair* featuring active female protagonists may not be able to claim membership of either of these categories, yet they do offer rewards that are not to be found elsewhere: a view into the inner life of the palace women who were the authors and audiences of these texts. Writing about the paucity of sources for gender history in Southeast Asia, Barbara Watson Andaya laments that on "the rare occasions when written material can be confidently ascribed to a woman, the cultural formulae which governed textual production obscures virtually any evidence of female involvement".⁷ This is not so in the case of the disguised heroine *syair*: the cultural formulae or conventions which governed their production are themselves an indication that the texts did not merely involve women, but were by and for them. The composer's individual voice is certainly obscured by the conventionality of the form — it is almost impossible to differentiate between the conventional verses of lamentation in, say, Daeng Wuh's *syair* and Raja Kalsum's — but the plots, characterisation and themes strongly imply a feminine viewpoint. In contrast, writing of old Javanese poetry, Creese notes that the *kakawin* poet's view of the inner court is almost exclusively male, and frequently voyeuristic. *Kakawin* rely heavily on masculine discourse and utilize metaphorical language and images that are overwhelmingly masculine in tone, particularly in the violence of the depiction of sexual relationships, the ongoing imagery of the defeat and death of women, their bodily reactions to the changes wrought by the transition from childhood to physical maturity, as well as the lack of attention to male embodiment.[8]

In the Riau disguised heroine *syair*, the reverse is true. Men are consistently depicted as less rational and less capable than women. The heroines are acknowledged as superior to their husbands, brothers and fathers in intellect, morality and military prowess. Sex does not involve violence. The heroines do return to the cloistered world of the palace once their great deeds are done, but there is no doubt that here, as in an early English novel that was wildly popular among women readers, "the direction of the plot ... outrageously flatters the imagination of readers of one sex and severely disciplines that of the other".[9] As the preferred reading of the women's quarters of the palace, the disguised heroine *syair* present distinctively feminine fictions.

I. Romantic *Syair* in Malay Literature

The origins of the *syair* form have been much debated, but the earliest and perhaps the most consummate example is the late 16th- or early 17th-century Sufi poetry of Hamzah Fansuri.[10] By the 19th century, the zenith of the *syair*'s popularity, the form was used not only for religious but also romantic allegories (*Syair Buah-Buahan*, *Syair Ikan Terubuk*, *Syair Kumbang Mengindera*), reportage (*Syair Kampung Gelam Terbakar*, *Syair Sultan Mahmud*, *Syair Inggeris Menyerang Kota*), and romantic narratives of all kinds (*Syair Bidasari*, *Syair Selindung Delima*, *Syair Sinyor Kosta*). The *syair* was indeed as Hooykaas remarked, "suitable for any occasion"; the multi-purpose form that could be used to convey a Malay scribe's parting advice to a Dutch philologist as well as a lover's complaint or Sufi allegory.[11] It appears that the romantic *syair* may be close kin to the teasing songs performed by *biduan*, or female court singers, such as Dang Saja and Dang Merdu in *Hikayat Hang Tuah*, and the erotic songs from which Hamzah Fansuri was at pains to distance himself.[12] That the *syair* was thought of as a genre of song is suggested by the description of a magical garden in one manuscript of the *Sejarah Melayu*:

> All the birds in the garden began to make sounds of various kinds: some like a person whistling, some like a person playing the flute, some like a person reciting *syair*, some like a person reciting verses, some like a person reciting couplets, some like a person reciting aphorisms, [and] the flowering lime cheered, the orchid cried out, the pomegranate smiled and the rose recited *pantun*.[13]

Music and voice are central to the aesthetic experience of the *syair*, and absent from the manuscript pages. Reading the lyrics of ballads or operatic libretti is a pallid experience compared to listening to a recording and even more so in comparison to watching a performance. Mindful of the centrality of oral performance in the Malay literary tradition, no discussion of romantic *syair* would willingly ignore this aspect.[14] The difficulty is that the silent manuscripts are all that remain of the original milieu of the *syair*. The experience of listening to the recitation of a romantic *syair* must be reconstructed, ironically enough, from textual sources. It should also be noted that though the *syair* may be oral forms in origin, by the time of their heyday in the 19th century, they took a definitely textual form. The scores, if not hundreds, of *syair* manuscripts that survive from the 19th century are not transcriptions of oral performances; rather, they are texts that were composed in writing. Though *syair* were intended to be read aloud rather than silently; they should be held distinct from types of narrative performance that were the province of the oral specialist, such as Sumatran *andai-andai* and *guritan*.[15] Contemporary accounts, such as that of Den Hamer in 1890s Banjar, make it clear that writing and reading were integral to the production and consumption of these *syair*.[16] This is significant because, as we will see, this indicates that women were not excluded from literacy or from engagement with written literature.

Romantic *syair* were not among the earliest lists of Malay works collected by European scholars, suggesting that the genre emerged in the late 17th or early 18th century.[17] They became the object of European scholarly interest in the 19th century, with the publications by Roorda van Eysinga (*Syair Ken Tambuhan*, 1838), Van Hoevell (*Syair Bidasari*, 1843), Hollander (*Syair Ken Tambuhan*, 1856) and Klinkert (*Syair Ken Tambuhan, Syair Bidasari, Syair Yatim Nestapa, Syair Sultan Mansur Syah Gempita, Syair Kahar Masyhur*, 1880–1886).[18] *Syair Ken Tambuhan* and *Syair Bidasari*, in particular, have since the time of Roorda van Eysinga and Van Hoevell attracted the notice of scholars as works of exceptional literary merit — though it has been pointed out that this had much to do with the apparent accordance of these works with Romantic tastes.[19] In his *History of Classical Malay Literature*, Winstedt contrasts *Syair Ken Tambuhan* and *Syair Selindung Delima* to other works such as *Syair Sultan Abdul Muluk* which "have more Muslim colouring, and are more suited to modern taste".[20] That the disguised heroine *syair* appealed to readers of his day would not have endeared them to Winstedt, for whom the greatest works of Malay literature were those of the "half-caste courts of the Sailendras and the Sultans of Malacca", which fell into neglect because of "Muslim prejudice".[21] Indeed, the disguised heroine *syair* do appear to be more profoundly Islamised than their predecessors, perhaps surprisingly given their heroines' subversive potential. There is, too, something to the charge that the later *syair* are less skilled artistic works than *Syair Bidasari* and *Syair Ken Tambuhan*. The disguised heroine *syair* are highly repetitive, in terms of word choice as well as tropes, and their plots abound in convention and coincidence. If *Syair Bidasari* and *Syair Ken Tambuhan* are operas by Verdi or Puccini, brimming with the sublime and the tragic, *Syair Siti Zubaidah* and *Syair Siti Zuhrah* have more in common with Gilbert and Sullivan operettas.[22] Yet, as we shall see, the emotional charge that these *syair* carried for their original audiences was no less than that of the great operas. And it is precisely the disjunctions between these *syair* and modern tastes and expectations of literature that are so revealing and rewarding for the present-day reader.

Since Winstedt's time, studies of the romantic *syair* have thankfully moved beyond culturally specific judgements of taste and value. The most notable publications on Malay *syair* are Gijs Koster's *Roaming Through Seductive Gardens*, Julian Millie's *Bidasari* and the study by Teeuw, Muhammad Haji Salleh and others of *Syair Sinyor Kosta*.[23] This last exemplifies the philological strand in the study of *syair*: it is a two-volume treatment, providing the complete texts of all four extant versions, as well as two English translations, a thorough discussion of the transmission history, and a comparison of the four versions. As a philological study, it leaves no stone unturned. Yet while applauding the achievements of this work, especially in making the text accessible to new readers, it is useful to note what it does *not* do and why there is some justice to Vickers' characterisation of the Leiden approach to Indonesian literature (in his case, Balinese) as "present[ing] texts as objects".[24]

The authors describe the various options open to the study of the four variants of *Syair Sinyor Kosta* as follows:

> One possible approach would be the study of the textual history. This involves a determination of the historical relationships between the variant forms on the basis of textual comparison, as well as the information regarding dates and places of provenance of the manuscripts and early prints, any other information contained in the preambles or colophons to the manuscripts, and external information of various kinds. A second approach is the structural analysis: a comparative study of the various texts on the basis of criteria such as internal coherence, 'logic' of the plot, consistence in the use of language, and so on. Then again, one might compare the different versions primarily from the point of view of the generic conventions as we know them to apply to the Malay syair in general or to certain types of syair in particular. Another possible approach is what one might call the mimetic or historical one, where one tries to discover to what extent the various versions of the story reflect historical situations or events or contain topographical or other factual information. One might also study the texts from a linguistic point of view ... Yet another kind of study would be primarily focused on the reception of the text in the society for which it was written, its readership, its distribution, and so on.[25]

Here, what is of interest is the systems of signification that operate within the text, between versions of the text, and between the text and society. It is essentially an exercise in comparison — holding up one text against another, or the text against "historical situations" — rather than interpretation. The meaning that the text held for its original readers, or for its readers today, seems to be beyond the pale of scholarship. Perhaps this meaning is so obvious that it is not worth scholarly attention; perhaps the text is too trivial to require any kind of exegesis. While such charges have been levelled at the romantic *syair* — with some justification — we will see that there is something to be gained in nevertheless considering them as complex literary texts, deserving of careful attention to questions of artistry and ambiguity.

Koster's *Roaming Through Seductive Gardens* addresses itself to such an approach, using structuralist literary analysis to elucidate the meanings of a range of Malay belles-lettrist texts. His stated aim is to "enter into a dialogue with the Malay textual heritage, notably with that part of it that consists of narrative, so that its texts may shake off the torpor of their long deathlike sleep and may awaken to a new lease of life and a new relevance, radiant once again with their own peculiar beauty".[26] The presence of the idea of beauty and of Koster himself as an active participant in a dialogue with the texts signal quite a different project from that of the contributors to *A Merry Senhor*. The texts do indeed gain a renewed vitality in his readings, at times precisely because these readings are at variance with received opinion about how they are to be interpreted. Moreover, Koster identifies and elucidates a particular tension at the very heart of the Malay tradition's view of fictional literature: the interplay of beauty, truth and moral profit. Koster's observation that within the paradigm of the Malay "Idea of the Book" "fiction can only be justified and be given an acknowledged status if it is seen to fulfill a subservient role as the handmaid of Truth. Fiction as a playful constructing of possible new worlds is allowed no place in it" is sensitive and illuminating.[27] As will become obvious, however, the present study of the disguised heroine *syair* does not adopt Koster's taxonomies of the workings of Malay literature, such as his association of the *dalang* narrator with Hindu-Javaneseness, orality and a soothing function, while the *dagang* narrator is Muslim, and representative of literacy and didacticism.[28] Koster's analysis, based on the hermeneutic approach of Jauss, presupposes a conception of Malay political culture that is the same in all places and at all times, what he calls "the Kerajaan Order", and a similarly fixed notion of Malay literary culture based on "the Idea of the Book".[29] It will be obvious that the following exploration of the disguised heroine *syair* does not share that vision but seeks rather to attend to the particularities of time and place. 19th-century Penyengat, where the Bugis-Malay aristocracy had lost all political and military power, cannot be seen as representative of "the Kerajaan Order". Similarly, romantic *syair* written for and in some cases by women are not invested with the authority inherent in "the Idea of the Book". Thus, Koster's theoretical framework and terminology, while an ambitious theoretical contribution to the study of traditional Malay literature, is not adopted here.

Julian Millie's *Bidasari* attempts to chart a course between Teeuw's philology and Koster's theory. In providing an edited transcription of a manuscript of *Syair Bidasari* and a lively English translation, Millie's book is most useful to students of Malay literature. His proposal that the *syair* should be read as a "theatre text" follows on from Sweeney's insistence on the importance of oral performance and from Dumas' work on *teater Dulmuluk*, a contemporary Sumatran theatre form that relates the story of *Syair Sultan Abdul Muluk*. As Millie himself notes, the *syair* predates the theatrical form, though he denies that this invalidates his approach. Millie rather scants the *syair*'s origins in the palace manuscript tradition, preferring to address the folk theatrical tradition. Millie's analysis conflates oral performance with theatrical performance, seeing no difference between reading a *syair* aloud (domestic, private, non-professional) to staging a play (commercial, public, professional). More significantly for the present study, Millie draws attention to the didacticism of the *syair*, noting that it is moreover directed exclusively at women.[30] Further analysis of the issue of gender in the *syair* would seem most apposite here, but Millie does not pursue it, all the more regrettable given the reproduction of gender stereotypes to be found on the book's cover.[31]

The romantic *syair* must be seen in the larger context of traditional Malay literature as a whole, a view that would scarcely be possible without the panorama provided by *The Heritage of Traditional Malay Literature*, as well as the deft readings of aesthetic aspects of the *syair* in *Keindahan Erti dan Erti Keindahan*.[32] The schematisation of the various functional spheres of traditional Malay literature — the spheres of benefit, beauty and spiritual perfection — allows individual works to be orientated and assessed in relation to the other works that make up the tradition. The reconstruction of the norms of traditional Malay poetics, particularly as explicated in Braginsky's essay on Safirin bin Usman Fadli's *Hikayat Anak Pengajian*, is a touchstone here. Most foundational for this exploration of the romantic *syair* is Braginsky's observation that the genre may originate at least partly in the "tradition of Malay female court singers, *biduan*", and that "the milieu of female palace singers, ladies-in-waiting and concubines of Malay rulers, as well as of their younger wives and relatives, was the preferred domain for the functioning of a considerable proportion of romantic *syair*. It is precisely in this domain and for this audience that they were often created, reflecting its ideals, norms and tastes".[33] While the question of gender is not a central concern of Braginsky's work, his encyclopaedic knowledge of traditional Malay literature and his conscientious attention to detail mean that he is perhaps the first scholar to have pointed out this very striking fact: that a major corpus of Malay literary texts was intended for female audiences.

Aside from scholars' judgements of the romantic *syair*, there are the opinions of the men and women who formed their original audiences, Malay speakers of the 19th century. Here there is a telling divergence of opinion, and one that falls along gender lines. As Chapter 2 sets out in detail, Malay men of letters such as Raja Ali Haji and Safirin bin Usman Fadli disparaged romantic *syair* as trivial, and in almost the same breath warned of them as morally dangerous. The recitation of romantic texts, they claimed, aroused dangerous emotions in listeners. What is more, women, with their impaired rationality, were particularly prone to falling under the spell of a seductive recitation. In Braginsky's reconstruction of the hierarchy of traditional Malay literary genres, the romantic *syair* fall neither into the sphere of benefit nor of spiritual perfection, but rather the lowest sphere, that of beauty.[34] While this low placement of the romantic *syair* is a convincing representation of how local literati like Raja Ali Haji might have viewed the genre, there are dissenting voices: those of readers themselves, who repeatedly declared their enjoyment of and devotion to romantic *syair*. It is no coincidence that avowed fans of romantic *syair* seem most often to be found among those groups which were themselves lowly placed in the 19th-century Malay social order: women and Chinese.[35]

This convergence of low philological opinion, the near contempt of local men of letters, and the wild enthusiasm of rank and file readers, is far from unusual in world literature. As with *syair*, medieval English prose romances were the product of a manuscript tradition and were read aloud; as with *syair*, they were widely enjoyed, supposedly by women and the "lower orders", and roundly condemned by men in positions of civil and religious authority. The 16th-century Spanish humanist Juan Luis Vives said of romances that they made readers "wylye and craftye, they kindle and styr up couetousnes, inflame angre, and all beastly and filthy desyre" — a charge that would have been familiar to 19th-century Malay readers of romances.[36] Many modern critics and scholars, too, have been unable to discern much merit in these English medieval romances. As Gilbert sardonically puts it, "[l]ife, medievalist literary critics generally seem to have felt, is too short to waste time on such mediocrities; there is more important work to be done on quality texts".[37] Quality texts are, by definition, produced and approved by those at the apex of the culture's symbolic order — in the Malay case, aristocratic *'alim* like Raja Ali Haji. Conversely, the literature produced and enjoyed by the lower orders, including court women, is stigmatised as of poor quality and dubious morals. Though romantic *syair* were said to be primarily of interest to women, they were also read and written by men. Even Raja Ali Haji himself admitted to enjoying *syair*, though only as a pleasant and trivial diversion from weightier intellectual pursuits.[38] The stereotypical association between women and romantic *syair* — in other words, the gendering of the romantic *syair* as female — was a consequence of the way value and status were assigned in that society. Just as the novel's origins as a low status genre in 18th-century England opened it to women as readers and writers, whereas the "high" genres of poetry and plays were the exclusive domain of men,[39] the romantic *syair* was a feminine genre because it was a low status genre, and vice versa. This low status should not, of course, be taken to mean that the *syair* lack interest or significance. Rather, that these *syair* so often defy the normative values of the society that produced them is part of why they are so enticing to study.

This book aims to explicate these *syair* as complex literary texts, affording a glimpse into the fictive world of the culture that produced them. In defence of the study of English medieval romance, McDonald argues that "popular romance provides us with a unique opportunity to explore the complex workings of the medieval imaginary and the world outside the text that feeds and supports it".[40] Likewise, the study of the romantic *syair* provides the opportunity to explore the "imaginary" of the women's world of the 19th-century Malay courts. The *syair* indicate the inner life and imaginative possibilities open to readers and writers of the 19th century. Literature was for them, as it is for us, a space of play, in which the realities of life could be temporarily stripped of their intractability, contested and reimagined. This imaginary is to be distinguished from actual social conditions: although texts are obviously related to lived experience, the relationship between text and life is not straightforward. Literary sources are not put to the best use simply to "*flesh out* what is available to us in terms of historical evidence" as Witcombe does in her study of *Syair Siti Zubaidah*.[41] Once the "fact that cultural expressions tend to idealize, exaggerate, or even romanticize reality" has been taken into account, though, it turns out that the *syair* — a romance, after all — does not furnish much flesh for the historical skeleton.[42] Attempts to mine texts such as these for information about the real lives of women in the past are stymied by the bare fact that these texts are fictions, governed by a poetics that imposes propriety and aesthetics onto unpredictable reality. Accounts of remarkable women are better found in historical than literary sources.[43] The subtitle of Creese's book, "marriage and sexuality in the Indic courts of Java and Bali", would be more accurate as "in the literature of the Indic courts of Java and Bali". These approaches are familiar strategies in the interpretation of traditional Malay literature, which has often been mined for historical information, not only by those interested in gender history, such as Creese and Witcombe, but also by, *inter alia*, Abdul Rahman al-Ahmadi who sought a historical precedent for the events described in *Syair Siti Zubaidah*, and by 19th-century scholars such as Newbold and

Low, who used *hikayat* to write political history.[44] Such a straightforward use of literary texts to fill in socio-political detail ignores the literariness of the texts themselves. As Sarra writes with respect to women's memoirs from Heian Japan,

> Texts from traditions remote in time provide the very basis on which we reconstruct social and political contexts. But texts do not simply and passively reflect their lost milieux. In its intertextual dimension, the text acts as a place where cultural fictions circulate according to the exigencies of desire — whether we locate that desire in the author herself or in the language and structure of the texts that now provide the basis for our reconstruction of her intentionality.[45]

The aim of this book is not to read outwards from the texts to historical or social contexts, but inwards from the contexts into the *syair* themselves. Moreover, the reading of the *syair* performed in this book does not claim to reproduce or even resemble one that a 19th-century reader might have performed. The author's intentions regarding the meaning of the text, or the original audience's understanding of what the text meant, are not taken as all that can or should be said. One cannot, of course, know more about Raja Ali Haji's world than Raja Ali Haji himself did. Nevertheless, his judgement of the romantic *syair* as trivial is not the last word on the subject — indeed, that judgement itself is ripe for questioning. Paying attention to the unspoken, incomplete, and repressed in order to explicate what a text means does not imply ignoring the normative reading but simply that the normative reading is not taken as the final word.

The feminist literary analysis of gender is integral to this investigation of romantic *syair*. This is not the project of looking for precursors, pioneers or heroines, of examining and cataloguing images of women, or of asserting that Raja Salihah was as great an exponent of traditional Malay literature as Raja Ali Haji, and that space should therefore be made for her in the canon. The work of Janice Radway on women reading romance novels and of Tanya Modleski on women and popular culture are important waymarkers. Modleski draws on psychoanalytic and reception theory's conception of art as a way of managing psychic conflict: the text "strategically arouses fantasy content within careful symbolic containment structures which defuse it, gratifying intolerable, unrealizable, properly imperishable desires only to the degree to which they can be laid to rest".[46] This means that women's popular fiction can be seen as both addressing real female concerns and reaffirming the oppressive gender order that gives rise to those concerns. In Modleski's words, it "is useless to deplore the texts for their omissions, distortions, and conservative affirmations. It is crucial to understand them: to let their very omissions and distortions speak, informing us of the contradictions they are meant to conceal and, equally importantly, of the fears that lie behind them".[47] Similarly, Radway writes of the contemporary romance novel that it "avoids questioning the institutionalised basis of patriarchal control over women even as it serves as a locus of protest against some of its emotional consequences".[48] The *syair* heroines who disguise themselves as men and become great kings or wise scholars, only to willingly return to a life of feminine seclusion, neatly express this combination of wish-fulfilment and denial, protest and acquiescence. Approaches such as those provided by Radway and Modleski allow the reader to link the text and its readers, the world of the *syair* and the socio-political world of the 19th century, without having to say that the one is the reflection of the other.

Penyengat mosque, 2004

II. Penyengat in the 19th Century

The seat of the Bugis Yamtuan Muda and his court, in 1849 Penyengat was home to some 600 people, including the Bugis-Malay aristocracy and their dependents, as well as 200 Hokkien Chinese.[49] The Dutch Resident of Riau was stationed a short boat trip across the water away, in the port of Tanjung Pinang on the far larger island of Bintan. A Dutch military officer who visited Penyengat in the early 1850s described the island as follows:

> An extensive campong lies on the south and east sides. The residence of the viceroy has many spacious buildings, amongst which the balei is conspicuous. A high gateway with a round roof, besides a wall on either side, protects the entrance. Not far from this stands the new mosque, a building, it is said, on the model of the great mosque at Mecca. With its four minarets and cupola, all covered with white plaster, this building has a striking appearance seen at a distance ... The mauseoleum of the late viceroy is situated at the foot of a hill. A capital stone jetty, with a landing place built on piles, having on either side a building for the receipt of import duties, is of the same date as the mosque, 1848–49.[50]

Thomson and De Bruyn's accounts offer several insights into Penyengat's "cultural ecology".[51] The famed Islamic piety of the island is evident in the building of the mosque, and the insistence that its plan followed that of Mecca. Although the Penyengat mosque does not much resemble the great mosque in Mecca, it is markedly different in style to earlier mosques in the Malay-Indonesian world, such as the one at Demak.[52] A close connection to Middle Eastern Islam was a central facet of Penyengat's identity. Less often acknowledged, both by Penyengat writers of the time and by later scholars, are European and Chinese cultural influences. Although many of the court attendants were in "Malay garb", Western influence was unpleasantly evident to Thomson, an English government surveyor who witnessed a royal wedding on Penyengat in 1847. This was manifested in the persons of the "quasi soldiers", with at their head a parade leader who was "though bare feeted wearing a cap with a gold band, military frock coat, and dirty white trowsers".[53] As in many royal courts in the Malay world during the age of encroaching European power, emblems of Western style were amalgamated into local ceremonial display. This was also the case in Penyengat, despite the claims of the Dutch Resident Netscher that Penyengat's leading thinker, Raja Ali Haji, was vehemently anti-European.[54] The significance of the Chinese presence on Penyengat is suggested by the remarkable claim that the mosque was funded by a

Chinese convert and returned pilgrim, as well as by Chinese participation in the royal wedding festivities.⁵⁵ The 1860 poem, *Syair Kahwin Tan Tik Cu*, relates the wedding ceremonies of the son of Tanjung Pinang's Kapitan Cina, the leader of the Chinese, and attests to a significant level of cultural interaction between the Malay and Chinese communities.⁵⁶

The central feature of the disguised heroine *syair* — the cross-dressed martial heroine — may well owe something to Chinese sources. This influence is especially discernable in *Syair Siti Zubaidah*'s seven warrior princesses. The cross-dressed martial heroine is such a stock figure of Chinese opera that there it comprises the "doamadan" genre, "sword and steed woman warrior plays".⁵⁷ The first appearance of this woman warrior is traced to two 16th-century plays by Xu Wei, themselves influenced by folktales such as the "Ballad of Mulan". Xu Wei's plays are thought to have inspired later writers — including women writers from Jiangnan — to include heroines disguised as men.⁵⁸ "In contrast with European opera and drama," Li writes, "the woman warrior role-type in Chinese opera is unique in its widespread presence in the general repertoire and in its imposing representation of the power of women — in terms of sociopolitical status, physicality and supernatural power, depending on the individual character depicted".⁵⁹ The description of Siti Jauhar Manikam's appearance in *Syair Sultan Yahya* recalls the make-up of the martial heroine in Chinese opera rather than the usual *putih kuning*, "yellow-white", Malay beauty.⁶⁰

Bercelak Siti bersifat alit	Siti's eyes were rimmed in kohl,
Putih berseri warnanya kulit	Her skin shone pale,
*Bibirnya merah bagai dihalit*⁶¹	Her lips were red as though rouged:

The Chinese princesses in *Syair Siti Zubaidah* are not, however, described in any remarkable way, but what is notable is that they are not in disguise but fight as women. Among the myriad entertainments at the Lingga royal court was a theatre form known as "wayang Cina".⁶² In Thomson's 1847 account of Penyengat, he noted "the screeching of Chinese wyangs [sic]" during wedding festivities.⁶³

Thus, despite the fact that Penyengat was held to be the site of the 19th century's purest Malay language and its finest Malay literature, it was profoundly hybrid. The settlement had been established in the first place to mark a rapprochement between rival Bugis and Malay factions, and was very mixed. The Bugis-Malay alliance had been forged in the chaotic aftermath of the 1699 regicide of the last scion of the Malacca dynasty,

Sultan Mahmud Syah. When Bugis mercenaries set up Raja Sulaiman, son of the murdered Sultan Abdul Jalil, as Johor Sultan, they were rewarded with the installation of one of their leaders, Daeng Marewa, as Yamtuan Muda, a viceregal position notionally subordinate to the Malay sultan. Thus, the Bugis succeeded in transforming themselves from pirates and mercenaries into courtiers, firmly ensconced in the Malay political order. The death of the Yamtuan Muda Raja Haji in the Bugis attack on Dutch-held Malacca in 1784 was a watershed in the decline of Riau's sovereignty. In the *Tuhfat al-Nafis*, Raja Haji's grandson Raja Ali Haji records that he died with a sword in one hand and a Qur'an in the other: an archetypal Muslim hero and the last Yamtuan Muda to take up arms. This ushered in an era of political and economic decline in Riau and the Malay states more generally. In 1787, the Dutch returned to Riau, and the Malay sultan moved his base to Daik, a day's journey from Penyengat. In 1818, both Malays and Bugis agreed to give the Dutch veto power over the choice of sultan, to allow the entry of warships into Riau, and to accept the presence of a Resident in Tanjung Pinang. "From the mid-nineteenth century," Matheson observes with regard to Riau, "effective control of trade, revenues, foreign affairs and most matters of policy were determined by Dutch rather than local administrators".[64] The British settlement of Singapore — leased from a brother of the Lingga Sultan — established a new mercantile centre that quickly overshadowed Riau. The division of the Malay world between the Dutch and the English in the Treaty of London of 1824 put the final nail in the coffin of indigenous sovereignty. The ancient kingdom of Johor was split between two European powers, and Riau, cut off from the thriving trade in Singapore, became an economic and political backwater.

Yet another blow for Riau sovereignty came in 1857, when Sultan Mahmud of Lingga was deposed by the Dutch, again with the backing of the Yamtuan Muda. Sultan Mahmud's offence was, as Matheson puts it, that he "tried to act as an independent ruler",[65] including making trips to Trengganu and Singapore without the permission of his Dutch masters. The Yamtuan Muda faction was opposed to him, ostensibly on moral grounds, but also no doubt because he refused to follow their lead. In the *Tuhfat al-Nafis*, Sultan Mahmud is depicted as a headstrong youth seduced by Westernisation and forgetful of *adat*, but in a text from his own court, *Syair Sultan Mahmud*, he appears as a raja in the old style, whose chief occupation and indeed duty is gorgeous display. Like his counterpart in Terengganu, who discussed theological matters with the English missionary Medhurst,⁶⁶ Sultan Mahmud took an interest in religious developments. He consorted with Christians and Zoroastrians and even joined a Masonic lodge in Singapore.⁶⁷ The palace Sultan Mahmud had built on Lingga in the Dutch style, with marble tables, spittoons and chequerboard floors imported from Singapore, can be seen as fulfilling the traditional role of the raja to adopt the most up-to-date trappings of power.⁶⁸ The deposition of Sultan Mahmud, in many ways a more traditional ruler than those of the Bugis faction, with their turn towards *syariah*-minded⁶⁹ Islam and political quietism, meant that the Lingga Malay dynasty irrevocably lost the cultural and moral high ground to the Penyengat Bugis. Part of the ideological project of the *Tuhfat al-Nafis* is to explain away this Bugis role in overthrowing a Malay ruler. Examining "local texts" from Lingga, Matheson shows that their depiction of the relations between Lingga and Penyengat are quite different from that of the *Tuhfat al-Nafis* and that a sense of rivalry between the two centres persisted late into the 20th century.⁷⁰

The Riau elite in the late 19th century continued to act as a cultural vanguard of the Malay world; being denied political and economic power, they turned instead to the accumulation of cultural capital. As Barnard observes, the "changing role of the Bugis in Riau society thus seems to have evolved from a military justification to one based on religion. The expression of this role is best seen in the renaissance in literature that occurred in nineteenth-century Riau".⁷¹ The Rusydiah Club, established on Penyengat from at least 1895, included both Penyengat Bugis and Lingga Malays, and adopted Western customs in the celebration of local festivities. Barnard's analysis of one surviving document of the Rusydiah Club, the *Taman Penghiburan*, details activities that would not go amiss at an English village fête, such as a sack race and a three-legged race.⁷² One of the club's members, Tengku Khalid Hitam, and his wife, Raja Aisyah Sulaiman, were important early modernists and activists for independence in the Malay world.⁷³ Tengku Khalid died in Tokyo, where he had gone to elicit help in the anti-imperial cause.

But the decline of Riau as a political power was in inverse proportion to its rise as a cultural and intellectual force. "The Dutch presence could be said to have had two positive effects on the production of Malay literature on Penyengat," Matheson writes. "Firstly by assuming responsibility for most areas of Riau's government the Dutch left the Bugis nobles more time to devote to religion, their studies and to their writing. Secondly, the Dutch interest in all aspects of literature stimulated the copying of old texts, and in some cases, the production of new ones".[74] Perhaps more importantly, Dutch philological collecting meant that Penyengat manuscripts that may otherwise have been lost survive to this day. In addition, Penyengat's proximity to Singapore and ties to the burgeoning publishing industry at the end of the 19th century aided the wider dispersion of Riau texts. More fundamentally, the Bugis nobility's loss of political and economic power may have prompted them to focus their activities on amassing cultural capital.

Another important factor in the literary activities of Penyengat was not fostered by the Dutch but rather by a force to which they were hostile: Islamic revivalism. The 19th century was a time of quickening change in the religious landscape of the Malay world. Increased traffic between the Malay-Indonesian archipelago and the Middle East, combined with the encroachment of "infidel" colonial powers, and the upsurge of revivalist Muslim movements, brought about a transition from the relatively syncretic practices of earlier eras to a more *syariah*-minded form of Islam. In the early part of the century, the pilgrimage to Mecca required extraordinary dedication or substantial means. Improved transportation links between the Arabian Peninsula and the Malay world meant that by mid-century some 2,000 Indonesian Muslims per year made the pilgrimage, increasing to more than 5,000 by 1890.[75] A party of nobles from Penyengat, including Raja Ali Haji and his father, performed the hajj in about 1829. At the same time, the number of Arabs in the Indonesian archipelago increased from 20,000 in 1860 to 61,000 in 1900.[76] It was clearly a mark of prestige for a Malay religious centre to have Arab scholars in residence, for they were handsomely rewarded. As the *Tuhfat al-Nafis* reports, Raja Ali Haji "selected several learned men, like Sayid Abdullah of Bahrain and others, to settle in Penyengat and teach for a year. When they left they were were given 400 to 500 dollars".[77] To these movements of people, Riddell adds that "Arab scholars in Arabia issued increasing numbers of long-distance legal opinions, or *fatwa*s, on wide-ranging topics in response to enquiries received from the Malay world".[78] The role of more stringently applied Middle Eastern standards to Malay political and social life, especially as regards gender roles, is suggested by the Meccan *fatwa* cited in the *Adat Aceh* as declaring rule by a woman illegal, thus ending the reign of the last woman raja of Aceh in 1699.[79]

No discussion of religious developments in the 19th-century Malay world — let alone one focused on Penyengat — can leave out Raja Ali Haji, perhaps the most influential and best known Islamic thinker of the Malay world in his time. Born in 1809, the son of Raja Ahmad and grandson of Raja Haji, Raja Ali Haji spent several years in the Middle East and soon became, in the words of the Dutch Resident Netscher, "a scholar of great renown among his countrymen".[80] After his cousin Raja Ali bin Raja Ja'afar became Yamtuan Muda in 1845, Raja Ali Haji became his advisor, both in matters of religion and in dealings with the Lingga court. He was also a leading member of the Naqshbandiyya Sufi order in Penyengat, headed by another cousin.[81] The Naqshbandiyya was opposed to pantheism (*wahdat al-wujud*) and innovation (*bid'ah*), and favoured engagement with the state through the provision of guidance to those in power.[82] This combination of theological conservatism and political cooperation is readily recognisable in Raja Ali Haji's works. He was a prolific writer on a diversity of subjects, from traditional topics of court thinkers such as kingship, to the proper conduct of women, to ribald *syair*, to a guide to writing and the beginnings of the first Malay dictionary. His *chef d'oeuvre*, however, is certainly the *Tuhfat al-Nafis*, a chronicle that, with its vision of the decline of Muslim states because of the moral covenants broken by their leaders, owes much to the historiography of the Muslim heartlands. Riddell characterises Raja Ali Haji as an "arch conservative in his views", who

> portrayed his society in an advanced state of decay, and presented the society of the prophet Muhammad as an ideal which individuals should strive to attain. He called for adherence to the *shari'a*, serious study of religious literature, and obedience to established scholarship. He called for the conduct of the state to be based on social harmony in the name of God, and attributed the decline of Riau to the failure of people — both rulers and subjects — to follow the teachings of the Prophet. In this way, he made a contribution to emerging reformist ideas which were spreading through the Malay world.[83]

Yet his writings may have been more severe than the man himself. Netscher's description of Raja Ali Haji as a "thoroughly fanatic scholar, who would quite willingly see the entire elimination of Christians and Christendom" and "no friend of the Europeans"[84] must be tempered by Raja Ali Haji as he appears in his correspondence with the European philologist Von de Wall. As the groundbreaking work of al-Azhar and Van der Putten shows, Raja Ali Haji was far from a dogmatic xenophobe. Rather, the "image that emerges from the letters is much more that of a pious teacher who devoted himself to his task of edifying the Malay people, who saw great benefit in working together with the colonial administration for educational purposes, and who became good friends with a European scholar".[85] The warmth and intimacy of Raja Ali Haji's friendship with Von de Wall — confiding not only his financial troubles and his grief at the death of family members, but also his sexual difficulties[86] — is perhaps the most surprising revelation of the correspondence.

In the Arab world itself, change was afoot. The Wahhabi movement rose up in the Arabian Peninsula, calling for a return to the ways of Muhammad and a purge of later accretions such as the saying of prayers at holy tombs.[87] The Wahhabi were to influence events on the distant island of Sumatra, as Dobbin describes in her history of the Paderi uprising in the Minangkabau lands. The Paderis were three Minangkabau pilgrims, named for the port of Pedir in north Sumatra, from which they had sailed on the hajj. They witnessed the fall of Mecca to the Wahhabis, and while there would have been subjected to Wahhabi laws, and brought their doctrine back to Southeast Asia.[88] Although the Turks drove the Wahhabis from Mecca in 1813, their doctrines may still have been current at the time of Raja Ali Haji's pilgrimage in 1829. At any rate, the Riau elite would not have been ignorant of the tumultuous events in the Minangkabau highlands. There is certainly some congruence between the Wahhabis' strict enforcement of the five prayers and ban on smoking tobacco and wearing silk clothing, on the one hand,[89] and on the other, Yamtuan Muda Raja Ali's prohibition of wearing gold or silk. The Yamtuan Muda also banned gambling, cock fighting — favourite targets of the Paderis' ire — and as the *Tuhfat* reports:

> abhorred those who indulged in pleasures which led to loose behaviour between men and women, and those who sang and crooned *pantun* with veiled invitations to adultery. On occasion he sent people to confiscate the lutes played by those who were serenading near the homes of decent folk so that the young would hear no scandal and so that there was nothing unseemly in the state.[90]

The Dutch Resident Angelbeek reported that the Riau nobles of 1826 competed with one another in matters of religion and regarded anything non-Muslim as "anathema".[91] Naturally enough, the Yamtuan Muda took his moral crusade to Lingga, where he enforced the five daily prayers and ordered women to put on the headscarf. Even a text of Sultan Mahmud's own court, Encik Kamariah's *Syair Sultan Mahmud*, shows the sultan taking the lead from the Yamtuan Muda:

Sultan pun menurut barang katanya	The sultan obeyed his words:
Hukum syari'a diajarkannya	[The Yamtuan Muda] instructed him in *syariah* law,
Mengerahkan segala isi negerinya	Commanded all the people of the land,
Disuruh sembahyang mereka sekaliannya[92]	And ordered them all to pray.

Just as Sultan Mahmud's response to the new regional order was to incorporate European ways, the Yamtuan Muda's turn towards *syariah*-minded Islam can similarly be seen not as an archaism — for like Wahhabism, it was a rejection of traditional practice — but as a response to change.

To replace the traditional amusements now deemed impious came entertainment from the Middle East. Matheson notes that Yamtuan Muda Ja'afar enjoyed listening to Arab *hikayat* related by sayyids, and that the songs from Mecca, Medinah and Cairo were part of the Ramadhan celebrations.[93] The romantic *syair* frequently mention the ability to recite or sing according to the styles (*lagham*) of these cities as one of the heroine's many accomplishments. Siti Jauhar Manikam, the heroine of *Syair Sultan Yahya*, for example, could recite in the styles of various places in the Islamic heartlands, including Egypt, Mecca, Arabia, Turkey, Medina and Yemen.[94] Even such religiously-oriented performances, however, could be viewed with suspicion. An 1892 collection of *fatwa*s — answers to questions put by Indonesian Muslims to Meccan religious leaders — contains two queries asking whether the use of tambourines during the recitation of the *mawlid* poem and of cymbals during *syair* recitation were permissible. Syeikh Ahmad Dahlan answered that they were, so long as their use was "not connected to anything else that is forbidden by the *syariah*" or in the absence of "forbidden activities".[95] It would seem that recitation accompanied by musical instruments was associated with activities — perhaps certain Sufi trance-inducing practices — that were condemned by the *syariah*-minded.

If Penyengat was a garden of writers and a centre of religious reform, it was also a rich field for European philologists to gather data about Malay language and literature. Like naturalists collecting specimens, Dutch philologists amassed quantities of manuscripts in the Riau archipelago, now preserved in the colonial archives. Although it is difficult to make an accurate estimate, the catalogues of the most important collections of Malay manuscripts in the world — Jakarta, Leiden and London — suggest that many can be traced to Riau. One of the reasons philological collecting focused on Riau was that it was (and is) said to be the home of the purest form of Malay. This has often been taken as an uncomplicated statement of fact, but any assertion about linguistic purity can hardly be divorced from claims about political legitimacy. The Riau dynasty figured itself as the heir to the Malacca sultanate of glorious memory, and thus — in spite of the radical hybridity of the population, including significant numbers of Bugis and Chinese — claimed that its language and customs were the most authentically Malay. No doubt inhabitants of other Malay states, whether on the peninsula, the east coast of Sumatra or southwestern Borneo, would have begged to differ. The fact that the Riau archipelago straddled the faultline created by the 1824 Treaty of London may also have contributed to the sense of its centrality shared by both Dutch and British. For the Dutch, Riau was the "surrogate for the lost Malacca".[96] A third and more mundane reason for the over-representation of Riau and Penyengat, in particular in the surviving archive materials, may have been the fact that Tanjung Pinang was a relatively congenial base for a European philologist. The Yamtuan Muda dynasty seemed to have given up any thought of opposing the Dutch and instead actively cooperated with them. Matheson points out that Europeans collected little data from 19th-century Lingga, perhaps because "it is very likely that on Lingga there were no intermediaries prepared to discuss with foreigners details of customary procedure which involved the Malay royal family. The Bugis on Riau seem to have been more prepared to act as informants on matters of language and custom".[97] In effect, the cordial relations between the Penyengat aristocracy and the Dutch have had a significant effect on establishing them as the cultural leaders of the Malay world. Beginning in 1830, Residents Elout and Walbeehm were active in commissioning copies of manuscripts in Tanjung Pinang.[98] The manuscript collections of H.C. Klinkert and Hermann von de Wall, both of whom were based for a time in Penyengat, are important repositories of romantic *syair*. Without the intervention of Klinkert, as Chapter 1 explores in more detail, it is likely that traditional Malay literature would be without any named women authors. In another instance of Dutch intervention, the publisher Roorda van Eysinga played a crucial role in bringing *Syair Sultan Abdul Muluk* to print, possibly altering its authorial attribution in the process. The role of European philologists in making Penyengat *the* centre of Malay literary culture must be borne in mind.[99] This of course begs the question of how many other literary centres, and how many authors, men and women alike, have been forgotten.

III. Women in the 19th-Century Malay World

If there is a popular perception of women in the Malay past, it is one of unrelenting patriarchal oppression.[100] Yet Gullick's analysis of what documentary evidence is available for the 19th century shows that there were Malay women who owned, inherited and disposed of property, engaged in trade and politics, and were people of consequence in their day.[101] Moreover, identifying gender as the fundamental cleavage in Malay society scants the fact that class — the distinction between slave and free, lord and commoner — was just as or perhaps more significant.

One of the few documentary glimpses of women at the Penyengat court is provided by Thomson, whose visit happened to coincide with a royal wedding. His account is worth quoting at length for the rare view it affords of the palace women:

> ... advancing into the enclosed court, we found several thousands of Malay and Chinese assembled, creating as much sound, discord, and music, on various instruments, as can be well imagined ... After the ceremonies were over, the bridegroom, a boy of fourteen dressed richly for a Malay, was carried on men's shoulders to the house, accompanied by the principal people attached to the Raja. On passing he was saluted by the quasi soldiers *à la militaire*. Next came the bride enclosed in scarlet curtains held extended by a frame, and excluding her from view. Immediately followed what we inferred to be matrons of noble blood, whose handsome appearance, fair complexions and peculiar gait, betokened them to be inmates of the Raja's harem. Then came groups of all sorts of ladies, young and old, black, brown and yellow, to the number of at least six or seven hundred. This stream of femininity poured from the audience chamber and filled the dwelling house, where no more could be seen of them.[102]

This procession of palace women would most probably have been not just residents of the surrounding kampung, but also the inhabitants of the *dalam*, the inner quarters of the palace, including wives, concubines and slaves. There were, it is clear from Thomson's description, a large number of women connected to the Penyengat court and centrally involved in the great ceremonial events that were the heart of the traditional Malay polity. In *Syair Sultan Mahmud*, a record of similar events during the reign of the last Lingga sultan, the author, a royal nursemaid named Encik Kamariah, notes just such mass participation of women:

Hampirkan siang rupanya hari	When the day was at hand,
Masuklah sekalian bini menteri	The ministers' wives entered,
Mengadap raja permaisuri	Presenting themselves to the queen,
Penuh sesak istana seri	Thronging the royal palace.
Ambalan segala orang perempuan	A procession of all the women,
Masuk ke dalam berkawan-kawan	Entered in groups together,
Berbagai jenis rupa kelakuan	Of many forms and manners,
Ada yang muda ada yang huban	Some were young, some were greying.
Ada tua ada yang muda	Some were old, some were young,
Ada yang bujang ada yang janda	Some were unmarried, some were widows,
Ada yang anum ada yang berida	Some were fresh, others aged,
Jikalau malam anak dara pun ada[103]	At night there were also maidens.

The similarity with Thomson's description is striking, as is the notable omission, in Encik Kamariah's account, of ethnic difference. It is as though the category did not exist for her — though it certainly did for him. These are two of very few descriptions of the women who would have formed the original audiences, and in some cases, authors of the Riau romantic *syair*, which may well have been recited on just such occasions as royal weddings.

Encik Kamariah's account provides a sense of the hierarchy and influence of royal and serving women within the inner quarters of the sultan's palace, but little other than their names can be gleaned of their individuality. The 19th-century Riau woman about whom the most is known is certainly Raja Hamidah, known as Engku Puteri. Penyengat had been ceded to her in 1804 by her husband, Sultan Mahmud. Engku Puteri's status was derived less from her marriage than from the fact that she was the daughter of that revered "witness to the way of Allah" and potent source of political legitimacy, Raja Haji.[104] Her brother, Raja Ja'afar, ruled as Yamtuan Muda. That the foundation of Penyengat was so tied to a woman acting as a broker between Malay and Bugis is typical of the pattern of politics in 19th-century Riau.[105] Andaya notes the marked difference between Engku Puteri as she is represented in Raja Ali Haji's *Tuhfat al-Nafis* — as "the quintessential matriarch, wise, supportive, and beloved of her family"[106] — and her role as described by the Indian Army officer Peter Begbie. According to Begbie, who met her in Malacca, Engku Puteri opposed the election of her stepson Tengku Abdul Rahman as sultan, taking the side of Tengku Husain, another stepson, instead.[107] In Begbie's account, family relations are not quite as harmonious as Raja Ali Haji would have it: the pro-Dutch faction apparently forcibly prevented Engku Puteri from leaving Riau with the royal regalia to attend Tengku Husain's installation in 1819 as Sultan of Singapore. The *Tuhfat* cannot, however, avoid reporting that in 1822, the Dutch removed the regalia from her keeping, thereby enabling the installation of their preferred candidate as sultan. Although Begbie claims that this took place at gunpoint, Raja Ali Haji will say only that, having duly consulted with the Yamtuan Muda, Timmerman Thyssen "took the Johor regalia from Engku Puteri in a way that did not undermine her position as princess".[108] Given the importance of royal regalia in establishing political legitimacy, removing it from Engku Puteri's keeping could not help but undermine her and any opposition to Dutch interests.

A Lingga text discussed by Matheson also throws up the intriguing case of Tengku Fatimah, Sultan Mahmud's daughter. In 1883, at least according to the *Keringkasan Sejarah Melayu* of 1930, Tengku Fatimah was elected regent on behalf of her son and ruled for two years, with Bugis and Dutch backing.[109] Raja Abdul Rahman, her son, was born in 1851, so he was hardly a minor at the time. However, the Dutch sources reported that Tengku Fatimah's rule lasted for only a month.[110] Her election would have been much more unusual in the 19th-century Malay world than it would have been in earlier eras: hereditary rule by women was practised in Patani between 1584 and 1688, and in Aceh between 1642 and 1699. The *Keringkasan Sejarah Melayu* registers disapproval on the question of Tengku Fatimah's election: "according to a compelling account there were still strong legitimate claimants to the sultanate like T[engku] Said, T. Husin and T. Mahmud. We do not know why the Sultanate did not go to them".[111] What is clear is that in 1930, when the *Keringkasan Sejarah Melayu* was composed, Tengku Fatimah was remembered, even by those who did not support her, as a political figure of note. On the one hand, this is hardly surprising: she was, after all, granddaughter of the Sultan of Johor, daughter of the Sultan of Lingga, and wife of the Yamtuan Muda Raja Muhammad Yusuf. On the other hand, her prominence is noteworthy, particularly as she may have been opposed to the more radical Muslim reforms promulgated by her husband.[112]

The stymied political careers of Engku Puteri and Tengku Fatimah are in part a result of encroaching European power, but also of the declining role of women in public life. Barbara Andaya suggests that the rise of the monotheistic world religions, including Islam, led to a decline in the public position of women, who had enjoyed a more prominent role in indigenous Southeast Asian religious systems.[113] Of course, Islam was long established in the Malay world, but in the 19th century it took on a new character that was less amenable to women in public life. It is no coincidence that while women rulers were a feature of the 17th and 18th centuries — in Aceh, Patani and Kelantan — there were none in the 19th century. The insistence of the Yamtuan Muda Raja Ali on the veiling of women during his visit to Lingga is an example of how women were literally to be removed from view. In *Syair Sultan Mahmud*, Encik Kamariah records the visiting Yamtuan Muda's religious reforms:

Di dalam negeri dipalukan canang	The gong was struck throughout the country,
Laki-laki perempuan disuruh sembahyang	Men and women were commanded to pray:
Lima waktu malam dan siang	Five times, day and night,
Seumur hidupnya jangan berselang	As long as they live, without omission.
Dengan titah sultan terala	By the command of the sultan the exalted,
Mendirikan hukum Allah Ta'ala	Upholding the law of Allah the most high,
Segala perempuan bertudung kepala	All the women covered their heads.
Mana yang tak mau disuruhnya hela[114]	Those unwilling he ordered to be punished.

The figure of the sultan enforcing religious reform is a literary trope, but more unusual are Encik Kamariah's further remarks that the only women who welcomed this development were those with thinning or greying hair, and that women complained that the *tudung* made them perspire. There is a greater focus on fashion rather than piety (against two stanzas in which religion and Allah are mentioned, there are four describing various styles of *tudung*), as well as the oblique acknowledgement in the verses quoted above that the edict had to be put into practice by force.[115] The cumulative effect is less of a wholehearted acceptance of new standards of female modesty than of a lot of foot-dragging and not-so-subtle acts of resistance. This is in stark contrast to the women depicted in Raja Ali Haji's didactic work for women, *Syair Siti Sianah*, who accept veiling before a male visitor as an unadulterated expression of pious modesty.[116] It would have been interesting to know how long these religious reforms at the Lingga court persisted after the Yamtuan Muda's return to Penyengat.

Perhaps, like the moral panics that have marked Malay society in later times,[117] veiling was fitfully and unevenly enforced. Aristocratic *ulama* such as Yamtuan Muda Raja Ali and his cousin Raja Ali Haji would most likely have attempted to start at home, enforcing public veiling within their own families and courts as a first step. Where there was the greatest pressure on women to change, there may also have been the greatest resistance: it is probably no coincidence that Raja Ali Haji's sisters and daughters produced the romantic *syair* which most fervently defend the ability of women to act in the public sphere. Nevertheless, these romantic *syair* do not simply reject the new religious standards. The same *syariah*-mindedness that guided Raja Ali Haji's works may be found in such traits of the disguised heroine *syair* as their Middle Eastern names and settings, their implicit opposition to the eroticism that suffused earlier texts, and the removal of any trace of un-Islamic religious practices. As we shall see, the disguised heroine *syair* attempt to negotiate a path between *syariah*-

Tomb of Engku Puteri, Penyengat, 2004

minded Islam, with its diminished public role for women, and older and still durable cultural norms in which a woman's sphere of activity is not merely the household or the bedroom.

The first two chapters of the book set out the context against which the disguised heroine *syair* may be read. The first examines the evidence for women's engagement in literary activities in the Malay world in the 19th century and earlier, showing that far from being illiterate and excluded from the literary community, they were active composers, copyists and readers of texts. In Chapter 2, the persistent association between romance, the feminine and emotional catharsis is explored, in order to understand the potent appeal of the romantic *syair*. The final three chapters are literary analyses of the theme of emotional control in *Syair Siti Zuhrah* and *Syair Sultan Yahya*; disguised wives at war in *Syair Sultan Abdul Muluk* and *Syair Siti Zubaidah*; and the division of reason and passion between the genders in *Syair Siti Dhawiyyah* and *Syair Saudagar Bodoh*. The choice of these themes arose from their prominence in the *syair* themselves and the fact that they reflect distinct permutations within the corpus of disguised heroine *syair* texts. The discussion of the texts in pairs allows a comparison of the same theme in different but closely related works. The arrangement of the chapters also reflects the development of the theme of the disguised heroine throughout the 19th century, from the strongly Panji-influenced type exemplified by *Syair Siti Zuhrah* and *Syair Sultan Yahya*, to a more prominent espousal of Islamic values in *Syair Siti Zubaidah* and *Syair Sultan Abdul Muluk*, to an even more markedly Middle Eastern milieu in *Syair Siti Dhawiyyah* and *Syair Saudagar Bodoh*. The conclusion discusses the disappearance of the *syair* as a popular form from contemporary Malay culture, and suggests some possible heirs.

1

Not Just Fryers of Bananas and Sweet Potatoes

Women in the Malay Literary Community

Criticising a reciter of *hikayat*, or prose romance, who allows himself to be carried away by the sound of his own voice, the 19th-century Batavian writer Safirin bin Usman Fadli describes how

> while reciting, he listens intently to voices and movements behind the partition, inside the house in which the recitation of *hikayat* has been arranged. And the ignorant reciter thinks in his heart: 'This must be women peeping from behind the partition in admiration of my voice. So crazy about it are they that they have stopped making coffee and frying bananas and sweet potato.' This is what is on the mind of the shameless fool![1]

In this, one of the very few contemporaneous Malay depictions of the scene of reading, a woman's place with respect to literature is segregated and subordinate. She neither reads herself nor sits in the reading assembly, but remains in the kitchen preparing food and drink for the men. Her relationship to literature is an illicit one, charged with prohibited erotic feelings for the male reciter's seductive voice, with all the perils that may bring — not least, a disruption in the supplies of refreshments. Echoing this vision of Malay literary culture as the preserve of men is the comment of the Malaysian scholar of Riau *syair*, Abu Hassan Sham, that the existence of *syair* by women "shows that women in Penyengat in the 19th and early 20th centuries were able to escape the image of mere secluded maidens or housewives and to stride towards giving birth to works, whether creative or didactic".[2] The introduction to an edition of *Syair Siti Zubaidah* by another scholar, Abdul Mutalib Abdul Ghani, identifies one of the text's major themes to be female emancipation, "by which is meant that the tribe of Eve should not necessarily only play a role in the kitchen".[3] In an article in the state-sponsored journal of Malay language and culture, *Dewan Sastera*, Jelani Harun asserts that in the 17th century, "literacy, generally speaking, was only possessed by men".[4] While Safirin bin Usman Fadli is at odds with his modern counterparts, Abu Hassan Sham, Abdul Mutalib Abdul Ghani and Jelani Harun, as to whether women ought to be confined to the kitchen, there is a consensus that they were confined there.

But what is really known about the status and activities of Malay women before the 20th century? Indeed, as Barbara Andaya laments, there is a lack of sources "like village registers, school records, memoirs, letters" for Southeast Asia "even in relatively recent times".[5] Yet while what the scholars just mentioned seem to envisage a past during which Malay women were tethered to the *kuali*, this obscures the fact that, whatever the arrangements in the urban Batavian home described by Safirin, the royal women of Penyengat would have had slaves and debtors aplenty to fry the bananas. As in other parts of the world, the crucial factors determining literary production were class as well as gender. Daeng Wuh, Raja Salihah, Raja Kalsum and Raja Safiah, four of the female authors of romantic *syair* from Penyengat, were all ruling-class women, with sufficient leisure and education to partake of literary activities. The case of Encik Kamariah, an *inang* or nursemaid, and therefore probably a slave or some sort of bondswoman, as well as of Encik Jamilah and Encik Tipah, about whom nothing is known other than their names, suggests that female palace retainers were also expected to have among their accomplishments the ability to compose poems. Female literary production in the 19th-century Malay world should not be seen as a sign of modernity, or as an eccentric activity undertaken by a few proto-feminists, or even as the sole preserve of members of the aristocracy, but as an accomplishment appropriate to educated ladies, including court attendants. Other examples of the practice of literature by court women include Heian Japan, which produced the ultimate work of female court literature, *The Tale of Genji*; the *precieuses* of 17th-century France; and the Chinese women poets, particularly of the Ming and Qing dynasties.[6] In contradiction to the association between modernity and female literacy that is commonly assumed, women's literacy and engagement with written literature has nothing necessarily to do with female emancipation or progress out of a patriarchal past.

The evidence of Malay women's participation in literary activities is not negligible. The most striking is the attribution of authorship of *syair* to women from Riau: Raja Safiah (*Syair Kumbang Mengindra*), Daeng Wuh (*Syair Sultan Yahya*), Raja Salihah (*Syair Sultan Abdul Muluk*), Raja Kalsum (*Syair Saudagar Bodoh*), Encik Kamariah (*Syair Sultan Mahmud*), Encik Tipah (*Syair Sultan Marit*), and Encik Jamilah (*Syair Yatim Nestapa*). Three of these women belonged to a single family: that of the famed writer and reformer, Raja Ali Haji bin Raja Ahmad — Raja Safiah and Raja Kalsum were his daughters, and Raja Salihah was his sister. Just as significantly, all but one of these attributions come from the Dutch philologist H.C. Klinkert, who, as we will see, seems to have taken special care to inquire who wrote a manuscript and when. The Klinkert connection underscores the fact that although all the known female authors came from Riau, these are not all the possible female authors. As Woolf observes, "Anon, who wrote so many poems without signing them, was often a woman".[7] Traditional Malay literature is well furnished with anonymous texts, and it should not be assumed that they are all by men. Many texts — especially from genres which were considered ephemeral, like the romantic *syair* — will not have survived. Collecting the evidence about female literary activities suggests that some women were literate, wrote literary texts, listened to and performed recitations, owned, copied and even rented out manuscripts. The picture is less of a few women from Penyengat, the vanguard of Islamic revivalism, shrugging off the shackles of tradition in order to write, than of a literary culture in which it was common for court women to produce, perform, consume and circulate literary texts. Their texts of choice, it would appear, were romantic *syair* and *hikayat*.

I. Women's Literacy and Education

Drawing on the admonitory introductory verses to a manuscript from a mid-19th-century Palembang lending library, Kratz describes how the library's "male and female customers" are sitting close to the oil-lamp, bending over the manuscript, talking about the story while rolling it up and opening it again, holding it tight to the breast submerged deeply into text and conversation and plainly forgetting such trivialities as the fears expressed by the owner.[8]

Women are addressed directly in these introductory verses as "all you noble matrons" when they are asked not to chew betel while reading.[9] As Kratz points out, the mention of women readers in these verses "is a very important inclusion, yet which is quite in line with the known fact that manuscripts very often were copied by women as well as by men".[10] Here we have quite a different depiction of communal reading from that delineated by Safirin: the women are not behind the screen or in the kitchen, but gathered around the same oil lamp and the same manuscript as the men. Just as there may have been all male groups, like that described by Safirin, and mixed groups, such as the one implied by Kratz's Palembang manuscript, there may also have been all-female groups, as recounted in *Syair Buah-Buahan*, by Safirin's nephew Muhammad Bakir. All the characters of this *syair* are anthropomorphised fruit — the heroine is Anggur (Grape) and her companions include Rambutan, Duku and Cempedak — and it seems clear that Muhammad Bakir is playing on a stereotype of women readers. As the *syair* observes,

> All women enjoy *hikayat*
> Reading *syair* and any kind of narrative
> At all times and at every moment
> For each one knows her letters.[11]

Literary depictions of aristocratic women from earlier times often mention their reading and recitation. An impeccably educated princess in the 16th-century or earlier *Hikayat Bayan Budiman* is described as "erudite, knowledgeable about the art of *syair*, writing in a good hand, and possessing an understanding of astronomy".[12] The heroine of *Hikayat Putra Jaya Pati* is depicted reading a Panji tale, while a court lady in *Hikayat Isma Yatim* is said to own a copy of *Hikayat Inderaputra*.[13] In *Syair Sultan Yahya*, the heroine Siti Jauhar Manikam studies religious texts (*mengaji*) and is able to recite the Qur'an in a pleasing voice.[14] The heroine of *Syair Saudagar Bodoh* even has the Qur'an memorised.[15] The depiction of women's reading is obviously idealised, a quality to accompany their always peerless beauty and occasional ability to fly. No less idealised is their choice of texts: romantic prose narratives show her reading other romantic prose narratives, while in the disguised heroine *syair*, she reads only the Qur'an.[16] Documentary sources, however, show that reading and writing — for pleasure or spiritual profit — were not merely literary tropes. Apart from the surviving manuscripts copied or attributed to women, discussed below, there are significant numbers of 19th-century letters by and from women still extant.[17] These letters suggest that far from being cut off from the wider world, women engaged in trade, politics and love affairs (love letters were a major epistolary genre).[18] Moreover, there are letters from non-aristocratic women, suggesting that literacy was not limited to the upper classes.[19]

Whereas literacy in many parts of the premodern world was the preserve of a small male elite, in his landmark study of "early modern" Southeast Asian society, Reid contends that the situation in maritime Southeast Asia may have been quite different, with widespread literacy in indigenous scripts among both men and women.[20] Reid argues that trade and courtship were the impetus behind the unexpectedly high levels of literacy in pre-colonial Southeast Asia, particularly among women. Women engaged in trade, for which basic literacy and numeracy were essential. The exchange of love poems — especially the *pantun* form — written on leaves or scraps of paper, was an important part of courtship in south Sumatra and elsewhere. Colonial censuses turn up some remarkable results with regard to female literacy. The 1920 and 1930 Censuses of Netherlands India "recorded the highest literacy anywhere in Indonesia not in those provinces where the modern school system was most widespread (North Sulawesi and Ambon) but in the Lampung districts of southern Sumatra. In 1930, 45 per cent of adult men and 34 per cent of adult women could write, and in contrast to the usual "modern" pattern the older age groups, had higher literacy than the younger".[21] Of course, 1930 was not 1830, and in any case, the colonial census must be handled with care. As Reid observes, there may have been a bias in favour of the languages and scripts known to the census takers, thus tending to suppress figures for local scripts.[22] Moreover, if the data were obtained by interviews with male heads of households, it would then be particularly suspect in the case of female literacy.[23] Yet both of these possible biases would tend to suppress rather than exaggerate the number of female literates. The 1921 British census of 15 large towns in the Malay peninsula similarly recorded such high levels of female literacy that the author of the report declared them "unduly" so, and cast aspersions on the ability of the census takers.[24]

Reid's theory is that from the 16th to the 20th centuries, literacy declined in Southeast Asia as indigenous scripts and patterns of education were replaced by those associated with Islam and Christianity.[25] However, it has been suggested that Islam may have played a definitive role in the spread of literacy outside courtly and priestly circles, and even to have been the prerequisite for the development of written Malay literature.[26] Islam's emphasis on the ability to read the Qur'an meant that reading, at least, was required of all believers.[27] If there is manuscript and anecdotal evidence of women's literacy from such places as Penyengat and Banjar, after all notable centres of Islamic learning, might this be due to the influence of Islam itself? How did Islam affect the transmission of female literacy in the Malay world?

A glance at the situation in other Islamic cultures might be helpful, though here, too, statistics are difficult to come by and making the comparison to the Malay case is not straightforward. Women's education in Egypt is, fortunately, relatively well-mapped. Here, according to Baron:

> Daughters of the ulama and others had occasionally been taught by tutors in medieval times, and this pattern persisted into the early nineteenth century. Edward Lane found in the 1830s that although female children were seldom taught to read and write, a *shaykha* (learned woman) sometimes instructed the girls of the wealthiest families, and that a few middle-class girls attended school with boys. The central text for these lessons was the Qur'an ... If taught to read at all — and few were — women were taught in order to read religious works.[28]

By the first half of the 19th century, members of the religious establishment had begun to lend their voices to promoting female education, but even so, the rates remained dismal.[29] An 1897 census in Egypt indicated that 8 per cent of men and 0.2 per cent of women were literate.[30] In other words, for every literate woman, there were 40 literate men. Literacy rates for women rose markedly — up 50 per cent by 1907 — with the spread of state-sponsored education for girls.[31] The Netherlands Indies census suggests that while literacy as a whole was more restricted in Riau in 1930 (5.56%) than in Egypt in 1897 (about 8%), the ratio of male to female literates was far more favourable in Riau (1:10) than in Egypt (1:40). This suggests that gender was less of a barrier in attaining the skills of reading and writing in Riau than it was in Egypt.

Of course, religion is but one of the myriad of interconnected factors that influence literacy levels, and it seems likely that when girls in places such as Penyengat learnt to read, it was as part of their religious education. The "traditional system", as described by Tucker for Egypt, has many resonances for the Malay case: "girls, particularly the daughters of literate parents, commonly studied with boys, at least until they reached age ten or twelve, in many of the *kuttab*s scattered throughout the country, or, if their parents could afford it, with private tutors at home".[32] Private tutoring seems to be implied in a marginal verse in Raja Ali Haji's *Syair Siti Sianah*, cautioning against allowing one's daughters to study Qur'an reading with a male teacher.[33] By implication, then, women were available to provide such instruction. Reporting on 1850s Penang, J.D. Vaughan remarked on two Malay women who supported themselves by teaching.[34] Of course, Abdullah bin Abdul Qadir Munsyi recorded in his famous memoir that it was his grandmother who first taught him the rudiments of writing and that she ran a school where over 200 students, both boys and girls, studied Qur'an reading and other subjects: "All sorts of people studied with her; some studied writing, others studied letters and Malay, each according to his or her wishes. Almost all the children in Malacca came to study with her".[35] The unusual aspect of Abdullah's grandmother's school was probably that it was so large and organised, rather than that it was run by a woman.

In classes such as those described by Abdullah Munsyi, both girls and boys learnt to recite the Qur'an, then as now considered an essential skill for Malay Muslims. (It should be noted, however, that learning to recite the Qur'an need not involve becoming functionally literate in Jawi.) More recent anecdotal evidence confirms the pattern of early childhood education — for both boys and girls — being provided by women teachers.[36] In his memoirs of growing up in an aristocratic Negeri Sembilan family at the beginning of the 20th century, Tan Sri Datuk Dr. Mohamad Said relates how he was sent to Qur'an reading classes taught by two women, Wan Neng and Wan Teh. He is careful to point out that these early teachers, with whom he studied until he completed the Qur'an at the age of nine, "had no special qualifications, and could not be considered authorities on how each word of the Koran should be pronounced".[37] Having escaped from Wan Neng's "unsparing use of the rattan", he passed on to more highly qualified male teachers, who had either studied in Mecca or were affiliated with revered religious leaders, in the company of other boys of good families.[38] It seems that those who continued on to further study (almost invariably boys) would then pass to a more highly qualified man for religious instruction, or, with the establishment of the colonial educational system, to a secular school. Women teachers could not, it seems, aspire to the same kind of status as their male counterparts. Female students, for their part, rarely continued their religious education beyond the basic level, nor did they enter the colonial school system.

Despite their exclusion from higher formal education, some girls in the Malay world learnt to read and write Jawi, and despite the fact that this skill was notionally intended for their religious benefit, they read romances. Tan Sri Mohamad Said recalls that his grandmother, mother and two aunts "were all avid readers of *hikayat* and *syair*".[39] Indeed, as Mohamad Said also notes, a colonial education, such as the one he received at the Malay College Kuala Kangsar, tended to lead one to scorn secular *hikayat* and *syair*, with their erotic scenes surpassing (in his estimation) the worst excesses of *Lady Chatterly's Lover*.[40] Mohamad Said's recollections of the popularity of these texts may temper Gullick's depiction of widespread illiteracy among the aristocracy.[41] Certainly, literacy was far from universal, even among the highest echelons of society, and manuscripts were rare and fragile. At a friend's house, Mohamad Said "noticed several pages of [*Hikayat Sultan Bustaman*] scattered about in his bedroom. On inquiring from him what had happened to the rest of the pages, he said they had been borrowed by various people and had never been returned to him".[42] When Mohamad Said at last came across a complete copy of this *hikayat*, it was through his aunt and his rattan-wielding Qur'an teachers: "one day my aunt Khatijah showed me a beautifully hand-written copy of this *hikayat* which she had, with the greatest difficulty, succeeded in borrowing from Sharifah Rogayah, the mother of my Koran-reading teachers, Wan Teh and Wan Neng".[43] It is an eloquent testimony of the way women acquired literacy, that barred from higher education, they turned instead to *hikayat* and *syair*.

While the spread of a more *syariah*-minded form of Islam through the Malay world in the 19th and early 20th centuries may have tended to work against older cultural patterns that encouraged female literacy,[44] girls still seem to have learnt to read as a central component of their basic religious education. Though their teachers often seem to have been women, it is clear that female students and teachers were barred from progressing up the traditional educational ladder.[45] This barrier would have contributed to the gendered construction of reading in 19th-century Malay literary culture, with romance marked out as the female domain, and religion marked out as the male domain. Of course, women continued to engage with religious discourse: Mohamad Said recalls how his grandmother, mother and aunt frequently discussed religious subjects,[46] and there are several surviving religious manuscripts that were copied by or belonged to women.[47] But romance was strongly marked as a feminine genre, as we will see. Perhaps it is no wonder that women readers were drawn to the disguised heroine *syair*, which attempt to bridge the gap between the old romances and the new religious requirements.

II. Authors and Copyists

The question of authorship is freighted with great importance in the context of women's writing. Feminists are sceptical that the death of the author was proclaimed at the very moment when women authors began to enter the canon. Once women were able to enter the establishment, it was declared meaningless and abolished. As Nancy Miller points out, the idea of the death of the author may be "a way of hiding a new, ingenious phallocentrism — it does matter who the author is to women, denied names and authority".[48] Central to the feminist literary critical project, has been the rediscovery and restitution of women writers. In the Malay manuscript tradition, authors of romantic *syair*, male and female, did not have the same authority as authors of religious or dynastic works, such that even their names are preserved only through outside intervention. Furthermore, little remains of these authors but their names and their texts — and even such bare biographical information is rare enough. As Klinkert lamented in 1866 with regard to the *syair* manuscripts he collected, "[f]or most of the MSS I am unable to mention either the name of the authors, or the time of composition, or the place of origin, for these are unknown".[49]

For the most part, Malay secular literature must do without authors. Furthermore, the distinction between author and copyist is often a vexed question in manuscript traditions and is particularly unclear in the case of Malay *syair*.[50] In traditional Malay literature in general, works such as religious texts have more stable attributions and were copied with greater fidelity than more popular works, which were subject to the embellishment and amendment of scribes.[51] Within the *syair* form itself, those with historical or religious content were held in higher esteem than "fictional" *syair*. It is extremely uncommon for a romantic *syair* to bear any attribution at all, whether to a man or a woman. The authorial persona of the romantic *syair* is usually styled as a *dagang*, a wandering merchant, alone and friendless, who claims to have copied the text or heard the story from elsewhere. In *Syair Sultan Yahya*, for instance, the *dagang* persona claims:

Suatu cerita sahaya suratkan	I am writing down a tale,
Sultan Yahya diceterakan	Telling the tale of Sultan Yahya
Karangan orang sahaya turunkan[52]	Handing down someone else's composition.

It cannot be overemphasised that this is a persona, and a highly conventional one, rather than any biographical revelation. It is known that *Syair Sultan Yahya* is attributed to Daeng Wuh, and that she was a woman atached to the Penyengat court, entirely due to the intervention of Klinkert in the usually anonymous manuscript tradition. Six of the seven known women authors of *syair* come from Klinkert: on his evidence, Daeng Wuh composed *Syair Sultan Yahya* around 1860; Encik Jamilah composed (or copied) *Syair Yatim Nestapa* in 1864; Encik Kamariah composed *Syair Sultan Mahmud*; Encik Tipah composed (or owned) *Syair Sultan Marit*; Raja Kalsum composed *Syair Saudagar Bodoh* in 1865; and Raja Safiah, who died in 1859, composed *Syair Kumbang Mengindera*.[53]

Klinkert's attention to provenance seems to have been unusual among European collectors, highlighted by Van Ronkel's belief, when he was compiling a catalogue of the Batavia Society's manuscript holdings in 1909, that information about previous owners and places of origin was irrelevant.[54] Just as unusual was Klinkert's interest in the low prestige texts of the Malay tradition: almost 60 per cent of his manuscripts, now held in the Leiden University library, are copies of romantic *syair* and *hikayat*.[55] Klinkert's interest in secular literature was probably prompted by his need to master a more literary style of Malay. He was engaged in translating the Bible into Malay, and had in fact already completed one version. The missionary society deemed its language too demotic, too redolent of urban Semarang, and therefore sent him to Riau, which European philogists of the time held to be the home of the purest Malay *Kitab* texts, with their frequent use of Arabic terminology, were intended to be read by religious students with assistance from their teachers — hardly a suitable model for a Bible translation intended to be widely accessible to lay people.[56] It seems that he intended his translation to be both accessible and literary, and his interest in *syair* — the popular form par excellence — should probably be seen in this context. That Klinkert's wife, Louisa Wilhemina Kahle, was an Indies-born woman of "mixed blood" who spoke only Malay and Javanese[57] may explain how he managed to get access to women's texts from the palaces of Siak, Penyengat and Lingga.

The name of the seventh woman author also comes from a Dutch philologist, Hermann von de Wall, who recorded on his copy of the manuscript that *Syair Sultan Abdul Muluk* was composed by Raja Salihah.[58] *Syair Sultan Abdul Muluk* appeared in print in the Dutch journal *Tijdschrift voor Neerlands Indië* in 1847. In this published version, Raja Ali Haji is given as the author, on the basis of a letter sent by him to the journal's editor, Roorda van Eysinga, in which Raja Ali Haji refers to "*Hikayat Sultan Abdul Muluk* which I myself have versified in Johor Malay".[59] Von de Wall lived for a time in Riau and knew Raja Ali Haji and his family circumstances very well, thus it is unlikely he would have made an error about the authorship of the poem. The Batavian publisher, Roorda van Eysinga, on the other hand, does not seem to have ever travelled to Penyengat or to have met Raja Ali Haji. Presumably, Raja Ali Haji or someone else in his family gave the manuscript to Von de Wall some time after the latter's arrival in Riau in 1857 and also gave him the name of Raja Salihah. One hypothesis is that Raja Ali Haji is the author, while Raja Salihah was the scribe who made Von de Wall's copy. In a letter to Von de Wall, Raja Ali Haji wrote of the manuscript of *Surat Kurais Raja Alam* he was sending his Dutch friend, that it "is a text in refined Malay, though the calligraphy is defective and many of the words are defective, because it is a woman's writing".[60] Both Raja Ali Haji and Haji Ibrahim complained about the difficulty and expense of finding competent copyists for the work they were doing for Von de Wall's dictionary.[61] It is possible that Raja Ali Haji pressed some of his female relatives into working in his home scriptorium. Certainly, he gave texts copied by women to Von de Wall as gifts (such as *Surat Kurais*) and loaned texts composed by women (such as his daughter Raja Kalsum's *Syair Saudagar Bodoh*) to Klinkert's own scribes to copy.

However, the alternative that Raja Salihah was responsible for a prose version or a different verse version of *Syair Sultan Abdul Muluk* which her brother revised or appropriated for publication seems on balance more likely. Raja Ali Haji was the indisputable author of numerous works, including many *syair*. However, none of the other *syair* belongs to the romantic adventure genre. Though they are often humorous, and in the case of *Syair Suluh Pegawai,* distinctly ribald, they all convey didactic messages about religious practice or law. With its completely different subject matter and much greater length, *Syair Sultan Abdul Muluk* sits rather oddly among Raja Ali Haji's other *syair*. It is also the most likely of all his known works to appeal to a European audience captivated by oriental literature (Goethe's

West-östlicher Diwan appeared in 1819, Lane's English translation of the Arabian Nights in 1839). In 1838, Van Eysinga published in Holland a Dutch version of *Syair Ken Tambuhan*, which he recommended to his readers as a specimen of poetry "encountered among peoples who, being neither literate nor civilized, express themselves naturally, following quite artlessly the promptings of their feeling and imagination": truly a Romantic recommendation.[62] One cannot therefore quite imagine Van Eysinga thrilling to the explanations in Raja Ali Haji's *Syair Siti Sianah* the necessity for ritual ablutions following a woman's menstrual period or to the risqué situations that arise from too-hurried divorce in his *Syair Suluh Pegawai*.[63] It is possible that *Syair Sultan Abdul Muluk* or a *hikayat* of that title was composed, read and copied by the women of Raja Ali Haji's household and that Raja Ali Haji appropriated it and reworked it, knowing the sort of thing Van Eysinga was after. On the other hand, Raja Ali Haji may simply have had a greater range of styles than one might first expect from a theologian, grammarian, linguist and historian. Though he regarded *syair* verses "as dealing in passion (*nafsu*) rather than addressing the intellect (*akal*), as conveying sentiment rather than substance", as Proudfoot gleans from Raja Ali Haji's comments on the interleaved *syair* passages in his *Silsilah Melayu dan Bugis*, nonetheless that work is brimming with *syair* and romantic *pantun*.[64] However, given the similarities of *Syair Sultan Abdul Muluk* to other romantic *syair* and its difference from the rest of Raja Ali Haji's oeuvre, it seems likely that, as Braginsky suggests, this was a text from the women's quarters of the palace that Raja Ali Haji edited.[65]

All seven of these manuscripts by women — the only pre-20th century texts in all of Malay literature to be attributed to named women authors — are *syair* from Riau. The connection between women and *syair*, especially romantic *syair*, has already been alluded to and will be discussed in more detail in the following chapter, but the Riau nexus raises the question of whether there was something special about the archipelago. Was there something about Penyengat that encouraged women's literary production? Abu Hassan Sham, for instance, proposes that the women of Raja Ali Haji's family were particularly imaginative.[66] While this hypothesis is impossible to substantiate, two factors that characterised Penyengat may have played a role in fostering women's engagement in literature there: the resurgence of *syariah*-minded Islam at the Yamtuan Muda's court, and the Bugis heritage of the viceregal family.

It is possible that royal women in Riau were more literary than women elsewhere in the Malay world because of this Bugis heritage. The Bugis had well-developed traditions of historiography and of palace women's involvement in the transmission of texts. A Dutch missionary searching for manuscripts in mid-19th century south Sulawesi observed:

> In general the Native women, especially the female chiefs, are much more expert in Bugis literature than the men ... Finally I looked no longer for the *guru* [religious teachers], but only for the *pasura*, i.e., those who occupy themselves with reading the *sura* or writings ... One finds such people only among the chiefly women and similar old women who have been associated with the court for a long time.[67]

But though the Penyengat aristocracy were proud of their Bugis roots, the cultural style and indeed the language of the court were Malay. Historical, *pasura*-type writings from Penyengat, whether by men or women, are not to be found. One of the *syair* attributed to a Riau woman, Encik Kamariah's *Syair Sultan Mahmud*, is a commemorative poem describing the journey of the sultan to Lingga. *Syair Sultan Mahmud* belongs to the well-established genre of the voyage *syair*,[68] and would not seem to owe anything to Bugis antecendents. Literary works from Penyengat appear to show no connection to Bugis forms. Raja Ali Haji's *Tuhfat al-Nafis*, while distinct from much of the Malay historiographical tradition, is shaped by Arabic rather than Bugis historiography.

Bugis cultural mores with regard to the position of women may be evident in the prominent role played by Engku Puteri, daughter of one Yamtuan Muda and wife of another, in the early 19th century. As well as being the custodian of the royal regalia, financing her younger brother's pilgrimage to Mecca, acting as a mediator between warring Bugis factions and playing a key role in brokering dynastic marriages, Engku Puteri also commissioned at least three literary works: *Syair Tengku Selangor, Syair Perang Johor* and *Kisah Engku Puteri*.[69] The first relates the visit of Tengku Selangor[70] to the Dutch Assistant Resident Walbeehm in Penyengat. The author, one Encik Ismail bin Datuk Kerkun, states on the first page of the manuscript:

Tengku Puteri suruh beta	Tengku Puteri instructed me
Karang syair suruh kata	To compose a *syair* and to relate [an account];
Baginda hendak buat cerita	
Kerana adinda pergi pesta	Her highness wished to have a story Because her sister has gone on a pleasure trip.

Dari titah tuan penghulu	From of the royal command of our leader,
Sebab takut serta malu	Because of [my] fear and reticence
Dia menyuruh sudah selalu	She commands me [to write it] constantly
Tidak boleh nanti dahulu[71]	[I] may not tarry.

Amidst the thoroughly conventional apologies and protestations of the authorial persona, it is striking to see Engku Puteri referred to as "tuan penghulu" and "seri paduka", words which are not used to describe her in Raja Ali Haji's *Tuhfat al-Nafis*. There is no doubt here that her commands were to be taken seriously. The second two works are extant now only in a copy made for Walbeehm in 1844, the year of Engku Puteri's death. *Kisah Engku Puteri* documents a voyage she made from Riau to visit her sick younger brother in Lingga in 1831. After a stay of some three months, during which her brother was cured and a thanksgiving feast was held, Engku Puteri returned to Penyengat. She was accompanied on her voyage by the author of the work, her brother Engku Haji Ahmad.[72] Engku Puteri was also the patron of Haji Abdul Wahab, "a Siamese by birth, although of Menangkabow heritage" who "went to Pulo Pinigad, where he sought and obtained the countenance of Tuankoo Pootri, the most influential of the widows of the deceased Sulthaun, and became the High Priest of herself and the Royal Family, as well as that of the nobility".[73] Haji Abdul Wahab is said to have translated the text now known as *Hikayat Ghulam* from Arabic into Malay, subsequently copied for Walbeehm and now in the Leiden collection.[74] All four of these texts survived only because of their connection to Walbeehm, so it is possible that there were more texts commissioned by Engku Puteri, or indeed by other royal women, that are now lost.

Yet even the striking prominence of Engku Puteri in public life may not be a specifically Bugis trait. Royal women who played central roles in politics and literature alike can be found elsewhere in Southeast Asia. In 18th-century Java, Ratu Pakubuwana was an important figure at the court of her grandson, Pakubuwana II. As Ricklefs has shown, Ratu Pakubuwana commissioned texts as a way of advancing her agenda at court.[75] Like Engku Puteri, Ratu Pakubuwana derived much of her authority from her exalted lineage and from personal spiritual prowess. Both women controlled access to the royal regalia, crucial for conveying dynastic legitimacy. Another example of a royal woman acting as a literary patron comes from 17th-century Aceh, where Taj al-'Alam, ruling in her own right as the daughter of one king and the widow of another, commissioned a work on religious law, *Mir'at al-Tullab*, from the Sumatran scholar Abdul Rauf al-Singkili. The next Acehnese queen, Inayat Shah, commissioned two works from him: *Risalat Adab Murid Akan Syeikh* and *Sharh Hadith Arba'in*, a commentary on a hadith collection.[76] Other religious works commissioned by the Acehnese queens are said to include *Tibyan fi Ma'rifat al-Adyan*, *Kifayat al-Muhtajin*, and *Akhbar al-Akhirat fi Ahwal al-Qiyamah*.[77] This suggests that the production of literary works at the behest of a spiritually and politically important woman was not unheard of in the royal courts of maritime Southeast Asia.[78]

But the most significant reason why Penyengat is exceptional in the Malay world as the home of all the known Malay women authors was the presence of Klinkert and Von de Wall. That the best evidence for female authors and copyists comes from Penyengat should not be taken to mean that such women were only to be found there. After all, Klinkert also collected manuscripts copied by women in Siak and Lingga, and Den Hamer witnessed Banjarese women copying out *syair*.[79] It is only when women authors and copyists are mentioned in passing in documents exchanged between men that a female authorial presence in traditional Malay literature can be proven. The Malay manuscripts that survive in libraries and archives today cannot be taken to be a complete or accurate representation of Malay literary culture, even of the relatively recent 19th century.[80] Ironically, Dutchmen like Klinkert and Von de Wall have bequeathed to us all the women authors known today.

III. Lenders and Borrowers

Colophons and accession records of manuscript collections indicate that women often owned books and circulated them between themselves, sometimes for a fee. Based on her research in Kedah, Kelantan and Terengganu, as well as recent offers of sales of manuscripts to the Malaysian National Library, Siti Hawa Haji Salleh remarks that *hikayat* were frequently read by palace women.[81] Indeed, better data on ownership may be gleaned from the catalogues of the younger manuscript collections — such as those in Malaysia and Indonesia — than from the older European collections. Although the manuscripts held in Malaysia and Indonesia themselves do not usually date from much before the late 19th century, they provide more information about a chirographic tradition that was still alive, if not flourishing, when they were copied. Among the manuscripts owned by women and now in the collection of Dewan Bahasa dan Pustaka, are a 1910 copy of *Hikayat Koris Mengindera* that belonged to al-Hajjah Mariam binti Muhammad Amin, Laksamana Perak;[82] *Syair Dewa Syah Syarif* donated by Cik Soda in 1963; *Syair Raja Muda Perlis* purchased from Sharifah Hanum binti Syed Hamzah; *Syair Sultan Mansur* bought from Tengku Zamzam; and three fragments of *Hikayat Syamsul Anwar*, collectively known as MS 90(A), that belonged to Tengku Zamzam, Sharifah Mastura binti Syed Shahabudin and Tengku Kalthum binti Sultan Abdul Hamid.[83] In the Malaysian National Library's holdings are a *Kitab Tawhid*, owned and possibly copied by Encik Zainab binti Tuan Khatib Abdul Karim al-Sambawa; *Bayan al-Shirk*, copied by Encik Aminah; and *Doa Kanzil 'Arasy* owned by Hajjah Fatimah binti al-Marhum Tuan Haji Abdul Hamid.[84] Other religious texts owned by women — suggesting that the depiction of them reading only romances is not quite the truth — are the didactic compendia of Nyonya Sawang, including tales directed at women, such as *Hikayat Darma Ta'siah* and *Hikayat Fatimah Bersuami*, as well as non-gender specific works like *Hikayat Raja Khandak* and *Kitab Seribu Masa'il*; a similar compendium of religious works belonging to Nyonya Halimah; and *Tarikah 'Alawiyyah* belonging to Nyonya Tasnim.[85] Klinkert acquired manuscripts from at least two other Penyengat women: Encik Seni, copyist and/or owner of *Syair Madhi*, and Encik Tipah, author or owner of *Syair Sultan Marit*.[86] The women's names confirm that, for the most part, they belonged to the most privileged strata of society — princesses and daughters of high court officials, sayyids, and religious notables.

How books circulated within this elite group in Riau is suggested by a note at the end of Klinkert's manuscript of *Hikayat Syah Firman*, one of eight bought from a *selir* or secondary wife of the Yamtuan Muda of Siak:

> *Hikayat Tuan Puteri Nurlela* was borrowed by Rasyimah on the fourth day of Rabia' al-Awwal in the Dutch year 1863, and was read for two nights. Just before the third night it was returned to its owner. For that we express our profuse thanks, because we greatly enjoyed hearing about the exploits of Syah Firman and his brother, together with their wives Tuan Puteri Indrasuka and Tuan Puteri Nurlela Cahaya.[87]

Another example of a text transmitted by a network of royal women is *Hikayat Syamsul Anwar*, written by Raja Aisyah Sulaiman, a granddaughter of Raja Ali Haji, in 1890. The text seems never to have been published. Out of the five surviving manuscript copies of the text, three come from royal women (the provenance of the other two is apparently unknown).[88] The three fragments belonging to Dewan Bahasa dan Pustaka that comprise MS 90(A), mentioned above, suggest that the text was literally parcelled out between various women. The conclusion of this manuscript traces its copying history: "This was composed by Raja Aisyah binti Raja Haji Sulaiman, Raja Pulau Penyengat, and copied by her humble close companion on the 14th of August, 1917, which equates with the first of Syawal, 1325. And the *hikayat* was copied once more by this humble servant in Alor Setar, the town of the country of Kedah, and was completed at 12.30 on Friday, the 18th of Dhu'l-Hijjah, 1351 [1933]".[89] The Kuala Terengganu manuscript of *Hikayat Syamsul Anwar* demonstrates a similar movement between royal women. Its colophon states that the *hikayat* was copied in Singapore in 1917 from a copy belonging to Tengku Fatimah Puteri al-Marhum Sultan Abu Bakar of Johor. Further on, the reader is informed that Tengku Ampuan Mariam had asked permission from Tengku Fatimah to copy the manuscript, and permission being granted, wrote it out into 33 notebooks in 1947. The manuscript, therefore, would seem to have come from Raja Aisyah or the Yamtuan Muda family in the first instance, before passing to and perhaps being copied by the Johor princess, and from there going to the Terengganu princess. Ties of blood are obviously important in the transfer of the manuscript — the three royal families of Terengganu, Johor and Riau were related. Just as significant is the absence of the print medium and of intervention by male relatives. Manuscripts evidently circulated through the personal connections between royal women, and were copied by the women themselves. Tengku Ampuan Mariam owned a number of other manuscripts, including *Hikayat Isma Yatim*, and also compiled a handbook of Terengganu court dance.[90] Rather than being a modern innovation, Tengku Ampuan Mariam's interest in *belles-lettres* was more probably part of a long-established tradition: literature, like dance, was a courtly pastime appropriate to royal women. Although these copies date from the dying days of the Malay manuscript tradition, it stands to reason that if Tengku Ampuan Mariam was willing to copy a manuscript by hand as late as 1947 when printed reading material was widely available, such a practice would have been even more widespread a century before.[91]

Of course, manuscripts were not always loaned disinterestedly — another common way for them to circulate was by being rented out for a fee. Encik Wuk binti Tuan Bilal Abu of Penyengat owned a copy of *Syair Sultan Mansur* (Klinkert 129) which she sold for six ringgit and two rupiah in 1863, as the buyer noted at the beginning of the manuscript. This new owner also warned that one should not allow the manuscript to be copied since "it is difficult to find and seldom available to buy, [and] because in this work a very beautiful story is related and of ten other copies not a single one is complete".[92] Manuscripts were obviously a valuable commodity, and owners did not scruple to restrict their circulation in order to maintain their rarity. As the daughter of Tuan Bilal Abu, to whom *Syair Siti Dhawiyyah* is sometimes attributed, Encik Wuk may have owned a number of manuscripts. Tengku Mariam's manuscript of *Hikayat Shams al-Anwar* also concludes with several stanzas which suggest that its owner rented it out for a fee:

Hendaklah tuan hal membaca	When you are reading,
Jangan tersirap walau di meja	Don't fling it down, even on a table.
Hikayat bukan didapat sahaja	*Hikayat* are not easily got,
Melainkan dengan keluar belanja	Without expenditure of money.
Sungguh tak elok karangan segala	Though the composition is unsatisfactory,
Tetapi banyak menuntutnya pula	Yet many ask to read it even so.
Harga pun lebih daripada mula	The price is more than it used to be,
Seratus enam puluh satu kepala[93]	One hundred and sixty per copy.

And:

Jelas dibayar tidak bersakit	Pay up in advance and you'll have no troubles,
Tiap-tiap sepenggal dua puluh ringgit	Each volume is twenty *ringgit*.
Yang membaca jagalah sedikit	You who are reading, take a bit of care:
Jangan terkena barang yang lekit	Don't let sticky things touch it.
Sampai tempoh janji dibilang	When the agreed time has elapsed,
Surat dipinjam segera akan pulang	The borrowed book should be returned promptly.
Namun jadi rosak hilang	Should it be damaged or lost,
Ukumnya kiamat bukan kepalang[94]	Great will be the punishment in the next world.

The observation that Malay manuscripts circulated mostly through interpersonal connections, there being neither libraries nor commercial booksellers, has been made before, notably by Proudfoot.[95] What has not been highlighted previously is the fact that royal women were also involved in a manuscript economy perhaps separate or parallel to a masculine one of martial-themed *hikayat*, religious and dynastic texts.[96]

* * * * *

Women in the 19th-century Malay world were not restricted to eavesdropping on men's *hikayat* recitation. They read, copied and indeed composed their own texts. They were both patrons and hirers of manuscripts. As we shall see in the next chapter, many works — most notably romantic *syair* and didactic texts — were addressed to female audiences. While the surviving evidence of Malay women's involvement in literary activities surveyed here is sparse, there is enough of it to prove that the assumption that literacy was the preserve of men in the premodern Malay world is unfounded. Moreover, the fact that there is any evidence at all is remarkable. The old Javanese literary tradition, to which the Malay may be compared if only because Creese's study of women in *kakawin* poetry is one of the few to discuss the issue of gender with regard to a traditional Southeast Asian literature, provides no such traces. According to Creese, women's literary activities in Javanese were restricted to the "social" — "the composition of lovers' laments and messages of secret assignation, written on nonpermanent surfaces such as the leaves of the *pudak* petal and *sumanasa* flowers, or the panels of buildings" — or the oral — "songs and lyrics of olden times as well as ancient stories collected together and passed on by word of mouth". Creese concludes that if "a distinctively women's writing ever existed in the Indic courts of Java and Bali, it has now been irretrievably lost".[97] The romantic *syair* is precisely the kind of distinctively women's writing that is lacking for Java and Bali, not only in its authors and audiences, but also in its viewpoint and its themes, and all the more notable because it would appear to be a particularly Malay phenomenon.

2

The Best Ones Make You Cry

Genre, Gender and Catharsis

The cluster of elements so persistently attached to the genre of the romantic *syair* throughout its history are encapsulated in Virginia Matheson's account of meeting a *syair* enthusiast in 1980s Riau. This was "Tengku Bun's second daughter, Tengku Sepiah, a lively lady in her forties", who

> explained to us how the horoscope books were used and told us anecdotes about personalities living and dead. When I expressed an interest in *syair*, she asked her brothers to find the copy of *Syair Seri Banian Selindung Delima* which the family owned. Eventually it was located at a neighbour's house, and Tengku Sepiah said she would read it. Bashfully at first, but then with more enthusiasm, she sang the *syair* for us. She repeated the tune every verse and her performance was enjoyed not only by all the family but also by the children who had gathered outside the house and stood watching, their heads thrust through the open windows. Tengku Sepiah remembered how in her youth she would devour a whole *syair* in one evening, and would weep over the best ones.[1]

Here, as so often, romantic *syair* are associated with aristocratic women, who are said to consume the texts compulsively, deriving from them a pleasure always close to tears. Many of these characteristics of the romantic *syair* as a genre are shared with forms of popular romance the world over, from medieval England, to tenth-century Japan, to present-day Mills and Boone. To these similarities must be added other charges often laid at the door of romance: that it is false and morally dangerous, and at the same time, paradoxically enough, trivial and aesthetically impoverished. Critics of romance in the Malay world, such as Abdullah Munsyi and the 19th-century Batavian scribe Safirin bin Usman Fadli, decried their power to befuddle the reader's intellectual and moral senses. Others, such as Raja Ali Haji, dismissed romantic *syair* as mere entertainment even as they register their enjoyment of such diversions from their more serious labours.

That the experience of literature is pleasurable is mostly obvious, but bears repeating in a scholarly context, where texts are works first and enjoyable a very distant second. As Leonard Jackson observes,

> All over the world, throughout the whole of history, people have been singing or reciting poems, acting in plays of various kinds, and telling stories ... All this time, other people have been watching these works and listening to them, and sometimes reading them — not through compulsion, not through languid acceptance of a social duty, not even as a formal religious or university study (though all these things exist), but avidly, for the sake of personal desire, and sometimes with a total, if temporary, loss of self.[2]

As Matheson's anecdote about Tengku Sepiah suggests, romantic *syair* were read for the pleasure to be gained from the "loss of self" described by Jackson. This is not, of course, to assert that romantic *syair* contained no trace of normative attitudes, no messages the text wished to impart to its audience. Since the text is shaped by the norms of its cultural milieu, it necessarily contains such attitudes and messages. The disguised heroine of the romantic *syair* is an exemplar of a sort, from whom one might take lessons for proper wifely conduct, but this was surely not the reason for its appeal. Rather, it is simply to point out that romantic *syair* were not primarily intended or understood to be for the provision of didactic instruction or the pursuit of spiritual perfection, usually taken to be the hierarchically superior values of traditional Malay literature.[3] Indeed, the *syair* heroines often act in defiance of the ideals of feminine conduct as promulgated in didactic texts of the period. This must be one source of their popularity among readers and of the disapproval they garnered among those readers' "betters". This chapter explores aspects of the genre of the romantic *syair* as a form of popular romance, and a particularly feminine one at that, before considering the power of *syair* recitation to call up listeners' emotions, ideally in order to provide a form of catharsis.

I. Heroine as Hero, Princess as Panji Prince

Women in male disguise are by no means scarce in world literature: randomly selected examples include the medieval English *Roman de Silence*, the Chinese folk ballad of Mulan, Shakespeare's *Twelfth Night*, and the *Arabian Nights*' story of Budur and Kamar al-Zaman. The comic and erotic possibilities of a woman in men's clothes must always have tempted writers, especially since male disguise greatly increases the plot possibilities for a female character in societies where women were not supposed to venture beyond the home. In Malay literature, this disguise takes a particular form, that of the princess who becomes a wandering knight, irresistible both in sexual attractiveness and force of arms. Her change into a man may be effected either by a simple donning of clothes, as is usual in the Riau *syair*, or by actual bodily metamorphosis effected by Batara Kala or a similar deity. Such heroines are rife in the Malay prose romances that go by the name of their usual hero, Panji. The vast corpus of Panji tales revolves around this hero, otherwise known as Raden Inu, prince of the kingdom of Kuripan, and his betrothed and beloved, Raden Galuh, princess of Daha. Their travels and adventures in search of each other, in various disguises and under a bewildering number of aliases, form the basis of the infinitely mutable storyline. Their adventures are often paralleled by those of their siblings and offspring, so that the plot may be multi-stranded and a conclusive ending infinitely deferred. Panji tales are of ancient provenance in Java, traceable through temple carvings to the 15th century,[4] and if Kumar is right about a connection between Panji in Java and Genji in Japan, both represented as a "radiant prince, peerlessly beautiful, superbly adorned, phenomenally accomplished, and of hyper-refined sensibility", to 500 BC.[5]

Panji tales seem to have spread from Java to the Malay courts during the period of Majapahit ascendancy in the 15th and 16th centuries.[6] They would have been well known to the readers of Penyengat. Klinkert's manuscript collection, gathered largely but not exclusively in Riau, includes *Hikayat Misa Kagungan Seri Panji Wila Kesuma* and *Hikayat Mesa Perabu Jaya*. Among Von de Wall's manuscripts are *Hikayat Cekel*

Waneng Pati, *Hikayat Nayakusuma*, and *Hikayat Mesa Gimang*.⁷ A *syair* commemorating notable events in the reign of Sultan Mahmud of Lingga makes reference several times to stock Panji characters and tropes: the sultan's palace is a suitable playground for Betara Kala and twice a princess' beauty is likened to that of Candra Kirana.⁸ During a royal wedding in Lingga, a Javanese theatrical company puts on a performance, possibly enacting stories of the Panji type.⁹ Their continuing popularity in Malay is attested by the manuscripts that were copied and composed into the 20th century.¹⁰

Establishing dates for particular versions of Panji tales in Malay or particular motif within the tale is subject to the usual pitfall of having a long literary tradition represented almost exclusively by 19th-century manuscripts. The heroine transformed into a man and the hero into a woman is found in at least two Javanese Panji tales, *Kuda Narawangsa* and *Panji Jayeng Tilam*, and in five of the ten Malay Panji tales examined by Harun Mat Piah.¹¹ But without hard chronological evidence — none of the texts discussed by Harun Mat Piah are dated — and given the paucity of heroines-as-heroes in the Javanese as distinct from the Malay Panji tales, it might seem probable that the motif came into Javanese and Malay literature from other sources. Perhaps the heroine-in-disguise is a late importation into Panji tales from, for instance, Urdu *masnavi* or the *Arabian Nights*?

Fortunately, Thai literary history proves to be more punctilious about recording dates. Two dramatic poems in Thai describing the adventures of Panji in Java are traceable to the mid-18th century, with the extant versions dated to 1809 at the latest.¹² In one of these poems, the heroine is transformed into a man by divine intervention and wanders as a prince, collecting several vassal states in her travels. When she meets with the hero again, the curse is lifted and they recognise each other. In the second poem, the heroine disguises herself as a man and is adopted as a son by a king. She wanders in search of her beloved, conquering a number of kingdoms in the process.¹³ Remarkably, these two poems are said to have been composed by Thai princesses, from the stories told to them by Malay serving women. Nilprapassorn writes that tradition attributes the poems to two daughters of Somdet Phra Chao Boromakot: "The Princesses had Malay maids who narrated different tales from the Panji cycle to them. Being inspired by the recitals, Princess Kunthon, the elder, composed *Dalang* while Princess Mongkut, the younger, composed *Inao* as dance-drama texts".¹⁴ Poerbatjaraka's observation that the source for Cambodian

Panji is Malay rather than Javanese because the form "Inao" rather than "Inu" appears to be influenced by Jawi orthography (a-y-n-w) would seem to apply here.[15] The significance of the Thai *Dalang* and *Inao*, apart from confirming the association between Malay palace women, secular court literature and recited performance, is that it makes it possible to state that the motif of the heroine as a warrior prince is already present in Malay literature in 1809.

An additional argument for Panji tales as the source of the disguised heroine in Riau *syair* is the close similarity of this motif between the two types of texts. In both, the heroine is after all not disguised as just any man, but as the perfect prince, exciting desire in all those who observe him, travelling in search of the lost beloved, conquering kingdoms and marrying princesses along the way. The disguise of the heroine not only as a hero, but as a Panji-type hero, occurs in several Malay Panji texts, including *Hikayat Kuda Semirang Sira Panji Pandai Rupa*, *Hikayat Panji Semirang*, *Hikayat Galuh Digantung*, *Hikayat Nayakusuma*, *Hikayat Misa Susupan*, and *Hikayat Carang Misa Kembar Sari*.[16] Harun Mat Piah proposes a number of typical features of Malay Panji tales, three of which are particularly prominent in the Riau *syair*: the heroine as Panji-type hero; battles between princesses; and the heroine's conflict with her mother-in-law. To this can be added the subplots involving siblings and the secondary disguise of the heroine as a dancer, musician or singer.[17] Mat Piah observes that the battles between princesses and the heroine's conflict with her mother-in-law are more characteristic of Malay than of Javanese Panji works.[18] Thus, even though the questing, bellicose heroine-in-disguise is present in Javanese Panji, she seems to have been more prominent in Malay Panji. The Malay tradition, in other words, amplified an element that was rather more minor in the Javanese source material. The Malay Panji heroine in disguise then became, in 19th-century Riau, the star of her own sub-genre of romantic *syair*.

Of the Panji texts just mentioned, few are easily available in published form or as scholarly editions, making reference to them for the purposes of source criticism problematic. There are, for instance, two very different modern published versions of *Panji Kuda Semirang*, and their relationship to the manuscript corpus is not at all clear. Nevertheless, it is significant that the character after whom *Panji Semirang* is named is not Raden Inu at all, but Candra Kirana.[19] She and her two handmaidens are not merely disguised as men, but have been turned into men by the god Betara Kala. Thus transformed and equipped with magic keris, they conquer the kingdoms of Tumasik, Angkar, Wirabumi, and Wirasab. Panji Semirang takes the two princesses of Wirasab captive. In another, significantly different, version of *Hikayat Panji Semirang*, Candra Kirana is the daughter of a king, competing for her father's affections with her half-sister Galuh Ajeng. Scorned by her father and stepmother, Candra Kirana runs away dressed as a man, and going by the name Panji Semirang Asmarantaka, founds a new kingdom.[20] The heroine of a Panji tale in a manuscript collected by Klinkert disguises herself as a man, and going by the name Mesa Perabu Jaya, becomes ruler of Mataram.[21] Another feature of Malay Panji works — though, again, not of the Javanese tales on which they are purportedly based — is battles between princesses. In *Hikayat Carang Mesa Kembar Sari*, Candra Kirana and another of Panji's wives do battle. While in male disguise, Candra Kirana is also known to fight Raden Inu himself, which always results in her victory.[22]

Though all these aspects of the heroine as hero are present in the female quest *syair* as a group, this is not the case with regard to the *syair* taken singly. The *syair* which most closely resemble Panji tales are *Syair Siti Zubaidah*, *Syair Sultan Abdul Muluk*, and *Syair Siti Zuhrah*. In these poems, the female protagonist is closest to the Panji heroine as hero, conquering kingdoms, and in two cases, marrying the princesses of vassal states. *Syair Sultan Yahya* has a more markedly Minangkabau or Malay folk flavour, while *Syair Saudagar Bodoh* and *Syair Siti Dhawiyyah* may be characterised as more Islamic, or at least more Middle Eastern, in their trappings. Nevertheless, Siti Jauhar Maknikam, heroine of *Syair Sultan Yahya*, engages in combat with her co-wife, Puteri Belanta Puri, as is characteristic of Malay Panji tales. Perhaps the clearest demonstration of kinship between the disguised heroine in Riau *syair* and the same figure in Panji tales is provided by Siti Zuhrah. Fleeing her home because of the ill treatment she suffers at the hands of her stepmother and half-siblings, Zuhrah and her sister Nurkiah disguise themselves as men. Their motive is not to rescue any male relative in distress, but because remaining at court and receiving scanting treatment from the queen is intolerable. The Panji heroine has a fine sense of her own dignity and would rather go into self-imposed exile — "abandoning herself to go wandering"[23] — than tolerate slights to her status. As *Hikayat Panji Semirang* describes Candra Kirana, "though she was young and still without reasoning, she was already aware of her own dignity".[24] Even in *Syair Siti Zubaidah*, much less influenced by Panji tales in other respects, the heroine's first motive for departing from her home is that she takes offence that her husband does not say goodbye to her before he goes into battle. She leaves in search of Zainal Abidin only later.

The numerous female attendants who accompany some of the heroines are also disguised. After the requisite wandering in the forest, Zuhrah and Nurkiah are adopted as the sons and heirs of the Sultan of Mesir. Not content to stay at home, however, Zuhrah continues her wandering, in a clear parallel with the Panji *kelana*, or knight-errant, and comes across her betrothed, Sidi Maulana, who is in pursuit of her.[25] She precipitously challenges him to battle — and Harun Mat Piah has noted several incidences of Galuh-in-disguise attacking and defeating Panji[26] — and wins easily. In fact, battle is avoided because Sidi Maulana is immediately infatuated. As one of his followers explains to the other members of the retinue, bemused as to why their leader has not put up the least bit of resistance:

Disahut oleh anak bendahara	In answer, the bendahara's son said:
Sebab pun Sidi menurut bicara	The reason Sidi obeys
Oleh terpandang Sultan mengindera	Is because he has looked on the royal Sultan
Tersemu di dalam manis suara	And is snared by a sweet voice.
Di mana Sidi tidak tertawan	How could Sidi not be captivated,
Terlalu elok Sultan bangsawan	When the noble Sultan is so lovely,
Sikap berani amat pahlawan	Brave and warriorlike in manner,
Gerak dan gaya bagai perempuan[27]	With the grace and bearing of a woman.

With their peerless beauty matched with martial abilities and their easily offended dignity, the romantic *syair*'s heroines in disguise are close kin to Panji princesses. An almost identical scene appears in *Hikayat Panji Semirang*, with the crucial difference that here the heroine too is struck by the hero's beauty: "the arrow she was holding almost fell to the ground because her heart was in such turmoil at the sight of Raden Inu".[28] The heroines of the female quest *syair*, as we shall see, never let their emotions get the better of them.

"Islamised Panji" Princesses

The disguised heroine *syair* of 19th-century Riau is in some sense a deliberate attempt to rework Panji tales for a more stringently Islamic milieu. Koster has termed these *syair*, in particular *Syair Sultan Abdul Muluk* and *Syair Siti Zubaidah*, "Islamised Panji romances ... in which the element of romantic desire and eroticism has been somewhat defused".[29] Islamic traits are certainly strongly present in the disguised heroine *syair*: Zubaidah, Rafiah and Jauhar Maknikam are all modest, pious, prayerful and skilled at reading the Qur'an. Indeed, it is Zubaidah's melodious recitation that first inflames Sultan Zainal Abidin's desire for her, in the linkage of (female) piety and (male) passion that is characteristic of these *syair*. Yet while the heroines excite desire, unlike Panji princesses, they have none themselves. Zubaidah also persuades Zainal Abidin to marry his full quota of four wives in the hopes of gaining *pahala*, religious merit, for herself. In perhaps the most Islamised works — *Syair Siti Zubaidah*, *Syair Sultan Abdul Muluk* and *Syair Siti Dhawiyyah* — the heroine loses her identity as sister, daughter and even as eroticised beloved, and becomes first and foremost a wife. The setting of the *syair* shifts from the four Javanese kingdoms where the Panji stories take place to either imaginary kingdoms like Barbaham and Barbari, Zamin Turan and Zamin Iran, or Middle Eastern locales such as Muscat and Damascus. The social setting too undergoes notable changes: sometimes the heroine is, as in Panji tales, a princess in a kingdom (Zubaidah, Rafiah, Zuhrah), but she may also be the daughter of a merchant who was once a king (Jauhar Manikam), or simply the daughter of a merchant (Dhawiyyah, Zainah). Needless to say, the common prologue to Panji tales, relating how the gods are incarnated on earth, is absent in the Riau *syair*. The anxiety this idea might provoke among reform-minded Muslims is obvious, and is attested by a caveat in a manuscript of *Hikayat Panji Semirang*, reassuring the reader that the account of gods descending to earth was merely a metaphor and not to be taken literally.[30] The usual Panji epilogue in which the kings renounce earthly desires and betake themselves to mountaintops to perform austerities, is likewise absent. The deities who make regular appearances in Panji narratives have made themselves scarce in the disguised heroine *syair*, except for the occasional comparison of the heroine to Rama, for instance. The destruction of kingdoms is accomplished in the Riau *syair* not by an attack of a mythical monster such as a *garuda* or a *bota* but that of a powerful foreign ruler, in retaliation for the mistreatment of a merchant subject to him.

A didactic poem for women by Raja Ali Haji contains a broadside against Panji literature that suggests why the old themes were becoming unacceptable in 19th-century Penyengat. The heroine of this text, *Syair Siti Sianah*, is a virtuous and pious woman, and an exemplary wife. Her preferred reading material is al-Ghazali's *Ihya 'Ulum al-Din*,[31] but her friends are stubbornly attached to the old romances.

Sianah berkata sambil tertawa	Laughing, Sianah said:
Salah daripada tuan-tuan semua	The fault is with your good selves,
Lengah membaca hikayat Jawa	Whiling your time away on Javanese tales,
Ilmu akhirat jadi kecewa	Harming your knowledge of the world to come.
Asyik membaca Koris Mengindera	Enraptured in reading of Koris Mengindera
Dengan permaisuri Indera	With queen Indera;
Hikayat itu dengan kira-kira	That tale with its conjurings,
Junjungan raja empunya bicara	Of the execution of the king's command.
Terkadang tertawa seorangnya diri	Sometimes laughing alone,
Mendengar laku Seri Sunan peri	Hearing of the behaviour of the *peri* Seri Sunan
Pergi merogol permaisuri	Going to ravish the queen
Diperdayakan dengan seorang puteri	But deceived by a princess.
Inilah disukakan abangnya Siti	This is what my elders delight in
Maka dibaca bermati-mati	And so read voraciously
Jika menaruh dendam di hati	But if there is passion stored up in your hearts
Hikayat itu pula menyakiti[32]	That *hikayat* will harm you.

The choice of the Panji-style *Hikayat Koris Mengindera* as the emblematically corrupting text is not accidental. It does in fact seem to have been popular with Penyengat women in Raja Ali Haji's day, for he gave a copy of it to Von de Wall in 1858. It was with regard to this manuscript that Raja Ali Haji remarked that its handwriting and spelling were defective because it was written by a woman. The manuscript was incomplete but Raja Ali Haji promised Von de Wall that he could obtain the rest of it from Lingga, so evidently it was also known at that court.[33] Klinkert obtained a copy of it (Kl. 39) and a Perak court woman owned another, dated 1910.[34] The tale of Koris Mengindera's adventures is just the sort of romance that would invite criticism from the *syariah*-minded: Koris is an incorrigibly amorous prince, always in pursuit of his cousin and beloved, Permaisuri Indera, but not averse to dallying with other women along the way.

In Sianah's assessment, reading romances leads directly to an impairment of the religious knowledge that is of such crucial value in the world to come ("ilmu akhirat"). The secular and the scriptural are starkly opposed, with women readers depicted as markedly more attracted to the former. This same opposition is apparent in a verse from the colophon of the Panji tale *Hikayat Kelana Jayeng Seteru*, copied by Muhammad Said bin Haji Muhammad Saman for his wife Cik Teh Afiah in 1910:

Tuntutlah tuan ilmu akhirat	Seek knowledge of the last days;
Jangan asyikkan membaca hikayat	Don't lose yourself in reading *hikayat*;
Amal ibadat itulah perbuat	Perform your duties and prayers;
Supaya jangan mati nan sesat.[35]	So that you do not die in confusion.

Reading secular literature is not so much a frivolous waste of time as a dangerous distraction from religious obligations. In addition, as Sianah points out in the *syair* that bears her name, the *hikayat* arouses the women's latent passions ("dendam di hati"), with potentially harmful ("menyakiti") results: not just erotic feelings but also insubordination towards male authority. Sianah accuses women readers of taking pleasure — indeed, laughing aloud — at the scenes of sexual intrigue depicted in *Hikayat Koris Mengindera*. Unable to control his desire, the *peri* or supernatural being in that text, Seri Sunan, enters the women's quarters of the palace in search of the heroine, Permaisuri Indera. Seeing him go into her bedchamber, Permaisuri Indera escapes in the guise of a palace servant. Seri Sunan lies down with another princess, Puteri Gangga Kuntum Seroja, only to discover his mistake. When his voice is heard, there is uproar in the palace. Koris rushes into the room in a fury, pushing aside Permaisuri Indera's attempts to prevent him. When he discovers Seri Sunan with Puteri Gangga, Koris regrets his public humiliation of Permaisuri Indera, but she shuns his apologies and spurns his advances.[36] In this passage, then, readers are invited to take delight in the fact that Permaisuri Indera succeeds in thwarting the desires of both Koris and Seri Sunan.

Needless to say, this would not have found favour with Raja Ali Haji, whose didactic works heap opprobrium on any demonstration of female independence or intransigence towards male authority. His collection of maxims known as *Gurindam Dua Belas* advises male readers to find a wife "who is able to submit".[37] Addressing women, his tone is even more ominous: "the Lord of Glory will be wrathful [if] you do not obey your husband's commands"; "sangatlah murka Rabb al-'Izzati perintah suamimu tiada dituruti". Rather, a wife should render her husband loyal and sincere service, *bakti*.[38] In *Syair Siti Sianah*, Raja Ali Haji condemns women's claims to their own property, persons or husbands, giving divine sanction to polygamy, female subservience and the use of violence against disobedient wives. *Syair Siti Sianah* teaches women the limitations of their rights and the onerousness of their responsibilities towards their husbands. In the section titled "the proper conduct of a wife towards her husband", among the failings singled out for censure are public demonstrations of distress at the news that the husband has taken another wife, turning the face away or scowling at him, speaking harshly and refusing sex (the sole stricture the text places on the husband, in contrast, is that he refrain from striking his wife on the face).[39] Perhaps it is no surprise that the women of Raja Ali Haji's own family — his sister and his daughters — composed *syair* in which the heroines observe Islamic norms but implicitly reject this extreme subordination.

Syair Siti Sianah is but one of a plethora of didactic works specifically directed at women and that were well known in the 19th-century Malay world.[40] These didactic works may be seen as the double of the secular romance, the two genres defining themselves against each other even as they are closely intertwined. Notable examples are *Hikayat Darma Ta'siah*, *Kisah Fatimah Berkata-kata dengan Pedang Ali*, *Kisah Nabi Mengajar Anaknya Fatimah* and *Hikayat Fatimah Bersuami*. Most, if not all, address women as wives, and stress obedience to husbands as a religious duty. As *Hikayat Sultan Ibrahim ibn Adham* puts it, "[w]e women believers should be devoted to our husbands, in the hope that we shall obtain the mercy of God the Exalted in the hereafter".[41] Other means of achieving spiritual merit, including fasting and prayer, are for nought if a woman's primary duty towards her husband is not faithfully carried out. As the Prophet Muhammad informs Fatimah in another text widely read during the period, "any woman who does not carry out her husband's instructions will arouse the wrath of Allah the Most High, and even if she prays and fasts, none of these deeds will be accepted by Allah the Most High, for her place will be in hell".[42] The punishment for anything less than sterling service — from doing laundry, cooking meals, perfuming the clothes one's husband intends to wear for the Friday prayer to acceding to sexual demands and bearing children — is eternal damnation.

Although this is generally the line taken by these didactic works, divergent opinions appear in unlikely places. A version of *Hikayat Darma Ta'siah* included in a compendium of 11 mostly religious texts has a rather surprising coda in which the heroine relates a story about Muhammad and his wife Aisyah, in order to argue for the importance of female initiative.[43] Not only does Aisyah leave the house without her husband's explicit permission, she also allows an old man to touch her breasts in exchange for some mangoes. Since her intentions were noble — to procure the out-of-season mangoes Muhammad had asked for — she is the object of his praise rather than his condemnation. Needless to say, this anecdote is not to be found in the canonical hadith collections — and most didactic texts take a very different view of female initiative. The question of women's intention and initiative are of course central to the disguised heroine *syair*. With such a diversity of opinions about the proper role of women, it is perhaps no wonder that Raja Ali Haji felt that there was a pressing need for works like his *Syair Siti Sianah*, with its devoted, pious wives who submit passively to their husbands' multiple marriages. The influence of al-Ghazali, whose *Ihya 'Ulum al-Din* included a book on women and marriage that states with admirable clarity that "marriage is a sort of slavery" for women and that a good Muslim woman is one who is obedient to her husband, may be discerned in *Syair Siti Sianah*. (After all, Sianah herself is depicted reading it.[44]) Nevertheless, the difference between the status of women in al-Ghazali's time and place and in Raja Ali Haji's was profound. Most telling of all is the fact that al-Ghazali's book on marriage is not addressed to women but to men, whereas Raja Ali Haji's *syair* most certainly exhorts women. In 19th-century Riau, women were readers and subjects, albeit recalcitrant ones. It seems likely, moreover, that this proliferation of Malay didactic works for women indicates that there was a struggle over the position of women in society, and a resistance to the importation of norms from other parts of the Islamic world.

One of the six *syair* discussed in this study is, of course, not a romance, but a didactic tale in disguise. The reason for *Syair Siti Dhawiyyah*'s attempt to pass itself off as a romance is set out in another *syair* from a hierarchically higher sphere of traditional Malay literature, *Syair Burung*. Also known as *Syair Unggas*, this poem has birds engaged in a theological discussion. A Penyengat manuscript of *Syair Burung*, copied by Raja Hasan bin Raja Ali Haji in 1859, explains why religious instruction might appear in the *syair* form:

Syair ini dengarkan olehmu	Listen to this *syair*,
Ibarat orang mencari ilmu	[As a] parable for those in search of wisdom.
Di dalam kitab banyak yang jemu	Many are bored by religious books,
Diperbuatkan syair supaya bertemu[45]	[I] created a *syair* so they may meet [with learning].

In other words, those who yawn over *kitab* and didactic texts may be enlightened, in spite of themselves, via *syair* renderings of religious or didactic messages. Conspicuous among the people who might avoid improving works and flock instead to romances are, as we have seen, women. *Syair Siti Dhawiyyah* shares many of the tropes of the disguised heroine *syair*, and was the third most frequently reissued title of its time.[46] However, as we will see in Chapter 5, Dhawiyyah is hardly a subversive figure. Though she does rescue her husband, she never dons a disguise nor even leaves her house. That her wifely devotion and moral probity suffice to bring her errant husband back to the right course makes her much closer to Sianah, Raja Ali Haji's ideal. Even so, the romantic guise of *Syair Siti Dhawiyyah* makes it a more appealing text than *Syair Siti Sianah*. But while *Syair Siti Dhawiyyah* is a didactic text disguised as a romance, the true romantic *syair* are also practising a kind of subterfuge, smuggling in arguments for women's authority and rationality under the cover of romance.

II. Feminine Susceptibilities

There are bad texts, and there are also bad readers. Readers unable to keep their passions in check could not be trusted to discern between truth and lies. Abdullah bin Abdul Qadir Munsyi, author of the famous 19th-century memoir, likened literature to a garden, from which the wise reader chose the fruits and flowers that would be beneficial to him. Ignorant readers, on the other hand, do not succeed in extracting didactic teachings from what they read, but instead abandon their critical faculties: "[he or she] daydreams and feels lazily drowsy, is amazed and wanders bewildered hither and yon".[47] Likewise, the Batavian writer Safirin bin Usman Fadli advises in the preface to his *Hikayat Anak Pengajian*, an 1871 collection of didactic stories for children learning to read the Qur'an:

> Whenever a servant of Allah who possesses rationality hears a tale, a *hikayat*, or a work of advice he takes it to heart just as someone entering a garden full of fruit and flowers of all kinds chooses from amongst all the fruits and the flowers, taking and eating those of the fruit which are wholesome. As for fruits which cause intoxication and unconsciousness when they are eaten, these he discards for fear of danger to himself.[48]

Safirin was so adamant that *hikayat* recitation possessed pernicious powers that he etymologically linked the words *hikayat* and *hikmat*, meaning magic.[49]

It is also clear that Safirin believes women are particularly at risk from the *hikmat* of romance. The feminine is here closely allied with a penchant for the fictional, and both are obstacles to rational men. Just like the stereotypically bad writer,[50] the stereotypically bad reader — the reader of bad fictions, the reader who reads badly — is also female. That women have a more precarious grip on their passions than men, due to their inherently weaker reason, is commonplace in Malay and other cultures.[51] Naturally enough, it follows that women are more susceptible to the iniquitous seductions of romance, consuming them compulsively, and unquestioningly believing them to be true. The hero of *The Tale of Genji* teases his stepdaughter that "women are obviously born to be duped" by romances in which there is "hardly a word of truth".[52] One of Chaucer's storytellers slyly asserts that the tale he has just told is "also trewe, I undertake / As is the booke of Launcelot de Lake / That wommen holde in ful greet reverence".[53] In the Malay world, romances, whether prose or verse, also tended to be discursively constructed as feminine. Malay men of letters were of the opinion that women were particularly vulnerable to the dangerous charms of romantic reading. As Safirin bin Usman Fadli warned:

> All men and women, when they hear a *hikayat* with a good story, are filled with passionate longing and feel desire in their hearts towards that *hikayat*. Some of them are filled with desire for the reader, especially if [he/she] has a good voice and modulation, then desire increases in the hearts of the listeners. Far from women not having their hearts inflamed, when most men find that their hearts beat in time with the reader's voice as they listen to the *hikayat*'s story.[54]

Both men and women may fall prey to the seductions of *hikayat* reading, but it is clear that in Safirin's view, women are more susceptible. Women, with their impaired rationality, are more likely to be carried away by *hikayat* recitation or indeed bewitched by magic spells (though we shall see in Chapter 7 that this formulation is reversed in the romantic *syair* themselves).

In *Syair Buah-Buahan*, Safirin's nephew, Muhammad Bakir, describes a reading assembly at which women recite and listen to a romantic *hikayat*, with a dramatic effect on their emotional state.[55] As a man in the book trade, it may be assumed that Muhammad Bakir knew his stock and his customers. No doubt he was also aware of the metaphorical usage of fruits and garden to represent literature, deployed both by his uncle Safirin and by Abdullah Munsyi, which *Syair Buah-Buahan* plays upon. Muhammad Bakir's description of female reading is one of absent rationality and uncontrolled emotions. The women here are feminine fruits, assembled to read from (in an admirable example of product placement, Muhammad Bakir's own) *Hikayat Sultan Taburat*. The fruits take turns reading aloud, and *Syair Buah-Buahan* even describes their different reading styles. Anggur, the heroine, reads sweetly and melodiously, of course, while the less refined character, Duku, reads so loudly that she can be heard several houses away. The effect of this reading is that the fruits become weepy, wistful and high strung, to say the least. Indeed, their emotional upheaval is contagious, for "whomever heard [their recitation] felt their hearts crushed".[56] Even when the gathering has concluded and they have returned to their respective houses, the fruits persist in their romantic melancholy:

Demikian akan sehari-hari	Thus it was day after day,
Membaca hikayat pagi sore	Reading *hikayat* morning and evening,
Sampai tiada ingat kanan kiri	Until they forgot left and right,
Selaku gila mabuk sendiri[57]	Behaving as though mad or drunk.

They are unable to sleep or indeed to do anything much other than reading *hikayat*, to the point that they turn pale from staying indoors. *Syair Buah-Buahan* is quite clear that such behaviour is only to be expected, for "all women enjoy *hikayat* / reading *syair* and any kind of narrative / at all times and at every moment".[58] Although Muhammad Bakir is far more sympathetic to his female characters than Safirin, there is no doubt that he depicts them as having a predilection for fiction which results in tears and upset. Moreover, the danger of illicit relationships with gentlemen fruits arises as a result of this *hikayat* reading, but Muhammad Bakir's humorous rather than moralising bent ensures that the turbulent emotions awakened in the lady fruits come to a happy conclusion when they are married to suitable partners.

The point is not so much that all readers of romantic *syair* were women — after all, there must have been plenty of men who read *syair*, if Raja Ali Haji could recommend it to the Dutch philologist Von de Wall as a diverting activity, and of course Safirin is primarily discussing male readers in his cautionary prologue.[59] Rather, what is important is that in the literary culture of the time, the consumption of romantic *syair* was constructed as a feminine activity and predilection. The reader who let himself be carried away by a romance would be placed, in spite of his gender, in the female subject position, thereby assuming, for the time being at least, the impaired rationality typical of women. In *Hikayat Hang Tuah*, for instance, when Hang Jebat reads aloud from a prose romance, not only the sultan's concubines but the sultan himself succumbs to the pleasures of the recited text:

> All the raja's concubines desired Hang Jebat. The raja too took pleasure from hearing Hang Jebat read the *hikayat*, because his voice was as sweet as a *buluh perindu*.[60] Hang Jebat knew how to modulate his voice so that all who heard him became sorrowful and melancholy; whomever heard him began to feel love in their hearts. Then the raja lay in Hang Jebat's lap. Hang Jebat ceased reading and began to sing a lullaby to the reclining raja, in the sweetest of voices. The raja fell soundly asleep in Hang Jebat's lap.[61]

While the palace women forget themselves so much as to throw Hang Jebat love tokens, it is the sultan who so loses his grip on his conscious mind that he falls asleep. Cradled in Hang Jebat's lap and serenaded with a lullaby, the sultan literally assumes a feminine position, that of Hang Jebat's beloved. This sultan is of course the one whose failings lead to the fall of Malacca to the Portuguese. The proper masculine response to *hikayat* reading, in contrast, was more likely the arousal of fighting spirit. The *Sejarah Melayu* relates how the "war-chiefs and young nobles" requested *Hikayat Muhammad Hanafiyah* from Sultan Ahmad, "in the hope that we may obtain profit [*faedah*] from it, for the Franks are attacking tomorrow".[62] It is masculine, then, to gain *faedah* from a text, whereas it is feminine to get emotional about it.

A number of features of the disguised heroine *syair* construct the reader's female subject position, and are shared in common with romances for women from other times and places. Perhaps the most obvious is the female protagonist, with whom the reader is invited to identify. Identifying with the heroine may be one of the chief pleasures of the female romance narrative, from the tenth-century Japanese *Sarashina Nikki* diarist's desire to become "a lady like the Shining Genji's Yugao, or the Uji Captain's Ukifune" to the readers of romance novels in our own time.[63] The *syair* heroine, like all good romance heroines, is a paradoxical figure: famous but cloistered, chaste but eroticised, defenceless but all-conquering. Most importantly, the romantic *syair*, like the 19th-century English novels which also took the name of the heroine as the title of the text, have at their centre "a conscious female protagonist".[64] The reader looks at the heroine even as she (or he) experiences the events of the narrative through the heroine's eyes. Yet the reader does not simply map herself onto the heroine, as Modleski shows in her analysis of romance novels. Part of the reader's pleasure is her foreknowledge, gleaned from her familiarity with the conventions of the genre: "Since the reader knows the formula, she is superior in wisdom to the heroine and thus detached from her. The reader, then, achieves a very close emotional identification with the heroine partly because she is intellectually *distanced* from her and does not have to suffer the heroine's confusion".[65] Thanks to the many other narratives, the reader already knows, the many other *syair* she has already read or heard, she is in a position of superior knowledge vis à vis the heroine even as she wholly sympathises with her. Knowing that the heroine will triumph, that her adventures will end in marriage to the one she has so long resisted, the reader is one step ahead of the heroine — she is distanced from her, in a move that is crucial to the *syair*'s emotional potency.

The feminine romance presents the events in the heroine's life as of essential significance — not only to her, but to her family and to the hero. In contrast, the hero is a marginalised figure, whose purpose is seemingly merely to be abducted, rescued and married. This is of course a reversal of what might be expected under a gender ideology which usually depicts women as marginal and passive. Raja Ali Haji's *Tuhfat al-Nafis*, for instance, does not depict women as actors in political events, and even sidelines his redoubtable aunt Engku Puteri in the historical record. In the case of many of the *syair*, the heroine's deeds are essential to the fate of the entire polity. In *Syair Siti Zubaidah*, for instance, the heroine's mistreatment by her mother-in-law is shown to be an act of gross injustice when she, Zubaidah, rescues her husband and defeats the enemy forces. As Abdul Mutalib Abdul Ghani aptly observes in his edition of the *syair*, Sultan Darman Syah sees relations between his wife and Zubaidah as "merely matters between women".[66] The ensuing events — the defeat of Kembayat at the hands of the Chinese princesses, and its restoration by Zubaidah — amply demonstrate that the feminine and domestic are of crucial importance to the state and the entire Muslim alliance. That "matters between women" determine the fate of nations is an eloquent tell-tale of female readership.

The heroines of the Riau romantic *syair* are in the habit of precipitously fleeing from their proper places, resulting in great alarm when their absence is discovered. Discussing this "disappearing act" in contemporary romance novels, Modleski describes it as the expression of an "infantile" (albeit common) revenge fantasy through which the hero is forced to admit the importance of the heroine to him. "A great deal of our satisfaction in reading these novels," Modleski writes, "comes from the elements of a revenge fantasy".[67] The different family dynamic of the Riau *syair* means that the heroine is often more concerned with impressing her importance on her mother-in-law or stepmother rather than her husband by this disappearing act. Nonetheless, a revenge fantasy is certainly involved (and this revenge is taken quite literally in the case of *Syair Siti Zuhrah*, in which the disguised heroine defeats her fiancé and makes him a vassal). The assumption of a disguise is a prelude to and prerequisite for the recognition of the heroine — not simply of her true identity but also of her true value and significance. Sultan Yunan is recognised by everyone not just as Zubaidah, but also as a peerless woman and wife, the heroic figure foreseen in prophecy, and far superior to Puteri Sajarah, whom her mother-in-law had favoured. The same is true of the other *syair*, in which the characters who have so unjustly victimised the heroine are inevitably forced to eat large helpings of humble pie. The reader, meanwhile, gets to have her cake and eat it too: enjoying the double satisfaction of identifying with a heroine who is both exemplary according to the terms of the conventional gender order and simultaneously overturns that order. While the heroine maintains the emotional control and self-effacement that are such admirable traits in women, the workings of the plot dramatise and fulfill her (and the reader's) rebellious desires on a spectacular scale.

Finally, the romantic *syair* may have appealed to women because they provide a symbolic representation of significant stages in a woman's life. *Syair Siti Zuhrah* and *Syair Sultan Yahya* trace the heroine's journey towards marriage, in the world of the *syair* conceived of as the state of adulthood. Her successful quest involves the denial of the hero's desire until the appropriate time (her own desire is so throughly denied that it is never present), on the one hand, and on the other, detaching herself from her natal family to find her place within her marital family. As a married woman, her co-wives become her new sisters, and her husband, as the dual usage of the word "kakanda" ("older sibling", but also used by a married woman when speaking to her husband) makes clear, is her new brother. Up to this point, the relationship between sisters is depicted as more intense and more fundamental than that of women and their husbands and also that of women and their brothers. It is telling that the "abang" whom Benzahara laments is not her husband, nor even her brother Jayaputera, but her sister Jauhar Manikam. All through her adventures as Juragan Budiman, Jauhar Manikam is tormented with distress for her sister left behind. Likewise, Zuhrah and Nurkiyah are never parted and for most of the *syair*, they are the only ones privy to their true identities. They form a closed circle of intimacy to which only their *inang*, a surrogate mother, is admitted. In the course of their travails, the sisters acquire and lose a succession of surrogate parents, from the *inang* to the syeikh who imparts magical knowledge to the sultan of Mesir and his wife who adopt them as heirs. Much grief springs from the inevitable parting of sisters after marriage, when the royal couples return to the husbands' domains. The relationship towards which the events of *Syair Siti Zuhrah* and *Syair Sultan Yahya* carry the heroines, however, is marriage: her final acceptance of the suitor she has hitherto done all in her power to escape. What is important in these texts is not the acquisition of magical animals or conquering one's foes in battle so much as learning to accept marriage as the ultimate feminine destiny. In *Syair Siti Zubaidah* and *Syair Sultan Abdul Muluk*, the heroine marries early in the narrative, and the plot concerns her attempts to manage wifehood and, especially, co-wifehood. Different *syair* can be seen as addressing distinct life stages.[68] The message of the *syair*'s conclusion is always that the gender status quo is both inevitable and desirable, despite the rejections of it that form the bulk of the story.

Yet the effectiveness of these *syair* in convincing their readers of the necessity of marriage and of peaceful coexistence with one's co-wives is called into question by the very proliferation of *syair*. As well as the five romantic *syair* considered in this thesis and well known examples such as *Syair Selindung Delima* and *Syair Ken Tambuhan*, there are dozens of other titles listed in the manuscript catalogues, including *Syair Kahar Masyhur*, *Syair Yatim Nestapa*, *Syair Dandan Setia*, *Syair Raja Nur Peri*, and so on, most of which seem to cover very similar narrative territory. The Riau romantic *syair* are variations on an entirely predictable theme: the blameless, exemplary heroine demonstrates her worth and is married, or is married and demonstrates her worth. There can be no surprise endings. The pleasure of predictability is evident even in our own time in such popular forms as the television detective drama or the romantic comedy, indicating that the desire for almost-identical repetition is an abiding one. Modleski suggests that the strong, indeed obsessive, tendency for plot repetition in romance novels indicates "ideological conflicts so profound that readers must constantly return to the same text (to texts which are virtually the same) in order to be reconvinced".[69] Or as Radway puts it, there is

> [a] deep irony hidden in the fact that women who are experiencing the consequences of patriarchal marriage's failure to address their needs turn to a story which ritually recites the history of a process by which those needs are constituted. They do so, it appears, because the fantasy resolution of the tale ensures the heroine's achievement of the very pleasure the readers endlessly long for.[70]

Thus Radway's interviewees' voracious consumption of romance novels. Thus also, perhaps, the feminine fruits' obsession with reading *hikayat* in *Syair Buah-Buahan* and Muhammad Bakir's claim that women constantly read romances. This is a potential explanation of the multiplication of plots with a high degree of similiarity in Riau women's *syair*: that they point to and work out, again and again, areas of perennial psychic difficulty in women's lives. For it cannot be doubted that although the *syair* are decked in the trappings of the impossible and improbable — talking animals, superhuman powers, effortless victories, justice done to all — they play themselves out against a backdrop of their readers' and authors' lives, in which marriage and co-wifehood were constants.

III. The Power of Poetry

In common with thinkers from Plato onwards (to take only one of the earliest and most familiar such polemic in world literature), Malay literati were uneasy about the power of poetry to make people lose their reason and believe in false notions.[71] In this, they took a similar line to Islamic philosophers who held that the pedagogical potential of poetry was most important. These include al-Farabi, who "reviles Arabic poetry as a school 'of cupidity and mendacity'" and Ibn Miskawayhi, who "advises that young people should not be instructed in the poetry of the *nasib*, since it encourages fornication; on the other hand, he sees educational merit in poems which celebrate courage and manliness".[72] The Malay *'alim* Bukhari al-Jauhari famously warned readers of his *Taj al-Salatin*, dedicated to the Acehnese sultan in 1603, to prevent their children from reading "other *hikayat* from among those which are popular in the Malay lands", which are "full of lies and disbelief, and those who read them or listen to them being read, verily, commit a sin".[73] Nur al-Din al-Raniri, the Gujarat-born scholar active at the Acehnese court in the 17th century, likewise warned against reading "worthless *hikayat*, in which there are many dangerous lies".⁷⁴ An important source of *ulama*'s objections to romantic *syair* and *hikayat* seems to have stemmed from the manner of their performance: evening recitation sessions, sometimes accompanied by music that induced trance-like or, at the very least, heightened emotional states. By the 19th century, anxious questions were being asked about the permissibility of certain Sufi practices that involved music and trance, and with which romance recitation would seem to have something in common. The dire warnings of these Malay literati about the deleterious effects of romance also stem from the content of such texts: deliberately false and all too often abounding in un-Islamic elements bound to irritate *syariah*-minded readers.

Syair were also often used in magical or ritual contexts. As late as the 1970s, *Syair Siti Zubaidah* was used in Banjar for divining the suitability of marriage partners, and *Syair Ikan Terubuk dan Puyu-Puyu* was used in an annual ritual in Bengkalis, to ensure a good harvest of the *terubuk* fish.⁷⁵ One of the female assistants in the Bengkalis ritual is even termed a *bidu*, like those early singers who may have been the originators of the *syair*.⁷⁶ According to Maxwell's account of "shamanism" in 1890s Perak, "in cases of royal séances", the medium's assistant is called a *biduan*.⁷⁷ Although in *syariah*-minded Penyengat, such magical uses of *syair* would presumably have been banished, recitation of literary texts during vigils kept for weddings, circumcisions and births, attested elsewhere in Indonesia to the present day, may still have been practised. In 1890s Banjar, *syair* were customarily read on the evening after a birth, to entertain people keeping vigil over the mother and the newborn.⁷⁸ Up to the 1970s, Malay *hikayat* were still being read aloud at circumcisions, weddings and funerals in Lombok.⁷⁹ That this recitation may have had some apotropeic function is suggested by Robson's surmise that "the singing of Javanese poetry [*kidung*] also has an application in what we may call a ritual context" on the occasion of liminal events such as pregnancy, birth or marriage.⁸⁰ Robson suggests that the *kidung*'s power to ward off danger and illness derives not from its content but from its metre, and perhaps the same was the case in the ritual uses of *syair*, although the narrative contents of both *Syair Siti Zubaidah* and *Syair Ikan Terubuk* have some relevance to marriage and *terubuk* fish respectively. Perhaps the fact of the event called for recitation, and the choice of *syair* would be made based on some connection between the nature of the event and the content of the text.

The most frequently attested effect of *syair* recitation is the release of emotion in the listeners — particularly the related and otherwise proscribed emotions of desire and distress, *berahi* and *rawan*. In the previous section, we have seen the kinds of emotions that recitation kindled in the hearts of unwary readers. But what was the effect of this emotional release? Scholars as diverse as R.J. Wilkinson, Muhammad Haji Salleh and Virginia Matheson have commented on the cathartic function of *syair*, brought about through the recitation techniques as well as their emotion-laden content.[81] Listening to *syair* was able to bring about, according to Braginsky, a "restoration of the balance of affects (emotions) in the soul".[82] A Minangkabau Malay told the German philologist Overbeck: "a *shaer* was read not so much for the story as for the delight one experiences from witty dialogue and in finding one's own feelings, passion or self-pity, well expressed".[83] As Wilkinson observed, "he [a Malay] loves the rhythm of poetry for its own sake and finds in it a relief for his feelings, especially his sense of melancholy and longing".[84] Clearly, the *syair* possess psychic potency, but as well as the potential to heal, descriptions of reciting and reading poetry within the literature itself tend to portray its disruptive and not its soothing powers.

In *Syair Buah-Buahan*, the desires awakened by reading spread uncontrollably: the fruits, abruptly de-anthropomorphised, are given by a man to his sick wife to eat but instead of healing her, they hasten her death. Heartbroken, the man then partakes of the same fruits and follows his wife to the grave. The fragrant plants that grow on their grave are the haunts of a pair of beetles, in Malay literature the incorrigible messengers of love.[85] The male beetle inscribes verses on flower petals and crafts them into a wreath that he then lets fall in front of a princess. There is a clear equivalence of food, fragrance and poetry as vectors of desire. Poetry sets desire loose in the world: on reading the verses, the princess is intoxicated with love and sets her ladies-in-waiting to crafting similar wreaths of amorous verses. The colophons that conclude romantic *syair* do not testify to a soothing function, but rather to the expression of emotional distress. Romantic *syair* begin in emotional turmoil, such as this example from *Syair Siti Zuhrah*:

Sebab maka madah dikarang	The reason I composed this poem
Gundahnya hati bukan sebarang	Was the unusual turmoil in my heart,
Terkenangkan masa zaman sekarang	Thinking on the present day,
Malulah muka memandang orang[86]	Ashamed to look others in the face.

As it began, so does it end, over 200 manuscript pages later:

Terkenangkan masa zaman sekarang	Thinking on the present day,
Gundahnya hati bukan sebarang	Unusual turmoil in my heart,
Aibnya miskin daripada orang	This wretch's shame before others,
Maka demikian diperbuatkan orang[87]	Thus am I treated by others.

Indeed, the *dagang* narrator's emotional state at the beginning and end of *Syair Siti Zuhrah* is so similar that several verses are repeated wholesale. Here, there is no resolution to the *dagang*'s distress.[88]

The reciting voices of the *syair* heroines are often mentioned as key elements of their attractiveness, even when they are reading from extremely sober texts. In *Syair Siti Zubaidah*, the hero is first attracted to the heroine when he hears her reading from the Qur'an. In this typical description of the erotic effect of poetic recitation, the heroine's voice awakens the hero's desires — it does not soothe them:

Langgamnya elok suaranya merdu	The melody was fine, the voice was lovely
Seperti bunyi buluh perindu	Like the sound of a *buluh perindu*[89]
Halus manis bunyi merdu	Fine, sweet, with a melodious sound
Seperti bercampur gula dan madu	Like sugar mixed with honey.
Sangatlah hairan raja bangsawan	Full of amazement, the noble king,
Ghairah berahi bercampur rawan	Desirous, passionate, mixed with distress,
Mendengar suara terlalu hairan	Utterly amazed at the sound of the voice,
Kalbunya gundah tiada ketahuan.[90]	His heart was in unspeakable turmoil.

This recalls Safirin's descriptions of "foolish readers" and Muhammad Bakir's satirical depiction of female *hikayat* addicts. Society's moral fibre is placed under intolerable strain by a few passages of *hikayat* reading. While prose and verse romance are supposed to enable their audiences to soothe their cares, *menglipur lara*, by inducing temporary forgetfulness, in fact the reverse seems to be the case. The fruits in *Syair Buah-Buahan* are *reminded* of their own sweethearts by the descriptions of the heroes in the *hikayat* they are reading.[91] Rather than forget their troubles, and far more dangerously, they forget the necessity of controlling their own emotions.

It has been suggested that Malay-Indonesian culture holds that emotions, particularly those thought to be negative or dangerous, must be suppressed. In her anthropological work in Bali, Wikkan shows that emotional control, specifically the repression of "bad" emotions and the projection of a "bright" and happy demeanour, are seen as essential to the maintenance of personal dignity and to the protection of bodily health.[92] Laderman's research in Terengganu confirms the importance placed on emotional repression in rural Malay society.[93] Strikingly, the symptoms of "soul-loss" caused by emotional incontinence listed by Wikkan's Balinese sources replicate those ascribed to both the writer and the heroines of the *syair*: confusion (*bingung*), weakness (*lemah*), dizziness (*pusing*). Moreover, a similar idea of the damaging effects of a lack of emotional control is expressed in *Syair Sultan Yahya* with respect to the smitten swains of the heroine and her sister:

Banyaklah orang bersakit hati	Many were heartsick;
Setengah bercinta bagaikan mati	Some so full of anxiety it seemed they would die;
Mana yang tidak tertahan hati	
Jatuhlah sakit membawa mati	Those who did not withhold their feelings,
	Fell ill, leading to death.
Setengah bercinta bukan kepalang	Some were so truly distressed,
Badan pun kurus tampaklah tulang	Their bodies so thin their bones were visible
Itu sebagai juga berulang	That, too, happened repeatedly
Sehingga bertongkat bergoyang-goyang.[94]	So that they walked with sticks, tottering.

Mental anguish is dangerous not simply or even primarily for the mind, but also for the body. In *Syair Sultan Yahya*, when Siti Benzahara realises her sister has gone to sea without so much as saying goodbye, she is so violently distressed that she loses consciousness: "she felt she could not endure [her suffering] / and so collapsed in a faint".[95] Later, her husband takes her on a pilgrimage to give thanks for the restoration of her health, in an explicit correlation of emotional and physical breakdown.

Kerana sakit baharu berhenti	Because her illness had just ended,
Sakitnya Siti bagaikan mati	Siti's illness that had brought her nigh unto death,

Daripada sangat berosak hati From her great heartsickness,
Bercintakan kanda sudahlah pasti.[96] Certainly caused by her anxiety for her sister.

In these *syair*, the control of extreme emotion is not so much a matter of seemliness as of physical health. If emotions are not controlled, then sickness and even death may be the result. It is no wonder, then, that critics of romantic reading like Safirin and Munsyi Abdullah denounced the awakening of emotions at reading assemblies. No wonder, too, that the word "cinta", glossed in modern Malay as "to love", at this time could just as easily mean "to sorrow".[97]

Defenders of romance present the opposing view: that the expression of emotion made possible by recitation is a prophylactic. The introduction to a manuscript of *Hikayat Misa Taman Sira Panji Jayeng Kusuma* explains that the composition is intended to soothe the passions in order to prevent dangers to the body that might otherwise cause illness: "so that each [person's] body is not harmed, for if it remains [in the same state] illness will result".[98] A preface to the romance *Hikayat Cekel Wanengpati* similarly indicates the benefits of listening to recitation: the text's intention, the narrator explains, is to "entertain the passionate heart". The narrator also seems to suggest that listening to this *hikayat* is better than simply expressing one's emotions: "even if [he/she] wishes to express what is in [his/her] heart, no good would come of this; therefore this *hikayat* called Cekel Wanengpati was composed".[99] Advocates of romance, then, argue that listening to *hikayat* or *syair* recitation provides a release for the turbulent emotions that the listeners have already stored up in their hearts. Critics, on the other hand, claim that recitation conjures up these emotions. Both, however, agree that emotional states have power over bodily health, and that recitation has power over emotional states.

The communal, sensory experience of the *syair* gave it additional potency. In this regard, *syair* recitation is strongly reminiscent of the *main puteri* shamanistic healing rituals witnessed by Laderman in Terengganu, which also involve narrative and performance in a group setting and which are also disapproved of by orthodox Muslims. These rituals involve the healing of patients' illnesses through emotional expression. Laderman stresses the necessity in *main puteri* of achieving "aesthetic distance", defined as "the balance point between feeling painful emotions that have been repressed in the past and reliving these feelings from a point of safety in the present". This distance is the prerequisite for catharsis, which occurs when people are given 'permission' to experience their feelings. This is especially important in a milieu — such as rural Malay society — where many emotions are regularly suppressed. Ritual, with its associated myths, provides a context that is both psychologically enabling and socially acceptable for repeated catharsis ... Techniques of aesthetic distancing often rely upon a willing suspension of disbelief, and combine experiences of pleasure and pain, as evidenced by the interweaving of awesome scenes with comic episodes that not only relieve tension but also provide critical comments about status, class, religion, politics, and relations between the sexes.[100]

In so far as *main puteri* involves ritual, spirit possession and trance, it is obviously different from *syair* recitation which is, as it were, secular. It is equally obvious that aesthetic distance, the suspension of disbelief, the appeal of the enactment of scenes of pleasure and pain at one remove from oneself, not to mention the opportunity for commentary on the status quo, play a major role in the experience of the *syair*. *Syair* may have been able to provide redactors and readers alike with a "psychologically enabling and socially acceptable" context for catharsis: a context in which the expression of emotions was permitted. *Syair* recitation may be thought of as on a continuum with *main puteri*, the literary form bearing the same relation to the therapeutic form as novel reading does to psychotherapy. That is, both have to do with the repressed desires, but literature is palliative, a pleasure that may lead to "a total, if temporary, loss of self", whereas *main puteri* and psychotherapy attempt, at least, to cure.[101] But poetry is ambiguous in its effects. As Jackson observes, "narrative and drama are much older, more widespread, and more flexible methods of therapy than psychoanalysis is, though they have the same ambiguous quality of sometimes making neurosis worse".[102] *Syair* recitation may restore the listener's psychic balance — or upset it still further. Modleski's observation of the narcotic effect of reading romances also comes to mind: "in presenting a heroine who has escaped psychic conflicts, [romances] inevitably increase the reader's own psychic conflicts, thus creating an even greater dependency on the literature".[103] Like opium and hallucinogenic mushrooms, frequently mentioned in the *syair* as causing states of emotional confusion, *syair* have the power to alleviate pain but may also be debilitating and addictive.

* * * * *

Romances were not the only kind of literature that women in the Malay world read. There are a few instances of women's ownership of other texts from more highly ranked spheres of Malay literature. *Kitab Tawhid*, *Bayan al-Shirk* and *Doa Kanzil 'Arasy* mentioned in Chapter 2 are three such examples. Likewise, men — even Raja Ali Haji — enjoyed *syair*. It does seem clear, however, that the discourse about literature in the 19th century held that women had a particular affinity for romance. This association is connected with the ability of recitation to evoke emotional responses, and with women's supposed impaired rationality and poor control of their passions. The appeal of romantic *syair* must have to do with a cathartic effect, along the lines described by Laderman for *main puteri*. Precisely because the romantic *syair* was thought of as trivial, otherwise proscribed emotions and perspectives could be expressed in it — such as resistance to the subordinance and co-wifehood so extolled by Raja Ali Haji. It is not by chance that the *syair*'s plot describes the transgression of the *ulama's* gender order, nor that, in the end, the status quo is restored. In this, it shares traits common to romance forms around the world: overturning and then reaffirming the rules that govern quotidian life, both subversive and conservative, both dangerously habit-forming and psychically necessary. It also furnishes a wealth of material for thematic analysis, treating as it does its readers' concerns and fantasies, the "imaginary" of 19th-century Malay aristocratic women. The following chapters address the most prominent of these themes: the struggle for emotional control, the figure of the heroine in disguise, and the gendering of reason and passion.

3

Ruling Passions

The Control of Emotion in *Syair Siti Zuhrah* and *Syair Sultan Yahya*

Passion and the necessity of its control are the warp and weft of *Syair Siti Zuhrah* and *Syair Sultan Yahya*. These *syair* are emotional at every stage of their creation and reception: the *syair* writer suffers great torment in the process of the text's composition, the heroes and heroines are racked by passion and sorrow, evoking echoing responses in the readers and auditors. In the character of the heroine, feeling takes precedence over thinking; her actions are dictated not by rational consideration or calculation, but by her emotions — shame, sorrow and the desire to avenge herself — and the necessity of their repression. The *rawan*, or emotional turmoil, which pervades these *syair*, comes from several sources: sorrow and fear at her vulnerability on the part of the heroine, desire for the heroine on the part of the hero, cathartic identification on the part of the composer or writer, and the intoxicating experience of *syair* recitation on the part of the audience. These texts foreground the romantic *syair*'s entanglement with the turbulent emotions awakened by beauty and desire, while at the same time they attempt to buttress the repression of emotion through the normative figure of the heroine.

Syair Siti Zuhrah and *Syair Sultan Yahya* are considered together here not only for the preponderance of *rawan* in their pages, but also because their plots have strong similarities, as the following summaries show.

Syair Siti Zuhrah[1]

Sultan Sahristan, Sultan Mengindera and Sultan Ma'rifat are cousins. Sultan Sahristan has five children. By his queen, he has two sons, Raja Ahmad Syah and Sulung Putera, and a daughter, Puteri Jamjam. By a minor wife, now deceased, he has two daughters, Zuhrah and Nurkiyah. Sultan Mengindera has two sons, Sidi Maulana and Haris Mengerna, and a daughter, Puteri Bendahara. Sultan Ma'rifat has four children: Puteri Semenyih, Puteri Khairani, Raja Indera and Raja Arifin. Much to the annoyance of his queen, Sultan Sahristan favours his two motherless daughters. The queen, egged on by her sister Ardhan, and assisted by her two children, intrigues against her stepdaughters. She dispatches the king and Raja Ahmad Syah on a hunting trip. Hostilities between the queen's camp and the stepdaughters, aided only by their *inang* or nursemaid, escalate. Ardhan and the *inang* exchange insults. The queen decides to confiscate all her stepdaughters' possessions and Ardhan plots to kill the girls. The princesses, accompanied by their *inang* and their serving-women, escape from the city into the forest by night — all dressed as men.

When the sultan returns, he is told that robbers have carried off his daughters. Distraught, he sends Sulung Putera and Raja Ahmad in search of them. Hearing of the abduction of Zuhrah, his betrothed, Sidi Maulana too sets off in pursuit.

The princesses and their retinue are caught in a storm, with the result that they are separated from their *inang*. The *inang* is discovered and adopted by a merchant and his wife. The princesses come across a holy man on a mountain and obtain *ilmu* (mystical knowledge) and magical objects from him. They then go to Mesir, where they are discovered and become the adopted sons of the childless king. They go by the names Syarif Istur and Muhammad Basri.

After the death of the king of Mesir, Syarif Istur assumes the throne. All is well in the kingdom, although the people wonder at "his" disinclination for marriage. Using the pretext of searching for a wife in Sahristan, Syarif Istur sets off, leaving Muhammad Basri in Mesir. By chance, Syarif Istur comes across Sidi Maulana and provokes him to battle. Having lost his heart to Syarif Istur, Sidi Maulana refuses to fight but returns with "him" to Mesir as a vassal king. On their journey, they skirmish with the seven fearsome warriors of Raja Andalan and Raja Serani. Next, they come across Sulung Putera and Raja Ahmad. Syarif Istur again provokes them to fight and this time, battle is joined. Syarif Istur easily captures Sulung Putera and takes him captive. In Mesir, the vassal princes are put in an exceptionally luxurious prison for two months, after which they are made members of Syarif Istur's retinue.

Meanwhile, Raja Serani's seven warriors plan to attack the kingdoms belonging to Sultan Sahristan, Sultan Mengindera and Sultan Ma'rifat (now described as "Raja Melayu"). The Serani — or sometimes called Olanda — soldiers are described drinking alcohol and otherwise enjoying themselves. They take the entire court of two kingdoms captive before moving on to Sahristan. Here, the king and queen have been smitten by grief at the loss of the two princesses, and Ardhan is suffering from a hideous illness. Wazir Omar is sent to get help, while the rest of the court is captured and jailed when they refuse to become Christians. Ardhan is abandoned in a ditch.

Raja Mesir has premonitions of disaster, quickly confirmed by the arrival of Wazir Omar. He and his vassals set off to the aid of the Malay kings. Happening upon Ardhan, Raja Mesir rescues and cures her. The two sides do battle, with much exchange of religious polemic. Inevitably, Raja Mesir's forces prevail. Some of the defeated Seranis agree to become Muslims, are renamed and absorbed into the retinue. Those who do not are jailed and swiftly die. The Malay captives are released, including Sultan Sahristan and his wife. However, the two princesses do not reveal their identity. Sidi Maulana tries and fails to seduce Raja Mesir.

Sultan Sahristan is still anxious to find his daughters. An astrologer knows the secret but fears to reveal it. Zuhrah, in the guise of yet another astrologer, reveals the true identity of Sultan Syarif and Muhammad Basri. The queen and Sulung Putera are alarmed that their dastardly deeds will be revealed, but Ardhan advises them to trust in Zuhrah's magnanimity. At last, all are reunited — including the *inang*. Marriages of all the cousins and various festivities take place, including a pleasure trip to the beach and to a garden. All return to their respective kingdoms.

Syair Sultan Yahya[2]

After a prologue in praise of Muhammad, the story begins with a king who, following the defeat of his country by his enemies, becomes a merchant in Zamin 'Ambar, ruled by Sultan Mu'tabar. The merchant has three children, all of exceptional beauty. The eldest is a son, Jaya Putera, while the two younger children are daughters, Siti Jauhar Manikam and Siti Benzahara. All the young men in Zamin 'Ambar are besotted with the two girls, who are, however, in seclusion and resolutely concentrate on their religious studies. Their father rejects all proposals on the grounds that they are too young to marry.

One day, Jaya Putera decides to go on a trading voyage to gain experience of the world. His parents reluctantly agree and furnish him with the ship Singa Melompat, complete with a hundred strong crew, cannons and ammunition. Jaya Putera and four companions sail to Zamin Turan, ruled by Sultan Yahya who is married to the jealous Puteri Belanta Puri. Sultan Yahya and Jaya Putera become fast friends, to the extent that the king will not permit Jaya Putera to leave Zamin Turan.

Seven months pass, during which the sisters are plagued by marriage offers and everyone becomes increasingly concerned by Jaya Putera's continued absence. The thwarted Encik S-t-n[3] poisons the merchant and his wife. Even a Dutch antidote administered by Sultan Mu'tabar is of no avail. After the death of the parents, the youngest daughter marries the heir apparent, Raja Hamzah. Fearing the king will marry her off too, Jauhar Manikam decides to go in search of her brother. She orders her four headmen to ready the ship Harimau Alam, including the cannon Leila Majnun. The men are unable, however, to push the ship down the rollers into the water. Despite the sacrifice of a buffalo and seven goats, Leila Majnun cannot be lifted. Jauhar Manikam and her seven handmaidens put on men's clothes, dressing as warriors. Once she invokes her royal origins, she and her 44 followers have no difficulty pushing the ship over the rollers. She departs without saying goodbye to her sister, lest the king detains her. The distressed Siti Benzahara is comforted by Raja Hamzah.

Jauhar Manikam decides to go by the name Saudagar Budiman Arif Laksana of Yemen. On her voyage, she acquires a magical beetle and a dove. Arriving in Zamin Turan, she immediately recognises Singa Melompat, whereas Jaya Putera fails to recognise both Harimau Alam and his sister. Saudagar Budiman tells Jaya Putera that "he" is a Yemeni merchant travelling in search of a relative. "He" also says that "he" was recently in Zamin Ambar, and reports the death of the merchant and his wife and the sad state of their daughters. Jaya Putera is overcome by sorrow and remorse, but just then, an emissary from Sultan Yahya arrives, summoning him to a hunting expedition. The messenger reports the arrival of the extraordinarily attractive merchant to Sultan Yahya, who is strangely affected by the news. Jaya Putera is reminded of his sister when he looks at Saudagar Budiman but fails to take this insight further.

When Sultan Yahya meets Saudagar Budiman, he at once suspects that "he" is a "she", since Jaya Putera is just as attractive but does not arouse the same desire in the king. Carried away, Sultan Yahya touches Saudagar Budiman's thigh as he leans over to examine "his" ring. Saudagar Budiman's discomfited reaction confirms Sultan Yahya's suspicions. The king's ministers advise him to test Saudagar Budiman further by various ruses, all of which Saudagar Budiman thwarts, with the help of "his" magical animals.

Saudagar Budiman resolves to return with her brother as soon as possible because of the danger that Sultan Yahya may unmask her. Sultan Yahya spends the night in his pavilion, neglecting his wife, who at once suspects that the merchant is a woman. When the two merchants ask permission to depart, Sultan Yahya delays them. Playing chess with Saudagar Budiman, the sultan makes further advances, and then suggests that they all go swimming. Saudagar Budiman makes "his" excuses, but while Sultan Yahya and Jaya Putera are bathing, a parrot arrives and recites *pantun* insinuating that Saudagar Budiman is a woman. Sultan Yahya resolves not to allow them to leave. They spend the night in the sultan's pavilion, where Sultan Yahya has ordered that Saudagar Budiman's bed be lined with banana leaves. The sultan's retinue tease Saudagar Budiman for never being separated from "his" *keris*. Saudagar Budiman spends a restless night, tearing up the banana leaves by tossing and turning.

The next day, when they are safely back on the ship, Saudagar Budiman reveals her true identity to Jaya Putera. The siblings decide to flee at once. When their escape is reported to Sultan Yahya, he immediately orders ships to be sent in pursuit. However, his men find that beetles have eaten the wood of the ships and birds have made nests in the sails. The people are conscripted to build another ship. Sultan Yahya is plunged into despair but is once again aided by the parrot, which tells him the name of Saudagar Budiman's country and of her royal origins. Puteri Belanta Puri is furious at her husband, but he departs nonetheless.

On their return voyage, Jaya Putera and Jauhar Manikam see a fruit floating in the sea. The four youths fail to retrieve it but Jaya Putera does so without difficulty. When the fruit is cut open, a beautiful princess emerges. Questioned by Jauhar Manikam, the princess reveals that she is Cahaya Mutia, the daughter of a Muslim jinn, that her country was attacked by an ogre and both her parents were killed. Jaya Putera falls in love with her but restrains his feelings. (This princess is plainly intended to become Jaya Putera's wife, so that all three siblings are married off satisfactorily, but after this initial appearance, she disappears completely from the narrative.)

They arrive at the river mouth leading to Zamin Iran, where by chance, Sultan Hamzah and Benzahara have come on a pilgrimage to a tomb to give thanks for her return to health after a serious illness. Benzahara sees a man casting a net and sends her handmaidens to buy fish from him. This man is none other than Jaya Putera, and the three siblings are reunited at last.

After some time, Sultan Yahya arrives, cannons blazing. The people of Zamin Iran are very much alarmed, believing themselves under attack, but Jaya Putera calms their fears. Sultan Yahya is royally welcomed and he, Jaya Putera and Raja Hamzah become great friends. In due course, Sultan Yahya sends his ministers to Jaya Putera and Sultan Mu'tabar to ask for Jauhar Manikam's hand in marriage. Permission is granted and much festivity ensues. The *syair* dwells at length on the preparations, processions and decorations of an unmistakeably Malay wedding. When left alone with her new husband for the first time, Jauhar Manikam cries but Sultan Yahya comforts her and sings her a lullaby.

One day, three ships arrive, captained by an old man who turns out to be the *bendahara* of Zamin Iran, of which Jaya Putera's father was king. Jaya Putera recognises the old man, who informs him that the country is now peaceful, prosperous and awaiting the return of its rightful ruler. This revelation of the royal origins of the sisters greatly pleases their husbands. Jaya Putera decides to return to Zamin Iran with the old man, and at the same time, Sultan Yahya decides to go back to Zamin Turan, taking Jauhar Manikam. All are sad at the parting but promise to exchange visits soon.

Jaya Putera becomes king and his country prospers, attracting merchants from China, Holland, India and Johor. After a rapturous welcome back to Zamin Turan, Siti Jauhar Manikam, out of concern for her good name, advises her husband to visit Puteri Belanta Puri. Sultan Yahya puts it off, with the result that Puteri Belanta Puri and her four handmaidens arm themselves, march to Siti Jauhar Manikam's residence and challenge her to a fight. To Sultan Yahya's alarm, Siti Jauhar Manikam takes up the gauntlet. The first to toss the other will be the winner. If Siti Jauhar Manikam loses, Puteri Belanta Puri will kill her, whereas if she wins, Puteri Belanta Puri will become her servant. Puteri Belanta Puri tries first but is unable to budge Jauhar Manikam, who having resigned herself to God, is being held down by angels. When Jauhar Manikam's turn comes, she invokes her royal origins once again and tosses Puteri Belanta Puri up into the sky. Jauhar Manikam shoots an arrow at her which shears off her hair. Puteri Belanta Puri falls unconscious to the ground. Sultan Yahya wants to kill her but Jauhar Manikam restrains him, tends to her fallen rival and even restores her hair. Puteri Belanta Puri is suitably contrite.

All being well, Sultan Yahya dispenses alms to the masses. Jauhar Manikam becomes queen and all three live happily. Friendly relations prevail between the rulers of Zamin Turan, Zamin Iran and Zamin Ambar.

* * * * *

The basic plots of both *syair* are identical, tracking the dissolution and subsequent reconstitution of the heroine's family in her journey towards marriage. In both, the heroine has a brother and a younger sister. Zuhrah's mother is dead when the *syair* begins; her stepmother contrives to send away her brother and father; Zuhrah and her sister Nurkiah remain together throughout their adventures; at last they are reunited with their father, brother and fiancé-cousins. Jauhar Manikam's brother leaves on a trading voyage; her parents are murdered; her sister marries the prince of the kingdom; she departs alone to find her brother. In the end, sisters and brother meet again, and all are married to appropriate, predetermined spouses. The multiple marriage plot is a common feature of traditional Malay narrative, most familiar from earlier Panji-style stories. However, another source that deserves mention is Malay folktales, with *Syair Sultan Yahya* in particular seeming to draw on south Sumatran narrative such as the story of Anggun Che Tunggal.[4] In this story, Gondan Gandariah sets sail in search of her beloved, Anggun Che Tunggal, with her 44 handmaidens, all disguised as men. The evocation of magic and animal sacrifice in the course of *Syair Sultan Yahya*'s plot sets it closer to Sumatran folk narrative and further apart from the more conscientiously Muslim means employed by the heroines of the other *syair*. Though Jauhar Manikam certainly does entrust herself to Allah (*berserah*) she just as often has recourse to the power conveyed upon her by her lineage. *Syair Sultan Yahya* is also notable for its frequent mentions of animal sacrifice, gambling and betting on horse- or elephant-races, again common in narratives like *Anggun Che Tunggal* but unthinkable in the more orthodox world of the other *syair*.

It may be assumed that *Syair Siti Zuhrah* and *Syair Sultan Yahya* come from Riau, since all extant manuscripts may be traced there.[5] Several more idiosyncratic characteristics point to a possible common redactor. Klinkert provides information only about *Syair Sultan Yahya*, which he says was probably composed by a Penyengat woman of aristocratic descent, Daeng Wuh, who was married to a certain Sayyid Muhassin Attas, and died in Pahang in about 1851. Klinkert's copy of the manuscript was made for him by his scribe in 1864. About the origins of *Syair Siti Zuhrah*, Klinkert is unfortunately silent, but it seems possible that his copies of *Syair Siti Zuhrah* and *Syair Sultan Yahya* were at the least copied by the same person: several verses common to both are so unusual that they may almost function as a signature. In *Syair Siti Zuhrah*, the *dagang* persona explains her miserable situation in the following stanzas:

Ya Illahi ya tuhanku	O my God, O my Lord,
Betapalah sudah gerangan untungku	What has become of me?
Jikalau ku kenang untung nasibku	When I think of my fate
Sepertikan hilang rasa nyawaku	I feel as though my life is lost.
Siang dan malam menanggung lara	Enduring sorrow day and night,
Seksanya badan duduk sengsara	Body tortured by pain,
Fitnahnya besar tiada terkira	Falsely accused by great calumny,
Duduk di dalam huru-hara	Residing in turmoil.
Jikalau kurang budi bicara	If wits and discernment are lacking,
Akhirnya dagang mendapat cedera	The wanderer will be harmed.
Besar percintaan tiada terkira	Great and incalculable troubles
Dagangnya miskin tiada bersaudara	[Will beset] the miserable, friendless wanderer.
Entahkan ya entahkan tidak	It may be true, it may be false,
Sahabat handai tiada yang jinak	No one close among friends or companions.
Miskin itu memeliharakan anak	The miserable one caring for [her?] child,
Tiadalah lulus sebarang kehendak[6]	With not a single wish coming to pass.

Compare *Syair Sultan Yahya*:

Ya Illahi ya tuhanku	O my God, O my Lord,
Betapalah sudah gerangan untungku	What has become of me?
Jikalau ku kenang akan nasibku	When I think of my fate
Sepertikan hilang rasa hatiku	I feel as though my heart is lost.
Siang dan malam menanggung lara	Enduring sorrow day and night,
Seksanya badan duduk sengsara	Body tortured by pain,
Jikalau kurang budi bicara	If wits and discernment are lacking,
Akhirnya dagang mendapat cedera	The wanderer will be harmed.
Difitnah oleh orang yang banyak	Falsely accused by many,
Saudara daging janganlah jinak	[My] blood relatives keeping far away,
Dagang nan leka meliharakan anak	The wanderer is absorbed in caring for [her?] child,
Tiadakan lulus sebarang kehendak[7]	With not a single wish coming to pass.

These verses do not appear in any of the other extant manuscripts of *Syair Sultan Yahya*. While the sentiments expressed in these verses are highly conventional, such a close sequence of them is unusual, especially given that the verses around them (though just as conventional) are different. The rhyme scheme ending in *–ak* is also relatively rare,[8] and certainly the description of the author caring for a child is very uncommon. It seems probable that the person self-described as "absorbed in caring for a child" was a woman. A further hint is the ambiguous phrase describing the *dagang* persona in *Syair Siti Zuhrah*: "living or abiding with women".[9] It appears that these manuscripts were among those that Klinkert noted as being copied for him by women.

Though hardly conclusive in themselves, other common features of the two *syair* taken together suggest that they may have come from the same copyist or redactor. In *Syair Siti Zuhrah*, the *inang* or royal nursemaid is a prominent and sympathetic character, in contrast to her usual portrayal in traditional Malay literature as either venal or a blank.[10] In *Syair Sultan Yahya*, the sultan's *pengasuh* or nurse has a long and moving speech in which she begs him not to leave his kingdom. Another common feature is the embedded and then abandoned minor plotline that can be found in both: the *inang*'s adventures in *Syair Siti Zuhrah* and the discovery of the princess in the *kelompang* fruit in *Syair Sultan Yahya* are subplots that begin but then disappear. It is as though the composer thought it sufficient to provide the familiar formulaic elements — the princess whose parents have been killed by a *bota* or ogre, the kindly merchant couple who rescue the wandering *inang* — and then simply to imply that these plots work themselves out in the expected way. In the end, the *inang* reappears and the *kelompang* princess marries Jauhar Manikam's brother, but their intervening adventures are not related. Furthermore, both manuscripts contain a character named B-n-d-h-r. While this could be read as Bendahara, this is hardly a common or particularly felicitous name in Malay; instead, the name may be the Indo-Persian Benazir, improperly understood by the copyist. To have the same foreign name in two texts reveals little, of course, but the same corruption of a foreign name suggests a link between the two.

Is the person responsible for the source manuscripts that became Klinkert 132 and 139 one and the same, a woman, perhaps Daeng Wuh, engaged in looking after children, shunned by her friends and kin? Such a supposition must remain just that, given the conventional aspects of the persona of the *dagang* as narrator — although it is interesting to note that the literary tradition does not necessarily figure the *dagang* as male. Ultimately, more significant than a possible common point of origin is that the two *syair* share a common sensibility, one that grafts an aesthetics of emotion onto a feminised romance of adventure, in which the overarching mood is one of *rawan*. Examining *rawan* as experienced by the heroine, the hero, and the readers and redactors of the *syair*, as well as the idea of the beautiful as that which provokes *rawan*, reveals the charm of the sorrowful, the pleasure of the painful in Malay romantic *syair*. Psychoanalytic theories of literature touched on in the previous chapter suggest how these *syair* may be seen as enabling the expression of otherwise prohibited emotions and as dramatising one of the central dramas of a woman's life, the loss of her natal family and its replacement by her husband. The acceptance of this change of status from daughter to wife is bound up with the necessity of emotional control, exemplified in the figure of the heroine. Only she, who has so many reasons to be wracked by the dangerous emotions of sorrow and anger, succeeds in governing her passions. As for erotic desire, though she inspires it in others, she herself is immune. As an exemplar, the heroine embodies the values deemed seemly in a woman, including emotional control. Meanwhile, the figures surrounding her — not only the other characters in the *syair* but also the audience and composer

— exhibit all the malign but irresistible effects of passion. They are the sites of the heroine's — and perhaps also the readers' — displaced emotions.

I. The *Rawan* Writer

Both these *syair* are introduced and concluded by the writer's emotional turmoil. Although assertions of the writer's *rawan* preceding, during and after the act of composition (or even of simple copying) are so ubiquitous in *syair* that the present-day reader tends to skip over them with impatience, they repay closer attention. Like the obligatory thanks offered to mentors and longsuffering family, coupled with the humble acknowledgement of all errors as the author's own, that precede almost every scholarly book of modern times, the claims may be no less heartfelt for being utterly conventional. But what does it mean to find the act of writing a heartrending experience? Why does a narrative about the sufferings and eventual triumph of a fictional princess cause the writer to dwell on his or her own personal grief? Despite the formulaic nature of the *dagang*'s complaint in *syair* prologues, they are by no means identical in temper. Some writers focus on the physical struggles of the act of copying, which can be well imagined — backache, neck ache, joint pain and fatigue are mentioned — while others protest their own lack of literary ability or poor handwriting.[11] Still, others extend their laments into the realm of quasi-comedic bathos, as does the copyist of *Syair Sultan Marit*:

Tidaklah dapat sajak yang molek	No pretty rhymes were to be had,
Hendak diatur supaya pelik	To be arranged in a choice fashion;
Daripada duduk rebah bergolek	From sitting upright [I] fell rolling,
Terlanggar pelita tumpah terbalik	Struck the oil lamp and spilled it upside-down.
Setelah melihat pelita tumpah	Seeing the spilt oil,
Datanglah hati hendak menyumpah	[I] wanted to curse,
Kerana kertas lagi bersepah	Because of the paper strewn about,
Berkaparan bagai seperti sampah.[12]	Scattered like rubbish.

The composer or composers of *Syair Sultan Yahya* and *Syair Siti Zuhrah*, however, suffer from more profound and more inward troubles, turning to writing because of, in Braginsky's words, "grief, sorrow, anxiety, and other depressive states of the soul".[13] The lament at the end of *Syair Sultan Yahya* may serve as a typical statement:

Suratan buruk tidak terperi	The handwriting is terribly bad
Jangan dikata muda bestari	[But] do not speak ill [of it], noble youth[s]
Tambahan banyak yang difikiri	
Serba salah duduk berdiri	For much weighed on [my] mind
	Standing and sitting, at a loss.
Kerana hati tiada bertentu	For my heart is unsettled,
Susah ditanggung bukan suatu	Enduring myriad torments,
Terkenangkan nasib miskin piatu	Thinking of [my] miserable, orphan state,
Segala makhluk tidak begitu	Unlike that of other creatures.
Tidaklah orang seperti sahaya	There is no one like me,
Menanggung duka seumur dunia	Enduring suffering for the age of the world.
Jangan dikenang bangsa dan kaya	
Sekalian itu luputlah dia[14]	Think not of lineage or wealth,
	For all that will pass.

In *Syair Siti Zuhrah*, the writer's epilogue takes up the themes treated in the narrative, seeming to adopt Zuhrah's tribulations as the writer's own. The writer laments her pain at her fatherless state and that she is thrown upon the tender mercies of her relatives, who, it seems, are in no hurry to help her ("hoping for the affection of [my] relatives / living as though amidst live embers").[15] One day, she hopes, her miserable state will change: "the day will come when the miserable wretch / is treated like a Chinese idol".[16] There are obvious parallels with Zuhrah and Nurkiah, motherless and fatherless, subject to the cruel treatment of their closest remaining kin and cast out into the wilderness, but at last gaining the elevated status of kings of Mesir, able to lord it over their former tormentors. Similarly, Benzahara's lament in *Syair Sultan Yahya* that "[my] blood relatives have no affection [for me]", is prefigured by the narrator's complaint that "[my] blood relatives keeping far away".[17] The composer or writer sees her own troubles in the heroine's, and it is perhaps this identification that unlocks the composer's own feelings. *Rawan* is bound up with a catharsis achieved through the otherwise sanctioned expression of malign emotions. On the evidence of the prologues and colophons to *Syair Siti Zuhrah* and *Syair Sultan Yahya*, the personal sorrows expressed by the composer are brought to the surface through a narrative involving the sufferings of the heroine. The composer laments not Zuhrah's fate — which has after all ended happily — but her own. Bookending the *syair* as they do, the prologue and colophon may not seem to be integral to the text, especially as the voice of the *dagang* persona does not intervene within the main body of the narrative, were it not that the heroine, the hero and the story itself are suffused with *rawan*.

II. The *Rawan* Heroine

The heroine, the focus of the *syair*'s interest and of the reader and writer's identification, is characterised by sorrow. Her *rawan* springs both from the loss of her family and from the vulnerable position in which this loss leaves her. Without protectors, she is forced to don the disguise of a man in order, as it were, to become her own male guardian. She cannot be said to enjoy the exploits permitted to her by her adoption of masculine disguise, experiencing at best a lugubrious satisfaction when her former tormenters are brought to heel. She is ever conscious of the shame of her pose — though, in Zuhrah's case, it is that of the most powerful king in the land — and longs to find a way to return to the cloistered safety of a royal woman's life. Despite her sorrows, she never abandons herself to them, for emotional control is a sign of her status as the *syair*'s heroine. Though her sense of resentment at being abandoned by her kin echoes that of the *dagang*, she does not permit herself the writer's miserable complaints. Instead, the heroine's sorrow manifests itself only discreetly, in tears and silences; while the more voluble laments go to subsidiary characters, it is she who demonstrates the emotional control that is so difficult and also so essential to achieve.

The heroines of these *syair* are exemplars, in the sense given to the term by Brownstein in her study of the heroines of the English novel, who unite the ideal qualities of the heroines of courtly romance with the search for identity in a bourgeois world.

> The paradigmatic heroine of courtly love poetry and aristocratic romance ... is unlike all other women, being important and unique, but she is also quintessentially feminine, therefore rightly representative of her sex. A paragon of paradoxes, she is both chaste and suggestive of erotic ecstasy, famous and private, embowered and imperiled; while she is pure idea, her outlines are hard and clear. Beautiful and virtuous as real people never are, she is the Ideal incarnate ... In a novel, a 'realistic' rewriting of romance, a conscious female protagonist takes

the [male] quester's place. It is a she who is the representative of a searching humanity: and she also continues to represent the obscure and vulnerable beautiful ideal.[18]

The *syair* heroine's partakes in many of these paradoxes: inspiring desire but without desire herself, the *orang pingitan* or secluded maiden famous throughout the kingdom, sheltered from the world until disaster sends her out into it defenceless. The romantic *syair* is far closer to the courtly romance than to the novel, but like the English novels of the 18th and 19th centuries which also took the names of the heroine as the title of the text, it has at its centre "a conscious female protagonist". In another fitting paradox, despite her consciousness, the heroine's exemplary qualities mean that she remains opaque, characterised chiefly by her perfection. While *Syair Sultan Yahya*, for instance, extolls the heroine's qualities at length — not only is she beautiful, she is also an accomplished weaver and embroiderer, pious, trustworthy, with an admirable voice for the recitation of the Qur'an, and so on — it hardly characterises her. The merest realist detail — Tun Kudu's squint in *Sejarah Melayu*, for instance, or Lela Mayang's wandering eye in *Syair Sinyor Kosta*[19] — is denied her. One might know her from her deeds, but these are paradoxical too: she is brave and resourceful though she has no wish to be, she retains an acute sense of her own dignity even while she appears to submit to the will of those more powerful, and she invariably weeps at the moment of her triumph.

A key component of the heroine's character is *malu*, a word glossed only inadequately as shame or embarrassment. *Malu* is, after all, usually a positive emotion, a sign of the modesty appropriate to an aristocratic woman — and not only to her, for to "know shame", *tahu malu*, is one of the crucial attributes of the civilised person. The only time Jauhar Manikam and her sister lose their *malu* ("hilanglah malu") is when they are so overcome by passionate grief at the murder of their parents that they lose consciousness.[20] For to be *malu* is to be supremely self-conscious, constantly aware of one's proper place, always curbing one's natural impulses. The heroine's main source of *malu* is her disguise, despite its splendour and the various adventures that it affords her. Of course, the disguise is adopted in the first place to avoid *malu*, since it would be highly inappropriate, not to mention dangerous, for her to wander the world as a woman. Thus, Zuhrah explains to her *inang*:

Beta nan hendak bersalin pakaian	I intend to change my clothes
Jangan diketahui orang sekalian	So as not to be discovered by people.
Perbuatan kita berbagai-bagaian	Our deeds will be various,
Mendapat malu akhirnya kemudian[21]	And may shame us in the end.

But this disguise becomes a source of *malu* as it attracts unwanted male attention, from which she cannot distance herself precisely because she is supposed to be a man. The heroine's characteristically feminine *malu* almost gives the game away when she is unable to join in the familiarities of her male companions. Sultan Yahya's frequent intimacies — touching Juragan Budiman's hand, leaning on "his" thigh, wiping the sweat from "his" face — cause Jauhar Manikam agonies of *malu* and prompt her flight from Zamin Turan. *Malu* is a better indicator of gender in these *syair* than physical appearance. While Syarif Istur and Muhammad Basri in *Syair Siti Zuhrah* appear sufficiently male to attract the attentions of all the women in Mesir, their *malu* behaviour in attempting to refuse costly gifts — having "the ways and manners like those of women" — marks them as female.[22]

In *Syair Siti Zuhrah*, this excessive *malu* — naturally, one of the heroine's most attractive qualities — is underlined when her true identity has been resolved and the assembled queens joke about her exploits as a man. Though the other women are highly amused at her great deeds ("without rival in the world / conquering infidels and Muslims"), Zuhrah herself responds with her usual reserve:

Puteri Zuhrah juga yang malu	Only Princess Zuhrah was ashamed,
Tunduk tidak mengangkatkan hulu	Lowering and not raising her head,
Sebab terkenangkan zaman dahulu	Because she remembered the past,
Orang bercetera bertalu-talu[23]	[Of which] people kept speaking.

The other women — and, one may assume, the readers too — relish the fact that Puteri Zuhrah gained mastery over all her royal siblings. As one of the queens says admiringly, "how mighty were you, my dear / able to conquer your older and younger siblings", also implying Zuhrah's husband in the term *kanda*, of course.[24] But the heroine herself does not overtly share in this pleasure. It is ambiguous, though, whether she hangs her head in shame in remembrance of her stepmother's cruelty, or in dismay that her now-storied adventures are consigned to the past. In yet another example of how closely the two *syair* parallel each other, in *Syair Sultan*

Yahya, the hero praises the heroine's exploits in male disguise, to which she responds with tears and shame:

Siti mendengar titah baginda	Siti heard his highness' words
Bertambah malu di dalam dada	And her shame only increased.
Mangkin menangis Siti yang shahada	Noble Siti wept all the more,
Hatinya malu geram pun ada[25]	Her heart ashamed but also angered.

The hint of anger may be significant here, for the occasion is her wedding night to Sultan Yahya, marking the end of her autonomy. Jauhar Manikam can now no longer resist him, as she could when she was Juragan Budiman. The power the heroine enjoyed while in disguise, never celebrated while she exercised it, is mourned when it has come to an end.

A remarkable aspect of the character of the heroine in these two *syair* is that she has a double, her younger sister. Benzahara and Nurkiah shadow their elder sisters in the narrative; though they too are indisputably beautiful, noble and deserving, they are peripheral characters whose lesser perfection serves to emphasise the heroine's exemplary nature. Not being exemplars, they express themselves more freely and so give voice to the emotional burden of the story. On her way to find her brother, Jauhar Manikam reflects sorrowfully on Benzahara, left behind in Zamin Iran. But while Jauhar Manikam weeps gently ("perlahan-lahan") over the dissolution of their family, Benzahara's reaction to her abandonment is far more impassioned, as we have seen above.[26] Whereas Jauhar Manikam's grief is wordless and solitary, at its most voluble extending to two stanzas, she utters to herself alone in her cabin, Benzahara's long lament in the presence of her husband Sultan Hamzah makes much more of the pathos of the situation:

Lalu menangis Siti bangsawan	Then noble Siti began to weep.
Wahai kakanda abangku tuan	O my older sister,
Meninggalkan adik tiada ketahuan	Leaving [me] without notice,
Duduk menanggung pilu dan rawan	To endure sorrow and suffering.
Sudahlah tiada ibu dan bapa	Already with neither mother nor father,
Abangku pulak tiada bersapa	Now my elder sibling spoke no word
Pergi pun tidak mahu berjumpa	But left without a [last] meeting,
Marahnya abang entahkan apa	What could be the cause of [your] anger?

Apa dosanya sahaya nan abang	What is my crime towards [you],
Makanya kanda pergi mengambang	That [you] went to sea,
Menempuh angin arus gelombang	Charging at the wind and rolling waves?
Meninggalkan sahaya tiadakah bimbang	Did you have no qualms at leaving me?
Tinggallah sahaya yatim piatu	I am left orphaned,
Saudara pun tidak barang suatu	Without kin at all,
Timbangnya belas duli tuanku	Only my lord's pity remains,
Tempat pertaruhkan diriku	To which I entrust myself.
Apakah gerangan celaka dan malang	What may be this accursed misfortune,
Makanya tinggal aku seorang	That leaves me all alone,
Ibu dan bapa tidak dipandang	Unable to see my mother and father,
Saudara daging tiadalah sayang	My blood relatives without affection?
Berbagai-bagai tangisnya Siti	Many were Siti's tears,
Serta meratap tiada berhenti	As well as her ceaseless laments,
Pilu dan rawan rasanya hati	Her heart sorrowful and distressed,
Cinta dan gundah bagaikan mati[27]	Worried and anxious like unto death.

Of course, Jauhar Manikam's departure had nothing to do with any fault on Benzahara's part — such a fault, Sultan Hamzah and anyone else listening well knows, is unthinkable in one so virtuous. Indeed, Benzahara's speech serves as a reminder of her innocence and vulnerability, thereby enjoining Sultan Hamzah to care for and protect her. It also makes explicit the central trauma of the plot, the dissolution of the family, which Jauhar Manikam's necessary stoicism tends to mute.

Similarly, Nurkiyah, too young to practise proper self-control, serves throughout *Syair Siti Zuhrah* as a foil to her sternly self-disciplined older sister. Where Zuhrah is reticent in the company of her stepmother, Nurkiyah says what she likes — thereby further inflaming the queen's anger. After all, she is still a child: "Princess Nurkiah did not yet understand / Did not yet know how to keep her feelings [to herself]".[28] With impeccable self-assurance, Nurkiyah flatly refuses to give her stepmother the jewelled doll she has been sent by her fiancé:

Permaisuri lalu berkata	The queen then said:
Wahai anakanda putera mahkota	'O [my] child, royal princess,
Mintaklah bonda patung permata	[Your] mother asks for the jewelled doll,
Bonda pun hendak bermain serta	For she too wants to play with it'.

Disahut oleh tuan puteri	The princess answered,
Seraya dipeluknya patung sendiri	While hugging her doll,
Tiadalah bonda patik memberi	'I won't give it to [my] mother,
Kerana permainan sehari-hari[29]	For I play with it all day long'.

Being older, Zuhrah must know how to "menaruh hati", conceal her feelings, and cannot exhibit her sister's candour. Thus, when her half-brother Sulung Putera demands that she give him a precious *kain* or cloth that she had inherited from her late mother, she is unable to refuse him. The younger, then, acts as an outward indicator of the emotions that the elder supresses as best she can.

The princesses' *inang*, too, acts as a mouthpiece for the feelings that they cannot themselves express, because of their superior status and exemplary nature. She and the queen's sister, Ardhan, engage in long exchanges of diatribe, speaking the words that Zuhrah and the queen suppress (although it must be said that the queen, being an antagonist, suppresses her feelings rather poorly). Both Ardhan and Seganda freely vent their anger and frustration; as Ardhan says of Seganda, "like a dog giving voice to its passion", in contrast to the sorrowful and appropriately aristocratic restraint shown by Zuhrah.[30] To give voice to passion, then, is bestial — or at best, lower class. Freed from the conventions of behaviour that govern high-status characters, Seganda and Ardhan are akin to the coarse and comic *panakawan* of traditional Javanese texts, and like them, they are unlikely speakers of truth. They are proxies who give voice to the emotions that Zuhrah and, to some extent, the queen, must suppress; the conflict between Ardhan and Seganda is likewise a displacement of the conflict between Zuhrah and the queen. All around the heroine, there are emotions in turmoil — quarrels over borrowed *kain*, palace intrigue, salty exchanges of insults — but she remains, as she must, aloof from all. Dismayed at the spectacle of her *inang* about to come to blows with Ardhan, Zuhrah attempts to remonstrate.

Puteri melihat laku inanganda	The princess saw her *inang*'s actions
Belas kasihan di dalam dada	And felt pity in her heart.
Dengan tangisnya puteri bersabda	In tears, the princess spoke:
Janganlah lagi bersungut bonda	'Complain no more, mother.
Mengapa demikian laku pekerti	Why do you act so,
Membuat Ardhan tidak seperti	Treating Ardhan improperly,
Tiada menaruh perasaan hati	Not keeping back your feelings?
Bukankah ibu hina yang jati[31]	Are you not truly base?'

Alas, Zuhrah's counsel of repression only fans the flames of Ardhan's ire:

Ardhan mendengar katanya puteri	Ardhan heard the princess' words,
Marahkan inang demikian peri	Scolding the *inang* in such a way,
Geramnya tidak lagi terperi	Her anger was unspeakable,
Disangkanya dia yang disindiri	Thinking that she was hinted at.
Seraya berkata suara tak tentu	While saying in an unsteady voice,
Mengapa Zuhrah berkata begitu	'Why do you speak so, Zuhrah?
Ku erti juga katamu itu	I understand your meaning:
Pukul anak sindir menantu[32]	Hitting the child but hinting at the in-law!'

The *syair* is not, after all, so wedded to the ideal of emotional control: it cannot resist milking the humour of its incorrigibly quarrelsome supporting characters who are so free with their passions. But it certainly does not allow Zuhrah to descend to name-calling herself. She remains, as she must, sorrowful but restrained.

III. The Rawan Hero

It is no surprise that another self-described "dagang yang rawan", miserable wanderer, in *Syair Sultan Yahya* is the hero, attempting to cajole Jauhar Manikam on their wedding night. Whereas *rawan* for the heroine usually springs from grief, for the hero, it is far more frequently related to desire. Desire — *dendam, cinta berahi* — is consistently attributed to the hero and never to the heroine. Whether appearing as a man or a woman, the heroine arouses desire in men and women alike, but gives no sign of being prey to it herself. Indeed, the only women who experience feelings of desire are from another class altogether, the commoners infatuated by Zuhrah and Nurkiyah in masculine disguise. Among the male characters, there are those who control their desires, like Jauhar Manikam's brother, Jaya Putera, and those who are controlled by them, like Sultan Yahya and Sidi Maulana. While the latter are certainly not vilified in the *syair*, they are depicted, to some extent, as antagonistic to the heroine, as well as morally inferior to her and the likes of Jaya Putera. On the whole, the *syair* view desire as dangerous, to be kept within the proper bounds — not for *Syair Siti Zuhrah* and *Syair Sultan Yahya* the delirious pleasures of the Balinese *malat*, Javanese *kakawin* or even Malay Panji romance.

The dangers of uncontrolled desire are set forth in the precipitating event of *Syair Sultan Yahya*. The fame (not the sight, for they are *orang pingitan*) of Jauhar Manikam and Benzahara has drawn young men from all around, but while most of them content themselves with befriending Jaya Putera, flying kites, spinning tops, conducting elephant fights, gazing about in lovesick abstraction, and parading themselves in their finery past the young ladies' window, a certain Encik S-t-n has a more sinister intent. His marriage proposal rejected and Jaya Putera safely away at sea, Encik S-t-n bribes a servant to poison the girls' parents. Their deaths set the plot of the *syair* in motion. Benzahara is swiftly married to the king's son Raja Hamzah, the highest-ranking eligible bachelor in Zamin Iran, thereby placing her maddening charms under the proper constraints. Jauhar Manikam remains unmarried, which, although the *syair* does not mention it, is contrary to the Malay custom that siblings marry in the order of their birth. The resolution of this disordered state of affairs forms the matter of the *syair*'s plot. Her quest for her brother is motivated by her wish to escape the continuing plague of suitors and her fear that the sultan will marry her off to an "alim pendita" or religious scholar.[33] That she never articulates why she does not want to marry such a man is a significant lacuna in the text. Throughout these *syair*, both Zuhrah and Jauhar Manikam strenuously resist marriage, which is in contrast to the other *syair*, in which marriage is very much a given and takes place early in the plot.

The double irony of Jauhar Manikam's predicament is that her male guardian is neglecting his duty to such an extent that she must go in search of him, and also that her search for him will bring her to Sultan Yahya, a textbook case of the hero unable to control his passion. Although he is a king, possessing all the usual attributes of nobility, youth, beauty and deportment, and the inevitable spouse of Jauhar Manikam, Sultan Yahya's comportment in most of the *syair* is hardly praiseworthy. Like Encik S-t-n, Sultan Yahya is crazed by desire for Jauhar Manikam, even when he first encounters her, disguised as the merchant Juragan Budiman.

Baginda melihat Juragan Budiman	His highness gazed at Juragan Budiman,
Di dalam hati sangatlah nyaman	Great pleasure in his heart,
Rasanya seperti tiada siuman	He felt as though insane,
Sepertikan luruh rasanya iman	As though he had lost his faith.

Tiadalah lepas kepada mata	Not letting 'him' from his sight,
Ghairah terkibar di dalam cita	Desire unfurled in his mind,
Di dalam fikiran sultan mahkota	The royal sultan thought to himself,
Juragan perempuan pasti kita	'I'm certain this shipmaster's a woman.'
Entahkan apa hendak dicari	'Who knows what she seeks,
Maka berlayar menyamarkan diri	That she has set sail in disguise;
Lemah lembut lengan dan jari	Gentle arms and fingers,
Halus manis mengeluarkan peri	Fine and sweet in speech.
Akan abang Jaya Putera	'As for my elder brother Jaya Putera,
Lemah lembut juga suara	His voice too is gentle,
Rupa pun elok tidak terkira	His appearance too is surpassingly lovely,
Tetapi tidak memberi asmara[34]	But he does not arouse desire.'

Thus, while Jauhar Manikam is presumably a credible man — "lemah lembut" and "elok" are not signs of effeminacy in these *syair* — there is something that gives her away. Desire here is depicted as a force that though overwhelming, has its own rules: Sultan Yahya immediately recognises Juragan Budiman and not Jaya Putera as an appropriate object of his passions, while Jaya Putera, for whom desire for Jauhar Manikam would be extremely inappropriate, does not.

Sultan Yahya's improper advances cause Jauhar Manikam to feel horror and revulsion; though she sails through the tests devised by Sultan Yahya to find her out, she is determined to flee from him. Madness takes hold of Sultan Yahya: not only does his faith fail, as the verses above indicate ("as though he had shed his faith"), he loses all sense of proper behaviour ("shame, embarrassment and manners all vanished").[35] This madness leads Sultan Yahya to neglect his wife, thus provoking her resentment and eventually the clash between her and Jauhar Manikam that takes place later in the narrative. As with Encik Setan, uncontrolled male desire is shown to lead to violence and familial rupture. When Sultan Yahya discovers Juragan Budiman has escaped, he is reduced to passionate tears — "weeping and sobbing madly / his heart longing for the shipmaster" — a pose at odds with proper aristocratic deportment and detachment.[36] While the amorous prince, exemplified by Panji and his avatars, is a paradigmatic character of traditional Malay literature, a counter-current of rationality and emotional continence is ever present — indeed, it is likely that this counter-current was gaining ascendance in 19th-century Penyengat. The great hero of *Hikayat Hang Tuah*, after all, never falls in love; it is Jebat and the Malacca sultan who are prey to their passions. However, it is striking that in *Syair Siti Zuhrah* and *Syair Sultan Yahya*, the hero's amorous passion is never termed *nafsu*, as it is in the didactic work *Syair Siti Dhawiyyah*, but rather *cinta berahi, dendam*, or other similarly less pejorative terms. The use of the Malay terms rather than the Arabic may be seen as a rejection of religious terminology, an attempt to clear a space in the *syair* of the imported discourse of religion, in which erotic desire is always stigmatised. *Nafsu* here connotes a passion for violence, and is explicitly associated with the heroine's female antagonist, the jealous first wife, Puteri Belanta Puri. Yet despite her attempt to kill Jauhar Manikam, the *syair* strongly implies that the blame for this lies at Sultan Yahya's door, since his unrestrained passion for Jauhar Manikam meant that he neglected Puteri Belanta Puri.

As though to compensate for the ambiguous figure of Sultan Yahya, and to give the reader a reassuring exponent of good masculine conduct, the *syair* provides Jaya Putera. Jaya Putera and his sisters are eventually revealed to be of just as noble a lineage as Sultan Yahya, a fact important in a discourse where virtue and political legitimacy are almost unfailingly coterminous. On their return voyage from Zamin Turan, Jaya Putera and Jauhar Manikam come across a *kelompang* fruit floating in the sea.[37] Despite the attempts of several of his companions, only Jaya Putera manages to secure the fruit, which turns out to contain the princess Cahaya Mutia — a sure sign that he is her intended. Jaya Putera is immediately inflamed with passion, but in contrast to Sultan Yahya, he keeps it in check:

Adapun akan Jaya Putera	As for Jaya Putera,
Berahinya tidak lagi terkira	His desire was incalculable;
Hendak pun ia berbuat angkara	[But] if he intended to make mischief,
Di akhirat j-m-d-h dapat cedera	He would suffer in the world to come.
Duduklah ia menahankan hati	He remained, restraining his heart,
Berhibur dengan berbuat bakti	Distracting himself with pious deeds,
Menanti sampai dengan seperti	Awaiting [their] proper arrival
Ke negeri adinda tempat Encik Siti[38]	In the kingdom of his younger sister Siti.

Upon their return to Zamin Iran, Jaya Putera and Cahaya Mutia are married and live happily ever after: "enjoying themselves day after day / having escaped from perilous danger".[39] Since they were in no danger from foes or storms or other external powers during their voyage, the "mara bahaya" from which they have escaped must be the volatile force of Jaya Putera's passion. Cahaya Mutia vanishes from the narrative after this point; it would seem that the only function of her presence is to enable Jaya Putera to provide a counterpoint to Sultan Yahya.

Among the ways Jaya Putera distracts himself during the voyage is by going fishing, and it is during the course of this expedition that he is reunited with his sister Benzahara. Here the control of passion leads directly to the reconstruction of the family, specifically of the sibling relationship. In contrast, Sultan Yahya's lack of control extends to neglecting the proper visits to his first wife, Puteri Belanta Puri, even against Jauhar Manikam's advice. Puteri Belanta Puri then challenges Jauhar Manikam to combat in the main square, thus at once endangering the life of the heroine and publicly exposing the collapse of marital harmony in the royal establishment. The fact that peaceful coexistence among the royal wives is most devoutly to be wished is demonstrated by Jauhar Manikam's mercy towards her fallen rival. Though Sultan Yahya wants to have Puteri Belanta Puri executed, Jauhar Manikam argues for clemency and ultimately restores a proper balance in marital relations. Puteri Belanta Puri becomes devoted to Jauhar Manikam, and Sultan Yahya divides his time equitably between his two wives (equitably at least according to their relative personal merit: he spends a week with Puteri Belanta Puri for every month with Jauhar Manikam). Once again, the management of desire averts danger — "having escaped from peril" — and the preferred sibling-style relationship between the erstwhile rivals is restored — Puteri Belanta Puri comes to think of Jauhar Manikam as "like her very own sister".[40]

In *Syair Siti Zuhrah*, there is the same pattern of the desiring hero attempting to transgress the boundaries of proper behaviour and of the emphatically non-desiring heroine thwarting him to keep desire within its proper bounds. Ruling Mesir in the guise of Sultan Syarif, Zuhrah collects her erstwhile persecutors and her betrothed, Sidi Maulana, as vassals at her court. Sidi Maulana is, of course, mad for love of Sultan Syarif, whom he suspects, by the *rawan* that struck him down at first sight, to be a woman. Like Sultan Yahya, Sidi Maulana cannot be quite sure whether his beloved is male or female but is nonetheless driven to tears by his unrequited passion: "*rawan* invaded his heart / so that he wept in his sheets".[41] Driven by the force of his passion, Sidi Maulana pushes his way into the royal sleeping quarters late at night, a serious violation of the sancitity of the *dalam*. He is amazed and yet more aroused to see Sultan Syarif asleep surrounded by women.

Sidi pun duduk di atas tilam	Sidi sat upon the bed,
Di hujung kaki sultan puhalam	At the feet of the alabaster sultan,
Tanglung pelita cahayanya kelam	The light of the lanterns and lamps
Bertambah gundah hati di dalam	was dim,
	The turmoil in his heart increased.
Serta dipegangnya kaki baginda	He took hold of his highness' foot,
Sangat berahi di dalam dada	Great desire aroused in him,
Sambil berkata bangunlah adinda	While saying: 'Arise, younger brother,
Tuan dipersilakan ayahanda[42]	Your father summons you.'

By this ruse, Sidi Maulana tricks Sultan Syarif into accompanying him into the night but is then forced to acknowledge that there has in fact been no summons from Sultan Sahristan. He resolves to tell Sultan Syarif (whom he apparently still believes to be a man) of his love, and admits that his purpose was to invite Sultan Syarif to amuse "himself" ("diajak bermain muda bangsawan").[43] What is meant by "bermain" (play) here may be gauged by the reaction of Sultan Syarif, who is not amused in the slightest. Furthermore, although the adjective "muda" belongs to the epithet "muda bangsawan" (noble youth), the phrase as a whole cannot help but recall "bermain muda" (youthful play), which in other Riau *syair* is used as a euphemism for illicit sexual intercourse.[44] Sultan Syarif's reaction to this ever more audacious series of trespasses by Sidi Maulana is, at first glance, surprisingly muted. With these heroines, emotions are conveyed less by what they say or do than by what they refrain from saying or doing, and by the great effort required to master their emotions.

Mendengarkan kata Sidi Maulana	Hearing Sidi Maulana's words,
Berkhabar benar dengan sempurna	Telling the complete truth,
Rasanya murka terlalu bina	'He' was full of wrath —
Disabarkan baginda raja yang ghana	But the mighty king controlled 'himself'.
Suatu pun tidak apa katanya	Not a word did 'he' say,
Kerana hati sangat marahnya	For 'he' was enraged,
Hendak digemparkan demikian lakunya	Wanting to create an uproar,
Malu didengar orang sekaliannya	[But] ashamed that others would hear.

Menjadi baginda berdiam juga	So 'his' majesty remained silent,
Sangat ditahan hatinya murka	Restraining 'his' anger.
Merah padam warnanya muka	Bright red 'his' face,
Pulang ke istana dengan seketika[45]	'He' returned to the palace at once.

Nevertheless, Sidi Maulana receives Sultan Syarif's message loud and clear, and descends into sleeplessness and lovesick anguish. By demonstrating impeccable self-control and suppressing "his" own anger at Sidi Maulana's conduct, Sultan Syarif maintains order. Of course, in doing so, Sultan Syarif fails to behave as a king would, for the discipline of patience and emotional repression pertains far more to royal women than to men.

In *Syair Sultan Yahya*, there is a corresponding scene in which the heroine-in-disguise is in danger of revealing her true gender because of sleeping arrangements. Sultan Yahya prevails on Jaya Putera and Juragan Budiman to spend the night with him and his male companions in the royal pavilion. This is Juragan Budiman's most vulnerable moment, when she is most at risk of discovery, and when the consequences of that discovery would be most dire. The sultan's companions tease Juragan Budiman about "his" obvious discomfort in their company:

Tuan seperti dikawal Inggeris	You are as though watched over by the English,
Tidur pun tidak bercerai keris	Not parting from your *keris* even in sleep.
Jikalau menggangu dirasuk iblis	If an evil spirit possesses you,
Orang di balai ditikam habis[46]	All the people in the pavilion will be stabbed.

Not giving up "his" *keris* — the symbolism is obvious here — is a sign of hypermasculinity that inevitably points to Juragan Budiman's femininity. That is, since "he" is really a woman, "he" does not relax "his" guard in male society, and this defensiveness cannot fail to mark "him" out to "his" companions. Moreover, Juragan Budiman's attachment to "his" *keris* is described as putting the men at risk of attack, if "he" is possessed — that is, if passion conquers reason. In defence of "his" unwillingness to part from "his" weapon, Juragan Budiman protests:

Hendaklah tidur tempat nan sempit	The place is too cramped for sleep:
Kiri dan kanan kawan diapit	Hemmed in by companions left and right,
Ada yang memunggung[47] *ada yang mengimpit*	Some spooning, some pressing in,
Ada yang memeluk ada yang menggamit	Some embracing, some fondling,
Duduk bergurau sama laki-laki	Bantering with other men,
Seperti tiada perempuan lagi	As though there are no more women.
Beta dipunggung tangan dan kaki	I am pressed upon by hands and feet;
Janganlah abang begitu lagi[48]	Older brothers, desist from this.

In this alternative scenario, reason is also at risk of defeat by passion, but here the result is not violence but sex. That both of these outcomes are avoided — eventually the men settle down to sleep — is testament to Juragan Budiman's control of "his" rationality. Indeed, Juragan Budiman does not even give in to the temporary suspension of the conscious mind that is sleep, remaining awake throughout the night. Just as in the case of Sultan Syarif, this extreme rationality marks Juragan Budiman as a woman. In an attempt to find out Juragan Budiman's true gender, Sultan Yahya had ordered that banana leaves be placed underneath "his" bed. When these leaves are examined the next day, the fact that they are torn and shredded indicates that Juragan Budiman passed a restless night and, ipso facto, that "he" is a "she". This proof that Juragan Budiman is a woman plunges Sultan Yahya into yet greater *rawan*, "great anxiety in his heart / silently brooding with mouth agape".[49] The stereotype of passionate women and rational men is well and truly reversed here, and enables Juragan Budiman to make good her escape.

That a dangerous moment has been headed off is clear from the relief expressed after Sultan Syarif is revealed to be Zuhrah and is married to Sidi Maulana at last: only then can they be said to be "escaped from catastrophe".[50] As in *Syair Sultan Yahya*, *Syair Siti Zuhrah* depicts the hero's desire as something which the heroine does not share and which is her role to thwart. Desire is male and it is dangerous. The *malapetaka* or *bencana* that is being averted in these *syair* is sexual relations outside marriage and it is a catastrophe for the heroine alone. The convention of traditional literary works in Javanese and Malay alike is that the heroine's first sexual encounter is forced upon her by the hero.[51] The extent to which this is a necessary pose that the bride must adopt is suggested by a contemporaneous Malay text, *Hikayat Panji Semirang*, in which the anti-heroine, Galuh Ajeng, is instructed by her mother to pretend to cry and protest on her wedding night.[52] But while Javanese *kakawin* consistently depict the wedding night as highly traumatic for the heroine, and necessarily, proscriptively so, the Riau *syair* usually draw a discrete veil over the goings-on in the nuptial bedchamber.

Syair Siti Zuhrah omits this type-scene altogether, in favour of a protracted account of the lavish wedding ceremonies that unite not only the hero and the heroine but also their various siblings and cousins. Concerned solely with marriage as a public performance, a great state event, the only hint of the more intimate aspects of it is that after four months and 12 days of festivities, "husband and wife came to agreement" ("muafakat").[53] In *Syair Saudagar Bodoh*, marital harmony, including sexual relations, is referred to as "muafakat" between husband and wife.[54] However, *Syair Sultan Yahya* includes a long account of the wedding night that is also significant for what it omits: the element of force and the sexual act itself. The scene is perhaps the apogee of the hero and the heroine's *rawan*, springing as they do from desire in the former case and distress in the latter:

Siti menangis tiada terperi	Siti wept violently,
Turun d[ar]i ribaan hendak lari	Got down from his lap to run away,
Segera dipegangkan raja bestari	But was swiftly caught by the noble king,
Sambil tersenyum manis berseri	Sweetly and radiantly smiling.
Ia berkata sambil memujuk	Coaxingly he said,
Diangkat diriba pinggang dipeluk	As he lifted her into his lap and embraced her waist,
Dicium pipi paras yang elok	And kissed the lovely one's cheek,
Tuan memberi abang nan mabuk[55]	'You intoxicate me.'

Sultan Yahya, though very much the "dagang yang rawan" beguiled by desire, behaves towards Jauhar Manikam in a manner that might best be described as maternal — singing a lullaby to her, covering her in a blanket, carrying her to her bath, tempting her to eat. These Malay conventions, which may also be found in *Hikayat Andaken Penurat* and *Syair Ken Tambuhan*, contrast strikingly with the wedding-night "battlefields" described by Creese and Vickers, where the heroine is left literally bleeding and defeated.[56] Thus, at the ultimate site of erotic *rawan*, the text reverts instead to a fantasy of infancy. Whether this is a reflection of the female audiences of Malay literature, who might have found the scene as it is depicted in the *syair* to be rather more appealing, or of a more reticent attitude towards sexually explicit material in Malay literary culture more generally must be left to further studies to decide.

IV. Beauty and *Rawan*

An important source of *rawan* and *berahi* in these *syair* is beauty, *keindahan*, usually of persons and their attributes, but also of landscapes, animals, and objects. The beautiful is that which causes forgetfulness of the self — making the spectators, as in *Syair Sultan Yahya* at the sight of Jauhar Maknikam's ship putting out to sea, "lose themselves in wonder".[57] The most prominent manifestation of beauty in these *syair* is that of people and their attributes — bodies, faces, voices, clothes. The hero and the heroine are, of course, the supreme exponents of this beauty, matchless in every regard, but lesser characters too are unfailingly beautiful, so long as they are noble. Beauty is less an indicator of moral worth than it is of lineage: thus Sulung Putera and his sisters, who terrorise their half-sisters, Zuhrah and Nurkiyah, are all described as attractive. Of course, even the nobility are not created equal: however beautiful Sultan Yahya's first wife Puteri Belanta Puri may be, Jauhar Maknikam has the edge over her. When they meet to do battle, the two walk together into the arena:

Ia berjalan berpegang jari	She walked hand in hand
Dengan puteri Belanta Puri	With Princess Belanta Puri;
Keduanya elok muda bestari	Both of them lovely, youthful, noble,
Seperti dewi dengan bidadari[58]	Like a goddess and a nymph.
Jauhar Manikam terlebih parasnya	Jauhar Manikam was the more beautiful,
Lemah lembut barang lakunya	All her actions gentle;
Belanta Puri pantas sajaknya	Belanta Puri's ways were brisker,
Terlalu petah gerak langkahnya[59]	Her steps and movements extremely smart.

As in a Hollywood film, it is axiomatic that the hero and heroine are the most beautiful of the beautiful people. And as in a Hollywood film, a large measure of the audience's enjoyment comes from the spectacle of this beauty, as well as from the luxury of the clothes, jewellery and *kerises* in which the hero and heroine are bedecked.

The scene in which the heroine dresses herself in men's clothes is something of a *locus classicus* of *syair* on this theme, and is treated at length in *Syair Sultan Yahya*. To quote only half of the description of Jauhar Maknikam dressing or *memakai*,

Bercelak Siti bersifat alit	Siti's eyes were rimmed in kohl,
Putih berseri warnanya kulit	Her skin shone pale,
Bibirnya merah bagai dihalit	Her lips were red as though rouged:
Cantiknya rupa Siti yang sulit	How lovely was the disguised Siti.
Giginya seperti sayap kumbang	Her teeth gleaming black like a beetle's wings,
Bersunting bunga melur yang kembang	Blossoming jasmine behind her ear,
Parasnya seperti dewa dan mambang	Her appearance like that of gods and spirits,
Cantik manis memberi bimbang	Pretty and sweet, arousing desire.
Eloknya tidak dapat dikata	Her loveliness indescribable,
Sepertikan lenyap dipandang mata	As if the viewer might disappear gazing upon it,
Seperti rupa peranakan danta	Like a doll of ivory,
Ditatah dengan pudi permata	Studded with gems and jewels.
Sudah memakai muda bangsawan	When the young noble had dressed,
Sajak dan sikah tiada berlawan	Her graceful movements without compare,
Sedikit tidak rupa perempuan	Not looking at all like a woman,
Seperti laki-laki yang pahlawan	But like a valiant man.
Elok mejelis barang kelakuan	All her ways fair and lovely,
Lemah lembut memberi rawan	Her gentleness stirring desire,
Rupanya seperti dewa di awan	Her appearance like a god in the clouds,
Laksana bulan diarak awan[60]	Like the moon escorted by clouds.

The classic tropes of the beautiful woman in traditional Malay literature — whose teeth are black, whose skin is so thin as to be transparent, and moreover is yellow or gold, not white — are absent. With her kohl, white skin and red lips, the heroine's beauty is of an exotic kind, perhaps owing something to Indo-Persian or Chinese models. Zuhrah and Nurkiyah, by contrast, are of a more familiar type: their skin is "like wrought gold", and dressed as men, they recall "[prince] Inu in the land of Java".[61] In both *syair*, there is a peculiar charm about a woman dressed as a man, a certain eroticism that stems from the gender ambiguity. Despite the descriptions of them that are hardly suggestive of masculinity to a modern audience, there is no doubt that the heroines are meant to be credible as men. Jauhar Maknikam, as quoted above, "does not look like a woman at all", and likewise, Zuhrah and her sister "look like real men".[62] Jauhar Maknikam is so convincing that her own brother fails to recognise her (though he does note her resemblance to himself!).

Poetry, whether *pantun* or *syair*, is also beautiful and *rawan*-provoking. Episodes of heightened emotion, such as the scene in which the parrot confirms to Sultan Yahya that Juragan Budiman is a woman and that in which Puteri Zuhrah and Puteri Nurkiah escape into the forest, bring together *rawan* and lyric description. The former scene features the single occurrence in these two *syair* of *pantun*, the verse form which may be said to be more closely associated with courtship and eroticism and also more formally complex than the *syair*. While *syair* verses interposed in prose may awaken desire, the irruption of *pantun* in the midst of *syair* has a similar effect of intensifying the emotional register. Juragan Budiman has just passed the tests laid for her by Sultan Yahya, intent on proving that "he" is in fact a woman. According to Sultan Yahya's advisors, a woman who throws a fishnet will shed blood. Juragan Budiman does indeed bleed, but warned of Sultan Yahya's ploy by the magic beetle, "he" disguises this as the blood of a dove "he" has sacrificed to ensure a good catch of fish. Similarly, Juragan Budiman leaps fearlessly over a canal, something Sultan Yahya is sure no woman could do. Having secured her disguise by dint of quick-wittedness and the *keramat* powers afforded by her noble lineage, Juragan Budiman seems at last to have gained a respite from Sultan Yahya's unwanted attention. But her disguise begins to unravel when a parrot alights on a tree and utters a series of *pantun*:

Terbanglah seekor unggas nuri	A parrot flew across,
Di atas pohon naga sari	And lit on the acacia tree,
Rupanya indah tidak terperi	Of surpassingly lovely appearance,
Sambil berpantun menyindiri	It uttered allusive verses.
Dari teluk mandi di jeram	From the bay to bathing in the rapids,
Singgah mengambil kuntum cempaka	Pausing to pick a *cempaka* posy;
Eloknya paras Jauhar Manikam	Jauhar Manikam's visage is lovely,
Di mana baginda tidakkan leka	How could his highness not be entranced?

Anak udang di dalam cawan	A young shrimp in a cup,
Emas ditempa dari Serati	Wrought gold from Surat;
Anak orang sabarlah tuan	Do not hurry after others' children,
Di dalam tangan sudah Encik Siti	For Siti is within your hands.
Indahnya bulan dengan matahari	How lovely is the moon and the sun,
Dipagar bintang sedang cuaca	Surrounded by stars on a clear night;
Bertemulah tuan sama jauhari	You have met with a jewel,
Jikalau ditentang hati binasa	If gazed at your heart will be crushed.
Dari Jirat ke Jerati [?]	From Jirat to Jerati
Singgah di Cina membeli pinggan	Pausing in China to buy plates
Sangatlah ghairah rasanya hati	How amorous is [your] heart
Menentang mengerna jadi juragan	Gazing at the bright one become a shipmaster
Pergi ke hutan menimbang berangan	Going to the jungle to weigh chestnuts,
Bunganya luruh di dalam perahu	Its flowers fall into the boat;
Patutlah tuan bida kayangan	No wonder you are a heavenly maiden,
Nujumnya nuri sudahlah tahu	The astrologer-parrot has found you out.
Eloknya Siti di Zamin Ambar	The loveliness of Siti of Zamin Ambar,
Cantik mejelis bagai digambar	As pretty as a picture,
Patutlah dengan duli mu'atabar	A fitting match for his dignified highness,
Jika terpandang memberi ghobar	The sight of her causing distraction.
Buah pauh dari sagara	A coconut from the ocean,
Buahnya jatuh di atas batu	Its fruit falling on a rock;
Jauhnya tidak berapa antara	She is not far distant,
Sungguhpun dekat belum bertentu[63]	But though close it is yet uncertain.

The parrot does not so much reveal all as drop hints, *sindiran*, for the beauty of a *pantun* is in its allusiveness. The first two lines or the *sampiran*, sometimes held to be merely nonsense phrases chosen for the sake of rhyme or other aural qualities, here refer obliquely and elegantly to the matter referred to in the *maksud* lines. Perhaps it is not too strained to read the image of the shrimp trapped in a cup and the rain of blossoms into the boat as Jauhar Manikam falling into the hands of Sultan Yahya. The travels from Jirat to Jerati to China recall the wanderings of Jaya Putera and Jauhar Manikam in the guise of merchants. The double coconut from the sea coming to land also looks forward to the discovery by Jaya Putera of Puteri Belanta Puri in the *kelompang* fruit. The *pantun* here effects a reversal of the plot, for up to this point it had seemed that Jauhar Manikam would be able to preserve her disguise. Whereas birds and insects are conventionally closely associated with facilitating romance (one thinks, for instance, of the *pungguk* or owl as a stock figure of yearning, the *pantun*-reciting parrot in *Syair Bidasari*, and the *kumbang* couple in *Syair Buah-Buahan*), Jauhar Manikam's dove and talking beetle keep her away from the amorous attentions of Sultan Yahya — only to be out-manoeuvred by the parrot. Indeed, Sultan Yahya's suit would have been stymied without the parrot's continued assistance, since once she has fled, it reveals to him further particulars about her identity, including the kingdom where she may be found. The first avian intervention precipitates the *syair*'s crisis: Sultan Yahya is resolved to make Juragan Budiman his, and Juragan Budiman is resolved to flee.

The depiction of beauty is prominent in one of *Syair Siti Zuhrah*'s most emotionally affecting scenes, the nocturnal escape of the heroine, her sister and their *inang* from Sahristan into the forest. This contains one of the rare lyrical passages of the *syair*, a sequence of verses in which the forest, through its birds, plants and even the night wind, responds with pity to the heroine's distress.

Bulan pun terang kilau-kilauan	The moon was shining bright
Memancar segenap daun kayuan	Its rays on all the leaves of the trees
Cahayanya persih di cela awan	Its light lustrous between the clouds
Seperti menyuluh puteri bangsawan	As though shining a torch for the well-born princesses.
Pungguk berbunyi di pohon angsana	A *pungguk* bird sang sweetly in an *angsana* tree
Merindu bulan cemerlang warna	Longing for the moon of glorious hue
Belaskan puteri kena bencana	Pitying the misfortune-struck princesses
Berjalan dengan gundah gulana	Walking in distress and turmoil.
Turunlah angin sipu bahasa	The gentle wind came down,
Teja membangun di atas angkasa	The shaft of light rose in the sky,
Selaku kasihankan puteri berbangsa	As though taking pity on the noble princesses,
Berjalan keluar dari [sic] dalam desa	Travelling on foot out of the city.
Murai bercerita bersahutan	The mynahs twittered to each other,
Riuh berkokok ayam di hutan	The jungle fowl crowed in uproar

Bagai belaskan puteri sultan	As though pitying the sultan's daughters.
Puteri pun pilu bukan buatan	The princesses were truly sorrowful.
Segala bunga berkembang-kembangan	All the flowers blossomed,
Diseri kumbang berlayang-layangan	Visited by beetles flying hither and yon
Persembahkan bau itu gerangan	As if they were presenting their fragrances
Keluar tidak dengan kenangan	So that the princesses did not depart without a sign of remembrance.
Terlalu pilu puteri mengindera	The royal princesses were so sorrowful.
Fajar merekah teranglah nyata	Dawn broke in clear light
Bertambah rawan emas juita	And increased the turmoil of those golden ones of life,
Berjalan dengan airnya mata[64]	Who walked in tears.

As frightening as the forest at night might be, in a reversal of the usual association of the forest with the feral and the city with the familiar, here the wilderness is beautiful, and far more sympathetic to the outcast princesses than their own kin. The natural world seems to share in the princesses' grief, the moon lighting their way, the flowers offering their scents and the birds crying as though in sympathy.

Old Javanese *kakawin*, as Creese shows, abounds both in lyric descriptions of nature and of eroticism, with both intended to evoke a sense of the sublime or *langö*: "a word that encapsulates not merely the subjective feeling of aesthetic delight but also its object, the beauty of women and the natural world. The emotions aroused by the luxuriant tropical landscape and the sensuality of women in it could scarcely be distinguished. Both allowed poet and audience to abandon themselves totally to poetic rapture".[65] Braginsky has extensively discussed the central role of the aesthetic experience of beauty in Malay literature.[66] However, lyric description as described by Creese and Braginsky is on the whole rather rare in the disguised heroine *syair*. This is not only because the poetics of the romantic *syair* privilege plot over description but also because, in spite of the pervasive discourse of *rawan*, eroticism is rather muted. *Pantun* verses, a rather reliable indicator in Malay literature of the erotic mood, are extremely scarce in the disguised heroine *syair*. The parrot's *pantun* are the only such verses in *Syair Sultan Yahya*, while in the more than 200 manuscript pages of *Syair Siti Zuhrah*, there are no *pantun* at all. It may also be significant that *pantun* are placed exclusively in the mouths of non-human creatures. *Pantun* are never exchanged between the human protagonists themselves, not even in the frequent *memujuk* scenes in which the hero cajoles the heroine. The erotic scenes that may be found elsewhere in traditional Malay literature — to say nothing of Javanese — are similarly conspicuous by their absence in the disguised heroine *syair*. The impression is that these *syair* are deliberately de-eroticised. Whether because of their female viewpoint or the *syariah*-minded tendencies of the Penyengat court is debatable. The former might militate against the male voyeurism that, according to Creese, pervades old Javanese *kakawin*, but it would by no means rule out eroticism per se. Whereas in *kakawin*, mood dominates over plot,[67] even in these highly emotional *syair*, plot holds sway and the relentless contest between passion and reason is won, always, by reason.

* * * * *

Syair Sultan Yahya and *Syair Siti Zuhrah* are replete with the paradoxes of desire: for the heroine, that the wished-for outcome is neither overtly sought nor celebrated; for the hero, that desire is depicted only in its dangerous and destabilising but never in its pleasurable aspects; for the copyist and author, that the *syair* unleashes repressed emotions without resolving them. The central paradox of these two *syair*, however, is the elevation of emotional repression as an ideal, exemplified in the figure of the heroine, even as *rawan* proliferates throughout the text, more often than not provoked by her. It is this unstable détente between opposing forces that prevents the texts from settling for the patness of didactic tales. *Syair Sultan Yahya* and *Syair Siti Zuhrah* have at their core, as their successors do not, an unresolvable emotional conflict. The crusading queens of *Syair Siti Zubaidah* and *Syair Sultan Abdul Muluk* are far less prone to twinges of *rawan*, while the thoroughly calculating and unsentimental merchants' daughters in *Syair Siti Dhawiyyah* and *Syair Saudagar Bodoh* shed hardly a tear.

4

From Battlefield to Bedroom

War and Marriage in *Syair Siti Zubaidah* and
Syair Sultan Abdul Muluk

The most well known of the Riau romantic adventure *syair* — the only ones to appear in modern editions or to be at all familiar to contemporary Malay readers — are also the most successful unions of the Panji motif of the martial heroine with the characteristic Riau theme of the *bakti* or service of wives. The victorious princesses, or *puteri jayeng*, of the previous chapter have become victorious wives, *isteri jayeng*, with the struggles of marriage transposed onto the battlefield.[1] The wars between the Chinese and the Kembayat "Malays" in *Syair Siti Zubaidah* as well as between Barbary and Hindustan in *Syair Sultan Abdul Muluk* are religious conflicts, pitting infidel against Muslim, and simultaneously demonstrations on a grand scale of the heroines' superior merit, their *sakti* or spiritual power that trumps that of all other women. In one of its modern edition, *Syair Siti Zubaidah* is subtitled *Perang Cina*, the war with China, and *Syair Sultan Abdul Muluk* could easily be subtitled *Perang Hindustan*, the importance of the heroine's bellicose role versus adversaries who are the ethnic others of the texts' Malay audiences. The heroine's assumption of the quintessentially masculine role as warrior means that the usual gender attributes are reversed more consistently here than in other *syair*: the heroine thwarts her foes through feats of arms and guile, collecting vassal princesses as she goes, while the hero spends much of the *syair* imprisoned, playing the passive role of patient endurance and fortitude. The heroes, Zainal Abidin and Abdul Muluk, fail in the ultimate male pursuit of war. The greatest warriors in these texts are women — no fewer than nine in *Syair Siti Zubaidah*, including the Chinese princesses — who abandon the usually feminine heroics of endurance for the usually masculine heroics of action. The familiar Malay literary trope of sexual encounter as battle, with the man always the victor, the woman always the vanquished, is here turned inside-out. The heroines are ever victorious on the battlefield, and the bedroom becomes an arena not for the demonstration of masculine potency but for the contestation of feminine worth.

Both *Syair Sultan Abdul Muluk* and *Syair Siti Zubaidah* are attributed to women of the Penyengat court. Some scholars have identified Tengku Bilik binti Raja Abdullah as the author of *Syair Siti Zubaidah*.[2] Nothing is known about her other than her name, which reveals that she was a daughter of the ninth Yang Dipertuan Muda of Riau (d. 1858). Of the surviving manuscripts of *Syair Siti Zubaidah*, only Klinkert's bears a date, 1864. Klinkert purchased it from a *selir* or minor wife of the Yamtuan Muda of the neighbouring kingdom of Siak, suggesting that if the text did originate in Penyengat, by the 1860s, it had spread elsewhere. *Syair Sultan Abdul Muluk* is better documented, appearing in print in a Dutch journal in 1847 under the name of Raja Ali Haji. We have already seen that the *syair* was likely to have originated among the women of Raja Ali Haji's household, and to have been merely edited by him.[3] Raja Ali Haji himself had been keen to get into print,[4] but probably would not have thought it appropriate for the name of one of his female relatives to be published. His appropriation of Raja Salihah's text may explain why *Syair Sultan Abdul Muluk* treats the disguised heroine theme far more conservatively than does its close kin *Syair Siti Zubaidah*. The plots of the two *syair* closely resemble each other. In both *syair*, a dispute between the king of a certain country and a foreign merchant leads to the foreign power's attack on the kingdom. In *Syair Sultan Abdul Muluk*, the enemy is the king of Hindustan, while in *Syair Siti Zubaidah*, it is the seven princesses of China. The princely hero is captured, while the heroine, his wife, manages to flee. Assuming male disguise, she conquers various kingdoms, amassing allies and followers, before vanquishing the enemy kingdom and rescuing her husband. The hand of Raja Ali Haji in reshaping *Syair Sultan Abdul Muluk* may be discerned in its relentless casting of the heroine's exploits as the *bakti*, or devoted service, of a wife to her husband.

Syair Sultan Abdul Muluk [5]

Sultan Abdul Hamid Syah rules over Barbari. His second-in-command is his wife's brother Mansur. The sultan's wife gives birth to a son, Abdul Muluk. Three years later, Mansur's wife has a daughter, named Siti Rahmah. She is brought up with her cousin Abdul Muluk.

Meanwhile, Hindustan is ruled by Raja Syahabuddin. Syahabuddin's uncle Bahauddin is a merchant who departs to Barbari to trade. There he sells his entire cargo to a local merchant. Some days later, the Barbari merchant discovers that the merchandise is defective and wants Bahauddin to take it back. The two merchants take the matter before the ruler of Barbari. Sultan Abdul Hamid Syah rules that, in accordance with local custom, Bahauddin should take the merchandise back. Enraged, Bahauddin draws a sword on the sultan, is thrown into prison, and there dies. The news reaches Raja Syahabuddin, who begins to plot his revenge.

By this time Abdul Muluk has reached the age of 13. His parents decide to marry him to Rahmah, now ten. The couple are married in a lavish ceremony. Two years later, Sultan Abdul Hamid Syah is on his deathbed and entrusts Abdul Muluk to Mansur's care. After his father's death, Abdul Muluk becomes king but cannot shake off his grief, which is only exacerbated by his mother's death soon thereafter. To improve his spirits, Abdul Muluk departs on a voyage, promising to return quickly.

The scene then shifts back in time and to the kingdom of Ban, where the queen is pregnant. Unusually heavy rain falls in the seven days preceding the birth of her daughter. According to the astrologer, this is a sign that the newborn princess, Siti Rafiah, will perform great deeds for her future husband. Indeed, the astrologer predicts that she will rescue her husband from distress.

One of the wazirs travelling with Abdul Muluk advises him to visit Ban, because of Rafiah's fame. Much excitement occurs over Abdul Muluk's arrival, with people thronging the streets and the princess and her attendants spying on the newcomers through her father's telescope. Abdul Muluk is welcomed by the Sultan of Ban and installed in a palace. There he stays for almost a year before deciding to return to Barbari. On his way to his morning bath, he catches sight of Rafiah, and from then on is in turmoil. At last, Abdul Muluk's wazir, guessing the situation, goes to the Sultan of Ban on Abdul Muluk's behalf. The wedding duly takes place, and the couple returns to Barbari. Rahmah gracefully accepts her husband's new wife.

Learning of Sultan Abdul Hamid's death and his replacement by Abdul Muluk, now aged 17, Raja Syahabuddin launches an attack on Barbari. He does so without sending notice of his belligerent intentions in advance. This breach of protocol upsets two of his ministers, whom Raja Syahabuddin then dismisses. Despite the valiant efforts of the Barbari forces, and the heroic exploits of the 14-year-old Wazir Suki, Raja Syahabuddin's troops have the upper hand. Abdul Muluk himself goes into battle but is captured. In the night, Rafiah invites a daughter of one of the wazirs to sleep in her bed, kills her, and escapes into the jungle. The following day, Raja Syahabuddin captures Rahmah and goes on to take Rafiah prisoner as well. Seeing a dead woman in Rafiah's bed, he assumes she has committed suicide. On his way back to Hindustan with his captives and booty, Raja Syahabuddin comes across a relief force sent from Ban, which he promptly annihilates.

In Hindustan, Abdul Muluk and three of his followers, including Wazir Suki, are jailed. Rahmah refuses to marry Raja Syahabuddin in spite of various tortures he inflicts upon her. Eventually, she too is thrown in jail with her husband Abdul Muluk.

Having given herself up to God, Rafiah wanders in the forest, lost and subsisting on leaves. Resting on a hillside one day, she sees all the animals fleeing, chased by a creature with blood-red fur. Rafiah kills this mysterious animal with Abdul Muluk's sword and cuts off its mane which she wraps around her waist. At once her fatigue disappears and she becomes strong. Being heavily pregnant, she is about to give birth alone in the jungle when she sees a light. She comes upon a house in which someone is reciting the names of God. When he has finished praying, a sheikh comes out and offers her shelter. In the care of the sheikh's wife, Rafiah gives birth to a son. She remains with the sheikh for 40 days, before asking that he care for her child until the baby reaches the age of seven, at which time he should be told who his parents are and sent in search of them. The sheikh teaches her various magical skills and sends her on her mission to avenge Abdul Muluk. Greatly distressed at having to leave her son, Rafiah nonetheless wanders in the forest until she comes across a group of sleeping hunters. She kills all seven of them, takes their clothes and horses, and continues on her quest, now dressed as a warrior.

Meanwhile, the Raja of Barbaham, yet another kingdom, has two children: a son, Jamaluddin Admani, and a daughter, Rahah al-Habbani. After the death of the raja, his uncle Bahasan usurps authority, taking control of the trade and edging out Jamaluddin. Bahasan wants to kill Jamaluddin, but the other nobles are unwilling to go so far. Rafiah, going by the name of Dura, arrives in Barbaham. "His" appearance attracts admiration and wonder from the inhabitants, one of whom invites "him" to stay at his house. Wandering through the town, Dura sees that the quarter occupied by Jamaluddin is deserted, while Bahasan's neighbourhood thrives. Dura's host explains the situation and advises "him" to attach "himself" to Bahasan, but Dura refuses and decides to serve Jamaluddin instead. Jamaluddin promises that if Dura cuts off Bahasan's head, he will give "him" his sister in marriage. After nightfall, Dura, in shabby dress and carrying a flute, goes into Bahasan's quarter. "His" flute-playing is much admired and eventually, "he" is summoned to Bahasan's presence. Bahasan tells Dura that if "he" succeeds in killing Jamaluddin, Dura will become chief of all the wazirs. Dura agrees, but remaining loyal to Jamaluddin, orders that explosives are set up around Bahasan's quarter. In an audience with Bahasan, Dura shoots him with a pistol. The sound of the shot is the signal for the explosives to be set off. Dura gains control, becomes sultan in place of Jamaluddin and duly marries Rahah. The complications inherent in this relationship are passed over in silence.

After a period of wedded bliss, Dura departs for Hindustan, where "he" makes contact with the two dissident wazirs out of favour with Raja Syahabuddin. These wazirs agree to assist the person they believe to be the Raja of Barbaham in disguise as a merchant (but who, to recap, is in fact the queen of Barbari in disguise as the Raja of Barbaham in disguise as a merchant). The attractive merchant's arrival is reported to Raja Syahabuddin, who summons Dura to court. Sensing something amiss, Syahabuddin asks for Dura's clothes. Dura refuses to hand them over then and there, on the grounds that it would be offensive to disrobe in the audience hall. When "he" later sends Syahabuddin the clothes, the raja asks why they have a feminine smell. Dura explains that "he" is so poor that "he" and "his" wife share their clothes. Dura then returns to Barbaham, where "he" persuades Jamaluddin to support her in attacking Hindustan. Barbaham forces infiltrate the market in Hindustan and launch a surprise attack. Dura and several companions slip into the city itself, and meet with the two wazirs. Then, as the Sultan of Barbaham, Dura goes to Syahabuddin and demands he give up Hindustan. Syahabuddin refuses, is then overpowered, imprisoned and dies soon after.

Dura takes over Hindustan, but is filled with concern about the fate of "his" son and Abdul Muluk. At length "he" learns that Abdul Muluk is still imprisoned and opens up the jail. Abdul Muluk, Siti Rahmah and Wazir Suki are barely alive. Dura is overcome with emotion, to the perplexity of "his" wazirs. "He" ministers to Abdul Muluk and Rahmah herself, brushing away the assistance offered by the ladies of the court. Abdul Muluk regains consciousness and notes the similarity between his rescuer and his wife, whom he believes is dead. Dura cryptically questions Abdul Muluk and Rahmah about Rafiah but they do not take the bait.

Jamaluddin and Rahah are summoned to Hindustan. Dura then asks Rahah if she will accept a divorce from Dura and remarriage to Abdul Muluk. Confused and upset, Rahah nonetheless agrees. Abdul Muluk likewise agrees to marry Rahah. Dura installs Jamaluddin as ruler of Barbaham in her place. Roaming the town at night, Dura hears people praising Abdul Muluk's just rule.

Abdul Muluk again notes the similarity between Dura and Rafiah, but still does not act. Dura becomes increasingly aggravated at his failure to recognise her. She withdraws from an audience with him and removes her headdress. When she returns, revealing her long hair, Abdul Muluk still says nothing. She goes away again and removes her outer garments. Again Abdul Muluk fails to react. Finally, Dura puts on women's clothes and at last Abdul Muluk recognises her. A joyful, if overdue, reunion ensues. Jamaluddin discovers the next day that Dura is a woman, to great amazement and merriment all around.

However, Rafiah is still tormented by worry for her son. Once he turns seven, the boy, named Abdul Ghani, asked the syeikh about the identity of his real parents. The syeikh tells him and sends him off in search of them. Abdul Ghani arrives in Barbaham, where he joins a group travelling to Hindustan. En route, Abdul Ghani is accused of theft, with the result that the leader of the group sells him to a miller. The miller and his wife adopt him. One day, the parents of another boy complain to the miller that Abdul Ghani has injured their son in a fight and demand compensation. Both fathers bring their sons to the sultan — none other than Abdul Muluk — to settle the issue. Abdul Ghani's true identity is revealed and he is reunited with his parents. Alms are distributed to the needy. The miller is given riches and appointed to an official post. The unfortunate individuals who falsely accused Abdul Ghani are beaten and thrown into the jungle. The sheikh is called forth and duly rewarded. Abdul Ghani's grandparents set him up as the ruler of Ban.

Syair Siti Zubaidah [6]

Kembayat is ruled by Sultan Darman Syah. He has a son after vowing to step down in favour of his heir while he is still young. A flood at the time of the son's birth prophesies a great future for him. The child is named Zainal Abidin. Astrologers foretell that he will rule over other kings, take four wives, and suffer a disaster from which one of his wives will rescue him. Darman Syah selects 120 boys as companions for his son, including Ja'afar Siddiq, 'Umarnya Baqi, Abdullah Sani and Muhammad Muhyiddin. From the age of six, they study with a qadi. After three years, they graduate to the study of the martial arts. Darman Syah decides to abdicate the throne. The young Sultan Abidin rules over a prosperous kingdom, thronged by merchants. A dispute, identical to the one in *Syair Sultan Abdul Muluk*, arises between a Chinese merchant and a Datuk Saudagar, and comes to Darman Syah for adjudication (Sultan Abidin is away on a hunt). The Chinese merchant is thrown into prison and his boats are seized. One sailor escapes to report the matter to the Raja of China, who is furious.

Raja Cina has seven daughters: Kilan Sura, who serves as Bendahara; Kilan Johan, *menteri* (minister) or *pahlawan* (warrior); Kilan Jali, *hakim*; Kilan Cahaya, *raja*; Kilan Suri, *jurutulis*; and Kilan Syamsu, *l-w y-a* (lawyer?).

Sultan Abidin returns from hunting but is not apprised of events in his absence. Three years later, Darman Syah proposes that Sultan Abidin marry. He is reluctant, but a dream of a beautiful woman prompts him to set sail in search of her, aboard the ship *Fath al-Zaman* with his companions and four *inang*. Zainal Abidin assumes the identity of a merchant, with his companions taking appropriate roles. They are threatened by a storm, which Zainal Abidin quells with his prayers.

Meanwhile, Pendita Ulama is the ruler of Iraqan Kastan but has retired to an island to concentrate on his devotions. His son Muhammad Tahir rules in his stead. Pendita Ulama lives on the island with his daughter Zubaidah. The approach of Zainal Abidin's ship causes much uproar on Pulau Peringgi, with Zubaidah and her ladies spying on the approaching ship through a telescope.

When Zainal Abidin lands on the island, he overhears Zubaidah reciting the Qur'an and falls in love with her. Dressed as a serving boy, he infiltrates the women's quarters with the help of his *inang* and sees that Zubaidah is indeed the woman he saw in his dream. The wedding duly takes place, although Zainal Abidin and his party are under the impression that Zubaidah is no more than the daughter of a holy man. On the return journey, the ship stops in Yemen, where Zainal Abidin assists the king, who is besieged by the infidel Raja Menggala. Rather than allow the princess of Yemen to marry this infidel, Zainal Abidin advises her father to proclaim that she has died. Raja Menggala departs in disappointment, while Zainal Abidin is obliged to marry Puteri Syajarah of Yemen.

In Kembayat once more, Zainal Abidin's status-conscious mother favours Puteri Syajarah over Zubaidah, though his own preference is the reverse. The old queen keeps Zainal Abidin away from Zubaidah, who retires to a modest house and teaches Qur'an reading to the populace.

The Chinese princesses decide to attack Kembayat in revenge. They banter and battle with Zainal Abidin's companions. Zainal Abidin takes the field without bidding farewell to Zubaidah, who then leaves her house to take up residence with an old woman on the edge of the town. Zainal Abidin is taken captive by the Chinese, and when he refuses to marry one of them, is imprisoned in a poisoned well with his companions. Hearing of this disaster, Zubaidah flees into the forest, although she is heavily pregnant. Giving birth in the wilderness, she abandons her infant son with a ring engraved with her father's name.

Her brother Muhammad Tahir continues to rule Iraqan Kastan. Together with five royal companions — including Raja Portugal — he travels to Pulau Peringgi and learns of Zubaidah's marriage. The rajas then go on a hunt, where they find and adopt Zubaidah's son, although of course they do not know his true identity. The child is named Raja Ahmad Syah.

Wandering in the forest, Zubaidah encounters Puteri Rukiah, orphaned daughter of Raja Yunan. They go to a syeikh to study. Rukiah asks for Zubaidah's help in expelling the usurpers to her throne. Dressed as men, they proceed to Yunan and succeed forthwith. Zubaidah rules as Syahar, while Rukiah is known as Nahar. They then set off to China, dressed as "joget" dancers, and attract the attention of the princesses. Eventually, they learn of Zainal Abidin's whereabouts, rescue him and his companions, and return to Kembayat. To restore Zainal Abidin's health, Syahar soaks him in a tub of onions for three days. Zainal Abidin, needless to say, does not recognise Syahar as his wife, although he does note a certain resemblance.

Syahar decides to attack China, with "his" allies: Rajas Farsi, Hindustan, Iraqan Kastan, and Handalan. Zainal Abidin learns from Muhammad Tahir of Zubaidah's royal origins. Syahar notices Raja Ahmad

Syah but does not recognise him as her son. After a spectacular battle, the Chinese princesses are defeated. The eldest princess flees to a cave in the mountains, from shame after her ears are cut off. The other six accept Islam and marry various of the Rajas. Syahar presses Zainal Abidin to marry Kilan Cahaya.

Zainal Abidin resolves to go in search of Zubaidah. Syahar asks him whether he would recognise Zubaidah now that eight years have passed. Syahar promises to help Zainal Abidin, but a week later, she presents herself to Zainal Abidin minus one layer of her clothing. However, she has to change her clothes completely before he recognises her and a joyful reunion takes place. Zubaidah insists that Zainal Abidin marry Rukiah, so that he has the full complement of four wives. Zubaidah is reluctant to return to Kembayat because of her mother-in-law, but upon their return, Zainal Abidin's mother is suitably repentant. Raja Ahmad Syah, who has been recognised as their son, marries a daughter of Sultan Olanda. A mass visit to Pendita Ulama on Pulau Peringgi takes place, after which all return to their respective kingdoms.

I. Heroism and Submission

If Rafiah and Zubaidah, the protagonists of these two *syair*, are the most heroic heroines of the Riau corpus, what constitutes the heroic? How does the difference between hero and heroine play out in texts in which the greatest warriors are women? In the *syair* generally there is a distinction between the heroics of action, usually male, and the heroics of endurance, usually female.[7] The two wives of Abdul Muluk neatly embody these two types of heroism, with Rafiah taking up arms against Raja Hindustan and Rahmah devotedly following her husband into prison. A heroic death may be achieved by both men and women; it is what precedes the glorious death that is gendered. Rahmah, who remains faithful to her husband despite the tortures she is subjected to by Sultan Hindustan is the "perfect woman".[8] To quote another *syair*, fighting unto death is seen as the definitive masculine trait, gaining one "a truly good death / a man's perfect fame".[9] The identification of the heroism of endurance with the feminine and that of action with the masculine is again borne out by Rahmah's advice to Rafiah that as women, they must submit rather than fight. Whatever disasters befall them are manifestations of Allah's will to be patiently borne, Rahmah counsels, for "what can we women do? /

whatever Almighty God commands / [we] may not avert".[10] Though it might be assumed that gender is irrelevant to the ability to defy God's will, Rahmah seems to argue that women are particularly impotent. Femininity is characterised by passive acceptance, and masculinity by actively striving and shaping one's own destiny. When Jamaluddin, the usurped king of Ban in *Syair Sultan Abdul Muluk*, protests that he cannot fight his cause because he must accept "the Lord of the Worlds' decree", the warrior Dura retorts that such passivity "is not the mark of a man".[11]

Since Dura is really Rafiah in disguise, "his" admonition to Jamaluddin can be understood as a subversion of precisely the gendering of heroism advocated by Rahmah. Both *syair* systematically reverse the usual gender order, placing the heroes in the conventionally feminine positions and the heroines in the conventionally masculine, thereby throwing Rahmah's characterisation of the heroic into question. Zubaidah and Rafiah both make their first flight from the palace in women's clothes, indicating that clothes and disguise are secondary to the very act of escaping in the assumption of the masculine heroic mode. The heroines are forced into action and into abandoning the secure domestic sphere for the threatening realm of the forest precisely because these spheres too have been reversed. When the heroines make their escapes, Barbary has fallen to Hindustan and Kembayat is about to fall to the Chinese princesses. The domestic is no longer safe and the wild forest has become a haven. The texts emphasise that necessity forces the heroines' hands; the reader is not to assume that either Zubaidah or Rafiah is a habitual cross-dresser or transgressor of the gender order like Puteri Cahaya Khairani *alias* Johan Ali Perkasa in the 17th-century or earlier Panji tale, *Hikayat Syah Kobat*:[12]

> The princess enjoyed playing the warrior. Every day she fought hundreds of valorous and brave fighters and champions, one after the other, and tested her power against numerous powerful princes. She defeated all of them. She was only 12 years old. When her father and mother forebade her from making war and testing her power, she wept and writhed until she fainted dead away, losing consciousness.[13]

In mid-19th-century Riau, heroines no longer dress as warriors because they like to, as Johan Ali Perkasa does, but because they have to, demonstrating the adaptation of an old motif for a more stringently Islamic milieu. Nor do Rafiah or Zuibaidah have to be prevailed upon to relinquish their disguises: they are only too happy to return to the palace as women (so long as they are installed as the preeminent wife).

If Zubaidah and Rafiah's transgressions are made necessary by the force of circumstance, they are legitimised by their evocation of the doctrine of *tawakal* and *berserah*, trusting in God. *Siyar al-Salikin*, the widely-used Malay redaction of al-Ghazali's *Ihya Ulum al-Din* by 'Abd al-Samad al-Palimbani, devotes a chapter to the topic of *tawakal* (Ar.: *tawakkul*) and distinguishes between three grades of it. The first, and the weakest, is trusting in God as one trusts in one's *wakil* or agent. The second is to trust in God as a child trusts in his or her mother, calling to mind the infants abandoned by Rafiah and Zubaidah. Of course, the children's trust — in their mothers and in God — is not betrayed, for they come to no harm. The final grade of *tawakal* is to trust in God "as a dead person in the hands of those washing [his/her] body, without any ability or free will at all, and this is highest among all kinds of *tawakal*".[14] The heroines are at this third and highest level of *tawakal*:

Berbagai dilalui Siti Arabi	Siti Arabi [Rafiah] traversed many [places],
Daripada padang bukit yang tinggi	From plains to high mountains,
Sangat tawakal di dalam qalbi	Greatly *tawakal* in her heart,
Berserah kepada Ilahi Rabbi[15]	Having given herself into the hands of God.

Zubaidah even quotes a Quranic injunction that also appears in the *Siyar al-Salikin*, "And trust thou in the Living One Who dieth not":

Kata Zubaidah lakunya gundah	Zubaidah spoke with distress,
Beta nan nenek sudah berserah	'Grandmother, I have given myself up,
Tawakallah beta kepada Allah	I have *tawakal* to Allah,
Untung dan janji sudah terjumlah	My fate and destiny have been allotted.
Di dalam Qur'an sudah tertentu	In the Qur'an it has been determined,
Dalil dan hadith semua di situ	Signs and traditions are all there,
[Ta]wakkal 'alayya alazhi la yamutu[16]	*[Ta]wakkal 'alayya alazhi la yamutu*
Hamba pun menurut dalilnya itu.[17]	This slave obeys that sign.'

Having entrusted herself and her son to God, Zubaidah reflects that forest and city are after all both in God's hands: "the forest is the same as the city / all are beneath the command of God the Great".[18] For the heroines, *tawakal* entails having the faith in Allah's providence such that they walk wherever their feet take them — "without knowing the destination / following the feet's inclination" — but with the ultimate aim of rescuing their husbands firmly in mind.[19] If one possesses the intention, then God provides the means. They have faith that Allah will provide them with the means to carry out their audacious ambitions, Rafiah's "very great wish".[20] But when other characters invoke *tawakal*, it seems that they have something else in mind, something closer to passive endurance. Abdul Muluk, for instance, reminds Rafiah of the necessity of submitting to God's will, "the decree of God the Powerful".[21] Jamaluddin, too, speaks of the impossibility of opposing events in God's plan as a reason for him not to rise up against the man who has usurped the throne: "the decree of the Lord of the Worlds ... cannot now be denied".[22] The heroines demonstrate that *tawakal* is not mere passivity. While their success is of course contingent upon God's approval, the heroines are confident that such approval is theirs. The doctrine of *tawakal* is used to throw a cloak of respectability over the heroine's cross-dressing exploits, and in so doing, delineates a space for female action.

Rafiah's ambition is the unimpeachably virtuous wish to rescue her husband, but Zubaidah's initial motives are murkier. She first leaves the palace for the humble home of a *nenek kebayan* — the stock old woman character of Malay romance, sometimes endowed with magical powers — before Zainal Abidin is captured, doing so, it should be noted, mainly on account of her own injured dignity. Zainal Abidin, prevented by his mother and his other wife, did not visit her before departing for battle, which Zubaidah takes an offence significant enough for her to leave her home:

Sampailah aku orang yang hina	This comes of a wretch like me
Hendak menyama raja yang ghana	Wanting to equal a great king.
Dipandangnya tidak betapa bina	He does not look much [on me],
Baik ku pergi barang ke mana	I should depart, no matter where.
Jikalau ia suatu peri	If something has befallen him,
Aku tak mahu diam di sini	I do not wish to remain here,
Belanya itu hendak ku cari	I want to avenge him,
Remuklah aku dibunuh puteri	[Even if] I am crushed, killed by the princess.
Kerana aku dagang piatu	For I am a miserable wanderer
Meng[h]arapkan kasih baginda itu	Hoping for his highness' affection
Sekarang datang peri suatu	Now something has befallen [him]
Aku pun menurut juga begitu	I will follow him yet.

Jikalau perangnya selamat sempurna	If his battle comes to a safe conclusion
Dicarinya aku barang ke mana	He will look for me everywhere.
Tahulah ia mula kerana	He will know the reason why:
Sebab tidak singgah ke sana.[23]	Because he did not visit [me] there.

If he is defeated, she intends to *bela* or avenge him, not by committing suicide, but by taking revenge upon the Chinese princesses. If he is victorious, on the other hand, she wants to teach him not to take her for granted. It is only later, living with the old woman, that she hears of Zainal Abidin's capture and declares "today I'll go in search [of him]".[24] Her first overriding reason for flight is not *bakti* towards her husband, but the preservation of her own dignity, and is strongly reminiscent of the Panji heroines who *membuang diri* or "cast themselves away" in response to insults. Indeed, she says as much herself when explaining her motives to her in-laws: she was "ashamed before the people of the kingdom / therefore I cast myself away", and her exploits were "not in order to look for [your] son".[25] Using the idea of *tawakal*, Zubaidah's Panjiesque wish to *membuang diri* may be domesticated, Islamised and shaped into the novel figure of the perfect wife as heroic warrior.

II. Gender in Wartime

Syair Siti Zubaidah and *Syair Sultan Abdul Muluk* thoroughly reverse the usual attributes of gender, masculinising the heroine and feminising the hero. The heroine's switch to the masculine mode of the heroic entails, as we have seen, the rejection of passivity but also the adoption of the masculine predilection for violence. This is explicitly depicted in the means through which Rafiah escapes from Barbari and gets hold of her disguise. Rather than surrendering to the overwhelming military force of Raja Hindustan, as Rahmah and Sultan Abdul Muluk himself do, Rafiah takes up arms. She stabs to death a palace attendant and places the knife in the dead girl's hands, in order to make it appear that the murdered girl is Rafiah herself, a devoted suicide.[26] Taking up her husband's sword — the unfavourable comparison to him is implicit, since he has just laid down his arms to Raja Hindustan — she climbs out of the window of her palace and flees into the forest. The acts of masculine boldness and violence that follow further empower her: the killing of a ferocious animal with blood-red fur gives her magical strength, and the murder of seven sleeping hunters furnishes her with men's clothing and a horse. This violence visited upon the innocent — for there is no suggestion that the *menteri*'s daughter and the hunters deserved their fates — goes without comment in the text and in no way impugns the perfect virtue and heroic deeds of Rafiah. A *jayeng perwira* or victorious hero, by definition, sheds blood, and by doing so, Rafiah transforms herself into one. Whereas heroines like Siti Zainah in *Syair Saudagar Bodoh* seem to simply produce their male disguises from their wardrobes, Rafiah must be initated into the warrior's life by murder of the hunters so that she may become "like a valiant man".[27] This type of violence is a marker of masculinity — after all, when women in the Malay romances commit murder, poison is their preferred means and other women their chosen victims.[28]

The disguise also entails the abandonment of two fundamentals of wifehood: obedience to one's husband and devotion to one's children. Both heroines are pregnant — a rather definitively female condition — when they abandon the mode of life usual to women. In their last meeting before he is captured, Zainal Abidin refuses to grant Zubaidah's request that she accompany him into battle but promises her that if their child is a son, he will be the heir to the throne. In effect, he denies Zubaidah's possible role as a warrior in favour of her role as a mother. Similarly, Abdul Muluk exhorts Rafiah to make the care of their unborn child her utmost responsibility,

Adalah suatu kakanda berpesan	One thing I ask of you:
Jikalau perang kakanda ketewasan	If I am defeated in battle,
Lamun selamat berputera tuan	But you are safely delivered of a son
Jangan tidak adinda peliharakan.[29]	Do not fail to care for him.

Here, the test of manhood is battle and that of womanhood is childbirth. In a direct contravention of this that goes unremarked in the text, Rafiah leaves her infant son in the care of a syeikh and his family in order to continue her search for Abdul Muluk. Even more cavalier about her maternal duties, Zubaidah abandons her baby in the forest, lest he encumber her in her quest for Zainal Abidin. The Riau *syair* are much more interested in women as wives than as mothers,[30] so it is no surprise that the husband's needs take precedence over the child's. Here, however, the heroine's role as wife is abandoned alongside her role as mother, since she contravenes her husband's wishes. Another Riau *syair* of the period calls obedience to one's husband a woman's religious duty: "this is women's sacred obligation / not to oppose their husbands' prohibitions".[31] As good

Muslim wives, the only way the heroines can embark on their great deeds is by abandoning womanhood entirely. In contrast, the Chinese princesses need no disguises or denials of femininity, since their bellicosity receives their father's full approval.

Along with the heroine's adoption of the masculine role comes the hero's adoption of the feminine — or rather, the imposition of the feminine role upon him. Zainal Abidin and Abdul Muluk are defeated, abducted, imprisoned, forced to endure and await rescue at the hands of their wives. Nor are the heroes the only male characters cast in a feminine light. On a hunting expedition, Zubaidah's brother, Muhammad Tahir, and a cohort of his allies discover her abandoned son; their tender affection for the child highlights Zubaidah's enforced denial of just such sentiments. In effect, the kings take the place of the absent mother. The king and queen of Kembayat, too, seem to have exchanged roles, with the king a passive and the queen an active figure. Raja Darman Syah does nothing to defend Zubaidah when his wife conducts a campaign against her, and as does not befit a king, delays Zainal Abidin from taking the field against the Chinese princesses. The fact that the king is ruled by his wife, that men are behaving like women and vice versa, indicates that matters in Kembayat are topsy-turvy and that the kingdom is ripe for defeat. The disguised heroine *syair* are careful not to endorse the rule of women.

The feminisation of the hero is particularly emphasised in *Syair Siti Zubaidah*, for whereas Abdul Muluk is at least defeated by the king of Hindustan, Zainal Abidin's foes are the seven Chinese princesses. Zainal Abidin is also placed in the typically female subject position — shared by Rahmah in *Syair Sultan Abdul Muluk* — of being pressed to accept an abhorrent marriage. The princesses try to persuade him to marry one of them, and like Rahmah vis à vis Raja Hindustan, he rejects them because they are infidels. Even before the princesses capture him, Zainal Abidin is repeatedly likened to a woman. In deference to his parents' pleas for his safety, he delays in taking the field against the princesses, with the result that, as he himself puts it:

Sedangkan ia anak perempuan	Though they are daughters
Datang ke mari mencari lawan	They come here looking for a fight.
Patik laki-laki muda bangsawan	I am a young nobleman,
Berdiam diri seperti perempuan[32]	[But] remain quiet like a girl.

Sangatlah patik menanggung malu	I endure terrible shame,
Dikata orang hilir dan hulu	Spoken of by people upriver and down,
Sultan Abidin takut terlalu	[Saying] Sultan Abidin is too afraid
Orang perempuan datang memalu.[33]	Of women come to attack him.

In the course of the battle itself, one of the Chinese princesses taunts him that it would be a shame for his beauty to be damaged, devaluing his martial abilities in favour of his physical attractions. Even Zubaidah reflects that the princesses' defeat of Zainal Abidin has emasculated him: "such is your fate / losing your valour [because] captured by women".[34] Languishing in the poisoned well, it is Zubaidah rather than any male figure Zainal Abidin calls on for help.

Whereas those Kembayat warriors who gave their lives in battle have gained the posthumous fame that is proof of their masculinity — "many great warriors died / how renowned were their names and the reports [of their deeds]" — Zainal Abidin is unmanned.[35] He and Abdul Muluk lack "the perfect renown of a man" or "a true man's renown".[36] When Zainal Abidin finally does challenge the princesses, he suffers the ultimate indignity of capture. Death would have been far preferable, for as the *syair* observed earlier, only cowards are taken alive: "the brave resisted / the cowards were all captured".[37] Although it cannot be alleged that Zainal Abidin is a coward — the Chinese princess Kilan Sura captures rather than kills him because she is so taken with his good looks that she wants to marry him to one of her sisters — it is this shame which Zubaidah is compelled to redress. Her quest is not simply to rescue him from physical suffering, for in that case she would reveal herself as soon as she had released him from the poisoned well. In order to "repay the shame", to rehabilitate his good name as a king and a man, she must remain in her masculine guise and enable him to defeat his enemies.[38] Likewise, Rafiah tells her mentor, the syeikh, that she wants to "repay", *balaskan*, her husband's defeat by Raja Hindustan, not to rescue her husband as such.[39] In both these *syair*, it falls to the heroine to redress the hero's failure to acquit himself as a man.

The irony of the reversal of gender roles here is epitomised by Zubaidah's comment on the naturalness of her alliance, as Sultan Yunan, with Sultan Kembayat. Both Sultan Yunan and Sultan Kembayat are, or seem to be, righteous Muslim kings, and so are quite properly opposed to the Chinese princesses, who are infidels and women to boot. Zubaidah remarks with regard to the princesses,

Ia perempuan tidak berdaya	They are incapable women
Lagipun besar nafsunya dia	And of great lusts.
Kita laki-laki tidak berbahaya	We men are not at risk
Hendak dijadikan takluknya dia[40]	Of being subjected to them.

The joke — that there is no "we men" at all — is between Zubaidah and the readers, for Zainal Abidin still does not know Sultan Yunan is a woman, and what is more, his wife. Not only does the male solidarity Zubaidah speaks of not exist, but her claims that women are powerless and excessively lustful are in her own case manifestly false. Part of Zubaidah's irony is her use of the Arabic-derived word *nafsu* rather than the less pejorative Malay terms *dendam* or *cinta berahi*. Even as she asserts it in her speech, in her person Zubaidah refutes the familiar stereotype of women as lustful and foolish. False too is the claim that Sultan Yunan and Sultan Kembayat, as men, are in no danger from the princesses, as Zainal Abidin knows all too well. But though Zubaidah is convincing as Sultan Yunan, adopting as she does here a posture so masculine as to be almost a caricature, the act of doing so suggests her true gender to her husband. Duly impressed by Sultan Yunan's intentions to fight the upstart Chinese princesses, Zainal Abidin is irresistibly reminded of his wife:

Dipandang baginda Sultan Yunan	His majesty gazed at Sultan Yunan,
Dengan Zubaidah tidak berlawan	No different to Zubaidah,
Tiada bersalahan rupa kelakuan	Nothing [amiss] in looks and manners,
Bezanya laki-laki dengan perempuan[41]	The difference that of a man and a woman.

Not only Sultan Yunan's looks, it seems, but also "his" speech ("'his' every word conferred profit"), behaviour ("the royal king's good conduct"), and above all, willingness to join in Zainal Abidin's cause recalls Zubaidah.[42] It is as though Zainal Abidin is dimly aware that any prince with such marvellous qualities cannot be a real man at all. But though he is struck by the similarity between Sultan Yunan and Zubaidah, the moment of recognition must be postponed until such a time as his shame has been wiped out by the defeat of the Chinese princesses and Zubaidah has given up her career as a conquering prince — that is, until the gender order has been reestablished.

III. The Field of Battle

If active struggle is inappropriate for women, it is even less proper for women to engage the enemy on the field of war. When Zubaidah asks to accompany him into battle and to die with him if necessary, Zainal Abidin protests that "war is not women's work".[43] His mother places a more censorious evaluation on a woman going into battle, saying that it is a *pemali*, a taboo that if broken would have dire consequences for Zainal Abidin in battle.

Kerana Zubaidah orang yang garang	For Zubaidah is valiant
Diikutnya pula' tuan sekarang	And will follow you now.
Menjadi sangkut pekerjaan orang	[Your] work will be obstructed;
Pemali konon petuanya orang[44]	People say it is a taboo.

However inappropriate or ill-omened it may be for women to fight, the princesses in these *syair* are ever victorious in battle. Since Zubaidah defeats the usurpers of the throne of Yunan with such ease that the incident is simply passed over in the text, the first time she truly displays her martial skills is in her encounter as Sultan Yunan with the Chinese princesses. Ushering Zainal Abidin to safety because he has still not fully recovered from his imprisonment in the poisoned well, Sultan Yunan engages four of the Chinese princesses in combat, assisted only by the "Raja Muda" or heir apparent of Yunan, Puteri Rukiah in disguise. Zubaidah defeats one princess after another, flinging them into the air, and slices off the ears of the eldest and most recalcitrant of them. The women warriors, Chinese and Malay alike, make liberal use of magical weapons — arrows in the case of the Chinese and a *cindai* cloth in Zubaidah's. Needless to say, Rafiah, Zubaidah and Rukiah all spend the requisite amount of time learning martial *ilmu* or esoteric knowledge from reclusive syeikhs, the usual source of fighting skill for heroes and heroines alike. While this helps to explain how they best the men, ultimately this magic is merely a manifestation of their *sakti*, magical powers accumulated by lineage, righteousness and ascetic practice. The defeat of Kembayat and Barbari may have something to do with the fact that right was not quite on their side: their opponents, going to war over the excessively harsh treatment of one of their merchants, have a good cause. Where combat is figured as *mengadu sakti*, "contesting *sakti*", if the women win, it follows that their *sakti* is greater.

Rafiah's military tactics are not those of all-out confrontation, the showdown on the battlefield favoured by both Zubaidah and the Chinese princesses, but of guile and trickery. As she puts it,

Tiada memadai senjata yang tajam	Sharp weapons will not suffice —
Panah senapang lela meriam	Arrows, rifles, cannons —
Sesungguhnya itu sempurna faham	Certainly perfect understanding
Serta bijaksana akalnya dalam[45]	[is needed],
	As well as wits and profound intelligence.

Rafiah's inclusion of *akal* in her arsenal is part of her appropriation of masculine attributes, and here again the woman in disguise is a better man than the princes she advises. By enlisting disaffected elements within the kingdom and secretly infiltrating the city with soldiers, Dura does indeed defeat the mighty raja of Hindustan. Dura's skill as a warrior is not limited to tactics and strategy, however; "his" beheading of the usurper Bahsan and "his" capture of Raja Hindustan and his allies amply demonstrate that Dura has no qualms about the use of brute force.

The martial women who do not need to disguise themselves are Chinese, which is less an indication of precedents for women warriors in Chinese literature than it is due to the otherness of the Chinese with respect to the Kembayat Malays. That women fight as women is no doubt intended as a demonstration of the barbarous nature of the Chinese. Even so, their motives are akin to those that propel Zubaidah and Rafiah. The Chinese princesses attack Kembayat out of filial duty: the merchant precipitously killed by Darman Syah was their uncle, and their father had been too ill when he received news of the outrage to respond appropriately. After his death, they take it upon themselves to avenge the offence to their father, to "seek revenge wholeheartedly".[46] Moreover, like the Malay heroes and heroines of the *syair*, the Chinese princesses combine bellicosity and beauty. Their movements while fighting are likened to dancing, and both their weapons and their persons are lavishly described:

Adapun Puteri Kilan Sura	As for Princess Kilan Sura,
Senjatanya daripada tembung cakera	Her weapon was a quarterstaff and discus,
Bersendi dengan emas udara	With mountings of 'heavenly' gold,
Bertatah intan pudi mutiara	Studded with diamonds, gems and pearls.

Lakunya pantas sikapnya kena	Her movements were swift, her bearing just so,
Memberi hati gundah gulana	Arousing turmoil in the heart.
Paras seperti patung cendana	Her appearance like that of a sandalwood doll,
Putih bersih gemilang warna	Pure white, of glorious hue.
Kilan Jali puteri yang bijak	Kilan Jali was a quick-witted princess,
Senjatanya tembung emas dimasak	Her weapon a quarterstaff of 'ripe' gold,
Keningnya seperti awan ditulis	Her eyebrows like an inscribed cloud,
Laksana bunga cempaka wilis	Like the *cempaka wilis* flower.
Parasnya elok sangat mejelis	Her appearance lovely and truly fair,
Anak rambutnya melentek wilis[47]	The wisps of her hair delicately curled.

Zubaidah, and indeed Zainal Abidin are described in much the same ways. That the warrior in these *syair* is praised for his or her beauty but is not eroticised or even sexually differentiated becomes more surprising when set against the treatment of women disguised as warriors in other texts. In the prose romance *Hikayat Panji Semirang*, for instance, the two handmaidens of the heroine who have dressed themselves as warriors are at pains to conceal their gender, in such a way that only accentuates it:

> Then they did battle, lunging and stabbing and striking, but Kuda Perwira and Kuda Perancha, while fighting, both behaved like women — that is, their hands did not cease holding their shirts to their chests. It seemed as though they feared [their shirts] would open and it would be seen that they were women. If it were seen then their secret would have be exposed and they would be ashamed, so as far as they could they shut away those two secrets on their chests, so that they would not be clearly seen by the people.[48]

The warrior women of the *syair*, in contrast, whether dressed in men's or women's clothes, have no such problems with their attire. The erotic flourishes that are so characteristic of earlier Malay literature are expunged in these *syair*.

The interreligious aspect of the wars waged in *Syair Siti Zubaidah* and *Syair Sultan Abdul Muluk* is also noteworthy, since it broadens the scope of the heroine's *bakti*. She is not only the saviour of her husband but also the defender of her people against infidel invaders. The world of these *syair* is bipolar: the interrelated and sometimes warring Panji kingdoms of

Daha, Kuripan, Gagelang and Singasari, in which religion does not figure as a distinguishing feature, are replaced by the Muslims on the one hand, and the infidels on the other. (This arrangement is not always particularly thorough, however, since Zubaidah after all becomes the sultan of Greece, one of her allies is Sultan Portugal and a Puteri Holanda becomes one of her daughters-in-law.) In *Syair Siti Zuhrah*, too, the heroine's enemies are also infidels — variously Dutch and Portuguese — and in all three *syair*, the defeated enemies are given the choice between embracing Islam or death. The novel element in these *syair*, reflecting the changing sentiments and political configurations of the mid-19th century Malay world, is not the woman warrior but the holy war, *perang sabil*. It may have been *de rigeur* by this time to emphasise interreligious contestation, and in particular, the conflict between Muslims and Christians. Those who do convert to Islam, like six of the seven Chinese princesses, are seemlessly integrated into the Malay elite. The crusade element of these *syair* is, like the Islamisation of the Panji heroine, a sign of their times.

Another instance of a change in courtly values may be sensed in these *syair*'s exploration of different meanings of *bela* for women. It can signify the taking of blood retribution, but it can also mean suicide, especially of a widow.[49] Suicide occupies an ambiguous place between the heroics of action and the heroics of endurance, for while it is the ultimate act of self-abnegation, it is also very much an act, the taking up of arms against a sea of troubles. In the Riau *syair* of female heroism, women's suicide is doubly ambiguous because while it is regarded as definitively un-Islamic, it retains a certain aura of legitimacy from earlier times, when the idea of royal women's loyalty unto death was considered acceptable and indeed praiseworthy. In the Panji tale *Hikayat Cekel Waneng Pati*, for instance, Raden Galuh greatly impresses Raden Inu when she promises to join him in death: "Someone will avenge your death. You will not die alone".[50] The ambiguity that suicidal devotion evokes in mid-19th-century Riau is eloquently expressed by Rahmah, who laments Rafiah's apparent suicide as an infidel death while simultaneously marvelling at this proof of Rafiah's devotion to their common husband:

Kasih sungguh Siti Arabi [Rafiah]	How great was Siti Arabi's love
Akan suaminya Sultan Barbari	For her husband Sultan Barbari,
Sampai membunuh diri sendiri	Such that she killed herself
Jadilah ia mati kafiri[51]	And died an infidel death.

Rafiah's fidelity to her husband is greater than her fidelity to her religion, as Rahmah notices. This is not a reason for censure but the predictable result of a value system in which a woman achieves religious merit through serving her husband, and religious demerit from failing to serve him.[52] As Milton put it, "he for God only, she for God in him".[53]

Rahmah goes on to contrast Abdul Muluk's devotion to Rafiah with hers to him, making it clear that the latter is the greater:

Wahai Rafiah yang bijaksana	Oh quick-witted Rafiah,
Tuan redakan mati yang hina	You were willing to die a wretched death.
Kasih tuan sudahlah sempurna	Your love is perfected,
Bagindalah yang tiada membalas guna[54]	His majesty has not equalled your qualities.

Rafiah's death is wretched in religious terms, but exalted in terms of her relationship to her husband. In *Syair Siti Zubaidah*, the Malay women of Kembayat, having been taken captive by the Chinese, arm themselves in resistance and are promptly killed. As such, they are glorious martyrs:

Matilah ia dibunuh Cina	They died at the hands of the Chinese,
Sabil ia dengan sempurna	Martyred perfectly.
Hidup pun apakah guna	For what use would life be,
Diperbuat gundik kafir yang hina[55]	As the concubine of a despicable infidel?

Although it is not quite turning the knife on themselves, the women plainly choose the "beautiful death" of martyrs in the cause of Islam over life.[56] It seems that while it is no longer fully acceptable to die with one's husband, it is the most noble of deeds to die for one's faith: *sabil* is replacing *bela* in the hierarchy of heroic deaths for women.

IV. War in the Bedroom

The proper battlefield for women is in the bedroom and their proper pose one of defeat, the amorous contest inevitably ending in masculine conquest. The trope of the first night of marriage as a bloody battle is familiar from the classical Javanese examples discussed by Creese and Vickers, though it has in any case a venerable and varied career in world literature. Vickers points out the metonymic relation between battle and sex in descriptions of the latter in Balinese *kidung* poetry, as well as the equation of the two "in the forms of the word *perang* (with its root meaning of 'to stab')".[57] As the taunts of Zainal Abidin's companion Abdullah Sani indicate, this dual meaning of *perang* also obtains in Malay *syair*. Confronting the Chinese princesses in battle, Abdullah Sani tells them that marriage, not war, is the proper vocation of women:

Lalu disahut Abdullah Sani:	Abdullah Sani then answered:
Menteri Cina sangat berani	The Chinese minister is very brave
Bukan menjadi bela di sini	[But I] am not to be sacrificed here,
Jadi suami patutnya ini	It is more fitting to become a husband.
Kerana tuan seorang perempuan	For you are a woman
Bukannya patut menjadi lawan	And ought not be an adversary;
Jikalau seperti di dalam peraduan	But if it were in the bedroom,
Puterilah patut menjadi kawan	The princess is fit to be my companion.
Patut berperang di dalam kelambu	[We] ought to fight beneath the mosquito net,
Keris dan lembing pujuk dan cumbu	Our krises and spears coaxes and caresses.
Sekarang berbuat benteng dan kubu	Now [you] put up parapets and stockades,
Membawa' laskar beribu-ribu	Bringing thousands of soldiers.
Itulah malu yang dipertuan	This is his highness' shame:
Berperang dengan raja perempuan	Fighting with women rulers,
Anak dara lagi perawan	Maidens and beauties,
Di tengah medan hendak dilawan[58]	Wanting to fight in the open field.

Abdullah Sani emphasises the inappropriateness of the Chinese princesses' martial actions by remarking on their defenses ("benteng dan kubu") and their cohorts of soldiers ("laskar beribu-ribu") — because, of course, in the nuptial chamber, the bride is unprotected and alone. He retains, meanwhile, the thrusting, attacking weapons ("keris dan lembing") for the groom's arsenal, transformed though they are into blandishments and caresses ("pujuk dan cumbu"). Ever the wit, Abdullah Sani goes on to entreat his adversary, Kilan Johar, using just such blandishments — "fruit of my heart, light of my eyes / do not be so angry". Yet in the same stanza, he presents himself to "those who possess weapons" and invites them to stab him if they please.⁵⁹ If the princess holds the weapons, then the warrior Abdullah Sani presents himself, albeit in jest, as the object of penetration.

Even as the controversies of marriage are elevated to the most public and prestigious arena of battle, the usual business of the bedroom — desire — is devalorised. Whereas Panji romances may be said to consist chiefly of wars on the battlefield alternated with wars in the bedroom, the latter are not much in evidence here. Only rather muted pangs of desire alert Zainal Abidin or Abdul Muluk to the presence of their long-lost beloveds, in contrast to the agonies suffered by Sidi Maulana and Sultan Yahya in the company of Zuhrah and Jauhar Manikam in their respective guises of Sultan Yunan and Juragan Budiman. In *Syair Sultan Abdul Muluk* and *Syair Siti Zubaidah*, the male antagonists are the most acutely sensitive to the *rawan* and *berahi* that so permeate *Syair Sultan Yahya* and *Syair Siti Zuhrah*: only the king of Hindustan detects the feminine aroma of Dura-aka-Rafiah's clothes. Dura's ally Jamaluddin and of course Abdul Muluk remain oblivious. The prodigiously amorous hero of Panji romance would not have been so obtuse, one imagines, and nor would he have resisted the offer of another wife, as Zainal Abidin does when Sultan Yunan presses him to marry Kilan Suri. Abdul Muluk, too, has to be prevailed upon by Dura before he agrees to marry again. Although the heroes are indeed provided — by the heroines — with numerous wives, as befits their status, there is no doubt that they marry multiply out of a sense of duty and that their affections for the heroine remain constant. When Zubaidah urges Zainal Abidin to marry yet a fourth time, he demurs:

Mohonlah kakanda tuan kurniakan	Permit me to excuse myself from
Beristeri tidak kanda niatkan	your bounty,
Tuan seorang sudah memada[i]kan	For I have no wish for a wife.
*Mangkin seribu tidak disamakan*⁶⁰	You alone suffice for me,
	A thousand others would not equal you.

These are heroes for a new age, quite different from the protagonist of *Hikayat Syah Kobat*, who despite his love for the heroine, is utterly unable to restrain himself from other dalliances.⁶¹

As usual in the Riau *syair*, female desire is entirely absent. Active feminine desire is given only to commoners and Chinese princesses, characters outside the values considered proper for the heroines. The louche behaviour of non-aristocratic women in the presence of the deliriously attractive hero is ubiquitous in traditional Malay literature, and the same is the case with commoners catching sight of the heroine-as-hero. Commoners, it would seem, need not even have a specified gender, so removed are they from the behavioural norms of their betters. Likewise, the Chinese princesses behave quite unlike their Malay counterparts. When the eldest of these princesses first catches sights of Zainal Abidin, she is so impressed by his beauty that she spares his life:

Kilan Samsu puteri yang jayang	Kilan Samsu the victorious princess
Di atas udara terlayang-layang	Flying in the air above
Kepada Sultan ia terpandang	Caught sight of the Sultan
Rasa hatinya terlalu sayang[62]	And was inflamed with love.

Zubaidah and Rukiah in their disguise as the *joget* or dancers, Syahar and Nahar, similarly set the princesses' hearts aflame. When the princesses set eyes on the two *joget*, they lose their hearts at once — "all the princesses were astonished / Feeling their lives flying away" — and then vie with one another to promise the dancers lavish gifts.[63]

Adapun puteri Kilan Suri	As for Princess Kilan Suri
Berahinya tidak lagi terperi	Her desire was indescribable
Gilakan Syahar muda bestari	Mad for the noble young Syahar
Memandang tidak sedarkan diri[64]	Gazing without coming to her senses.

That such expressions of desire are inappropriate and ought to be punished is clear not only from Zubaidah-as-Sultan-Yunan's remark that the princesses have great *nafsu*, but also by the fact that Zubaidah-as-Syahar uses this *nafsu* to hoodwink them, infiltrating the Chinese palace in order to find and free Zainal Abidin. If the Chinese princesses are both *jayeng* and *sayang*, martial and amorous, the heroines certainly are not.

The residual Panji element of the heroine-in-disguise marrying other princesses is emptied in the Riau *syair* of any erotic qualities and transformed, instead, into yet another demonstration of wifely *bakti*. Though Rahah is married to Dura, she apparently entertains no suspicions about her husband's sexual reticence. The marriage night is left decorously undescribed — "the story will not be elaborated / for it's too difficult to find rhymes" — but it would seem that there has been no sexual contact between Dura and Rahah, as Abdul Muluk's suspicions regarding Dura's identity are roused once he has *berdamai*, "made peace", with Rahah.[65] The repressed metaphor of the marriage night as battle resurfaces in the use, common in these *syair*, of "peace-making" as a euphemism for intercourse. Rahah herself is plunged into shame by the revelation that her erstwhile husband is really a woman, to be consoled by Rafiah who evokes their shared malign fate. Against this chaste account, one might compare the far more sexually interested and informed women to be found in *Hikayat Panji Kuda Semirang*, in which the heroine Raden Galuh (also known as Panji Semirang) has two wives, who speculate about "his" shirking of "his" conjugal duties:

> The Princesses Sang Nata Wirasab Raden Cendera Kesu'ma and Raden Anglang Mendira were brought along with 'him'. Both the princesses were amazed that Panji Semirang did not molest them at all. They thought, 'He must be impotent, for he does not enjoy women. What a pity that such a handsome man has no desire.' They smiled to one another.[66]

The Islamised discourse of *Syair Sultan Abdul Muluk* in comparison is plain to see in the contrast between these two princesses' knowing smiles and Rahah's mute shame and quiescence. When Dura divorces Rahah and prevails upon Abdul Muluk to take her as his third wife, this is yet again a demonstration of her *bakti* to her husband. Likewise, while *Syair Siti Zubaidah* sidesteps the matter by making Puteri Rukiah into Zubaidah's deputy and companion-in-disguise rather than her wife, Rukiah ends in the same position as Rahah, transferred to the hero in yet another demonstration of selfless devotion by Zubaidah.

Though polygamy can be seen as the root of all Zubaidah's problems — her frustration that she was passed over in the palace hierarchy in favour of her co-wife was the reason she ran away in the first place — she must come to see that it is a necessary good. The more the merrier, or, as Rahmah puts it in *Syair Sultan Abdul Muluk*, "if his royal highness had wives by the score / they would all be kin to us".[67] Thus, Zubaidah points out that the thrice-married Zainal Abidin has yet to fulfill the "hukum syarak", religious law, enjoining four wives:

Cukupkan empat apa salahnya	Completing the quartet is no error,
Kerana laki-laki sudah adatnya	For that is a man's custom,
Sunat konon menurut Nabinya	The blessed practice of the Prophet.
Janganlah kakanda memungkirkannya[68]	Do not breach it, [my] husband.

When Zainal Abidin returns to her after only one night with his new bride, she counsels him to go back again: "that is the custom of newlyweds / a day does not suffice to make certain".[69] Of course, the *sunnah* of marrying four times is recommended rather than required, and the spiritual benefit of it accrues not just to the husband but perhaps even more so to the wife. Zubaidah's motive for such selfless sharing of her husband, "readily giving her husband", is the merit she thereby acquires for the afterlife, "gaining great blessings".[70] In these *syair*, the hero must not desire other women for their own sake but for the sake of the fulfilment of religious law; the heroine, meanwhile, desires her advancement, in this life and the next, more than she does her husband's undivided affections.

Syair Siti Zubaidah and *Syair Sultan Abdul Muluk* downplay desire between cosmically predestined lovers in favour of an idealisation of marriage as a partnership of (almost) equals. On Zubaidah and Zainal Abidin's first night together after so many years apart, husband and wife retire to the bedroom and the curtain is let down around the bed. The scene is set for what the text tastefully elides when describing a later nuptials, since after all, "one knows [the ways] of the amorous / when they achieve their hearts' desires / For when will passionate hearts be extinguished?"[71] Passionate hearts are not much in evidence here, however, for rather than responding to Zainal Abidin's kisses, Zubaidah launches into 13 stanzas recapitulating her sufferings at the hands of his mother and the great deeds she has carried out for his sake. Reduced to tears, Zainal Abidin admits his and his mother's fault:

Berbagailah pujuk raja bestari	The noble king coaxed her,
Minta' ampun kepada isteri	Asked pardon of his wife.
Perkataan belas juga diberi	Speaking affectionate words,
Serta dengan merendahkan diri[72]	And abasing himself.

Ever gracious, Zubaidah forgives him — "my lord's sins have been forgiven" — leading Zainal Abidin to implore her not to use the honorific language that a subordinate should use towards a king, "do not use the language of slave and lord".[73] His abasement before his wife is the counterpart of hers before him when she reveals her identity, but is far more unexpected given that he is the king and her husband, doubly her master. In part, his request that she speak to him as an equal is because her royal lineage has been established but it is also in recognition of her heroism, which she has just recounted at length. Because she is an exceptional woman, the text seems to argue, she should be accorded equal status with her husband: she bows to him but he to her also.

Though authority is in the hands of the heroine when in her guise as *puteri jayeng*, and is wrested away from the hero by his defeat in battle, the question of who is in charge once all has been put to rights is answered only ambiguously. Once Rafiah has given up her identity as Dura, she cedes control over Barbaham to Jamaluddin: "the country of Barbaham is my gift / my husband shall own whatever is there".[74] Nonetheless, Jamaluddin remains in her (and not Abdul Muluk's) debt, once again swearing his fealty to her and requesting her permission to return to his kingdom. Zubaidah is acknowledged by her brother, the Sultan of Iraq, as the ruler of Yunan:

Kerana bukan negerinya kita	For it is not our country,
Adinda Zubaidah rajanya yang nyata	My sister Zubaidah is the true raja.
Apa bicaranya ikutlah serta	Whatever her decision I will follow it;
Kita sekadar menurutkan kata[75]	We only obey instructions.

Hearing this, Zainal Abidin agrees: "the country belonged to his wife".[76] As is proper, Zubaidah responds by denying that she has any authority but again, her husband refers the matter of who should rule in Yunan in her stead back to her. At last, she appoints Raja Mahiran, whom she and Rukiah had deposed in the first place — thereby literally restoring the status quo. Zubaidah retains the final say in the matter of who is to rule, but it is evident that she is now the king-maker rather than the king.

Greater glories are hers when her father-in-law urges her to accept the rulership of Kembayat:

Akan sekarang apa bicara	What now is the decision?
Ayahanda hendak memulangkan negara	Your father wishes to restore the country
Kepada tuan lela mengindera	To your noble self,
Isi negeri rakyat tentera	[Together with] the country's people and soldiers.

Barang yang ada di negeri Kembayat	Whatever there is in the land of Kembayat,
Menteri hulubalang laskar rakyat	Ministers, warriors, soldiers, subjects,
Perintahan tuan baik dan jahat	For you to govern, for good or ill,
Ayahanda sekalian sekadarkan melihat	Your father and others will only look on.

Rumput rampai sampah dan abuk	The grass, trash and dust,
Semuanya punya paras yang elok	All belong to your lovely self.
Sebarang ada semuanya takluk	Whatever is there is subject to you,
Seorang tak boleh lagi menolok	No one will compare to you.
Demikianlan tuan niat ayahanda	That is your father's wish
Kepada tuan lela yang syahda	For you, noble and fair
Adapun akan paduka kakanda	As for his highness, your husband,
Menjadi wazir kepada anakada[77]	He will become an advisor to you, my child.

It would seem that what the old king of Kembayat is offering her is not, as might be expected, the position of queen or principal wife — *permaisuri* or *isteri gahara* — but of raja, with her husband merely an advisor. When Zubaidah refuses this as too great an honour for a miserable wretch or impoverished wanderer — "pacal yang hina", "dagang miskin" — her husband and father-in-law take this as a sign that she is still upset over her mother-in-law's former slights![78] After much diplomacy, Zubaidah is prevailed upon to accept the throne of Kembayat and is crowned, *dirajakan*. But, as we have seen, she no longer has the autonomy that she possessed as Sultan Yunan.

Later descriptions of the disposition of authority within Kembayat seem to belie this glorious triumph. Although Zubaidah rules, it appears that she rules only the palace, the usual realm of the queen: all that her heroic deeds have achieved, in this case, is getting the upper hand over her mother-in-law and Puteri Syajarah. Moreover, Zubaidah's dealings with her three co-wives seem to be more those of a skilled tactician of the *dalam*, the women's quarters of the palace, than of an indisputed raja:

Dengan suaminya terlalu bakti	To her husband she rendered great service
Madunya ketiga disukakan hati	And pleased the hearts of her co-wives.
Barang kehendak semua dituruti	Whatever their wish, she fulfilled it,
Menjadilah kasih sampai ke mati	Giving rise to affection till their dying day.
Segala madunya tunduk belaka	All her co-wives bowed to her,
Sopan dan malu tidak terhingga	Extremely well mannered and reticent.
Sekalian takut menentang muka	All were afraid to look her in the face,
Apa katanya diturutnya juga	Whatever she asked, that they did.

Zubaidah itu orang berakal	Zubaidah was intelligent,
Mengadap seteru sangat tawakal	Trusting in God when facing her enemies,
Jalan bermadu hatinya cekal	Stoic in the path of co-wifehood,
Mengaji sembahyang tidaklah tinggal	Never omitting her prayers or religious study.
Terlalu sangat kasih suaminya	Her husband loved her greatly
Tidaklah dilalui barang kehendaknya	And did not cross her wishes,
Terlalu hormat akan isterinya	Having so much respect for his wife
Tidak berani melalui katanya	That he did not dare disobey her.
Tambahan pandai pulak memelihara	And she was skillful at looking after them —
Madunya ketiga sama setara	The three co-wives equal in status —
Sedikit tidak diberinya cedera	Not giving them the least cause for offence,
Lakunya seperti sanak saudara[79]	Treating them like her own kin.

Syair Siti Zubaidah contradicts itself in its attempts to imagine a happily-ever-after for its heroine that also abides by societal norms. *Syair Sultan Abdul Muluk* is far more coherent on this matter: Rafiah and Rahmah were never in conflict; Rafiah unambiguously cedes the powers she collected as Dura to her husband and returns to her supreme destiny as wife. In both texts, heroinism consists in equal parts of valour on the battlefield and the exercise of diplomacy in the polygamous household. In the end, the victorious heroine is once more in a position to be advised by her father, as Pendita Ulama advises Zubaidah, to "obey her husband's wishes".[80]

V. Disguise and Recognition

Kembayat is brought down by the failures of its king, Zainal Abidin's father Darman Syah, whose botched adjudication of the matter of the Chinese merchant precipitates the seven princesses' revenge attack. His greatest error, however, is in failing to notice that the tension between his wife and his daughter-in-law Zubaidah, while feminine and domestic, is not at all trivial. As we have seen, romances for women place the heroine front and centre, giving her significance that she lacks in other genres of literature where women are marginal. The greatest revelation of the plot is the heroine's true worth, in spite of her apparently humble birth. The old queen disdained Zubaidah out of a belief that she was a commoner but the revelations of Zubaidah's great deeds and, no less importantly, of her descent from the throne of Iraqan Kastan, force her to recognise her daughter-in-law for what she is — a jewel beyond compare. The penitent queen declares:

[Di] atas bumi, di bawah awan	On the earth, beneath the clouds,
Seorang tak lebih daripada bangsawan	There is no one greater than your
Bangsa martabat sudah ketahuan	noble self,
Bangsa yang mulia emas tempawan	Lineage and standing now known,
	The noble lineage of [you, like] beaten gold.
Daripada bonda belum mengerti	Because I [lit.: mother] did not yet
Bangsa yang mulia tiadalah pasti	understand,
Disangkakan hina tuanku gusti	And your noble lineage was not certain,
Jadilah bonda bergundah hati[81]	[I] assumed you, my lady, were lowly
	And so I was distressed at heart.

All erroneous assumptions, misunderstandings and uncertainties are swept away. For Rafiah, too, the revelation of her identity also brings greater appreciation of her worth: her husband's "love and affection increased / as though [he] had won a mountain of jewels".[82] The heroine is disguised so that the truth about her may be revealed with more striking force.

As in other romances for women, the heroine's transgression of the orthodox gender order ends in a return to convention. The moment she is recognised as the ultimate heroic figure, her brilliant career is over. This moment of recognition is so deferred that it strains credibility, even within the narrative conventions of the *syair*. Although the heroine is utterly convincing as "a famous man", the blindness of Zainal Abidin and Abdul Muluk is significant.[83] In their case, it is not a question of the lack of *akal*. Both notice the resemblances between their apparently male saviours and their wives, but fail to act upon that insight. The scenes in which recognition finally dawns and they acknowledge their wives follow precisely the same pattern in both *Syair Siti Zubaidah* and *Syair Sultan Abdul Muluk*. First, the heroine secludes herself within the palace, removes her outer garments, and then, clad only in "fine inner garments" in Rafiah's case and "a single garment" in Zubaidah's, shows herself to the hero.[84] Startled that his rescuer is evidently not a king but a woman, and moreover uncannily resembles his wife, the hero nonetheless remains silent, ostensibly out of shame, *malu*, lest he be mistaken. This curious shame and even a species of fear inspire the hero's reticence: "he wished to speak to her but felt terror".[85] Since it is not enough to show herself to be a biological woman, which the thin inner garments presumably reveal plainly enough, the heroine then dresses herself in women's clothes, assuming once more the cultural accoutrements of womanhood. But again, the hero does not speak. In *Syair Siti Zubaidah*:

Sultan Abidin melihat nyata	Sultan Abidin saw clearly,
Terlalu hairan rasanya cita	His thoughts exceedingly amazed,
Melihat paras seperti dipeta	Seeing the appearance as though painted,
Rupa Zubaidah demikian serta	And the very image of Zubaidah.
Tetapi tidak juga diteguri	But he did not greet her,
Sehingga memandang berdiam diri	Only gazed in silence.
Zubaidah pun datang menghampiri	Zubaidah then came close to him,
Tunduk menyembah sepuluh jari	Bent and made ten-fingered obeisance.
Sujud di kaki sultan paduka	Prostrated herself at the sultan's feet,
Seraya menangis tidak terhingga	While weeping uncontrollably:
Wahai tuanku indera mastika	Oh my lord, my talisman,
Patik nan tidak tuanku peka[86]	You did not [sense] me, my lord.

The same scene is recounted in *Syair Sultan Abdul Muluk*:

Setelah dilihat Dura bangsawan	Once noble Dura had seen
Tiada ditegur sultan dermawan	That the generous sultan did not speak to her,
Ia pun masuk ke dalam peraduan	She went into the bedroom
Lalu memakai seperti perempuan.	And dressed as a woman.
Keluar pulak siti bestari	The well-born lady emerged,
Sujud di kaki Sultan Barbari	Prostrated herself at the Barbari Sultan's feet,
Dengan tangis puteri bestari	The well-born princess in tears.
Baginda terkejut dilihatnya isteri[87]	His highness was startled to see his wife.

Thus, both *Syair Siti Zubaidah* and *Syair Sultan Abdul Muluk* make explicit the fact that the heroine must make herself subject to her husband once more, must prostrate herself in front of him and weep, before he can (bring himself to) acknowledge her as his wife. At the very moment when she is recognised as a *puteri jayeng*, she must return herself to her primary identity as her husband's wife if he is to recognise her at all.

* * * * *

In combining the older motif of the disguised heroine with the new imperative that women devote themselves to their husbands, *Syair Siti Zubaidah* and *Syair Sultan Abdul Muluk* protest against, and finally acquiesce to the idea that marriage is the ultimate arena of female heroism. With respect to *Syair Sultan Abdul Muluk* as a product of the Riau court, Barbara Watson Andaya asks whether Siti Rafiah's disguise and her adventures may "be interpreted as a statement on the unrealised potential of 'femaleness'? On the other hand, what are we to make of the recurring motif whereby women achieve success only when they disguise themselves as men?"[88] The meaning of success in Andaya's question requires more attention, for the victory that is achieved is basically a marital one: the heroine's demonstration of her fitness to be the first of all her husband's wives. Her exploits outside the home are only means to that end. These *syair* do not truly subvert the status quo: while the gender order is destabilised by the heroines' adventures in masculine guise, the texts end with her resumption of the conventional feminine role and the reaffirmation of the legitimacy of polygamous marriage. In a characteristic gesture that further demonstrates her exemplariness, the heroine takes it upon herself to furnish her husband with other wives. The hero's protracted, if not rather preposterous, failure to recognise the heroine until she falls on her knees before him is a sign of the limits of these *syair* as subversive imaginings. In the end, the transgressive potential of the martial heroine, the *puteri jayeng*, is forsaken for the reassuring figure of the heroine as exemplary wife, the first among equals of the polygamous establishment.

5

Calculating Women, Foolish Men

Reason in *Syair Siti Dhawiyyah* and *Syair Saudagar Bodoh*

The dichotomy between *akal* and *nafsu*, reason and passion, is a familiar one in the Malay world, with women usually allocated to the side of irrationality, error, and seductive danger.[1] This formulation is reversed by the intelligent women and foolish men in *Syair Siti Dhawiyyah* and *Syair Saudagar Bodoh*, both of which make much of the superiority of the heroine's *akal* over her husband's. These *syair* are further distinguished from others current in mid-19th-century Riau because although they take place in milieux Middle Eastern in name and Malay in character they are bereft of the fantastical elements — flying Chinese princesses, magical weapons, portentous omens, and animals reciting *pantun* — that are so frequently met with elsewhere. This difference is encapsulated in the character of their heroines, who are not the daughters of kings pretending to be the daughters of merchants, like Siti Zubaidah, nor even the daughters of merchants who were once kings, like Siti Jauhar Maknikam, but simply the daughters of merchants. In moving from aristocratic heroines who triumph through the magical powers granted to them by their elevated lineage to mercantile heroines who succeed by their own good sense and fortitude; from the restitution of the status proper to the heroine's noble birth to the establishment of justice according to ideas derived from Islamic law; from heroes rescued from the clutches of hostile monarchs to heroes saved from unfortunate situations brought on by their own flaws; the scene shifts from the values and norms of the palace towards those of the marketplace, from the courtly towards the commonplace. Dhawiyyah and Zainah are rather distant from Panji princesses, so quick to offence and to arms. Instead, they are clever, canny, and delight in outwitting their dull husbands. The clever woman who saves her husband, especially in a mercantile Middle Eastern setting such as Basra or Muscat, has close parallels in Arabic stories about a clever slavegirl who saves her master.[2]

The discourse of *akal* is central to this move. Divergent ideas of *akal* — its very definition, how it is to be obtained and its proper uses — play a central role in *Syair Saudagar Bodoh*'s response to its probable predecessor, *Syair Siti Dhawiyyah*. For *Syair Saudagar Bodoh*, *akal* is common sense, the command of practical matters, having a head for business; in *Syair Siti Dhawiyyah*, it is of a more rarified variety, entailing the ability to judge between right and wrong, and the self-discipline to forsake vain earthly satisfactions in the hope of heavenly rewards. As representations of the conduct of wives, one is an exemplar and the other is a farce, therefore occupying very different positions in the hierarchy of Malay literature. *Syair Saudagar Bodoh*, an unfilial descendant of *Syair Siti Dhawiyyah*, uses humour to unsettle the authority of the didactic text.

Syair Saudagar Bodoh[3]

A fabulously wealthy merchant in Damascus has only one child, a good-looking son who has never done a day's work in his life. The boy spends his days in idleness, which stunts his intellect. His father has a palatial home, with gold walls and ceilings and pillars filled with jewels. All the other merchants know of the house's riches and are anxious to get their hands on them. The merchant also has an adopted relative in Muscat, Malik Hasani, who captains his fleet of trading ships.

One day, the merchant falls ill and summons his son to his bedside. His parting advice to the young man is that if he wants to get married, he must choose a virgin. After his father's death, the son sets about implementing his father's advice. He marries but being uncertain whether the woman is a virgin, he divorces her after 20 days. Indeed, the young merchant (called simply Saudagar Muda) seems to be unclear on the concept, because he goes on to marry and divorce 100 women in succession. At last, he marries a woman from Kampung Dagang: she is of obscure origin, her parents being dead, and works as a servant, but is very beautiful. Unbeknownst to the young merchant, she has a lover. The young merchant and the woman marry, and he hands over his assets to her. Revelling in her new wealth, the woman becomes proud and arrogant, even wearing a silk *sarung* to bathe. At night she steals her husband's possessions and passes them to her lover. The young merchant is at a loss to explain the disappearance of his wealth and since he is not trading but simply relying on his inheritance, soon there is nothing left. The house is stripped bare and he is even forced to sell his slaves.

Just in time, Malik Hasani arrives with four ships. Discovering the young merchant's dire straits, Malik Hasani advises him to come to Muscat, leaving his wife behind. The young merchant readily agrees, but first Malik Hasani has the gold removed from the walls and ceilings of the house, replacing it with stone painted gold, and empties the pillars of their jewels. These riches are transported in secret to Malik Hasani's ships. The house is then sold to a consortium of eight merchants eager to get their hands on its riches. After the deal is concluded, Malik Hasani and the young merchant sail away, leaving the other merchants to discover that they have been duped. They are outraged but decide that the young merchant is too noble (or perhaps too stupid) to have tricked them and that his wife must have removed the gold and jewels without his knowledge. The merchants seize the wife and haul her before the sultan, who sentences her to be exposed to the sun without food or drink, as a result of which she shortly dies.

Meanwhile, the young merchant has begun a life of ease in Muscat under the care of Malik Hasani. Malik Hasani has a daughter of exceptional beauty, piety and intelligence, Siti Zainah. In due course, he proposes to the young merchant that they marry. Due to his previous unfortunate matrimonial experiences, the young merchant is reluctant, but Malik Hasani advises him that if he bases his choice of a woman on four signs, he will not go wrong. These signs are the four long, four short, four black and four white characteristics of the ideal wife ("long" body, long hair, long fingers and "long" wits, and so on). The young merchant declares that if there is any such woman, he would surely marry her. It will not surprise the reader to learn that Malik Hasani promptly claims that his daughter Siti Zainah fulfills all these criteria. She is then married to the young merchant, with much ensuing festivity.

Unfortunately, she then refuses to have anything to do with him, causing her parents to suffer much embarrassment and the young merchant the pangs of unrequited desire. Her father decides that she must be inhibited by living in the same house with her parents, and so builds the newlyweds a lavish new home. However, after they move in, the situation deteriorates, with Zainah even refusing to let the young merchant speak to her. At last, Malik Hasani remonstrates with her and she explains that her aversion to her husband is due to his extreme stupidity. In order for the young merchant to learn the ways of the world, Zainah asks Malik Hasani to furnish him with 40 camels loaded with goods and send him on a trading mission.

No sooner has the young merchant arrived at Yemen with his camels and a large retinue than a crafty merchant takes hold of the ear of the leading camel. He asks the price, and the young merchant, innocently assuming that he meant the single camel and its load, answers that it is 1,000 dinars. But when the Yemeni merchant pays the thousand dinars, he seizes all 40 camels and their loads. The young merchant's protestations are in vain, with witnesses and a local notable all ruling in the Yemeni's favour. Dejectedly, the young merchant sends his retinue back to Muscat but remains behind himself, too afraid of what his wife and father-in-law would say. In Yemen, he lives a life of poverty and homelessness, reduced to doing manual labour such as pounding rice and carrying sweet potatoes.

Back in Muscat, Siti Zainah is troubled not so much by her conscience but by her worries about the damage to her good name, should her husband's plight be known. Dressed as a religious scholar, complete with robe and turban, she travels to Yemen. Calling herself the young khatib (Khatib Muda), she claims she has come to study with the qadi. The qadi is flattered, not to mention charmed by the young scholar's attractive appearance, and the two spend their days in study and teaching.

One day, the young khatib catches sight of the young merchant hauling grass for horse fodder. Needless to say, the young merchant fails to recognise his wife but after some coaxing, tells the khatib how he fell upon such bad times and agrees to do as "he" advises in order to restore his wealth. The khatib has the merchant dressed in a manner befitting his former station and sends him off to the Yemeni. The Yemeni, failing to recognise the man he duped, is delighted at the appearance of another rich gull. When the young merchant takes hold of the Yemeni's finger and asks the price, the Yemeni assumes he means his rings and answers that it is 100 dinars. Thereupon the young merchant draws his *keris* and tries to cut off the Yemeni's finger. Great uproar ensues, and all parties repair to the qadi for judgement. The qadi rules in favour of the Yemeni, but the khatib intervenes, arguing from the precedent of the camels. The qadi then orders the Yemeni to return all the camels and their goods, which he does, in fear of the matter reaching the ears of the king.

The khatib returns to Muscat, leaving the young merchant to follow behind. When he meets his wife again, he is astonished and delighted to learn from her that she was the young khatib. Zainah resigns herself to her husband's great stupidity and the couple live henceforth in marital harmony.

The lithograph version, published in 1880, contains a much longer and more dramatically satisfying ending, going into greater detail about the niceties of the case argued by the khatib. The khatib and the young merchant then return to Muscat together, and when they arrive there, the khatib tells "his" companion that "he" will visit him the next day — and that he very much looks forward to meeting "his" companion's wife. Zainah beats the young merchant to the house and gives him a warm reception. When the khatib turns up the next day, however, she is nowhere to be found, having apparently gone to visit her sick mother. No sooner does the khatib leave than Zainah reappears, exasperating her husband. The same thing happens on the second day, but on the third day, she does not change out of her disguise. When the young merchant finds the khatib sitting in his wife's room, the penny finally drops. After upbraiding her husband for his stupidity, cataloguing his various blunders, Zainah relents and the marriage is consummated at last.

Syair Siti Dhawiyyah[4]

Siti Dhawiyyah is the beautiful daughter of a merchant in Basra and an only child. On his deathbed, her father bequeaths all his wealth to her, but cautions her that it is useless. He tells her to seek "ilmu perempuan" and take care about whom she marries. Dhawiyyah gives her *inang* or nurse money to purchase *ilmu*. Her *inang* returns with various magical charms for fascinating one's husband, but Dhawiyyah doubts that this was what her father had in mind. Her relatives try to coax her into marriage but she is reluctant as she has not fulfilled her father's wishes. In a pleasure garden, she chances on an old woman whom she asks for "adat bersuami", the customs or norms of having a husband. The old woman advises her that the husband is always right, no matter what. Dhawiyyah is grateful for this information. Meanwhile, the king's son is introduced: the handsome and feckless Haris Fadhilah. Four beautiful women are particularly taken with him: Siti Hafsah, Siti Fatimah, Siti Arabi and Siti Maramah. Siti Hafsah causes herself to be seen by Haris Fadhilah, who is immediately besotted and begins a dalliance with her (and eventually with the other three as well). The king finds out about this from his courtiers and is furious with them for standing by while his son is corrupted. The courtiers advise him to go easy on Haris Fadhilah, seeing as he is the sole heir to the throne. The king charges the courtiers with finding Haris Fadhilah a suitable wife. They propose Dhawiyyah. Haris Fadhilah comes to see his parents, attributing his absence to illness. He is reluctant to marry his parents' choice, but has no option in the matter. Dhawiyyah agrees to the marriage, on the condition that she remains in her own home. A lavish wedding is conducted, but Haris Fadhilah flees from the nuptial bedchamber to his mistress without so much as looking at Dhawiyyah. She takes this calmly, in line with the old woman's advice. While Haris Fadhilah disports himself with his four mistresses, Dhawiyyah bribes her servants to keep the matter quiet. She makes sure that food and clothes are kept ready for him. To her relatives, she claims her husband is in bed and too shy to come out to meet them, and on subsequent visits, that he is visiting his father and other such ruses, meanwhile singing her husband's praises to her relatives. When Haris Fadhilah's mother comes to visit, Dhawiyyah tells her he is out horse riding, and defends him against the queen's accusations of bad conduct. However, the king is not taken in as he has heard reports from the ministers about his son's doings. The courtiers again dissuade the king from killing Haris Fadhilah, advising him to send his wayward son on a sailing mission instead. Having no other options, Haris Fadhilah agrees.

The four mistresses ask him to bring back various costly items from his travels. Dhawiyyah's obliging relatives assemble at her house with supplies for Haris Fadhilah's voyage. He sends a messenger to Dhawiyyah, asking what she would like him to bring from abroad. She gives the messenger money ("four *duit*") from her purse and asks that her husband purchase some *akal* or rationality. Haris Fadhilah goes to Surat, where he does a brisk trade in the goods he has brought with him. On leaving Surat, a storm blows up and prevents the ship from moving. The sailors advise him that this is because he has forgotten a promise. Only then does Haris Fadhilah recall his promise to Dhawiyyah. He goes ashore and tries to buy *akal*, much to everyone's merriment. At last, he finds an old man willing to sell him "the lore of husbands having wives", which amounts to being careful in one's choice of wife, avoiding women who are only interested in wealth and choosing one who is dutiful no matter what her husband's financial circumstances. In order to test the character of his women, the old man tells Haris Fadhilah to appear to them dressed in torn and dirty clothes, as though he has lost his fortune. Then the old man requests payment of exactly four *duit*. Haris Fadhilah returns to Basra, where he tries out the ruse, with predictable results: he is spurned by his four mistresses but given a royal welcome by his wife. Overcome by remorse, he takes to his bed for a week. Dhawiyyah and Haris Fadhilah are reconciled, he confesses to his parents, and everyone is amazed by and full of praise for Dhawiyyah's conduct. The four women are drowned in the sea.

I. An Undutiful Daughter

A dying man imparts a few last words of wisdom to his only child: find the wisdom necessary for marriage. The child's misunderstanding of this advice then sets the plot in motion. Marriage takes place, but due to the husband's lack of *akal*, is no state of bliss. The wife strives to put matters right. The husband is sent on a trading journey precisely in order to acquire *akal*. All difficulties are resolved in the end, with the heroine, by dint of her superior *akal*, definitely the dominant partner in the marriage. Moreover and unusually, the heroine ends the *syair* as the hero's only wife. Thus, both *Syair Siti Dhawiyyah* and *Syair Saudagar Bodoh* are about marriage, not as a goal, but as a problem: what is the nature of a wife's *bakti*, service, to her husband, particularly when she is the more intelligent partner in the marriage? The closeness of the plots of the two *syair* — utilising not only the same tropes but in the same order — suggests that the later text, *Syair Saudagar Bodoh*, may have been a response to the earlier *Syair Siti Dhawiyyah*. However, *Syair Saudagar Bodoh* hardly shows the proper filial respect due to a progenitor.

This undutiful relationship expresses itself forcefully in the depiction of the husband. Haris Fadhilah, Dhawiyyah's husband, is a philanderer but in other respects, is very satisfactory, making a brilliant success of a trading voyage. When Dhawiyyah has reformed him from his licentious ways, there is no doubt that he is a changed man. Saudagar Muda, on the other hand, has hundreds of failed marriages and a botched trading mission behind him. Even after Zainah rescues him from poverty in a strange land, he remains as foolish as before. Whereas Haris Fadhilah abandons Dhawiyyah on her wedding night in favour of his more alluring concubines,

Saudagar Muda spends most of the *syair* experiencing considerable sexual frustration after he is categorically rejected by Zainah. Wifely *bakti* for Dhawiyyah is selfless submission; in Zainah's case, it involves her taking charge of their affairs and not letting her husband too far out of her sight. In answer to the patient acceptances and tearful repentances in *Syair Siti Dhawiyyah*, *Syair Saudagar Bodoh* proposes sharp retorts and impudent tricks. Though Dhawiyyah would never dream of such a remark, Zainah does not hesitate to say "I told you so". The po-faced Dhawiyyah invites parody by Zainah.

Klinkert attributed *Syair Siti Dhawiyyah* to a Tuan Bilal Abu, who died in the 1830s and had been attached to the mosque on Penyengat.[5] Whether or not Klinkert's identification of the author is correct, two other manuscripts indicate a possible connection to Riau. One, perhaps once belonging to Roorda van Eysinga, was copied in Singapore in 1857 "behind the mosque of Encik Fatimah Riau", and another was made by Husain bin Ismail, a Bugis scribe.[6] That there are seven extant manuscripts suggests that *Syair Siti Dhawiyyah* was quite a popular work, current in Riau and the surrounding areas from at least the 1850s. This is borne out by the 17 lithograph editions that appeared between 1870 and 1913, all of which were published in Singapore, the major outlet for Riau texts. Indeed, *Syair Siti Dhawiyyah* was one of the ten most frequently reissued lithographs in the early period of Malay printing.[7] *Syair Saudagar Bodoh*, by contrast, exists in a single manuscript, which probably only survived through the intervention of Klinkert, and in two lithograph editions by unknown publishers dating from 1880 and some time in the 1890s.[8] Once again, a note by Klinkert provides the earliest information about the author, that she was Raja Kalsum binti Raja Ali Haji, and the date, 1861.[9] (The attribution of *Syair Saudagar Bodoh* to her in the 1879 lithograph edition probably makes her the first named female Malay author in print.) Unlike the widely-read *Syair Siti Dhawiyyah* then, *Syair Saudagar Bodoh* is a text that may have initially circulated only within Raja Kalsum's family or household, coming to wider attention only after traditional Malay literature crossed what Proudfoot has called the print threshold.[10] If *Syair Saudagar Bodoh* had been written a generation earlier, beyond the reach of the printing press, or if Klinkert had not chanced upon a copy of it, it would most probably be unknown today. This may go some way towards explaining the non-canonical approach to the subject of an intelligent woman married to a foolish man in *Syair Saudagar Bodoh* versus the basically conservative outlook of *Syair Siti Dhawiyyah* to the same material. Klinkert's intervention and the spread of print publication may have had the effect of capturing a marginal text that might otherwise have disappeared.

Contests of intelligence between husbands and wives may be found elsewhere in Malay narrative, from folktales about Pak Pandir and Mak Andeh to other popular Riau texts like *Syair Puteri Akal* to more canonical, Islamicate works like *Hikayat Nakhoda Muda*.[11] The striking parallels between the two *syair*, as well as the likelihood that Raja Kalsum knew *Syair Siti Dhawiyyah*, suggests that her text could have been at least in part a response to Tuan Bilal Abu's. At any rate, it is not impossible that readers of both texts in 19th-century Penyengat would have taken *Syair Saudagar Bodoh* as a reworking of the themes of the well-known *Syair Siti Dhawiyyah*. The nature of this response may be gauged by the claims the texts make for themselves. *Syair Siti Dhawiyyah* proclaims itself at the outset as not simply idle reading material but "syair tamthil ibarat", "a *syair* [of] models and parables":

Syair dikarang dagang yang fakir	This *syair* is composed by a poor wanderer,
Diambil ibarat di sinilah fikir	To take as an parable, to think upon it here,
Dari dahulu sampai ke akhir	From the past to the end,
Perkataan jangan diberi mungkir[12]	These words must not be gainsaid.

The *syair* is not to be read simply for pleasure or to distract oneself from quotidian worries but as a *tamthil*, an example, an allegory or parable to teach proper conduct. A profound religious message is promulgated in its pages: a woman who submits patiently and wisely to her husband will attain spiritual merit. Despite the assertions of cataloguers, it is not a poem about love.[13] There are the trappings of the romantic *syair* or the Panji romance, certainly: a supremely attractive hero and heroine, jealous rivals for the hero's affections, kings and queens, an exotic location. But the hero is animated only by lust and the heroine solely by duty. The plot concerns the contest between the two, eventually resolved into marital harmony. *Syair Siti Dhawiyyah* is in fact a didactic text disguised as a romance, the sugar-coated pill prescribed to women by such diagnosers of moral ills as Raja Ali Haji and Safirin bin Usman Fadli. As far as its message is concerned, this text has more in common with other didactic fables for women of the period, such as *Hikayat Darma Ta'siah*, *Hikayat Fatimah Bersuami* and especially *Syair Sultan Mansur*, with its finger-wagging tale about the dangers of concubinage, than it does with a romantic *syair* like *Syair Siti Zubaidah*.[14]

Syair Saudagar Bodoh, by contrast, begins simply with "listen to a certain matter / seemingly the tale of people of yore", making no claims for the veracity or virtue of the story while firmly distancing it from the reader's reality.[15] The text is guilty of both crimes for which fictional literature stands accused by such writers as Safirin: it is comprised of lies, and attractive ones at that. The narrator makes it clear that the willful heroine of *Syair Saudagar Bodoh*, who makes a fool of her husband, is not to be taken as worthy of imitation or *tamthil*. However, neither is she a negative example, a cautionary figure who misbehaves and is punished, for Zainah gets away with it all. The *syair* containing a didactic message to women demands to be taken seriously ("these words must not be gainsaid"), whereas that sending up the foolishness of a husband is rather more self-deprecating ("the story is foolish").[16] Only the lithograph version, though, assesses the text as *bodoh*, foolish or ignorant; in the manuscript, that attribute is firmly attached to the person of Zainah's husband. Thus, a text that diverges from canonical norms is brought into line when it is presented to a wider audience. Nowhere is this divergence more evident than in the discourse of *akal*.

II. *Akal* and its Others

A standard definition of *'aql*, the Arabic word from which the Malay is derived, denotes intellect, intelligence, reasoning or "a natural way of knowing, independent of the authority of revelation, what is right and wrong".[17] *Akal* was a substantial topic in traditional Malay literature, meriting a chapter of its own in Bukhari al-Jauhari's *Taj al-Salatin*, where it is termed the greatest of all God's creations because from it proceeds all good and evil in the world.[18] To Bukhari, *akal* is not morally neutral: the man who possesses *akal* (or *budi*, which is used interchangeably) strives to commit good deeds and shuns evil acts; conversely, the man who lacks *akal* has no fear of the Day of Judgement and acts with impunity. At the same time, it is possible to have *ilmu*, or knowledge, but to lack *budi/akal*, in which case that knowledge is in vain.[19] Thus, *akal* is not the possession of knowledge but of wise judgement, which necessarily implies adherence to religious law.

Syair Siti Dhawiyyah adheres to this canonical definition of *akal*, where it is the means to make the moral choice between good and evil conduct, and even demonstrates the perils of wielding knowledge without *akal* as a guide. However, in *Syair Saudagar Bodoh*, *akal* is simply intelligence or wits, the means of achieving an end, whatever that might be. The second variety — the use of *akal* for getting one's own way and especially for securing financial gain — is particularly associated in both *syair* with women but only in *Syair Siti Dhawiyyah* is it termed ignoble *akal*, *akal yang leta*. Furthermore, the possession of *akal* in *Syair Siti Dhawiyyah* is opposed to desire, *nafsu*, whereas in *Syair Saudagar Bodoh*, its antithesis is stupidity, *bodoh*. Thus, those who lack *akal* in *Syair Siti Dhawiyyah* give unbridled rein to their passions, whereas those who lack it in *Syair Saudagar Bodoh* are simply foolish. In both cases, the most *akal*-free characters are the heroines' husbands: Haris Fadhilah leads a profligate life of lechery, committing crimes against God's law, while Saudagar Muda mismanages his financial affairs and bankrupts himself repeatedly, after all not a sin but only incompetence.

Syair Siti Dhawiyyah begins with the very question: what is *akal*? On his deathbed, the heroine's father instructs her to seek out "clear *akal*", specifically "women's knowledge".[20] *Ilmu* is a red herring that sets Dhawiyyah off on the wrong track, connoting as it does esoteric and especially magical knowledge. Despite her misgivings, she sets her nurse to gathering *ilmu* and ends up with a rich haul of magical means for strengthening a woman's attractive power over a man (*hikmat*, *guna* and *ilmu pesona*). Faced by this collection of *ilmu*, however, Dhawiyyah rejects it, reflecting that this sort of thing is beneath her: "in the end it will not be [proper] / [I] will be ashamed and gain a bad name".[21] The text is shot through with polemic against magic.[22] True *ilmu*, which in Dhawiyyah's case turns out to be the knowledge of how to exercise self-control to the point of abjection, is repeatedly opposed to the morally and physically degrading effects of *ilmu hikmat* or magic. Haris Fadhilah's four concubines first charm him with music, then maintain their hold over him by dosing him with unwholesome foods. When these women are sentenced to death, it is to a great extent for their practice of magic:

Inilah orang menaruh hikmat	Such are people who have gained
Memakai ilmu tidak berhemat	magical powers,
Seketika juga merasa nikmat	Using this lore carelessly.
Mangkin lama tidak selamat[23]	They enjoy it only for a moment,
	As time passes, it grows perilous.

Transitory carnal pleasures enjoyed through *ilmu* are implicitly contrasted here to the eternal bliss of heaven enjoyed by the virtuous (it may be assumed that Dhawiyyah takes the long view of the "akhirnya kelak" quoted above as the world to come itself).

Dhawiyyah finally gains the knowledge she seeks from a most unlikely source, an impoverished old woman living alone in a garden. The old woman's *ilmu*, or *adat bersuami*, "the customs of having a husband", amounts to a doctrine of keeping up appearances at all costs: the wife must never complain or speak ill of the husband to himself or others, even if he neglects her, is violent or wicked. The wife has a greater duty of care with respect to her husband's reputation than he does himself. These pearls of wisdom, which could have been cribbed from the numerous didactic texts for women that abounded at the time, serve Dhawiyyah well. Although Haris Fadhilah abandons her on their wedding night, Dhawiyyah conceals this from her family and his. He always happens to have just stepped out the door when relatives come to call, or so she tells them. She is patient, resigned to her fate, crafty only in concealing her husband's misdeeds. At the critical moment in the *syair*, when he has returned, unwashed and clad in rags, she welcomes him into her home:

Hatinya malu ditahankan	Her shamed heart she steadied
Sebab pahalanya dikehendakkan	Because she wished for blessings;
Ilmu bakti yang dikerjakan	The lore of devotion she carried out,
Jalan khairat yang digemarkan[24]	The way of glory she admired.

The admiration of her in-laws and the repentance of her husband are sweet, no doubt, but Dhawiyyah's ultimate aim is other-worldly: religious merit acquired through acts of devotion, a foot on the path of spiritual glory. The proper use of *akal* for a woman, this text argues, is the accumulation of merit through suffering in silence.

The improper use of *akal* by women is the pursuit of wealth. According to the old man who finally provides Haris Fadhilah with some much needed enlightenment, women have two types of *akal*, "some are noble, some are base".[25] Base *akal* is represented by the four concubines, and its aim is not so much the gratification of lust but of greed for material possessions: "if a woman is very intelligent / she likes only our wealth".[26] The quartet of infamous Sitis makes a speciality of leading men on and rejecting them once they have got what they are after:

Banyaklah rosak orang muda-muda	Many youths were ruined,
Gilakan Siti keempat yang ada	Out of madness for the four Sitis,
Sudah diambil harta dan benda	[Who] took their wealth and goods,
Dia tak mahu lawan bersenda[27]	Then did not want to banter with them.

Siti Hafsah initially seduces Haris Fadhilah out of desire for his person but this quickly transforms into desire for his wealth. Accordingly, when he returns from his trading voyage and pretends to have lost all his money, she turns him out of her house. The other three women follow suit, driving home the lesson about the perfidious quality of women with base *akal*. Whereas ignoble or base *akal* for women is emphatically connected to greed and only secondarily to lust, men who lack *akal* are unable to control their sexual passions. Due to his permissive upbringing, Haris Fadhilah is "caught up in his lusts / his discernment and intelligence quite gone".[28] He is not a fool in the way that Saudagar Muda is; he would not be duped into selling 40 camels for the price of one, he simply is incapable of governing his lust, taking up with not one but all four Sitis, despite his father's threats to execute him.

Akal in *Syair Saudagar Bodoh*, however, is less freighted with religious burden and is not subdivided by gender. The acquisition of wealth and money, even through rather fast dealings, is seen as a worthy aim for men and women. Zainah concerns herself not at all with spiritual matters; on the contrary, she is most interested in her reputation and financial security. Business sense is seen as a positive attribute and one that does not go amiss in a woman. The two most intelligent characters are the heroine and her father; their intelligence consists not in distinguishing between right and wrong, but in identifying and securing their interests. Malik Hasani — "his intelligence was complete and he was brave / rendering service to Our Lord God" — does not scruple to mislead a group of merchants who buy Saudagar Muda's house.[29] The merchants, knowing of the hidden treasures and believing that these would be theirs with the house, offer him a huge sum of money. The deal is sealed with a feast, but the next day, after the departure of Malik Hasani's ship, the other merchants discover that the treasures, down to the gold floors and walls of the house, are gone.

Malik Hasani is guilty of a second piece of sharp dealing when he persuades Saudagar Muda to marry his daughter. He first describes the four sets of four ideal characteristics of women, which are, he claims, all present in his daughter. These qualities — the four short, long, white and black traits — emphasise physical beauty, which Siti Zainah certainly possesses. She also indubitably has "long" wits, one of the four "long" traits. However, under the "short" category, which exemplifies obedience and pliability, Zainah is not quite as advertised.

Pertama pendek pemandangannya	First, short is her gaze;
Serta pula pendek suaranya	And short is her voice;
Ketiga perempuan pendek langkahnya	Third, short are a woman's steps;
Keempat pendek pendengarannya[30]	Fourth, short is her hearing.

A woman with a short gaze, it may be assumed, will not have too sharp an eye for her husband's shortcomings; one with a short voice will not raise it in rancour or in airing her opinions; one with short steps will not stray far from the home; one with short hearing will not listen in on the affairs of others. Siti Zainah wastes no time in subverting all the qualities her father has given Saudagar Muda to expect, refusing to so much as look at or speak to him.

Zainah's main objection to her husband is a thoroughly practical one, that he has no idea of finances:

Meskipun kaya dengan sentosa	Though rich and at ease,
Menaruh emas kati dan laksa	With gold by the *kati* and the tens of thousands,
Jikalau akal kurang periksa	If his *akal* is not attended to,
Semuanya itu habis binasa	All of that will be destroyed.

Jikalau tulus[31] *hati yang bebal*	If he follows his doltish heart,
Harta benda jadikan timbal	Wealth and goods are in the balance.
Jikalau mati bicara akal	If *akal* and discernment die,
Wang habis badan yang tinggal[32]	Money will be spent, leaving only the body.

To Zainah's proposal that her husband be dispatched on a trading mission to learn the ways of the world, her father, Malik Hasani, responds very favourably: "his daughter's *akal* was very obvious / and he was pleased at heart".[33] Thus, Zainah's money-mindedness receives her father's full support. Moreoever, she goes to the rescue of her husband not out of wifely duty but because of her fear that her reputation will suffer. Saudagar Muda is so ashamed to have been duped by the Yemeni that he refuses to return to his in-laws: "he wished to return but hadn't the courage / afraid of being scolded by his inlaws and wife".³⁴ Quite correctly, he fears that Zainah will behave exactly as Haris Fadhilah's four concubines did and expell him from the house for the failure of his business venture. Zainah's response to this is not to reflect on her own attachment to earthly success but to lament yet again her husband's stupidity: "her husband was so incredibly foolish / that he had ruined himself".³⁵

Stupidity is of course exemplified by Saudagar Muda. Despite his some 102 marriages, sexual incontinence is not identified in the text as his particular problem. He married and divorced a hundred women in quick succession because he was uncertain whether he was carrying out his father's instructions to marry a virgin (the reader too is left somewhat bemused on this point). Although Zainah's resistance to consummating the marriage provokes some distress, far from forcing his attentions upon her, he restrains her father Malik Hasani from beating her into obedience. In *Syair Saudagar Bodoh*, true stupidity is failure in money matters: falling for the Yemeni merchant's ruse of taking the price of one camel for the price of the whole caravan. Likewise, the financial misdeeds of Saudagar Muda's penultimate wife are given more significance than her sexual infidelity. Her death sentence is effectively for theft rather than for adultery — in contrast to the fates suffered by the four Sitis of *Syair Siti Dhawiyyah*. The lack of *akal* in *Syair Saudagar Bodoh* is manifested in purely pragmatic terms, whereas in *Syair Siti Dhawiyyah*, it has strong moral overtones. These differences in the meaning of *akal* in the two *syair* bear upon how it is to be acquired and to what end.

III. The Getting and Spending of Wisdom

The first source of *akal* for the heroes and heroines of these *syair* is their parents. Zainah's ready intelligence is no doubt the result of her tutelage by her canny father Malik Hasani. However, this method seems rather prone to failure, with the other main protagonists failing to imbibe the wisdom of their *orang tua*. Dhawiyyah's father leaves it rather late to pass on his words of wisdom, instructing her on his deathbed, with the result that she is somewhat at sea. Young men in particular slip through the gaps of this pedagogical system, with both Haris Fadhilah and Saudagar Muda's lack of *akal* attributed to the over-fondness of their parents. In *Syair Saudagar Bodoh*, "the merchant loved him exceedingly / too fond of his only son", with the result that

Suatu kerja tidak mengerti	He didn't know how to do a thing
Sehingga ke duduk bersuka hati	Except enjoy himself.
Sebarang kehendak semua dituruti	Whatever he wished was done;
Jadilah akal fikiran mati[36]	So his thinking and *akal* died.

As for Haris Fadhilah, "he didn't know a thing / his only task besporting himself".[37] Fortunately, where parents fail, there are other elders on hand to provide guidance: Siti Dhawiyyah receives instruction on "the customs of having a husband" from an old woman, while Haris Fadhilah finds an elderly farmer who tutors him on "the lore of men with wives".[38] These wise old people are acting *in loco parentis*, as Haris Fadhilah aptly observes: "you, grandfather, are in my mother and father's stead / teaching this *akal*".[39]

The second major source of *akal*, for men at least, is trade. Haris Fadhilah and Saudagar Muda are despatched on trading voyages not just to learn the ways of the world but also the control of their own errant passions. As the king of Basra's ministers advise him with regard to Haris Fadhilah:

Apabila ia ke negeri orang	When he travels to a foreign land,
Dapatlah ia akal yang terang	He will obtain clear *akal*,
Akal yang bodoh dapatlah kurang	The foolish *akal* will be reduced,
Nafsu syaitani dapat dilarang[40]	Devilish lusts will be banished.

Haris Fadhilah proves to be a gifted entrepreneur: he arrives in Surat with a shipload of fragrant oils, resins and incense, which he sells to the eager local merchants and makes a several hundred per cent profit. The Surati merchants are so taken — with the attractive young trader as much as with his wares — that they do not even try to bargain down the asking price. Both Haris Fadhilah himself and the perfumes he has for sale excite their desire: "the judicious merchant spoke to all of them / all were astonished and gazed in turmoil", and "their passion was increased by the fragrances / all were astonished at his looks".[41] Unlike when his beauty attracted Siti Hafsah and he was then entrapped by her, in this instance, Haris Fadhilah is able to manipulate the desire he awakens in others to his own advantage. But his most important financial transaction is a petty one, at least in monetary terms: the purchase of four *duit* worth of *akal* from the old man, at Dhawiyyah's behest.

The miniscule amount of money involved points to the fact that in *Syair Siti Dhawiyyah*, financial profit is not an end in itself. The old woman similarly let Dhawiyyah have her *akal* at a knockdown price, and when Dhawiyyah spent thousands of dinars in the hopes of acquiring *akal*, all she got was useless and potentially harmful *guna* and *hikmat*. While this suggests that the *akal* the two young people seek is in fact common sense — ubiquitous and therefore cheap — it also serves to remove these transactions from marketplace considerations of profit and loss. The asceticism of these wise old people points to rewards in the world to come. Their liminality, dwelling as they do on the fringes of human society, scorning worldly comforts and profit, calls to mind the jungle-dwelling ascetics of earlier literature — the oldest sister of the Daha kingdom in Panji tales, for instance, who never marries but accumulates great spiritual power — to whom the hero turns for esoteric knowledge. Thus, while trade and financial profit are important in *Syair Siti Dhawiyyah*, the heroine, and under her influence, the hero, have their eyes trained on greater prizes, and their feet on the "jalan khairat" or "the road of glory".

Not so in *Syair Saudagar Bodoh*, where, in any case, the trading mission fails to edify Saudagar Muda. Zainah's sole considerations, wealth and reputation, are unashamedly part of the transient *alam fana*. Her plan to educate her husband, so that "he will understand profit and loss", spectacularly backfires, with Saudagar Muda reduced to carrying fodder for horses and being beaten like a slave.[42] Perhaps the only edification gained from this débacle comes to Zainah herself, when she realises her husband's true limitations: "the Young Khatib [i.e., Zainah] thought to herself / my husband seems extremely foolish".[43] Despite his failure, Zainah reconciles herself to him and they live as a married couple at last. Thus, neither the advice of his father and the avuncular Malik Hasani nor experience of trade has any effect on Saudagar Muda's *akal* — a comic commentary on the traditional pedagogical methods presented in *Syair Siti Dhawiyyah*. *Syair Saudagar Bodoh* presents no avenues for improving the *akal* one was born with.

In these *syair*, women play a prominent role in brokering men's quest for *akal*. Women are the means through which men acquire or lose it. The acquisition of a wife is synonymous with obtaining *akal*: "my son ought to be given a wife / so that he may obtain noble *akal*" in *Syair Siti Dhawiyyah*, and "the custom of men with perfect *akal* / is to search for an intelligent woman", in *Syair Saudagar Bodoh*.[44] Such predictions come good at least in the case of Dhawiyyah and Haris Fadhilah, but the influence of women on men's *akal* is also considerable in its negative capacity. Haris Fadhilah lost his *akal* in the first place at the hands of Hafsah and her spells. As the text observes sagely:

Adat laki-laki sahaja begitu	Men's custom is always such:
Terkena hikmat menjadi mutu	Spell-struck they become melancholy,
Akal dan budi tiada bertentu	*Akal* and intelligence are disorded,
Tiadalah ingat barang suatu[45]	They don't remember a thing.

Men are consistently depicted as the victims of women's practice of dubious *ilmu* — a development of the idea that men are the victims of their uncontrollable passions, which are incited by women. As pejorative as this description is, the emphasis placed on women's agency is worthy of note.

The two *syair* propose divergent purposes of *akal*, with *Syair Siti Dhawiyyah* focused on spiritual reward in the *dunia akhirat* and *Syair Saudagar Bodoh* looking no further than the here and now. Haris Fadhilah's father's greatest concern is that his son is transgressing religious law by committing adultery, *zina*. The king is on the point of ordering his son's execution, lest it appear that he is an unjust ruler who punishes the lowly but lets his son get away with the same crimes. As the king declares,

Di dalam kitab sudah terjanji	In the Book it has been promised,
Hukum syarak sangat terpuji	Religious law most praised:
Meski pun anak memasuk keji	Though one's own child incur censure,
Hukumkan dahulu supaya cuci[46]	Sentence [him] so that [sin] may be wiped away.

In *Syair Saudagar Bodoh*, though, the law is commercial above all. Although Saudagar Muda's adulterous wife is tortured to death at the king's command, it is for the charge of theft rather than for her sexual immorality. The other brushes with the law also have to do with business transactions: the qadi's ruling which upheld the Yemeni merchant's claim to Saudagar Muda's 40 camels, and the counter-ruling by the young *khatib* which restored the camels to Saudagar Muda. It is telling that the law is adduced with very different emphasis in the two texts: in *Syair Siti Dhawiyyah*, the king's main concern appears to be policing sexual immorality whereas in *Syair Saudagar Bodoh*, the regulation of commercial transactions is uppermost. Here, again, the relatively secular outlook of *Syair Saudagar Bodoh*, where *akal* is purely pragmatic, contrasts with the thoroughly religious one of *Syair Siti Dhawiyyah*, where *akal* must be used for a moral purpose.

IV. Guides for Wives

Both *syair* end on the same note of marital concord achieved at last. But while Dhawiyyah acts within the boundaries of proper feminine behaviour proscribed in the many didactic texts for women of the time, Zainah flouts them. She does exactly what Raja Ali Haji in *Syair Siti Sianah* identifies as signs of *derhaka* or treason in a wife: turning her face away, speaking harshly, refusing conjugal relations and leaving the house without his permission.[47] It bears reiterating that Zainah is not the female villain of the piece. That lot falls to Saudagar Muda's nameless penultimate wife, the prime example in the text of *akal yang leta* ("ignoble *akal*") who meets a suitably sticky end. Nor is Zainah a comical figure; the butt of the text's joke is ever the unfortunate Saudagar Muda. An indulged daughter revered (and feared) by her husband, she disobeys male authority and yet is not chastised — all the more surprising in a literature where the wicked are punished and the good are rewarded with a heavy hand.

Despite the differences between the two *syair* in their depictions of the attitude of the wife towards her *akal*-deficient husband, there are significant similarities that assert the rights of the married woman. Both Dhawiyyah and Zainah remain in their own homes, which although was the practice in probably the majority of Malay marriages, was not the rule among the aristocracy, to say nothing of how irregular uxorilocality is in the Middle Eastern lands where the *syair* are set. In the other Riau romantic adventure *syair*, there is a tear-stained scene in which the heroine bids farewell to her native home and sets off for her husband's kingdom. Dhawiyyah's sole condition for marrying Haris Fadhilah is that she be permitted to remain in her own home. Thus, while appearing to be the model of pliability and meekness, deferring humbly to her relations' wishes regarding the choice of marriage partner, she defends the most important ground for securing her agency. Were she not in her own home, able to call upon her devoted servants and draw upon her considerable fortune, Dhawiyyah would never have been able to carry off the feat of dissimulation that hides her husband's bad behaviour from her relatives and in-laws. In effect, her financial independence is a prerequisite for her selfless *bakti* to her husband. Unlike all the other heroines, Dhawiyyah never leaves her home and despite that she is able to make her will felt in the world. Zainah too remains in her own home after her marriage, moving only to a new house built by her father where she is still indisputably on her own turf. Saudagar Muda is very much the interloper, the cucumber among durians, as one 19th-century Negeri Sembilan saying describes the man among his wife's family.[48]

In other romantic *syair*, there are inevitably other wives against whom the heroine struggles to assert her primacy. Some of the heroines even assist their husbands in acquiring further wives, to his — and consequently to her own — greater glory and prestige. However, even these heroines view polygamy with distress, and accept it only by asserting their superior standing in the hero's affections or in the state hierarchy. The four Sitis who enthrall Haris Fadhilah call to mind the four wives permissible to him under Islamic law; their destruction at the end of the *syair* removes all rivals to Dhawiyyah. Saudagar Bodoh marries and divorces 101 times before settling down with Zainah. Given her dominance in their relationship, it would seem unlikely that he would have the temerity to take another wife. Different as they are in temperament, both heroines assert themselves as the hero's sole wife. In *Syair Siti Zubaidah* and *Syair Sultan Abdul Muluk*, in contrast, the heroine's great deeds result in her becoming the recognised queen, first among equals but not the only wife. Encik Wan Upik, a character in Raja Ali Haji's *Syair Siti Sianah*, argues that the wise man has only one wife and that polygamy should only be the prerogative of aristocracy.[49] Needless to say, Encik Wan Upik's opinion is argued down by the text's heroine and moral authority, Siti Sianah. In this didactic text intended to enforce social norms, Encik Wan Upik's views are derided by the other women as arrogant and even impious. Perhaps these polemics in *Syair Siti Sianah*, and the various depictions of wifehood and co-wifehood in the romantic *syair*, are traces of a dispute on this subject in Malay society of the time.

As we have seen, fictional literature was disapproved of on the grounds that it spread lies, and potentially dangerous ones at that.[50] The wise reader chooses what is beneficial from the text and discards what is harmful. Returning to Safirin bin Usman Fadli's likening of the text to a garden and the wise reader to someone entering that garden, taking the beneficial flowers and fruit while discarding those which induce intoxication and forgetfulness, it is easy to see how such an approach could be taken to reading *Syair Siti Dhawiyyah*.[51] Indeed, that text seems to enact this very scene, when Siti Dhawiyyah goes to the pleasure garden with her companions, finds there the true *akal* she has been looking for and definitively discards false and dangerous *ilmu*. At the same time, *Syair Saudagar Bodoh* cannot be shelved with the heady romantic fantasies governed by *nafsu* which seem to be the theoreticians' implied targets, such as *Hikayat Koris Mengindera* and *Hikayat Indraputra*, since this text partakes of and is structured by the discourse of *akal*. In his preface to *Hikayat Anak Pengajian*, Safirin explains that its intention is to "be profitable for all those who possess *akal* and to cast blame on those who are foolish".[52] *Syair Saudagar Bodoh* likewise recounts how profit accrues to those who possess *akal*, at the expense of those who are *bodoh*. It is not a text of forgetfulness but of pragmatism, a work concerned not with soothing the troubled soul but with maintaining a healthy balance sheet. *Syair Saudagar Bodoh* argues against the prevailing gender ideology — under which, as *Syair Siti Sianah* claims, most women are ignorant because they do not resist their passions — in its depiction of the triumph of an *akal*-endowed woman:

Itulah kebanyakan ramai perempuan	That is the case with most women:
Hawa nafsu tiada dilawan	Lusts and passions are unopposed,
Jadilah tidak dapat pengetahuan.[53]	Thus they do not gain knowledge.

As such, the text may not be a fruit that induces intoxication and dreams, but more dangerously, one that reflects an alternative construction of reality, a set of values declaring the worth of women's *akal*. But as a humorous text, can *Syair Saudagar Bodoh* possibly be weighed on the same scales as the didactic *Syair Siti Dhawiyyah*?

The relationship between humour and didacticism in *Syair Siti Dhawiyyah* and *Syair Saudagar Bodoh* demands attention. Despite its didactic burden, *Syair Siti Dhawiyyah* is not devoid of humorous episodes; likewise, *Syair Saudagar Bodoh*'s gleeful inversion of the proper relations between husband and wife does not preclude a certain serious intent. Do humourous or parodic episodes, in which the accepted order of society is turned on its head, simply reinforce that very social order either by acting as a safety valve or by arguing from the negative example? Studies of humour in Malay culture have suggested an affirmative answer, with the result that Haris Fadhilah's risible request to purchase *akal* serves merely to make the text, and therefore its didactic message, more palatable. Following this argument, the absurd conduct of Saudagar Muda is simply an entertaining demonstration of how not to behave.

Didacticism has been granted a position near the apex of the hierarchy of traditional Malay literature, just beneath the texts of spiritual benefit and the sacred books. In this view, good literature provides *faedah*: benefit or profit. Laughter has no place in literature except as a means of obtaining that benefit, and episodes in which the accepted social order is overturned are instances of negative didacticism. Hang Jebat's rebellion is a prime example, but the follies of Pak Pandir, Pak Kadok, Lebai Malang and company are likewise included, as Braginsky writes: "sometimes directly and sometimes *ab adversum*, by means of the 'humorous inversion' of established norms of behaviour, these stories all the more emphatically affirmed the truth of the norms and moral values they seemed to reject and the dignity of the intellect overcoming all obstacles".[54] In this case, Saudagar Muda's bumbling exploits ultimately reaffirm the superiority of the husband within marriage, and even humorous traditional Malay literature supports what Bakhtin, in his study of the grotesque in Rabelais, termed "the official culture of the ruling classes".[55]

In the context of traditional Malay literature, official culture was epitomised by texts which upheld the primacy of the feudal state, of which *Hikayat Hang Tuah* is a notable example. Here, overturning the accepted relationship between feudal lord and subject is most often read as a negative example, a cautionary didactic message.[56] However, such court-centred texts are distinct from folk culture, which owes allegiance to no authority. Perhaps the images of Malay folk culture, no less than those of Renaissance France which informed Rabelais' work, "have a certain undestroyable unofficial nature ... opposed to all that is finished and polished, to all pomposity, to every ready-made solution in the sphere of thought and world-outlook".[57] It cannot be that the function of the grotesque stupidity of the folk character Pak Pandir, for instance, is to demonstrate, as one scholar has argued, "that people should possess at least a simple ability to think and a minimum knowledge of the skills needed to survive in daily life".[58] To insist on the same kind of didacticism in both official and folk culture is to equate chalk with cheese. While there may certainly be readers who need persuading that loyalty is due to an unjust ruler, there are surely none who need to be instructed that the baby should not be bathed in boiling water. (Or to put it another way, if there were people in need of such instruction, folktales would be unlikely to assist their education.) Folk humour is not simply a palliative for the grimness of life or a pedagogical tool for the particularly dim, but also carriers of subversive messages. The wives of folk culture are somewhat more astute than their doltish husbands, on whose heads they rain curses and blows — a far cry indeed from the deferential Siti Dhawiyyah and from the standards of female behaviour promulgated in texts like *Hikayat Nabi Mengajar Anaknya Fatimah*, but not so distant from the self-willed Siti

Zainah. Malay court culture, although ideologically distinct from village culture, was by no means sealed off from it; the boundary between the two was permeable, with slaves and and people of rural origins coming to serve within the palace, no doubt bringing their stories with them. As a *syair* recited for amusement rather than edification, *Syair Saudagar Bodoh* may draw upon oral tradition and village values.

Travesty plays a role not just between these texts — with *Syair Saudagar Bodoh* a non-official, parodic version of *Syair Siti Dhawiyyah* — but within them. In both, women usurp masculine positions of intelligence and authority: in order of transgressiveness, the saint (*keramat*), the doctor (*tabib*) and the preacher (*khatib*). The saint is, of course, Dhawiyyah, while the doctor is Hafsah, and the preacher is Zainah in disguise. In every case, travesty reverses the expected social order with humorous effect. Being a respectable woman, Dhawiyyah does not do anything so outré as dress in men's clothes. Her *keramat* powers manifest themselves *in absentia*, when Haris Fadhilah's ship is prevented by wind and waves from leaving Surat. His companions believe this is because he has neglected to fulfill the request (*pesan*) of a spiritually powerful person: "who knows who it was who made the request / a learned person it would seem".[59] Dhawiyyah held the ship and the lives of its passengers in her hands: "we all were on the verge of death / for forgetting the request of a holy woman".[60] These *keramat* powers are confirmed once again when the only person willing to sell *akal* to Haris Fadhilah asks for four *duit*, precisely the amount she had given her husband. The strength of Dhawiyyah's injunction comes from the strength, indeed invulnerability, of her prayers: "truly infallible are her prayers / to Allah the One".[61] Up to that moment Dhawiyyah has demonstrated exemplary control over her passions but has appeared neglected and sidelined, powerless to effect a change in her husband's behaviour and unable to claim the rights due to her as his wife. This is, therefore, a demonstration that through faith and self-control — through complete quietism, in other words — a woman may achieve spiritual potency.[62] In so far as the spiritually potent individual is usually a man, Dhawiyyah is reversing the gender status quo, but in the most unthreatening manner possible, and certainly without outraging her modesty by putting on a turban or travelling to a distant land.

Her antithesis in the text similarly eschews a change of attire when she assumes a man's role. Hafsah does not herself claim to be a *tabib* or doctor; she is so called in jest by Haris Fadhilah's mother, who sees straight through her son's claims to have been ill and under a doctor's prohibition (*pantang*) not to look at the sun, the moon or people. His symptoms, dizziness and turbulent emotions ("a dizzy head and troubled heart"),[63] are rather more reminiscent of lovesickness than disease, and his mother hits the mark when she remarks that Haris Fadhilah must have been receiving treatment from a woman doctor:

Tabib perempuan keras pantangnya	A woman doctor's prohibitions are severe,
Penyakit besar diubatkannya	Great ailments are treated by her.
Banyaklah hadiah gerangan diberinya	He gave her many gifts, it seems,
Sudahlah baik segala penyakitnya	For now his ailment is cured.
Puteraku itu berkat sungguh	My son is truly fortunate:
Tabib perempuan segera sembuh	A woman doctor healed him quickly.
Meski sedikit ubat dibubuh	Though only a little medicine was applied,
Dengan seketika sihatlah tubuh[64]	At once his health is restored.

Haris Fadhilah's lust is figured as the disease of which the female doctor cures him, naturally without much recourse to medicine and in exchange for handsome gifts. With her knowledge of *guna* and *hikmat*, Hafsah could well be considered a *tabib*, except that her expertise is not in healing but in harming. The two terms, *tabib perempuan* and *keramat perempuan*, mirror each other: the powers of the former stemming in this case from esoteric knowledge condemned by religion, and those of the latter from personal merit accumulated according to the codes of the faith.

Hafsah, the false *tabib*, is executed, while Dhawiyyah, the true *keramat*, is exalted. Zainah, the false *khatib*, is an unqualified success, despite the fact that her impersonation of a male religious leader is by far the most transgressive of these usurpations. In her robe and turban, carrying a bundle of theological texts, she is completely convincing. Just like Dhawiyyah, Zainah is another *alim pendita*, but here, this does not mean stored-up spiritual power but the ability to study religious texts, to discourse on theological matters, and to manipulate legal arguments. Moreover, Zainah's actions are not premised on quietism, as are those of Dhawiyyah, but are actively transgressive. Sitting in the circle of theological students, Zainah has penetrated to the heart of the male establishment, where women must not be — because of the desires they evoke in otherwise righteous men as well as because of the deficiency of feminine *akal*. The terrible scene of unmasking and punishment that one might expect simply does not take place; on the contrary, Zainah demonstrates that she understands the law better than the old qadi himself does, using his own argument against him. A counterfeit *khatib*, and a woman to boot, bests the venerable qadi.

The reverse travesty, where a man is given the guise of woman, is conjured up when Dhawiyyah attributes Haris Fadhilah's failure to appear before her relatives to shyness:

Anak raja itu lain kelakuan	The prince's behaviour is unusual:
Sangat pemalu bagai perempuan	As shy as a woman,
Duduk bersembunyi di dalam peraduan	Staying hidden in the bedroom,
Malu dilihat teman dan kawan[65]	Ashamed to be seen by friends and companions.

This reversal operates to similar satirical effect, with the great debaucher of women figured as a bashful bride. All these episodes of travesty and reversal are met with laughter, whether by the characters themselves, as in the case of the queen's joke about her son's *tabib perempuan*, or by the *syair*'s audience. Laughter, as Maier has observed, is rather rare in traditional Malay literature. The stiff postures of stock heroes and heroines of romances do not make for rollicking comedy.[66] Aristocratic smiles are usually not a matter of amusement; the proverbial expression *senyum raja* conveys an unsettling sense of ambiguity and inscrutability.[67] The smiling mouth should be covered by a modest hand to hide the bestial teeth, while laughing out loud betrays an alarming lack of self-control.

Needless to say, most of the laughs in *Syair Saudagar Bodoh* are at Saudagar Muda's expense: Malik Hasani laughs when Saudagar Muda confesses that, after all his failed marriages, he is afraid of women; the Yemeni merchant laughs at the second approach of Saudaga Muda, apparently to be duped once again; Khatib Muda laughs when her husband and the Yemeni come to her for adjudication. Strikingly, though, the punchline of the entire *syair* — the revelation to Saudagar Muda that his saviour, the young *khatib*, is none other than his wife in disguise — gets no laughs from the characters in the manuscript version. Zainah breaks the news with admirable restraint:

Menyahut madah kakanda nan tuan	She answered her husband,
Seraya berkata perlahan-lahan	Speaking softly,

Khatib Muda itu membicarakan	'The young *khatib* who argued for you
Itulah hamba yang mendapatkan	Was me come to find you.'
Saudagar mendengar kata isterinya	The merchant heard his wife's words,
Disambut dipangku diciumnya	Embraced her, took her on his lap and
Kasih sangat tuan rupanya	kissed her,
Kepada dianya dimuliakannya[68]	'It seems you truly love me.'
	He paid her honour.

Their long estrangement and the succession of Saudagar Muda's misadventures come to an end in a moment of tranquility rather than hilarity, a retreat from the topsy-turvy gender relations that held sway in the rest of the *syair*. The redactor of the 1880 lithograph version evidently felt that this ending was out of keeping and prolonged the conceit, having Saudagar Muda repeatedly attempt to bring about a meeting between Khatib Muda and Zainah, with the final result that

Ditariknya hidung ditampar muka	She pulled his nose and slapped his
Bodoh apakah tidak terhingga	face:
Bini sendiri tidak disangka.[69]	'What is this incredible stupidity?
	Your own wife [and] you don't
	realise it.'

At last, when the truth is revealed, both Zainah and Saudagar Muda laugh at his stupidity, with this very laughter a sign of some kind of self-awareness on the part of Saudagar Muda.

The moment of reconciliation is also marked by laughter in *Syair Siti Dhawiyyah*. When the queen jokes that Haris Fadhilah has been receiving treatment from a *tabib perempuan*,

Tertawa besar ayahanda bonda	His mother and father laughed greatly,
Dengan puteranya dilawan bersenda	Bantering with their son.
Haris pun malu di dalam dada	Haris was ashamed,
Sekalian kelakuan diketahui ayahanda[70]	All his deeds were known by his father.

Not only does this laughter cut Haris Fadhilah down to size, it helps to save his life. The king had been ready to execute him for his adulteries, but the sight of his only child and his wife's witticism melts his bloodthirsty resolve. Laughter defuses the tensions surrounding proper behaviour. It also reverses the usual hierarchy of prince and commoner. When Haris

Fadhilah goes from village to village in Surat, his slave boy preceding him to announce his wish to buy *akal*, he is met with amazed laughter from the common people:

Setelah didengar orang segala	Once the people had heard,
Tertawa mengilai berkata pula	They shrieked with laughter and said:
Orang ini selaku gila	'This man seems mad!
Akal siapa berjual pula[71]	Who would sell *akal*?'

Far from being offended by this laughter, Haris Fadhilah smiles, and in acknowledging his own foolishness, takes the first step towards acquiring wisdom. The hilarity of the villagers calls to mind the laughter of Kemala Arifin and his wife in *Hikayat Musang Berjanggut*, both moments during which the fear that usually governs the relations between commoners and aristocrats is banished. That this moment is fleeting testifies to the undiminished authority of royalty in the milieux where both *Syair Siti Dhawiyyah* and *Hikayat Musang Berjanggut* were related. The story on which the latter is based, "The Lady and her Five Suitors" in the *Arabian Nights*, follows its Rabelaisian instincts to the end, with the carpenter, the chief of police, the wali, the qadi, the wazir and the king imprisoned in a cabinet for three days until they void their bladders on one another. They are at last released by the neighbours, who "fell a-laughing at them".[72]

But if laughter in Malay aristocratic texts like *Syair Saudagar Bodoh*, *Syair Siti Dhawiyyah* and *Hikayat Musang Berjanggut* ultimately draws back from the subversive possibilities of Rabelais or the *Arabian Nights*, this does not mean that it has no effect: the very occurrence of these instances of laughter destabilises the status quo. Though their plots restore the normative social order, *Syair Siti Dhawiyyah* and *Syair Saudagar Bodoh* are quite different in tenor from unsmiling works such as *Hikayat Nabi Muhammad Mengajar Anaknya*. When Raja Ali Haji burlesques the laws of marriage in his *Syair Suluh Pegawai*, the pious dicta governing the relationship between husband and wife in his *Syair Siti Sianah* appear in a different light. If even Raja Ali Haji, perhaps the writer of his age who most adeptly merges the values of the court with those of resurgent Islam, was not immune to the allure of other sources of culture, it is perhaps not so obligatory to take as read the hierarchical taxonomy of Malay literature as implied by its leading practitioners. As Bakhtin writes, "[w]hile analyzing past ages we are all too often obliged to 'take each epoch at its word', that is, to believe its official ideologists".[73] Applying

Bakhtin's point here, one's understanding of traditional Malay literature should not be based solely on the claims of male aristocrats in their serious mode. Court women and commoners also have something to say, and their views, necessarily different from those of the likes of Raja Ali Haji, are as compelling. *Syair Saudagar Bodoh* and still less *Syair Siti Dhawiyyah* are not texts of folk culture, but they contain echoes of a different, non-official ideology, glimmers of resistance, that undermine easy didactic certainties.

* * * * *

For every *Syair Siti Dhawiyyah*, claiming that the only way for a woman to attain heaven is through *bakti* to her husband, there is a *Syair Saudagar Bodoh*, pointing out that men have no monopoly on intelligence. This formulation of *akal* — and the depiction of the heroines as more pragmatic with regard to money and more concerned with religious obligations than their husbands — echoes recent anthropological work on gender ideologies in Malay and Javanese societies, where it is has been termed the counter-hegemonic view.[74] In her discussion of alternative Javanese ideologies of gender, under which men are perceived to be less able to control their passions, especially in matters of sex and money, than women, Brenner points out that this view is held by both men and women. She also cautions against trying to "reconcile these conflicting images of female and male nature and behaviour. All cultural systems embody such contradictions and ambiguity, and to try to resolve or ignore the contradictions gives priority to our own desire for order rather than to the realities of complex social phenomena".[75] *Syair Saudagar Bodoh*, and to a lesser extent, *Syair Siti Dhawiyyah*, represent a counter-hegemonic, marketplace perspective of women, men and *akal* that runs against the hierarchically superior ideology of the palace. But where *Syair Siti Dhawiyyah*, as a serious text in all senses of the word, depicts female rationality conquering masculine passion while remaining thoroughly conventional, *Syair Saudagar Bodoh* uses humour to vault the boundaries of approved female behaviour.

Conclusion

The Heritage of the Disguised Heroine *Syair*

This investigation of six *syair* began by sketching why these texts are of interest and how they may be read, before exploring the milieu from which they came. Two factors were constitutive in shaping women's literary production in 19th-century Penyengat, and in the survival of their texts into the present day. First, the intervention of Dutch philologists, who took an interest in the less prestigious genres of Malay literature and who noted down the manuscript owners and scribes who provided them with texts, thereby bringing romantic *syair* by women into the historical record. Once again, six of the seven attributions of female authorship in 19th-century Malay literature come from Klinkert, while the eighth comes from Von de Wall. While six of these women seem to have belonged to the Penyengat court, Encik Kamariah was from Lingga, suggesting that women in other parts of the Malay world may also have composed, copied and read texts. The proximity of Penyengat to Singapore, and indeed the move of many members of the Penyengat aristocracy to Singapore following the abolition of the Riau sultanate in 1913, probably meant that Penyengat texts made the transition to lithograph printing more rapidly than texts from other areas. This in turn helps to explain why the most frequently reissued books of the era of lithograph printing are Penyengat texts. Secondly, the characteristic form taken by these *syair* — the heroine in disguise going to the rescue of her husband, father or brother — may have arisen in response to the increasing pressures on women to retreat from the public to the domestic sphere. The changing ideas about the role of women are exemplified in the writings of Raja Ali Haji, father and brother of women *syair* authors.

The first chapter gathers the documentary evidence for women's involvement in literature — as composers, owners of manuscripts, patrons, lenders and borrowers — to suggest that literacy and reading were not confined to Penyengat, but were quite strikingly widespread. While depictions of women reading in literature are briefly examined, more conclusive are the many surviving letters by and to women, as well as the extensive evidence of women's ownership of manuscripts. Examples of women owners of manuscripts come from Bengkulu, Perak, Batavia, Kuala Terengganu, Kedah and Siak, from the 19th century into the 20th, indicating that women readers were to be found across the Malay world. In addition, Engku Puteri of Penyengat commissioned texts, in an example of female literary patronage. While Reid's claim that premodern island Southeast Asia had unusually high levels of female literacy has attracted criticism, the evidence considered in this chapter suggests that literacy in Jawi among aristocratic Malay women was not rare. Of course, these literate court women would have formed a tiny percentage of the population as a whole, but their presence is nonetheless significant. The Riau *syair* attributed to women should not be seen, as has previously been the case, as evidence of Penyengat's position in the vanguard of progress or modernity. Instead, these manuscripts may be the few known surviving testaments to what was once a thriving culture of female engagement in literature in courts and urban centres across the Malay world.

The association between the genre of the romance and women is explored in Chapter 2, as a prelude to the thematic readings that form the second part of this book. The chapter delineates the romantic *syair* as a form of popular romance, sharing features with popular romances from other literary traditions. The dominant Malay literary discourse of the 19th century figured romance as a vice particular to those of impaired rationality, and was therefore thought to be especially appealing to women. Recitation of *syair* and *hikayat* were believed to have the power to unleash listeners' latent emotions — for good or ill, depending upon the orientation of the commentator. The disguised heroine *syair* are situated between Panji romance on the one hand, and didactic literature for women on the other. The dangers of literature to the reader of impaired rationality, and its cathartic powers, are also discussed here.

Chapter 3 begins the analysis of the texts themselves in detail, with a consideration of the tension between emotions and the necessity of their repression in *Syair Siti Zuhrah* and *Syair Sultan Yahya*. The copyist or redactor of these two *syair* may well be the same person, as the introductory verses share certain idiosyncracies and the two texts as a whole have a common tenor of ever-present *rawan*, or psychic distress. Here the heroine is the still centre in a whirlwind of emotional upheaval, the character who most successfully puts into practice the doctrine of emotional repression considered so essential to aristocratic women, and yet the source of much of the turmoil suffered by the other characters. Supporting characters voice the anger or distress that the heroine represses, while the hero is filled with a destabilising ardour for her, even (or especially) in her guise as a man. While these *syair* include *pantun* and episodes in which the beauty of nature is evoked, familiar features from earlier Malay romance, on the whole the erotic mood is rather dampened. In their relentless evocation of psychic distress, or *rawan*, these *syair* demonstrate the unresolvable tension between emotional repression and catharsis.

The best known examples of the heroine-in-disguise genre, *Syair Sultan Abdul Muluk* and *Syair Siti Zubaidah*, are discussed in Chapter 4. Here, the theme of a woman's *bakti*, or devoted service, comes to the fore, although not in the way that *bakti* was interpreted in the didactic texts for women so amply represented in 19th-century Malay literature. Instead of passive endurance, submitting to suffering and hardship while remaining steadfastly loyal to her husband, this heroine refuses the female role: changing her dress, abandoning her child, taking up arms and excelling in the male domain of battle and violence. The doctrine of *tawakal*, or submitting oneself to God, is invoked as a means of legitimising the heroine's radical actions. At the same time, the hero is feminised: captured and incarcerated, he can merely endure his torments and await rescue by his wife. This reversal of gender roles is most comprehensive in *Syair Siti Zubaidah*, where even the antagonists are women, and men are reduced to minor characters. The "war in bedroom" trope, which depicts the heroine as the defeated victim of the hero's amorous assault, is here turned on its head. However, despite this subversive interlude, once she has restored order, the heroine prostrates herself before her husband, returns to her feminine role and restricts her campaigns to the *dalam*. These *syair* demonstrate how popular romance opens up a space in which the dominant gender order is challenged, only to retreat from those possibilities into a pat and conventional ending.

In the final chapter, the arena is not the battlefield but the marketplace, and the heroines demonstrate their superiority over their husbands not in military strategy but in the calculation of profit and loss. The fate from which the wives rescue their husbands is moral bankruptcy in *Syair Siti Dhawiyyah*, and financial bankruptcy in *Syair Saudagar Bodoh*. In *Syair Siti Dhawiyyah*, the only didactic *syair* considered among the six core texts, this calculation is of religious merit rather than simply money, as it is the case in *Syair Saudagar Bodoh*. Indeed, the latter *syair* seems to be responding to, and poking fun at, the didacticism of the former. However, both *syair* overturn the usual distribution of *akal* and *nafsu*, reason and passion, between the genders. Rather than assigning *akal* to men and *nafsu* to women, as more authoritative texts do, here and throughout the disguised heroine *syair*, women are eminently reasonable, while men are prey to passion. This presentation of what Peletz terms the counter-hegemonic view of gender[1] underscores the fact that the culture that produced these texts was not univocal on the subject. Even the ultimately conservative endings of these *syair*, and the consistently conservative didactic message of *Syair Siti Dhawiyyah* in particular, do not belie the importance of female agency and rationality in their pages.

Inscription of verses from Raja Ali Haji's "Gurindam Dua Belas", Penyengat, 2004

But what became of this most popular of 19th-century genres in the 20th? Early Malay novels, such as Marah Roesli's *Sitti Noerbaya* (1922), Merari Siregar's *'Azab dan Sengsara* (1920), and Syeikh Hadi's *Hikayat Faridah Hanum* (1925), included *syair* and *pantun* verses, and narrative *syair* themselves remained popular into the 1920s.[2] Early Indonesian novels in particular seem to have retained some of the romantic *syair*'s interest in the central female protagonist, perhaps indicating that female readership was also a feature of modern literary forms. Examples include *Sitti Noerbaya*, Haji Mukti's *Hikayat Siti Mariah* and the Batak language novel *Sitti Djaoerah* by M.J. Soetan Hasoendoetan.[3] However, by and large, modern Malay literature has disowned its past. Ungku Maimunah Mohd Tahir shows that the literary scene in British Malaya was the product of the graduates of Sultan Idris Training College, who saw themselves as quite distinct from and indeed opposed to the scions of the aristocracy who received an English-language education at the Malay College Kuala Kangsar. Thus, the practice of Malay literature passed from the aristocracy to a rising class of schoolteachers, journalists, policemen and others who aligned themselves with the rural and working classes.[4] The diverging strands of Malay literature are perhaps exemplified by the fact that when Tengku Ampuan Mariam made her own manuscript copy of *Hikayat Shamsul Anwar* in Kuala Terengganu in 1947, Ishak Haji Mohamad had published his novels, *Putra Gunung Tahan* (1938) and *Anak Mat Lela Gila* (1941). In these novels, it is clear that the author has achieved a critical distance from the traditional styles and motifs that he strategically deploys.[5] Ishak's affection for traditional literature and his willingness to experiment with its forms in his own work were unusual; most of the new breed of Malay writers turned their backs on the courtly heritage. In Ungku Maimunah's words, Za'aba's 1926 definition of the short story "perhaps best demonstrates the ground rules which governed literary writings of the time". As he wrote in *Majalah Guru*: "Stories which can serve as lessons, examples, models and the like. Not fairy tales or fantasies which are unacceptable to the minds of the people in this age".[6] And yet, despite Za'aba's association of the fantastic or fictional with the archaic, his position is not much different from that of Safirin bin Usman Fadli or Abdullah Munshi in the previous century. Literature for the sake of pleasure remains unacceptable: it must have a higher purpose, impart moral lessons and *faedah*. The growth of the market in popular fiction — and pornographic novels in particular — in the 1960s only entrenched the moralists' occupation of the high ground.[7] Moreover, the literary avant-garde was just as male-dominated as the high prestige genres of traditional Malay literature. Of the 95 members of Angkatan Sasterawan '50, better known as ASAS 50, the organisation that went on to set the literary agenda for independent Malaya, there was but a single woman.[8] The number of Malay women writers in the first half of the 20th century seems to have been even fewer than that of Malay court women who composed *syair*. Zaini-Lajoubert names as pioneers Hamidah, Selasih, Saadah Alim, Hajjah Zainon Sulaiman (Ibu Zain), Hafsah and Rafiah Yusof.[9]

If romantic *syair* and *hikayat* have no place in modern Malaysia, there is one Riau writer who yet enjoys a privileged place. Raja Ali Haji and the Riau heritage are frequently invoked by members of the political elite in Malaysia as a way of defining Malay identity. In 1984, the then Deputy Prime Minister, Musa Hitam, provoked a rift with the Yang Dipertuan Agung when he publicly quoted Raja Ali Haji to the effect that "the king should not delay government legislation".[10] More recently, in a speech reiterating the constant refrain of Malaysian government ministers and Dewan Bahasa dan Pustaka, the state agency for the promotion of Malay language and literature, that any day now there will be a Malay winner of the Nobel Prize for Literature, current Malaysian Prime Minister Najib Tun Razak quoted from Raja Ali Haji's "Gurindam Dua Belas".[11] This is indeed the best known work of Raja Ali Haji's *oeuvre*, though it is the slightest: anodyne couplets extolling the virtues of refined speech, polite behaviour, and finding a submissive wife. The popularity of Raja Ali Haji — conservative, elite, *syariah*-minded — in modern Malaysia comes as no surprise. The situation in Indonesia, where "Melayu" is one ethnic identity among many, and not a very significant one at that, is of course quite different. Modern political alignments mean that Malaysia — rather than Indonesia, and still less Singapore — is the keenest to lay hold of the Riau legacy.

But while serious and prestigious literature largely abandoned the forms and themes of "traditional" *syair* and *hikayat*, these continued to flourish in Malay popular culture up to the 1960s. The 20th-century analogues to the romantic *syair* are after all not novels or modern poetry — read by a tiny segment of society and ever preoccupied by the necessity of improving their readers — but mass cultural forms such as *bangsawan* theatre and the cinema, shaped for the tastes and pleasures of the audience. Romantic *syair* were used as source material for the *bangsawan* plays that were all the rage from the early 1900s to the 30s and 40s, and in which *syair* verses were sung.[12] When the new medium of cinema began to take over both *bangsawan* audiences and actors, it also took on *bangsawan* plots. A 1953 survey showed that cinema-going was the "primary leisure activity" in Malaya: 20% of the residents of a particular area of Singapore went to the cinema once or twice per week, and 50% at least once or twice per month.[13] Films of romantic *syair* include *Selindung Delima* (1958), *Dandan Setia* (1959), *Siti Zubaidah* (1961) and *Bidasari* (1965). The only film based on a prose romance was *Panji Semerang* (1961), although there were several treatments of the Hang Tuah story.[14] The *syair* plots have, of course, undergone some changes in their filmed manifestations: Hicks has shown that the Maria Menado film version of *Selindung Delima* depicts the heroine as a passive object of the male gaze in contrast to her more active portrayal in the *syair*.[15] Modernity, after all, does not necessarily imply progress towards gender equality.

The status of the romantic *syair* and traditional literature in general by the latter half of the 20th century is elucidated in Adibah Amin's 1968 novel, *Seroja Masih di Kolam*. The novel relates the re-education of the heroine, Diana, away from her false Western consciousness and back to her authentic Malay identity. Comfortable behind the wheel of a car or in a swimsuit — sure signs of deracination in the novel — the English-language educated Diana has failed the Malay examination that is required for her to enter university. Her cousin and tutor Ridhwan gives her a number of "classical" texts to study: *Hikayat Raja Muda*, *Sejarah Melayu*, *Hikayat Seri Rama*, "as well as *syair* like Siti Zabidah, Panji Semerang and the like".[16] Here various distinct types of literature — royal chronicle, prose and verse romances — from a variety of periods and contexts are thrown together, their differences obviated by the fact that they are all set texts for the examination and, amounting to the same thing, all signifiers of Malayness. The achievement of Malay identity quite literally requires passing a test. For *Syair Siti Zubaidah* and *Syair Panji Semirang* to enter the canon and rub shoulders with the likes of *Sejarah Melayu* would probably have surprised the readers of the 19th century. Though Diana comes to find that "slowly the words, sentence structures and old phrases became agreeable to her, and she felt how sweet it was to repeat them",[17] the reason for the appearance of these works in the novel is pedagogical rather than pleasurable. Reading *Syair Siti Zubaidah* has become a test of identity rather than the enjoyable, addictive experience that brought delicious tears to the eyes of its listeners and reciters. Indeed, the "traditional" texts remain in print only through the state publishing house, Dewan Bahasa dan Pustaka, and are read chiefly as set texts in the secondary school leaving examination in Bahasa Malaysia.

The more likely descendants of the romantic *syair* are the popular Malay romance novels with such impressive sales figures that they have been ceded shelf space in Kuala Lumpur's premier bookshops, usually dominated by English-language books, and been given column inches in English-language newspapers. In five years, Alaf 21, the leading publisher of Malay romance novels, sold half a million copies of seven titles on its list. In stark contrast to the Malay literary establishment, the leading authors of popular literature are all women: Sharifah Abu Salem (*Tak Seindah Mimpi*, 70,000 copies; *Pesona Rindu*, 70,000), Damya Hanna (*Bicara Hati*, 100,000; *Sepi Tanpa Cinta*, 70,000), Aisya Sofea (*Kau Untukku*, 80,000; *Sehangat Asmara*, 70,000), and Nia Azalea (*Kau Yang Satu*, 75,000).[18] These are sales figures unheard of in the world of literary publishing (even Shahnon Ahmad's 1999 satire guaranteed huge sales by the author's eminence and its scatalogical treatment of the then Prime Minister, had a first print run of a mere 15,000 copies).[19] Such is the phenomenon of these novels that the literary establishment was unable to ignore them. In the words of an article in the Malay daily *Utusan Malaysia*: "These works can sell in the hundreds of thousands and their writers can become wealthy. This is in contrast to serious literary works published by DBP itself which do not make a profit and are not enjoyed, unless they are chosen as text books".[20] The article revealed that DBP was holding a special workshop on the Malaysian popular novel, entitled "Between Commercialism and Intellectualism". According to another report in the Malay media,

> The workshop proved that popular works contain literary values that can be taken up and, if they are honed and buffed, the talents of their writers may be able to give rise to serious literary works with intellectual characteristics. Their work is not just about love but is full of information that can increase the reader's knowledge, though there are some writers who write purely in order to make money, giving no thought to literary values.[21]

Once again, Malay popular fiction is damned with faint praise: it is good if it confers information or moral benefit, and it is bad if it is entertaining, or only about love, or too commercially successful. In Indonesia, there has been a similar explosion of popular novels written by women, most notably Ayu Utami, Dewi Lestari and Nova Riyanti Yusuf. As some of these novelists have observed, the label applied to their work — *sastera wangi*, or fragrant literature — is derogatory, a back-handed compliment to the writers' looks at the expense of their ability.[22] These women novelists' popular success is, predictably enough, taken by the literary old guard as evidence of their superficiality. As Pramoedya Ananta Toer is supposed to have said, "All they write about is themselves and sex".[23] While the Malaysian novels are likely to be more aesthetically conventional and politically conservative than the Indonesian ones, both groups point to a huge female audience avidly consuming fictions of emotion and desire that are frowned upon by the establishment. The connection with the romantic *syair* is plain to see.

If the popular culture of the present is of interest as a countervailing voice that at times chimes with official rhetoric and at other times defies it, expressing simultaneously the utopian fantasies of its admirers and the norms enforced by the peculiar synthesis of capitalism and feudalism that obtains in Malaysia, then much the same is true of the popular culture of the past. There is, in addition, the fact that while contemporary popular culture is ubiquitous, that of even a decade ago, let alone a century or more, seems to have vanished and left no trace. By its very nature — closely attuned to the interests of its audience, readily consumable — popular culture is ephemeral. According to the hierarchies of aesthetic and moral values that obtained both in its time and still obtain in the present, it ranks low. But for precisely these reasons, 19th-century Malay popular literature is a legitimate and indeed necessary subject of study, lest the only voices of the past be official ones, in Bakhtin's sense — those of male Malay aristocrats and religious leaders. The absorption of works of popular literature like *Syair Sultan Abdul Muluk* and *Syair Siti Zubaidah* into the canon — demonstrated by the attribution of the former to Raja Ali Haji and the two recent editions of the latter by major Malaysian cultural institutions, as much as by Adibah Amin's telling reading list — is a misleading anachronism. This is not, of course, to assert that the perspectives contained in works such as the romantic *syair* are to be espoused in the present day, which would be to commit precisely the same error as those who present canonical texts as worthy of study because of the moral or didactic lessons they impart to today's readers. Just as there is no reason for the modern Malaysian woman to tailor her behaviour according to the views of Nur al-Din al-Raniri,[24] there is equally no reason for her to take Siti Zubaidah, say, as a role model. While the search for foremothers and pioneers — for heroines, in fact — was a defining feature of the early feminist movement, it now appears naive. The point is not to seek out role models but to try to discover the past as it was, which is inevitably to challenge received ideas.

In the case of traditional Malay literature, these received ideas amount to an ideology formulated by Malaysian state institutions for their own ends. For even though the literary heritage of the past appears marginal to modern life, it is highly politically charged, especially as regards the question of the identity of its heirs and the basis for their claim. As Judith Nagata writes with regard to "heritage" architecture in Penang,

> [o]n the surface, 'heritage' is a benign, non-threatening concept, generally having positive associations with conservation and preservation, usually of (the more impressive and older) examples of the built environment, but also of arts and crafts and other items of material culture. It conveys a comforting sense of continuity between past and present, an iconic representation of ancestry in a pleasing visual and tangible form. In many societies today, heritage is groomed and sponsored by the establishment, as one form of cultural hegemony, to enhance its own credibility and venerable historical credentials, in what Handler calls 'a nationalist objectification of culture.'[25]

The Malay literary heritage, as it is constructed by Dewan Bahasa dan Pustaka and by the national curriculum, has certainly been subjected to just such a "nationalist objectification". Moreover, it is nationalist more in the sense of *bangsa*, race, than *kebangsaan*, nationality. Matheson Hooker calls the focus on the Malay rather than the Malaysian — to say nothing of the human — condition in Malay novels "ethno-nationalism", as distinct from nationalism.[26] Despite repeated pleas for Dewan Bahasa to publish writing in other Malaysian languages, this remains most unlikely.[27] That the heritage is constructed by the institutions of the supposedly multiethnic state as the product or the possession of one ethnicity alone guarantees that it will be regarded with either suspicion or disinterest by many Malaysians. Traditional Malay literature is in danger of becoming a series of faux leatherbound facsimiles exalting the achievements of the Malay race — a symptom of what has been called "traditionalism: the manipulation, invention, and recombination of cultural patterns, symbols, and motifs so as to legitimate contemporary social realities by imbuing them with a patina of venerable historicity".[28] Of the *Karya Agung* or *Great Works* book series launched in Kuala Lumpur in 1996, Proudfoot observes that the "extravagantly produced volumes are destined for the display cases — perhaps more often than the bookshelves — of the rising Malay middle class who are industriously engaged in manufacturing a sanitized national past".[29] Archaic symbols of Malay identity are, as in the case of the then head of UMNO Youth, Hishamuddin Hussein, brandishing a *keris* at the 2005 Annual General Meeting of the party, quite literally used to threaten those who dare to challenge Malay hegemony. The Malay past has become, depending on the task at hand, either a bucolic if backward rural idyll or a glorious time in which everyone knew their place and kept to it.[30] In the usual formulation of Malaysian history, the Malay polities succumbed to the devious machinations of European imperialists; there was a Malay race that understood its identity in just the same way as it does now; the "other" races are latecomers, without long roots in the archipelago, and they are lucky to be tolerated; women were pious, modest, veiled, illiterate, and confined to the kitchen. It is a small but critical move to set against such falsifications of history what emerges from the disguised heroine *syair*: that there were women readers and writers, and that the most widely-read literary works of the 19th century were romances that showed women to be rational subjects.

Appendix I

Women Authors and Copyists

Table 1. 19th-century Malay women authors

Name	Text	Date	Place	Source
Raja Salihah bt Raja Haji Ahmad	*Syair Sultan Abdul Muluk*	Before 1847	Penyengat	Von de Wall
Daeng Wuh	*Syair Sultan Yahya*	Before 1851	Penyengat	Klinkert
Raja Kalsum bt Raja Ali Haji	*Syair Saudagar Bodoh*	1865	Penyengat	Klinkert
Encik Kamariah	*Syair Sultan Mahmud*	After 1856	Lingga	Klinkert
Raja Safiah bt Raja Ali Haji	*Syair Kumbang Mengindera*	Before 1859	Penyengat	Klinkert
Encik Tipah (or copyist?)	*Syair Sultan Marit*	No date, probably collected 1864–1867	Penyengat	Klinkert
Encik Jamilah (or copyist?)	*Syair Yatim Nestapa*	1864	Riau	Klinkert
Engku Bilik bt Raja Abdullah	*Syair Siti Zubaidah*; *Syair Yatim Nestapa* (but see En. Jamilah); *Syair Muhibbat al-Zaman*		Penyengat	Abu Hassan Sham

Table 2. 19th-century Malay women copyists and manuscript owners

Name	Title	Date	Place	Source
Anon	Misc. *syair*	1890s	Banjar	Den Hamer
Cik Soda	*Syair Dewa Syah Syarif*	Before 1963		DBP
Encik Seni	*Syair Madhi*	1860s?	Penyengat	Klinkert
Encik Zainab bt Tuan Khatib Abdul Karim al-Sambawa	*Kitab Tawhid*			PNM
Encik Lena	*Syair Selindung Delima*	1780s	Bengkulu	Marsden letters
Encik Wuk bt Tuan Bilal Abu	*Syair Sultan Mansur*	Before 1863	Penyengat	Klinkert
Hajjah Fatimah bt Tuan Haji Abdul Hamid	*Doa Kanzil 'Arasy*			PNM
Mariam bt Muhammad Amin	*Hikayat Koris Mengindera*	1910	Perak?	DBP
Nyonya Alperes Hakim	*Hikayat Amir Hamzah*	MS dated 1792	?	Iskandar
Nyonya Haji Da'ima	Misc. religious	1863	Kampung Tanah Tinggi	Iskandar
Nyonya Halimah	Misc. didactic/religious	1840s?	Batavia	Iskandar
Nyonya Rahimah	*Hikayat Pandawa Lima*	1820	Batavia?	Iskandar
Nyonya Sawang	Misc. didactic/religious	Before 1849	Batavia	Iskandar
Nyonya Tasnim	*Tarikah 'Alawiyyah*			Iskandar
Siak *selir*	*Hikayat Syah Firman* and eight others	Before 1863	Siak	Klinkert
Syarifah Hanum bt Syed Hamzah	*Syair Raja Muda Perlis*			DBP
Syarifah Mastura bt Syed Syahabudin	*Hikayat Syams al-Anwar* (fragment)			DBP
Tengku Kalthum bt Sultan Abdul Hamid	*Hikayat Syams al-Anwar* (fragment)			DBP
Tengku Zamzam	*Syair Sultan Mansur*; *Hikayat Syams al-Anwar* (fragment)			DBP

Appendix II

List of Manuscripts

1. *Syair Sultan Yahya* (also known as *Syair Saudagar Budiman*)
   a. UBL Klinkert 139. 20 cm by 16 cm, 18 lines per page, 140 pp (Iskandar, *Catalogue*, p. 731). Copied by one of Klinkert's clerks, Penyengat, 1864. Attributed by Klinkert to Daeng Wuh, d. 1851.
   b. PNRI W. 249. 33 cm by 21 cm, 19 lines per page, 130 pp (Van Ronkel, Catalogus, p. 322). Perhaps a Bataviaasch Genootschaap copy of a manuscript from a Singapore lending library.
   c. PNRI W. 250. 33 cm by 17 cm, 17 lines per page, 289 pp (Van Ronkel, *Catalogus*, p. 323). Watermark is of a beetle, K&S, 1863. Continues past the ending of Klinkert 139, but ends abruptly.
   d. UBL Cod Or 1777. 23 cm by 18 cm, 20 lines per page, 125 pp (Iskandar, *Catalogue*, p. 40). Copied Sungai Batang, possibly Palembang, "di dalam istana". Copied malam "Ahad, 18 Rabi' al-Awwal", no year. Came from the Royal Academy of Delft in 1864.
   e. Bibliothèque Nationale Mal-Pol. 268. 19 cm by 16 cm, 14 lines per page, 180 pp (Voorhoeve, "Manuscrits", p. 69). Dated 1275 AH (1858–9).

2. *Syair Siti Zuhrah* (also known as *Syair Sultan Syarif* or *Syair Ardhan*)
   a. UBL Klinkert 132. 19 cm by 15.5 cm, 18 lines per page, 274 pp (Iskandar, *Catalogue*, p. 729).

b. PNRI W. 261. 24 cm by 21 cm, 19 lines per page, 247 pp (Van Ronkel, *Catalogus*, p. 326). Date of copying given in European numerals as "128", i.e., sometime in the 1280s (1863 onwards?).
c. PNRI W. 262. 33 cm by 220.5 cm, 19 lines per page, 254 pp (Van Ronkel, *Catalogus*, p. 328).
d. PNRI W. 263. Watermark is Beetle, K&S, 1863. 20 cm by 17 cm, 15 lines per page, 319 pp (Van Ronkel, *Catalogus*, pp. 328–9).

3. *Syair Sultan Abdul Muluk*
a. PNRI W. 257. 33 cm by 21 cm, 19 lines per page, 190 pp (Van Ronkel, pp. 321–2). Van Ronkel reports that, according to Van den Berg, there was once a note by Von de Wall attached to this manuscript, giving Raja Salehah as the author. By Van Ronkel's time, this note was lost. Van Ronkel also says that this manuscript is better than Van Eysinga's text. Watermark: around the edge of the medallion CONCORDIA RESPARVAE CRESCUNT. Next page: WS TZ. Iskandar dates this watermark to ca. 1865.
b. UBL Cod. Or. 1740. 20.5 cm by 16 cm, 19 lines per page, 189 pp (Iskandar, p. 25). Watermark: Britannia with LLOYD JAMES and 1840. From Royal Academy Delft 1864.
c. UBL Cod. Or. 1748. 22 cm by 16.5 cm, 15 lines per page, 237 pp (Iskandar, p. 28). From Royal Academy Delft 1864.
d. UBL Cod. Or. 3368. 20 cm by 15 cm, 19 lines per page, 202 pp (Iskandar, p. 176). Watermark is also Britannia with LLOYD JAMES and 1840, but also crowned eagle in scrollwork with GIOR MAGNANI and AL MASSO. Copied July 1846, Kampung Kota Renteng, Penyengat. Van der Tuuk bequest.
e. UBL Cod. Or. 7342 19.5 cm by 16 cm, 15 lines per page, 132 pp (Iskandar, p. 426). Copied by Mat Ali of Palembang Timur. First owner his nephew (or niece?), Encik Itam. Later owned by Musa of Kg Kebun Kelapa, Betawi. A copy of the printed text, including letters. Bought by Snouck Hurgronje in 1892.
f. PNM MS 450. 20.2 cm by 16.7 cm, 26 lines per page, 144 pp (*Manuskrip Melayu Koleksi Perpustakaan Negara Malaysia*, p. 34).

4. *Syair Siti Zubaidah* (also known as *Syair Kembayat*)
   a. UBL Klinkert 130. 20.5 cm by 15.5 cm, 19–20 lines per page, 379 pp (Iskandar, p. 728). Watermarks: Britannia with MUNRO and 1862, Horn/SM and SMITH & MEYNIER/FIUME, JAMES [?], GLASGOW, BELGIQUE, Sailing ship, 1860 and 1861. Bought by Klinkert from *selir* of Siak Yamtuan Muda, 2 September, 1864.
   b. PNRI Ml. 450. 508 pp (Behrend, p. 291). No watermarks. Incomplete: missing pages (including beginning) are noted in Dutch inside front cover.
   c. PNRI W. 255. 33 cm by 21 cm, 19 lines per page, 422 pp (Van Ronkel, pp. 324–6).
   d. PNM MSS 25. 20.9 cm by 17 cm, 19 lines per page, 154 pp (Katalog Ringkas, p. 3).
   e. PNM MSS 1075. 21 cm by 16.6 cm, 14 lines per page, 26 pp (Katalog Manuskrip Tambahan Kedua, p. 5).
   f. DBP MSS 24. 25 cm by 18 cm, 138 pp (Katalog Induk, p. 2).

5. *Syair Saudagar Bodoh*
   a. UBL Klinkert 164. 20.5 cm by 17 cm, 15 lines per page, 23 pp (Iskandar, p. 740). Note by Klinkert gives author as Raja Kalsum and date of composition as 1861, with date of copy 1865. Watermark is Beetle, K&S, 1863.

6. *Syair Siti Dhawiyyah* (also known as *Syair Haris Fadhilah*)
   a. UBL Klinkert 157. 20 cm by 15.5 cm, 18 lines per page, 102 pp (Iskandar, p. 738). Copy bought by Klinkert in Penyengat, 1856–7. Tuan Bilal Abu (d. 1830s) given by Klinkert as the author, woman copyist.
   b. PNRI Ml. 214. 19.5 cm by 16.5 cm, 14 lines per page, 180 pp (Van Ronkel, pp. 340–1). Judging by the note at the beginning, mentioning "babou-babou" in "Kampung Tanah Boengoer", perhaps a manuscript from a lending library. However, is on the CONCORDIA paper apparently commonly used by the Bataviaasch Genootschaap.
   c. PNRI Ml. 255. 20.5 cm by 16 cm, 16 lines per page, 147 pp (Van Ronkel, pp. 341–2). 1893 copy by Muhammad Bakir, who rented it out, of an 1864 Pontianak MS. "Yang menukil" the Pontianak MS was one Tuan Syarif Muhammad ibn Ahmad al-Qadri. Has an additional seven pages at the end.

d. PNRI W. 259. 33 cm by 20.5 cm, 19 lines per page, 88 pp (Van Ronkel, p. 342). 1272 AH. Continues with *Syair Ikan Terubuk*.
e. Bibliothèque Nationale Mal-Pol. 278. 19.5 cm by 15 cm, 16 lines per page, 114 pp (Voorhoeve, "Manuscrits", p. 72). Copied in Singapore, behind Masjid Encik Fatimah Riau, 1858. Legal contract, copied in the same hand, pasted in the back.
f. SOAS MS 36559. 19.5 cm by 14.5 cm, 15 lines per page, 55 pp (Ricklefs and Voorhoeve, p. 161). Scribe: al-Husain bin Ismail "orang Bugis".
g. PNM MSS 2119. 51 pp (*Manuskrip Melayu Koleski Perpustakaan Negara Malaysia Tambahan Keempat*, p. 29). Copied 21 Safar 1293 AH (18 March 1876). Tanjung Hilir, Pontianak.

Appendix III

Extracts and Translations

The episodes were selected because they are of particular interest with reference to the book's discussion of the disguised heroine motif, and because they highlight points of connection or divergence between the various texts. From these citations, more extended than was practical to include in the main part of the book, I hope that the reader will be able to gain for him- or herself a deeper sense of the *syair*, and of their diverse subjects, styles and attitudes. These range from the sublime to the ridiculous, from pathos to humour, and from piety to impertinence.

The excerpts are based on transliterations from single manuscripts, those which most probably came from Riau. For the sake of clarity or for comparison, reference has been made to other manuscripts or editions, but these excerpts are intended to be transcripts for the non-specialist rather than philological editions.

Similarly, the intention of the translations is to allow interested readers who do not know Malay access to the texts. I have not attempted to reproduce the rhyme scheme of the Malay quatrains in English, although I have tried to retain a flavour of the verses' original tone and style (including repetition). Readers comparing the Malay original and the English will also note the problem of dealing with the "filler" words often used to pad out the metre or complete the rhyme (most notably *nin* and *nan*). To the same end, epithets (such as *bestari, pokta, syahda, berida*) are used widely in the *syair*, taking a variety of meanings. I have therefore been guided by context in taking some creative licence in translating these words.

To facilitate comprehension, spelling has been standardised to match that of modern Bahasa Malaysia. Arabic words are represented as they appear in Jawi (that is, they have not been changed to correct Arabic). Page numbers given refer to page numbers on the manuscripts.

I. Klinkert 139 *Syair Sultan Yahya*   I. Klinkert 139 *Syair Sultan Yahya*

After the death of her parents and the marriage of her sister, Siti Jauhar Manikam decides to go in search of her brother, Jaya Putera.

Ada kepada suatunya hari
Lalu berfikir Siti bestari
Apalah sudah demikian peri
Baiklah aku pergi mencari

On a certain day,
Noble Siti thought to herself:
"What shall become of this?
I'd better go in search of him myself."

Lalu menangis Siti bangsawan
Hati di dalam pilu dan rawan
Datanglah fikir tiada ketahuan
Air matanya bercucuran

Then well-born Siti wept,
Her heart sorrowful and tumultuous.
Uncertain thoughts came to her,
Her tears spilled forth.

Tambahan segala isi negeri
Datang menyuruh sehari-hari
Hendak dipinang jadi isteri
Ada yang setengah datang sendiri

And all the inhabitants of the kingdom
Sent messengers daily,
Asking for her hand in marriage;
Some even came in person.

Hendak pun ia ke dalam kota
Terlalu takut di dalam cita
Jikalau dikahwinkan duli mahkota
Dengan segala alim pendita

Even if she wished to enter the city,
She was too afraid,
Lest she be married off by his highness
To some learned holy man.

Duduklah ia dengan bercinta
Berbuat ibadah juga semata
Diserahkan dirinya sudahlah nyata
Jangan beroleh nama yang leta

She remained in anxiety,
And all she did was pray,
Resigning herself to God, that was certain,
So she did not gain a base name.

24.
Mintak doa pagi dan petang
Menadahkan tangan lepas sembahyang

24.
Sending up prayers morning and evening
Hands uplifted after her devotions,

Jangan mendapat aral melintang Dengan kakanda segera bertentang	That she would not meet with misfortune, But soon see her brother.
Lalu bermadah Siti bestari Wahai dayang pergilah diri Penghulu keempat panggil ke mari Aku nin hendak bertemu sendiri	Then noble Siti spoke: "O, handmaids, go you And call hither the four headmen. I wish to meet with them."
Pergilah dayang dengan segera Mendapat penghulu empat saudara Datuk dipanggil Siti mengindera Entahkan apa gerangan bicara	The handmaids went at once To meet with the four brother headmen. "Datuks, you are summoned by the royal Siti, We know not on what matter."
Segeralah pergi penghulu keempat Sambil berjalan terlalu cepat Datang kehadapan Siti bersifat Tunduk menyembah bersila rapat	At once the four headmen went, Walking at speed To the presence of illustrious Siti. They sat with heads bent in obeisance.
Segera ditegur Siti dermawan Sambil memberi sireh di puan Segera disambut keempat pahlawan Belas memandang Siti bangsawan	At once munificient Siti addressed them, While offering sireh in its tray. At once the four warriors accepted it, Compassionately regarding well-born Siti.
Siti bermadah perlahan suara Bapak keempat apa bicara Beta nin hendak berlayar segera Mencari abang Jaya Putera	Siti spoke in a low voice: "My fathers four, what is your council? We wish to sail at once In search of our brother Jaya Putera.
Entahkan hidup entahkan mati Selama ini belumlah pasti Berbalik hairan rasanya hati Apakah sebab demikian pekerti	If he is dead or alive, we know not, Thus far all is uncertain. Our heart feels overturned by wonder. What can be the cause of this?

Harimau Alam kapal ayahanda
Itulah turunkan oleh mamanda
Gedung yang tiga mana yang ada
Isikan kapal jangan tiada
	Harimau Alam is our father's ship:
	That one, respected uncles, bring
	   down to the sea.
	From whatever is in the three
	   storehouses,
	Fill the ship, do not be remiss.

Leila Majnun meriam pusaka	Leila Majnun, the cannon inherited,
Itupun hendak dibawak juga	That too we wish to bring with us.
Muatkan di kapal lapis tembaga	Load it onto the brass-sheathed ship.
Mamanda keempat pergi belaka	Go about this, respected uncles.

25.
Pahlawan keempat segeralah pergi
Mendapatkan kapal galangnya tinggi
Berapa banyak segala laki-laki
Hendak menyorong kapal Peringgi

25.
The four warriors went at once
To the ship high on its slipway,
Bringing many men
To push the Frankish ship to the water,

Berapa disorong orang yang banyak
Sedikit tidak kapal bergerak
Banyaklah orang terberak-berak
Ada yang jatuh bagai ditolak

But though the men shoved hard as
   they might,
The ship did not budge.
Many were stuck in the mud,
Some fell as though pushed.

Penghulu keempat terlalu hairan
Peluh di badan bercucuran
Diambilnya kerbau disembelihkan
Kambing tujuh disemahkan

The four headmen were amazed,
Their bodies pouring with sweat.
They took a buffalo and slaughtered it,
Seven goats they sacrificed.

Leila Majnun hendak diangkat
Rasanya itu terlalu berat
Sekalian orang sangat gelorat
Inilah pekerjaan memberi mudharat

Wanting to lift up Leila Majnun,
They felt it too heavy.
All the people were in uproar:
"This work brings danger."

Habislah tipu penghulu keempat
Lela tu tiada boleh diangkat
Kapal disorong lunasnya lekat
Di atas galangan tiada terangkat

The ruses of the four headmen were
   at an end,
The cannon could not be lifted.
The keel of the ship was stuck fast,
Unable to be moved along the slipway.

Habislah tipu daya upaya
Kapal tak boleh menyorong dia
Sekalian orang tiada bergaya
Di atas galangan kapalnya sedia

The ruses and stratagems were at an end,
The ship could not be pushed.
All the people were helpless,
And the ship remained on the slipway.

Penghulu pun sudah hilang bicara
Lalu kembali keempat saudara
Mengadap Siti lela mengindera
Duduk menyembah dengannya segera

The headmen were at their wits' end,
And returned, the four brothers,
To face Siti, lovely and royal,
At once they sat in obeisance.

Katanya aduh tuan puteri	They said: "Alas, princess,
Kapal nin lekat tiada terperi	The ship is stuck fast.
Disorong tidak mau memberi	When pushed it will not give,
Semah pun sudah patik nin beri	Though sacrifices have been offered."
Demi didengar Siti mengerna	When bright Siti heard this,
Tersenyum manis laku tak bena	She smiled sweetly and without a care,
Lalu bermadah dengan sempurna	Then spoke appropriately:
Janganlah bapak gundah gulana	"Fathers, do not be troubled.

26.
Janganlah bapakku berhati sali
Keempat bapakku baiklah kembali
Baikkan sauh tali temali
Nyorong kapal beta tak ghali

26.
My fathers, you need not have
   steadfast hearts.
Best you return, all four of you,
Repair the anchor and rigging.
To push the ship we are not averse."

Penghulu pun turun lalu berjalan
Membaikkan sauh di pangkalan
Sauhnya besi mata sembilan
Tali temali perbuatan Silan

The headmen then went on their way
To repair the anchor at the launching-
   place.
The anchor was of iron, with nine points;
The rigging of Ceylon make.

Adapun akan Siti bangsawan
Lalu memakai selengkap pakaian
Bersama dayang tujuh sekawan
Empat puluh empat sekawan

As for the well-born Siti:
She arrayed herself in a complete outfit,
With her seven handmaids,
And forty-four attendants.

Mematut pakaian cara laki-laki
Berseluar panjang berkancing kaki
Berbaju antelas bunga beragi
Berkancing dada intan pelangi

Suited in the manner of a man,
In long trousers fastened at the feet,
Satin jacket with a flowered pattern,
Fastened at the chest with iridescent
   gems.

Berlilit ramping limar angsana
Bergelang emas berastakona
Berkeris terapang emas kencana
Berhulukan intan sembilan warna

Slender waist-wrap in *angsana*[10]
   patterned cloth
Octagonal bracelets of gold,
A gold-sheathed keris,
With a handle of nine kinds of diamonds.

---

[10] A tree, *pterocarpus indicus*. See Wilkinson, *Dictionary*, p. 19.

Berdestar ungu shahdan berkalok	A headdress of purple, curved,
Terkenalah malai sunting dan tajuk	Adorned with flowers, pendent and aigrette:
Parasnya Siti terlalu elok	Siti's appearance was so lovely,
Cantik mejelis tiada bertolok	Pretty and beauteous, without compare.
Beramal pelangi bertelepuk perada	With a rainbow kerchief stamped in gold-leaf flowers,
Selepa tersampai di hulu khanda	Trailing over the hilt of her dagger,
Bercincin zamrut ikatan Olanda	An emerald ring in a Dutch design,
Bertali leher bersawit dada	A necklace, twisted across her chest.
Muzahnya datang ke mata duli	Her shoes came up to the ankle,
Berkapan jong sarat berkaus duli	Royal footgear shaped like loaded ships[11]
Elok mejelis muda terjali	Lovely and pretty, the lovely youth,
Sekalian yang memandang mendam khayali	All who saw her lost their heads.
Bercelak Siti bersifat alit	Siti's eyes were rimmed in kohl,
Putih berseri warnanya kulit	Her skin shone pale,
Bibirnya merah bagai dihalit	Her lips were red as though rouged:
Cantiknya rupa Siti yang sulit	How lovely was the disguised Siti.
27.	27.
Giginya seperti sayap kumbang	Her teeth gleaming black like a beetle's wings,[12]
Bersunting bunga melur yang kembang	Blossoming jasmine behind her ear,
Parasnya seperti dewa dan mambang	Her appearance like that of gods and spirits,
Cantik manis memberi bimbang	Pretty and sweet, arousing desire.
Eloknya tidak dapat dikata	Her loveliness indescribable,
Sepertikan lenyap dipandang mata	As if the viewer might disappear gazing upon it,[13]
Seperti rupa peranakan danta	Like a doll of ivory,
Ditatah dengan pudi permata	Studded with gems and jewels.

---

[11] The translation of this line is extremely provisional.
[12] Blackened teeth were considered a mark of beauty. See Zumbroich, "Teeth as Black as a Bumble Bee's Wings".
[13] For a similar usage in *Hikayat Isma Yatim*, see Braginsky, *Heritage*, p. 251.

Sudah memakai muda bangsawan Sajak dan sikah tiada berlawan Sedikit tidak rupa perempuan Seperti laki-laki yang pahlawan	When the young noble had dressed, Her graceful movements and bearing without compare, Not looking at all like a woman, But like a valiant man.
Elok mejelis barang kelakuan Lemah lembut memberi rawan Rupanya seperti dewa di awan Laksana bulan diarak awan	All her ways fair and lovely, Her gentleness stirring desire, Her appearance like a god in the clouds, Like the moon escorted by clouds.
Dayang ketujuh memakai juga Dara sekalian memakai belaka Sekaliannya elok tiada terhingga Sekalian memandang berhati duka	The seven handmaids dressed themselves too, Maidens all arrayed completely, All boundlessly lovely, All who gazed on them felt wistful.
Eloknya paras Siti dayang-dayang Sikap seperti laki-laki yang jayang Keris meniarap tersiap di pinggang Keris panjang suatu dipegang	Lovely of visage was Siti and her handmaids, Carrying themselves like victorious men, Equipped with a keris at the waist, And another long keris in the hand.
Empat puluh empat sama sebaya Pantas manis sama bergaya Patutlah pengiring Siti yang mulia Sama tahu menyimpan rahsia	Forty-four, of the same age, Graceful, sweet, all of one air, Fit to accompany the distinguished Siti, All knowing how to keep a secret.
Bermadah manis Siti bangsawan Kepada segala muda pilihan Marilah kita turun berjalan Menurunkan kapal ke pangkalan	Well-born Siti spoke sweetly To all the choice young ones: "Let us now go on foot To bring the ship down to the launching-place."
Lalu berangkat Siti yang bijak Diiringkan dayang sama bersajak Sambil berlenggang terlalu kacak Sekalian terkejut orang yang banyak	Then intelligent Siti set off, Accompanied by handmaids, all in step, While swaying so smartly, Astonishing the common people.

28.
Sekaliannya orang hairan tercengang
Tiada berkelip mata memandang
Di dalam hatinya siapakah gerang
Eloknya bukan sebarang-barang

Sekaliannya tidak terkata-kata
Sangatlah hairan di dalam cita
Memandang muda ramai semata
Seperti tulisan di dalam peta

Adapun akan muda sekalian
Sampailah ia pergi di pangkalan
Berhimpunlah muda sama handalan
Harimau Alam lalu disorongkan

Jauhar Manikam Siti bestari
Menyorong kapal ia sendiri
Ditenungnya kapal kanan dan kiri
Mencitakan namanya orang yang
   bahari

Sambil berkata perlahan-lahan
Suaranya halus memberi rawan
Jikalau aku asal bangsawan
Raja bertahta di Zamin Iran

Tujuh lapis turun menurun
Empunya meriam Lela Majnun
Harimau Alam segeralah turun
Engkaulah kapal bernama Anusirwan

Kapal pun turun dengan seketika
Mengembang di laut seperti naga
Terkenalah temberang layar terbuka
Kiri dan kanan meriam tembaga

28.
All the people were agog in
   astonishment,
Their gazing eyes unblinking,
In their hearts they thought: "Who can
   this be?
Their loveliness is of no ordinary kind."

Not a one said a word,
So amazed were their hearts,
Simply gazing at the many youths,
As though at a drawing on a picture.

As for all the youths,
They arrived at the landing stage.
The youths, alike in ability,
Then pushed Harimau Alam.

Jauhar Manikam, noble Siti,
Herself pushed the ship,
Casting spells to the left and right of it,
Summoning her glorious forebears by
   name.

While saying quietly,
Her refined voice stirring the heart:
"If I am indeed of well-born origin,
From rajas enthroned in Zamin Iran

Seven generations in succession,
Owning the cannon Leila Majnun,
Harimau Alam, at once descend.
You are the ship named Anusirwan."[14]

In a moment the ship descended,
Spread its sails in the sea like a dragon.
Equipped with stays and unfurled sails,
To left and right the brass cannons.

---

[14] Anushirvan or Khosrau I was the sixth-century Persian Sassanid king, known in the Malay world from the *Taj al-Salatin* and similar texts.

Tali-temali daripada rantai	The rigging made of chains,
Layarnya kapal daripada cindai	The ship's sails of fine cloth,
Indahnya kapal terlalu bisai	The ship's beauty so gallant,
Sekalian yang terlihat hairan terlalai	All who saw it were amazedly distracted.
Bilik dan kamar berdinding cermin	The cabins and chambers were walled with mirrors,
Dibuat jendela tempat berangin	Windows were made to let in the breeze,
Perbuatan tukang di atas angin	Made by craftsmen from above the winds,
Berapa banyak raja yang ingin	The desire of so many rajas.
29.	29.
Tanju dan kandil digantungkan pula	Hung with sconces and lanterns
Segenap sekat pintu jendela	On all the partitions, walls and windows,
Diselangnya dengan intan gemala	Alternated with jewels and diamonds,
Berjuraikan emas berjala-jala	Tasselled with gold trelliswork.
Katil gading ranjang perada	The mattress of ivory, the bedstead of goldleaf,
Digantungkan kelambu kasa Olanda	Hung with draperies of Dutch muslin,
Berdaun budi emas bernila	With a leaf-pattern fringe in sapphire-studded gold:
Tempat peraduan Siti yang syahda	The sleeping place of lovely Siti.
Perhiasan kapal lengkaplah sudah	The adornment of the ship complete,
Berangkatlah turun Siti yang indah	Siti the beauteous made her way down.
Hatinya Siti terlalu gundah	Siti's heart was so melancholy,
Seperti rasa akan berpindah	It felt as it might leave her body.
Terlalu sebal di dalam dada	So dejected at heart,
Olehnya terkenangkan paduka adinda	In memory of her royal sister,
Tidaklah bertemu dengan kakanda	Whom she could not meet with,
Takut ditahan oleh baginda	For fear of being detained by his highness.
Siti pun duduk di atas geta	Siti then sat upon a divan,
Dihadap dayang sekalian rata	Faced by all the handmaids.
Penghulu keempat adalah serta	The four headmen, there too,
Menyuruh membongkar sauh berganta	She commanded to weigh the anchor and strike the bell.

Siti pun menyuruh berlayar segera	Siti instructed them to set sail at once;
Terlalu kencang angin utara	So strong was the north wind,
Lagipun takut kalau ketara	And she feared to be noticed,
Takut ditahan oleh saudara	Feared to be detained by her brother-in-law.
Lalu berlayar Harimau Alam	Then Harimau Alam set sail,
Dibawak Siti Jauhar Manikam	Carrying away Siti Jauhar Manikam,
Ombak berdengung arus yang dalam	Waves booming, the current deep.
Berlayarlah ia siang dan malam	They sailed night and day.
Bermadahlah Siti nila utama	Siti, excellent sapphire, spoke
Kepada dayang ada bersama	To the handmaids with her:
Marilah kita bersalin nama	"Let us change our names.
Ke negeri yang jauh tempat menjelma	A distant land is where we arose.
Sebutlah kami Juragan Budiman	Call us Juragan Budiman,
Arif laksana saudagar Yaman	The wise, a merchant of Yemen."
Suka tertawa sekaliannya teman	All her companions laughed in pleasure:
Pandai menggelar usul budiman	"How good you are at naming, wise one."

30.

Berlayarlah Siti berhati duka	Siti sailed, heartsick,
Siti Benzahara dikenangkan juga	Remembering Siti Benzahara.
Apakah gerangan mala petaka	"What sort of a disaster is this,
Adik dan kakak bercerai belaka	That sunders older and younger siblings?
Wahai adikku emas tempawan	O little sister, o beaten gold,
Dengan kakanda berceraillah tuan	From me you are parted.
Tinggallah adikku muda bangsawan	My young noble sister, left behind,
Kekal tinggal diatas kerajaan	Remain forever on your throne.
Dari kecil abang pelihara	From infancy have I tended you.
Tidak bercerai bertiga saudara	The three siblings never separated.
Sudahlah sampai masa sengsara	Now the time of suffering has come,
Abanglah seorang menanggung lara	I alone bear the pain."
Juragan pun masuk ke dalam peraduan	The ship's captain then entered the bedroom,
Rasanya hati terlalu rawan	Her heart in such tumult.
Lalu menangis perlahan-lahan	She wept gently,
Terkenangkan adinda Siti rupawan	Thinking of her lovely sister.

....	Juragan Budiman passes the night in Sultan Yahya's *balai*.
Setelah malam sudahlah hari Baginda bertitah kepada menteri Mintak peraduan di rumah diri Suruhlah mamanda bawak ke mari	Once night had become day His highness spoke to his councillors: "Bring a pallet from your house. Command one of my noble uncles to bring it hither."
Perlahan-lahan baginda berkata Sepertikan tidak kedengaran nyata Hendak pun mintak di istana beta Kerana puteri terlalu menta	His highness said, in a voice low So that it could not clearly be heard: "I'd ask for it to be brought to my own palace But the princess will be enraged."
69. Jikalau peraduan mamanda bawakkan Daun pisang suruh alaskan Akan peraduan tempat Juragan Kerana hendak beta lihatkan	69. Should my noble uncle bring a bed, Let it be underlaid with banana leaves, To be the sleeping place of Juragan, For we wish to make a test."
Lalu menyambut menteri terbilang Lalulah segera berjalan pulang Menghiaskan peraduan wajah gemilang Suatu dialaskan pucuk pisang	The esteemed courtiers accepted the command, At once returned home, Adorned the sleeping place of glorious aspect, One bed underlain with banana sprouts.
Setelah sudah lalu dibawakkan Di atas balai disuruh bentangkan Baginda bertitah kepada Juragan Marilah beradu janganlah segan	Once finished they brought it To the pavilion and ordered it be spread out. His highness spoke to Juragan: "Come and sleep, do not hesitate.
Kanda adinda marilah tidur Janganlah banyak kata dan tutur Beta mendengar hati nin hancur Di manakan boleh lagi terlipur	Brothers old and young, come to bed. Do not talk and chatter. We hear it and our heart is crushed— And how can it be soothed?

Kerana kita akan bercerai	For we shall be parted.
Marilah tidur kita nin ramai	Come, sleep, all together.
Janganlah malu usul yang permai	Do not be shy, pretty one.
Penyudah kasih tidur di balai	The ultimate mark of affection is to sleep in our pavilion."
Adapun baginda berkata-kata	His highness spoke these words
Sambil berhamburan airnya mata	While his eyes streamed with tears
Pilu dan rawan rasanya cita	Sorrowful and moved in his emotions,
Sepertikan hendak menurut serta	As if he wished to follow them.
Juragan kedua belasnya rasa	The two merchants felt pity for him,
Melihatkan laku raja berbangsa	Seeing the demeanour of the noble king.
Kerana sudah kenal biasa	From their familiarity with him
Air mata cucur tiada berasa	They did not sense their own tears falling.
Lalulah ia rebah beradu	Then they laid themselves down to sleep,
Tiga sebanjar ketiganya itu	In a row, the three of them.
Baginda menangis tersedu-sedu	His highness wept and sobbed,
Tidak tertahan hatinya pilu	Unable to restrain his sorrowful heart.
Sekalian bujang muda jauhari	All the noble young men,
Ramai berlampar kanan dan kiri	So many stretched out to right and left,
Dengan segala anak menteri	With all the courtiers' sons,
Sangatlah ia bersiap diri	All of them had readied themselves.
70.	70.
Anak menteri yang muda-muda	The young sons of the courtiers
Ramailah tidur sambil bersenda	Lay there all together, teasing:
Marilah dekat wahai adinda	"Come close, little one,
Bersama tidur dengan kakanda	Come and sleep with your brother.
Tuan seperti dikawal Inggeris	You're as though watched over by the English,
Tidur pun tidak bercerai keris	Not parting from your *keris* even in sleep.
Jikalau mengigau dirasuk iblis	If an evil spirit possesses you,
Orang di balai ditikam habis	All the people in the pavilion will be stabbed.

Mintaklah keris bawak ke mari	Give us your keris, bring it here.
Tiada kan datang orang pencuri	No thieves will approach."
Bujang pun marah tidak terperi	The youth was greatly angered,
Ditepisnya tangan anak menteri	Pushing away the young courtier's hand.
Ia memalis seraya berkata	'He' looked away and said:
Tiadakan boleh tidurnya mata	"I cannot shut my eyes,
Mulutnya ingar sangat gempita	For the riotous clamour of mouths.
Murka sekarang duli mahkota	His highness will be angered.
Hendaklah tidur tempat nin sempit	The place is too cramped for sleep:
Kiri dan kanan kawan diapit	Hemmed in by companions left and right,
Ada yang memunggung ada yang mengimpit	Some spooning, some pressing in,
Ada yang memeluk ada yang menggamit	Some embracing, some fondling.
Duduk bergurau sama laki-laki	Bantering with other men,
Seperti tiada perempuan lagi	As though there were no more women.
Beta dipunggung tangan dan kaki	My back is pushed by hands and feet;
Janganlah abang begitu lagi	Brothers, desist from this.
Apa yang disusahkan sahaya berkhanda	What is the trouble if I am armed
Bukannya hendak menikam kanda	It's not that I'll stab you, brothers.
Selamanya sahaya demikian ada	As long as I am as I am,
Bercerai senjata haram tiada	I'll not part from my weapon."
Suka tertawa segala teruna	The young men laughed with glee,
Mendengarkan sungut bujang sekaliannya	Hearing all the plaints of the youth.
Berkata dengan pujuk cumbuannya	They spoke cajoling sweet words,
Terlalu berahi melihat parasnya	Aroused at 'his' good looks.
Lalu berkata indra pahlawan	Then one of the royal warriors said:
Janganlah marah adikku tuan	"Don't be angry, little brother.
Jikalau seperti adinda perempuan	If you were a woman,
Biarlah abang timbal bangsawan	Then let me be your partner."

71.
Bujang sekalian mendengar kata
Terlalu marah di dalam cita
Tunduk menjeling lakunya menta
Sampailah sahaya dagang yang leta

Apatah daya sahaya nin tuan
Sebab di hadapan yang dipertuan
Jikalau seperti pasar dan jalan
Tahulah sahaya membalaskan

Sekaliannya muda suka tertawa
Janganlah marah utama jiwa
Abang sekadar bergurau jua
Bukannya pulak jadi kecewa

Setelah sudah bergurau senda
Lalulah tidur sekaliannya muda
Sunyilah sudah balai yang syahda
Habislah tidur mana yang ada

Adapun akan Juragan Budiman
Tidur pun tidak berasa nyaman
Terkenangkan pantun burung di taman
Habislah disindir laku dan roman

Keluh kesah Juragan nin tidur
Di daun pisang habislah hancur
Juragan pun bangun duduk terpekur
Lalulah makan sireh sekapur

Duduklah ia menantikan siang
Duduk bersandar di balik tiang
Fajar pun sudah berbayang
Pergilah mandi lalu sembahyang

71.
When the youths heard these words,
They were greatly angered,
Bent their heads, looked sidelong,
  their manner enraged:
"So it is with me, a base stranger—

What can I do, sirs,
For I am before his majesty.
Were this the market or the street,
Then I'd know how to answer."

All the young men laughed with glee:
"Do not be angry, excellent soul.
Your brother is merely jesting,
And by no means intends to hurt you."

When they had teased and jested,
Then all the young men slept.
The splendid pavilion was silent,
All there were fast asleep.

As for Juragan Budiman,
Sleep was uncomfortable,
Thinking of the garden bird's *pantun*,
The hints dropped in ways and looks.[15]

Sighing and uneasy Juragan slept,
The banana leaves all shredded.
Juragan rose and sat deep in thought,
Then took a quid of sireh.

'He' sat awaiting day,
Leaning against a pillar.
When dawn began to break,
'He' went to bathe and pray.

---

[15] This refers to the prior incident, during which Juragan Budiman and Sultan Yahya are in a pleasure garden, when a bird starts reciting pantun alluding to Juragan Budiman's true female identity.

Setelah hari siang nin nyata	Once it was clear day,
Baginda terkejut membukakan mata	His highness opened his eyes with a start.
Dilihat Juragan adalah serta	Seeing that Juragan was there,
Segeralah bangun duli mahkota	The royal king arose at once.
Baginda tersenyum seraya memandang	His highness smiled as he gazed.
Sudahkah mandi paras yang sedang	"Have you already bathed, perfect lovely one?
Mengapakah bangun tuan seorang	Why did you arise alone?
Tiada mau membangunkan abang	Did you not wish to wake me?"
72.	72.
Juragan tersenyum seraya berkata	Juragan smiled and answered:
Takutlah patik hamba yang leta	"Your humble servant was afraid,
Takut murka duli mahkota	Afraid to anger the royal king,
Kerana tuanku sedang bertahta	For you are the one upon the throne."
Baginda tersenyum terlalu suka	His highness smiled with pleasure,
Memandang Juragan rasanya leka	Absorbed in gazing at Juragan.
Lalu baginda berbasuh muka	Then he washed his face,
Datanglah hidangan dengan seketika	And refreshment was served at once.
Santaplah baginda raja bangsawan	His highness the well-born king partook of food,
Dengan Juragan menteri sekalian	With Juragan and his courtiers all.
Sudahlah santap baginda tuan	Once his highness had eaten,
Santaplah sireh di dalam puan	He partook of sireh from its dish.
Juragan kedua lalu bermohon	The two merchants then took their leave.
Patik hendak dahulu turun	"We wish to return first.
Petang sekarang naik berhimpun	In the afternoon we will meet again,
Ke bawah duli mohonkan ampun	For this we ask the king's forgiveness.
Hendak berlayar lagi dua hari	We wish to set sail in two days.
Naiklah juga patik ke mari	We shall return again hence."
Baginda tersenyum durja berseri	His highness smiled with radiant countenance.
Baiklah tuan muda jauhari	"Very well, young nobles."

Lalulah turun muda handalan	Then the two clever youths went down,
Menuju sekoci di pangkalan	Heading for the ship's cutter at the jetty,
Orang menonton sepanjang jalan	People watched them along the way,
Laki-laki perempuan berlari-larian	Men and women running to see.
Juragan berdayung dengan segera	Juragan rowed at once,
Berlumba dengan Jaya Putera	Racing with Jaya Putera,
Sorak gemuruh tiada terkira	With great cheers and shouts,
Sekoci Juragan dahulu mara	Juragan's cutter came first.
Setelah sampai Juragan bestari	Once the noble Juragan had arrived,
Jaya Putera muda jauhari	Jaya Putera, intelligent youth,
Lalulah naik di kapal sendiri	Boarded the ship himself.
Silakan abang masuk ke mari	"Please, brother, come here."
Lalulah duduk Jaya Putera	Then Jaya Putera sat down,
Di atas kerusi dua setara	On one of two identical chairs,
Tunduk menyembah Siti mengindera	Noble Siti bent in obeisance,
Sambil menangis tidak terkira	While weeping incalculably.

73.

Terlalulah sangat menangis dia	She wept greatly
Di atas ribaan muda yang cura	On the lap of the jovial youth
Tidakkah abang mengenal sahaya	"Do you not recognise me, brother,
Makanya tidak bertanyakan rahsia	That you do not ask my secret?
Sebab adinda jadi begini	The reason your sister is thus,
Mencari abang ke sana sini	Searching for you hither and yon,
Ayahanda bonda semuanya fani	Father and mother are both passed away,
Makanya adinda selaku ini	Therefore your sister is in this state."
Sangatlah terkejut Jaya Putera	Jaya Putera was greatly astonished,
Segera dicium kepala saudara	At once kissed his sister's head,
Sambil menangis tiada terkira	While weeping incessantly,
Melihat adinda sangat sengsara	Seeing his sister in such distress.
Wahai adikku Siti dermawan	"O my sister, generous Siti,
Sampailah kasih rupanya tuan	How great, it seems, is your love.
Patutlah kasih abang kan tuan	How right it was I felt affection for you,
Tetapi tidak abang sangkakan	But I had no inkling it was you.

Abang nin tuan sangat celaka Tiada mengenal adik dan kaka Ibu dan bapak mati belaka Sedikit tidak disangka-sangka	I am most unfortunate, Not recognising my sibling, either elder or younger, Mother and father both dead, Not a bit of this did I imagine.
Wahai tuan Siti bestari Marilah kita pulang ke negeri Takut diketahui raja yang bahari Tentulah tidak kita diberi	O noble Siti, Let us at once return to our land, Lest this be known by the splendid king, For he surely will not permit us to depart.
Jika diketahuinya tuan perempuan Tentulah diambilnya adikku tuan Apatah daya abang nin tuan Selaku kita dapat ditawan	If he knows that you are a woman, He will certainly make you his. Then what will your brother be able to do? For we will be captives.
Lalu disahut Siti yang syahda Benar sekali sabdanya kanda Sementara belum diketahui baginda Segera berlayar jangan tiada	Then lovely Siti answered: "True indeed are my brother's words. So long as it is not known by his highness, Let us set sail at once."
Adapun akan Jaya Putera Menyuruhkan bujang empat setara Menyuruh layarkan kapal dengan segera Beta di sini dengan saudara	As for Jaya Putera, He ordered the four youths To set sail at once. "I am here with my sister."

74.

Penghulu keempat sudah berkerah Menyuruh menarik bendera merah Tiada memalu gong pengerah Dengan perlahan kapal berpindah	The four headmen were set to work, Ordering that the red flag be hoisted. The summoning gong was not struck. Quietly the ship began to move.
Sauh dibongkar layar terbuka Berlayarlah kapal dengan seketika Lajunya tidak lagi terhingga Lepaslah teluk tanjung yang tiga	The anchor was weighed, the sails unfurled, The ship set sail at once. Its speed was limitless, Leaving the bay and the three capes.

Berlayarlah ia berperi-peri	It sailed in that manner,
Lajunya kapal tidak terperi	The ship's speed incomparable,
Keduanya kapal samalah seri	The two ships equal in radiance,
Terlalu jauh tinggalnya negeri	The city left far behind.
Adapun akan sultan yang ghana	As for the powerful sultan,
Turunlah sudah Juragan mengerna	Once the noble Juragan had departed,
Hati baginda gundah gulana	His heart was in great turmoil,
Seperti orang terkena guna	Like that of someone struck by black magic.
Dilihatnya peraduan tempat Juragan	Gazing at the place Juragan had slept,
Daun pisang yang dilihatkan	He caught sight of the banana leaves.
Seketika baginda hairan terpegan	At once his highness was stunned by surprise.
Daun ini sahaja dicarikkan	These leaves alone were in shreds.
Duduklah baginda tersedu-sedu	His highness sat sobbing,
Seperti orang menaruh rindu	Like someone full of longing,
Terlalu gundah di dalam qalbu	Too melancholy in his heart,
Diam termenung termangu-mangu	In silent thought, full of confusion.
Hati baginda rasa tak sedap	His heart felt uneasy
Terkenangkan Juragan hati tak tetap	Recalling Juragan his heart was uncertain.
Sekalian orang datang mengadap	All the people sought audience with him
Kelakuan baginda semua tak tetap	But his behaviour was all unsettled.
Datanglah dayang tuan puteri	The handmaids of the princess came
Persilakan baginda sultan bestari	Inviting his highness, the noble king.
Baginda pun tunduk berdiam diri	His highness bent his head in silence
Tiada diendahkan kata isteri	And paid no heed to his wife's words.
Setelah hari sudahlah petang	Once the day had turned to evening,
Dinanti Juragan tiadalah datang	He awaited Juragan who did not come.
Baginda berjalan pergi datang	His highness walked to and fro,
Ke pintu gerbang mata menentang	His eyes gazing at the doorway.

75.
Sehingga sampai malamnya hari
Tiadalah datang Juragan jauhari
Baginda pun bimbang[1] tidak terperi
Lalu menyuruh anak menteri

Ia pun pergi dengan segera
Pergi berkayuh ke tengah segara
Dilihatnya kapal Jaya Putera
Sudah berlayar kedua saudara

Lalulah ia pergi bertanya
Perahu yang banyak tempat bertanya
Kapal dua buah ke mana perginya
Tiadakah tuan melihatnya

Lalulah disahut orang di situ
Sudah berlayar kapalnya itu
Jam berbunyi pukul satu
Kapal berlayar sudahlah tentu

Setelah didengar anak menteri
Kembalilah ia berperi-peri
Mengadap baginda sultan bestari
Khidmat menyembah sepuluh jari

Ampun tuanku sultan muda
Kapal Juragan sudah tiada
Patik tanyakan segala nakhoda
Sudah berlayar kapal yang ada

Setelah baginda mendengarkan sembah
Arwah melayang durja berubah
Hati kejut rasanya gundah
Air mata turun mencurah

75.
When night had fallen
And the clever Juragan had not come
His highness was greatly concerned
And gave orders to a young courtier.

He went at once,
Rowing out into the sea,
Saw that Jaya Putera's ship
Had set sail, with the two siblings.

Then he went to ask,
At the place where there were many
  boats:
"The two ships, where have they gone?
Did you, sirs, not see them?"

Then the people there answered:
"Those ships have set sail
When the clock struck one.
The ships set sail, for certain."

The young courtier, having heard,
Returned to tell of it.
Faced his highness the noble sultan,
Saluted and made ten-fingered
  obeisance.

"Forgive me, my lord, youthful sultan,
Juragan's ship is gone.
Your servant enquired of the captains,
Who said the ships have set sail."

When his highness had heard those
  words
His soul took flight and his
  countenance transformed,
His heart was alarmed and distressed,
His tears fell in floods.

---

[1] MS: d a t-ng.

Tiadalah baginda terkata-kata
Sehingga berhamburan airnya mata
Pilu dan rawan di dalam cita
Terkenangkan Juragan muda yang
    pokta

His highness said nothing
But his tears streamed down.
Sorrow and distress in his thoughts,
Remembering the matchless young
    Juragan.

Baginda bertitah perlahan-lahan
Sampainya hati Juragan nin tuan
Di manakan gerangan negerinya tuan
Supaya abang mengadap bangsawan

His highness spoke in a low voice:
"So you've had the heart to do this,
    Juragan.
Where, perchance, may be your
    homeland,
That I may meet with you there?"

II. Klinkert 132 *Syair Siti Zuhrah*

II. Excerpt from *Syair Siti Zuhrah* (Klinkert 132)

Hounded out by their stepmother, Zuhrah leaves the city for the wilderness, taking with her Nurkiyah, her sister, and their attendants.

Sudah musta'ib sekaliannya rata
Kepada inang puteri berkata
Waktu inilah perginya kita
Sementara belum terang nin nyata

Once all had been made ready,
To her nursemaid the princess said:
"Now is the time for us to depart,
Before it is fully light.

Beta nin hendak bersalin pakaian
Jangan diketahui orang sekalian
Perbuatan kita berbagai-bagaian
Mendapat malu akhirnya kemudian

We wish to change our clothes
So that we are not recognised by the
    people.
If we behave otherwise,
In the end we may be shamed."

Lalu memakai puteri bangsawan
Berseluar panjang tulis berawan
Berkancing kaki intan kilauan
Mukanya seperti bulan di awan

So the well-born princess dressed
In long trousers with a pattern of clouds
Buttoned at the feet with sparkling
    diamonds,
Her face like a moon in clouds.

Berbaju antelas kain Olanda
Bercincin intan berkancing dada
Berbulang unggu telapak perada
Elok mejelis bangsawan muda

A jacket of Dutch satin,
Diamond rings and buttons on the chest,
A sash of purple with ?owers in gold leaf,
Lovely and fair, the young noble.

82.
Sudah memakai dengannya segera
Diambilkan pulak pakai saudara
Puteri Nurkiyah lela mengindera
Kerana ia beradu cendera

Telah selesai memakainya puteri
Diambilnya pedang hulu baiduri
Khanjar tersisip sebelah kiri
Ramal pelangi berseri-seri

Puteri Zuhrah lalu bersabda
Sambil memandang kepada adinda
Bangunlah tuan jiwa kakanda
Kita pergi mendapat ayahanda

Segeralah bangun tuan puteri
Sukanya tidak lagi terperi
Seraya berbasuh muka sendiri
Wajahnya persih amat berseri

Puteri Zuhrah muda bangsawan
Segera dipakaikan adinda tuan
Diberi memakai cara pahlawan
Elok mejelis usul dermawan

Sudah memberi pakai saudara
Dikenakan keris hulu mutiara
Parasnya mejelis tiada terkira
Duduk semayam dua setara

Puteri Zuhrah lalu berkata
Wahai adinda emas juita
Janganlah tuan khabarkan warta
Kepada orang sekalian rata

Jikalau temu dengannya orang
Jangan berkhabar suatu barang
Jika ditanya tuan sekarang
Katakan kita bangsa yang kurang

82.
Having dressed at once,
She then took up her sister's clothes—
Princess Nurkiyah, the royal one,
For she was fast asleep.

When the princess had dressed,
She took a sword with a hilt of opal,
A dagger at her waist on the left,
Tucked beneath a gleaming rainbow kerchief.

Princess Zuhrah then spoke,
While gazing at her sister:
"Wake, o my life,
We go to meet with our father."

The princess got up at once,
Her delight indescribable,
Washed her face herself,
Her countenance lustrous and shining.

Princess Zuhrah, young and noble,
At once dressed her little sister,
Giving her the style of a warrior,
Lovely and fair, of munificent origin.

Once she had dressed her sister,
She gave her a keris with a hilt of pearls,
Her appearance was incalculably fair.
Of like beauty, the two sat together.

Princess Zuhrah then said:
"O, little sister, gold of my life,
Do not tell about us
To any other people.

Should we meet with someone,
Tell them nothing at all.
If you are questioned now,
Say that we are of humble lineage.

Jikalau berkhabar emas juita
Diketahui oranglah bangsanya kita
Sangatlah malu rasanya beta
Kepada orang sekaliannya rata

If you tell them, o gold of my life,
And they know of our lineage,
We shall be greatly shamed
Before the general populace."

83.
Puteri Nurkiyah menjawab sabda
Patik menurut titahnya kanda
Beta pun suka di dalam dada
Supaya segera bertemu ayahanda

83.
Princess Nurkiyah answered those
   words:
"I obey my elder's command.
We are indeed pleased
That we will soon meet our father."

Akan segala dayang dan siti
Sekalian memakai dengan seperti
Pakaian perempuan sudah berganti
Seperti laku laki-laki yang jati

As for the handmaids and attendants,
All dressed appropriately,
Replacing their women's clothes
For those of true men.

Hanyalah kedua siti bestari
Tidak bersalin pakai sendiri
Bersama dengan inang yang bahari
Jadi pelayan kanan dan kiri

Only the two noble attendants
Did not change their own clothes,
Together with the old nursemaid.
They were to serve on the right and left.

Sudah memakai sekaliannya rata
Lalu berangkat puteri yang pokta
Sambil berhamburan airnya mata
Pilu dan rawan rasanya cita

Once all had dressed,
The peerless princesses then departed,
While shedding copious tears,
Sorrow and turmoil in their thoughts.

Turun dari maligai ratna
Diiringkan segala muda teruna
Puteri kedua gundah gulana
Terkenangkan ayahanda raja yang
   ghana

They descended from the jewelled
   palace,
Accompanied by all the young
   'bachelors'.
The two princesses were melancholy,
Thinking of their father the mighty raja.

Memakai kasut tatah permata
Lalu berjalan keluar kota
Kepada mata-mata inang berkata
Bukakan pintu apalah beta

Wearing shoes studded with jewels,
They walked out of the city.
To the watchman the nursemaid said:
"Will you open the gate for us?"

Mata-mata berkata suaranya seni
Hendak ke mana ibuku ini
Membukakan pintu tiada berani

The watchman said in a high-pitched
   voice:
"Where are you off to, mother?

Kalaukan murka raja yang ghani	I don't dare to open the gate—
	What if the mighty raja is angered?"
Inang menjawab laku tak tentu	The nursemaid answered impatiently:
Bukakan aku segeranya pintu	"Open the gate for me at once,
Kerana aku hendak ke situ	For I wish to go out.
Tidakkan murka baginda itu	His highness will not be angered.
Sebentar sahaja aku berjalan	I only want to go out for a moment
Mencari ubat puteri handalan	To look for medicine for the
Apa ditakutkan terangnya bulan	renowned princess.
Aku pun pergi dengan bertaulan	What is there to fear when the moon shines bright?
	And I go with companions."
84.	84.
Mata-mata mendengarkan katanya	The watchman heard her words
Sangat percaya rasa hatinya	And completely believed
Hendak ubatkan tuannya	That she wished to get medicine for her mistress,
Dibuka pintu dengan segeranya	So he opened the gate at once.
Keluarlah inang serta puteri	Nursemaid and princesses went out
Diiringkan dayang agus jauhari	Accompanied by the fine precious handmaids,
Serta berjalan berperi-peri	As they walked they conversed,
Menuju ke dalam hutan dan duri	Heading into the thorny forest.
Bulan pun terang kilau-kilauan	The moon was shining bright
Memancar segenap daun kayuan	Its rays on all the leaves of the trees
Cahayanya persih di cela awan	Its light lustrous between the clouds
Seperti menyuluh puteri bangsawan	As though shining a torch for the well-born princesses.
Pungguk berbunyi di pohon angsana	A *pungguk*[16] bird sang sweetly in an *angsana* tree
Merindu bulan cemerlang warna	Longing for the moon of glorious hue
Belaskan puteri kena bencana	Pitying the misfortune-struck princesses
Berjalan dengan gundah gulana	Walking in distress and turmoil.

---

[16] A small owl that is supposed to pine for the moon and is therefore used in Malay *pantun* as a stock figure of the unrequited lover. See Wilkinson, *Dictionary*, p. 464.

Turunlah angin sepoi bahasa Teja membangun di atas angkasa Selaku kasihankan puteri berbangsa Berjalan keluar dari dalam desa	The gentle wind came down, The shaft of light rose in the sky, As though taking pity on the noble princesses, Travelling on foot out of the city.
Murai bercerita bersahutan Riuh berkokok ayam di hutan Bagai belaskan puteri sultan Puteri pun pilu bukan buatan	The mynahs twittered to each other, The jungle fowl crowed in uproar As though pitying the sultan's daughters. The princesses were truly sorrowful.
Segala bunga berkembang-kembangan Diseri kumbang berlayang-layangan Persembahkan bau itu gerangan Keluar tidak dengan kenangan	All the flowers blossomed, Visited by beetles flying hither and yon As if they were presenting their fragrances So that the princesses did not depart without a sign of remembrance.
Terlalu pilu puteri mengindera Fajar merekah teranglah nyata Bertambah rawan emas juita Berjalan dengan airnya mata	The royal princesses were so sorrowful. Dawn broke in clear light And increased the turmoil of those golden ones of life, Who walked in tears.
85. Berjalan tidak berhenti lagi Menurutkan barang kehendak kaki Naik segenap gunung yang tinggi Padang yang luas semua dipergi	85. They walked without stopping Following the inclination of their steps Climbing all the high mountains Traversing all the wide plains.
Puteri Nurkiyah lalu berkata Kepada kanda dipandangnya mata Apa diperbuat di sini kita Terlalu takut rasanya beta	Princess Nurkiyah then spoke, Looking at her elder sister: "What is it that we do here? We feel so frightened.
Seumur hidup tidak merasa Di dalam negeri senang sentosa Sudahlah takdir Tuhan yang Esa Baharulah ini mendapat seksa	In all our life we have never felt so, In the easeful, peaceful city— This the decree of God the One, Only now do we experience suffering.

Semalam mengapa katanya kanda Hendak mendapatkan akan ayahanda Sekarang mengapa di sini tiada Terlalu takut hati adinda	Last night why did my sister say That we were going in search of our father? Now why is he not here? Your little sister is so frightened."
Disahut oleh tuan puteri Diamlah tuan jangan berperi Jalan tak dapat lagi dicari Sesat lalu kita ke mari	The princess answered: "Hush, speak no more. We cannot find the road, We were lost and so came hither."
Berhentilah cetera puteri mengerna Di dalam hutan berjalan lena Tersebut perkataan raja yang ghana Hati di dalam gundah gulana	Leaving the tale of the royal princesses Walking tiredly in the forest, Let us speak of the mighty king, His heart full of melancholy.
Berburu sudah berapa lama Seekor binatang tidak menjelma Terlalu hairan raja 'ulama Menteri pengulu sertalah sama	Having hunted for some time, Not a single animal appeared. The wise raja was astonished, Likewise his courtiers and headmen.

Titah baginda kepada menteri
Kita berburu berapa hari
Tiada kuasa demikian peri
Marilah kita pulang ke negeri
	His highness spoke to the courtiers:
	"We have been hunting for many
	   days,
	And there is nothing in our power to
	   be done.
	Let us return to the city."

Tidaklah dagang berbanyak reka Kembalilah sultan seri paduka Hati baginda rasanya duka Sampai ke negeri dengan seketika	The tale-teller will not be roundabout: His royal highness the Sultan decided to return, With his heart sorrowful, And arrived at the city not long after.

86.
Gemparlah orang sekaliannya rata
Mengatakan datang duli baginda
Terlalu susah permai yang pokta
Jangan dikata Ardan yang dusta
	86.
	Hubbub arose among the people,
	Saying that his highness was
	   approaching.
	The peerless queen was thrown into
	   disquiet,
	To say nothing of the deceitful Ardan.

Tatkala datang duli yang ghana	When the mighty king approached,
Orang pun gempar di istana	The people in the palace were in uproar,
Mencari puteri lela mengerna	Looking for the royal princesses,
Orang sekalian ke sini sana	Everyone rushing hither and yon.
Lalu bertitah permaisuri	The queen then spoke
Kepada anakanda Jamjam Puteri	To her daughter Princess Jamjam:
Apa bicara muda bestari	"What is your counsel, young noble?
Kerana ayahanda sudah kembali	For your father has returned.
Ayahanda tuan tentu bertanya	Your father is certain to ask
Akan puteri kedua-duanya	After those two princesses.
Sekarang apa gerangan jawabnya	Now what shall we answer?
Terlalu susah bonda memikirnya	Your mother is unquiet at the thought."
Disahut puteri merdu suara	The princess answered in a sweet voice:
Patik pun sudah hilang kira-kira	"I too am at a loss.
Jikalau ditanya ayahanda betara	If asked by my revered father,
Apa hendak dijawabkan segera	What ready answer shall I have?"
Bertitah permai raja perempuan	The queen consort spoke
Kepada Sulung Putera bangsawan	To well-born Sulung Putera:
Apa bicara sekarangnya tuan	"What now is your opinion,
Ditanya ayahanda raja pahlawan	If we are questioned by your valiant father the king?"
Sulung Putera menjawab sabda	Sulung Putera answered her words:
Apa bicara semuanya bonda	"And what is your counsel for all this, mother?
Hilang fikiran di dalam dada	I am at a loss to know what to do.
Sebarang perintah menurut anakanda	Whatever you command your son shall obey."
Setelah Ardan mendengarkan kata	When Ardan heard those words,
Keduanya hilang bicara yang nyata	That both were at a loss,
Dengan marahnya memberi warta	Angrily she uttered her tidings:
Anakanda dan kanda akalnya buta	"My children and my sister have blunted their wits.

Apa disusahkan olehnya kanda
Jikalau datang tanya baginda
Jawablah kanda serta anakanda
Katakan puteri sudah tiada

87.
Kerana anakanda keduanya hilang
Disamun oleh Badui jembalang
Diambilnya kedua wajah gemilang
Dibawanya lalu ke hutan lalang

Demikianlah kata paduka suri
Kepada kakanda mahkota negeri
Tambahi lagi sebarang peri
Harta dan benda semua dicuri

Seketika duduk ia di situ
Datang baginda paduka ratu
Ahmad Syah bersamalah itu
Semayam di geta bertatah mutu

Belum pun sempat baginda bertahta
Datanglah permaisuri mahkota
Ardhan puteri bersamalah serta
Datanglah dengan airnya mata

Dengan tangisnya permai bersabda
Apa bicara kanda anakanda
Keduanya puteri sudah tiada
Dicuri Badui orang berida

Mana segala harta bendanya
Belumlah sempat lagi diambilnya
Sulung Putera segera merampasnya
Kedua anakanda sudah dibawanya

What has my sister to fear?
If his highness makes question,
Answer, sister and children,
Say that the princesses are gone.

87.
For the two children are lost
Attacked by the cursed Bedouin tribe.
They snatched away the two radiant-
    faced ones,
Took them away into the wild-grass
    forest.

That is what the queen should say
To your husband, crown of the realm.
And add to that some such story
That treasure and goods have also
    been stolen."

They had sat there for a moment,
When his highness the king arrived,
Together with Ahmad Syah,
And was seated on the jewel-studded
    divan.

His highness had not yet seated
    himself on his throne
When the crown consort arrived,
Princess Ardan along with her,
Arriving streaming with tears.

Weeping, the queen spoke:
"What shall we do, husband and children,
For the two princesses are gone,
Stolen by the Bedouin, experienced
    thieves,

As for all their treasure and goods,
They had not the chance to take them.
Since Sulung Putera at once snatched
    them back.
But the two children they have carried
    off.

Belumlah sempat gerangan peri Diambil Sulung keduanya puteri Kerana Badui segeralah lari Membawa segala siti bestari	It seems that there was no time For Sulung to rescue the two princesses, For the Bedouin fled at once, Taking all the noble attendants."
Demikianlah kata permai mengindera Serta dengan Sulung Putera Sangat terkejut sultan perwira Baginda menangis tidak terkira	Thus said the royal queen, Together with Sulung Putera. The heroic sultan was stunned And wept incalculably,
Sambil bertitah lakunya duka Wahai adinda permai mastika Tidakkah ada orang berjaga Pintu kota maka terbuka	While speaking, with sorrowful demeanour, "O my wife, talisman queen, Was there no one on guard, That the gate of the city was open?
88. Mengapa tiada dijagakan orang Jadilah Badui membuat garang Dapat menyamun di tengah terang Kota diperbuat sebarang-barang	88. Why was it unguarded, Such that the Bedouin menaced, Were able to attack in broad day, The city treated as they pleased?"

Raja Ahmad menangislah juga
Terkenangkan adinda gemala mastika
Kerana tidak disangka-sangka
Sudahlah datang bala celaka
	Raja Ahmad also wept,
	Thinking of his sisters, talisman
	   jewels,
	For it had not occurred to him
	That disastrous misfortune could
	   befall them.

Seraya bermadah perlahan suara Kepada adinda Sulung Putera Wahai adinda muda perwira Tiada berjaga hulubalang bentara	Then he spoke in a low voice To his brother Sulung Putera: "O my brother, valiant youth, Were there no warriors or attendants on guard?
Kerana tuan yang tinggalkan Barang apa suruh jagakan Tidakkah boleh adinda suruhkan Di dalam kota suruh kawalkan	For you were the one left behind, Asked to guard what was here. Could you not have instructed That the city within be watched?"

Sulung Putera mendengarkan kata	Sulung Putera heard those words,
Sabda kakanda muda yang pokta	The speech of his brother the peerless youth.
Tunduk curah airnya mata	He bent his head and tears poured down.
Kakanda jangan menyalahkan beta	"Brother, do not blame us.
Baginda pun gundah bukan suatu	We too are exceeding melancholy."
Menyuruh memanggil penunggu pintu	He ordered the gate-keeper summoned.
Mata-mata datang mengadap ratu	The watchman came to face the king,
Rasanya takut bukan suatu	Full of no little fear.
Baginda semayam di tengah puri	His highness was seated in the middle of the palace,
Serta dengan putera sendiri	Together with his sons.
Sultan bertitah muka berseri	The Sultan spoke with shining countenance:
Mata-mata juga hampir ke mari	"Let the watchman approach."
Mata-mata duduk di bawah ketapakan	The watchman sat at the foot of the throne,
Serta menyembah dengan ketakutan	And made fearful obeisance.
Menjunjung duli paduka sultan	Placing the royal sultan's foot upon his head,
Gentarnya hati bukan buatan	His heart quivering in no small way.
Titah baginda kepada mata-mata	His highness spoke to the watchman:
Hai penunggu pintunya kota	"Gate-keeper of the palace,
Suatu malam waktu yang nyata	On that certain night, at a particular time,
Siapakah masuk ke negeri kita	Who was it who entered our domain?

89.

Pintu kota siapa membuka	Who opened the gates of the city?
Engkau sekalian tidak berjaga	You all were not keeping watch,
Badui masuk tiada ditegah	So that the Bedouin entered unchallenged.
Hampirlah engkau sertanya juga	Perhaps you were in league with them."

Mata-mata mendengar titahnya ratu Terkejutnya hati bukan suatu Tunduk menyembah penunggu pintu Harapkan ampun telah tertentu	The watchman heard the words of the king, Startled in no small way. The gate-keeper bent in obeisance: "Craving your pardon, that is certain,
Beribu ampun duli syah alam Sultan mahkota memutar alam Tuanku tinggalkan berapa malam Seorang tidak masuk ke dalam	A thousand pardons, your royal highness, Crown sultan who revolves the world. My lord was absent for several nights, Not a soul entered within."
Baginda murka bukan kepalang Mukanya merah gilang gemilang Pembohong engkau hai jembalang Puteriku kedua mengapakah hilang	His highness was exceptionally enraged, His face shone gleaming red: "You are a liar, you devil! Why are my two princesses lost?
Jikalau tidak orang mencuri Mengapatah hilang anakanda puteri Khabarnya Badui masuk ke mari Dialah konon membawa lari	If not because someone has stolen them away, Why then are my daughters the princesses lost? I am told the Bedouin entered here; They are the ones who took them away.
Hampirmu muafakat penunggu pintu Maka engkau berkata begitu Anakanda bunuhlah dianya itu Kerana derhaka nyata tertentu	You were in cahoots with them, gate-keeper, That is why you speak thus. My son, kill him, For his clear treason."
Raja Ahmad Syah mendengarkan sabda Sangat murka laku ayahanda Menyuruh membunuh mata-mata berida Terlalu gundah bangsawan muda	Raja Ahmad Syah heard those words, His father greatly enraged, Commanding him to kill the old watchman. The young noble was greatly upset.
Kepada mata-mata ia berkata Berkhabarlah engkau hai mata-mata Jangan sekali engkau dusta Siapa yang masuk ke dalam kota	To the watchman he said: "Tell us, watchman, Don't dare to lie, Who was it who entered the city?"

Mata-mata pun takut bukan kepalang	The watchman was exceptionally
Gemetar segala sendi dan tulang	afraid,
Kerana murka raja terbilang	His joints and bones all aquiver,
Tunduk menyembah lakunya walang	Because of the rage of that famous king.
	He bent in obeisance with dejected demeanour.

90.

Daulat tuanku daulat syah alam	"Long may my lord reign, ruler of the world,
Adalah tuanku suatu malam	There was a certain night,
Tatkala bulan terangnya kelam	When the light of the moon was obscure,
Hanya inanganda keluar di dalam	Only the royal nursemaid left the city.

Serta dayang ada berdua	Together with two handmaids.
Keluar kota inang yang tua	The old nursemaid left the city.
Tidak melihat anakanda kedua	I did not see your two children,
Hanyalah inang seorang jua	Only that one nursemaid."

Permaisuri mendengarkan kata	The queen heard those words
Akan sembah itu mata-mata	Presented by the watchman
Sangat terkejut rasanya cita	And was terrified in her thoughts,
Kalau diketahui puteranya serta	Lest her son's involvement be known.

Permai bermadah lakunya suka	The queen spoke with pleasure:
Kata mata-mata benarlah juga	"The watchman's words are true.
Tatkala hilang usul mastika	For when the talismanic ones were lost,
Inang dan dayang tinggal belaka	The nursemaid and handmaids were left behind

Belum sempat inanganda bertanya	Before the nursemaid could be questioned,
Inanganda sudah keluar dianya	She too had already gone.
Entah ke mana gerangan perginya	No one knows where she may have gone.
Anakanda puteri konon dicarinya	Perhaps in search of the princesses."

Baginda mendengar kata isteri	His highness heard his wife's words
Sangatlah yakin raja bestari	And the royal king was convinced.
Suatupun tidak baginda berperi	Not a word did his highness utter,
Duduk menangiskan anakanda puteri	But sat lamenting his daughters the princesses.

III. PNRI W. 257 *Syair Sultan Abdul Muluk*

III. *Syair Sultan Abdul Muluk*

After her husband's defeat and capture at the hands of Raja Hindustan, Rafiah escapes from her palace into the forest.

Setelah petang sudahlah hari
Rafiah bermohon lalu kembali
Serta sampai ke istana sendiri
Masuk ke peraduan Rafiah puteri

Once it was evening
Rafiah took her leave and returned,
Arrived at her own palace,
And entered her bedchamber.

87.
Lalu menangis tiada berhentinya
Datang kepada malam harinya
Diajaknya seorang anak menterinya
Tidur bersama dengan dianya

87.
Then she wept without cease
All the way until night,
Invited a daughter of one of her councillors,
To sleep together with her.

Anak wazir tidur sangat cenderalah
Lalulah bangun Siti Rafiah
Dengan sikin disembelihnyalah
Tangannya dipegangkan sikin sebilah

The councillor's daughter slept soundly,
And Siti Rafiah got up,
Slaughtered her with a knife,
And put the knife in her hand.

Ia pun mengambil pedang suaminya
Yang tinggal di tempat peraduannya
Keluarlah ia dari jendelanya
Berjalan tu dengan air matanya

Then she took her husband's sword,
Left behind in his sleeping place,
Climbed out of the window,
Going with tears in her eyes.

Disuruh oleh Sultan Hindi
Mengawali sekalian orang Barbari

Sultan Hindi had ordered
That the Barbari people be kept under guard.

Menyamarlah ia sambil berjalan
Seorang pun tiada yang menegurkan
Sudahlah dengan yang demikian
Lepaslah ia ke dalam hutan

Disguising herself as she walked,
Not a single person spoke to her.
And in this manner
She escaped into the forest.

....

The dead girl is discovered and is presumed to be Rafiah. Rahmah is tortured and then imprisoned with her husband.

94.
Sebermula tersebut suatu perkataan
Akan Rafiah puteranya sultan
Membawa dirinya ke dalam hutan
Menurutkan kehendak kakinya
 berjalan

Beberapa yang dilalui Siti 'Arabi
Daripada padang bukit yang tinggi
Sangat tawakkal di dalam qalbi
Serta berserah kepada Ilahi Rabbi

Apabila lapar rasa perutnya
Daun kayu juga yang dimakannya
Terlalu letih rasa badannya
Tambahan pula dengan hamilnya

Rafiah pun menangis berkata ia
Letihlah sudah tiada bergaya
Wahai nasib apakan daya
Dengan perintah Tuhan yang kaya

Tangislah ia sambil berjalan
Tiada terangkat rasanya badan
Laparnya lagi tidak tertahan
Tambahan pula dengan keberatan

95.
Adalah kepada suatu hari
Di tepi bukit baringlah puteri
Hatinya masyghul tiada terperi
Terkenangkan nasib Sultan Barbari

Seketika lagi tampak kelihatan
Segala binatang berlari-larian
Menderu seperti bunyinya taufan
Rafiah terkejut bangkit perlahan

94.
Now a certain matter is related
Regarding Rafiah, daughter of the
 sultan,
She went into the forest,
Walking according to her feet's
 inclination.

Many places did Siti 'Arabi pass,
Of plains and high hills,
Her heart full of surrender to God,
Having entrusted herself to the Lord
 her God.

When she felt pangs of hunger
Leaves of trees alone she ate.
Her body felt extreme fatigue,
Especially as she was with child.

Rafiah wept and said:
"Exhausted and powerless,
O fate, what can I do?
This is the decree of God the
 Almighty.

She lamented as she walked,
Feeling as though she could not lift
 her feet,
Her hunger she could not endure,
Nor the weight of her pregnancy.

95.
On a certain day,
The princess lay down on a hillside,
Unbearably distressed at heart,
Thinking of the fate of Sultan
 Barbari.

A moment later appeared
The animals all in flight,
Roaring like the typhoon.
Startled, Rafiah rose cautiously.

Ia mendengar serta dilihatnya	She heard and saw
Binatang yang lari ada mengejarkan	That the fleeing animals were chased
Seekor binatang hebat rupanya	By an animal of terrible appearance
Seperti darah rupa bulunya	Its fur red as blood.
Rafiah pun sangat rasanya ngeri	Rafiah was full of terror,
Mengunus pedangnya bangkit berdiri	Unsheathed her sword and stood,
Binatang menerkam datang berlari	The animal ran and lunged at her.
Ditahankan pedangnya oleh puteri	The princess held it off with her sword.
Setelah mati sudahlah binatang	Once the animal was dead
Kepada misainya ia terpandang	To its whisker she glanced—
Hanyalah sehelai terlalu panjang	But a single long strand.
Diikatnya puteri kepada pinggang	The princess tied it to her waist.
Misai binatang sudah diambilnya	Having taken the animal's whisker
Lalu diikatkan kepada pinggangnya	And tied it to her waist,
Hilanglah segala letih lesunya	All her fatigue and tiredness vanished,
Jadilah kuat pada saatnya	And at once she became strong.
Madah tiada dipanjangkan lagi	This story will not be drawn out—
Berjalanlah pula Siti 'Arabi	Siti 'Arabi went on,
Tiada berketahuan tempatnya pergi	Not knowing where she was bound,
Menurutkan mana kehendaknya kaki	Following her feet's inclination.
Enam bulan lamanya sudah	Six months passed,
Di dalam hutan Rafiah menyerapah	While in the forest Rafiah uttered
Serta tawakkal kepada Allah	spells against evil spirits,
Hamilnya itu sangat beratlah	She surrendered herself to Allah.
	Her pregnancy had much advanced.
Suatu malam kepada cetera	One night, the story goes,
Rafiah sakit hendak berputera	Rafiah felt the pains of childbirth.
Gundahnya tiada lagi terkira	Her distress was unimaginable,
Harapkan Allah juga yang memelihara	Her hope only in Allah to care for her.
Tambahan terkenangkan nasib badannya	When she thought of her fate,
Hancurlah luluh rasa hatinya	Her heart felt utterly crushed.
96.	96.
Teringatlah akan ayah bondanya	Remembering her father and mother,
Rafiah pun tangis seorang dirinya	Rafiah wept all alone.

Dengan takdir Ilahi Rabbi	According to the decree of the Lord God,
Memandang jauh Siti 'Arabi	Siti 'Arabi looked into the distance,
Dilihatnya ada sinaran api	Saw that there was a ray of fire,
Berjalanlah ia pergi mendapati	And walked towards it.
Berjalanlah ia tiadalah lengah	She walked without tarrying
Bertemulah dengan sebuah rumah	And came to a house.
Lalu berhenti Siti Rafiah	Then Siti Rafiah halted
Di luar pintu duduk di tanah	Outside the door and sat upon the ground.
Didengarkan oleh Rafiah puteri	Princess Rafiah heard
Rumah tu ada orang pasti	That the house was certainly occupied
Tengah dhikr Allah belum berhenti	By someone ceaselessly reciting Allah's name
Rafiah menangis duduk menanti	Rafiah wept as she sat waiting.
Siti menangis tersedu-sedu	Siti wept and sobbed,
Sambil berkata suaranya merdu	Saying in a melodious voice,
Ya Allah ya Tuhanku Ya Rabbi	"O Allah, o my lord, o my God,
Engkau juga yang menolongi aku	You alone assist me."
Kata orang yang menceritakan	The teller of the tale said:
Adapun yang empunya rumah di hutan	The owner of the house in the forest
Seorang syeikh 'ulama pilihan	Was a sheikh, a renowned sage,
Doanya maqbul tiada terlawan	Unrivalled in fulfilment of his prayers.
Telah tuan syeikh sudah sembahyang	Once the sheikh had finished his prayer,
Kepada anaknya dia memandang	He gazed at his daughter.
Bukakan pintu olehmu dayang	"Maiden, open the door.
Ada seorang gharib yang datang	A stranger has arrived."
Anak tuan syeikh bangkit berdiri	The sheikh's daughter rose up
Membuka pintu dia sendiri	And opened the door herself.
Bertemu dengan Rafiah puteri	She met with Princess Rafiah,
Sama bersalaman berpegang jari	Greeting her and taking her hand.

Sudah bersalaman muda utama
Keduanya naik bersama-sama
Rafiah mencium kaki 'ulama
Oleh tuan syeikh segera diterima
	Once the excellent young women had
	    greeted each other
	The two went up to the house
	    together.
	Rafiah kissed the feet of the sage
	And was at once welcomed by the
	    sheikh.

Tuan syeikh melihat belas dan
    sayang
Ia berkata sambil memandang
Dari mana gerangan anakku datang
Sampaikan ke mari seorang-orang
	The sheikh looked at her with pity
	    and compassion,
	And said while he gazed upon her:
	"From whence have you come, my
	    child,
	Such that you arrive here all alone?"

97. Siti Rafiah menjawab kata Sambil terhambur airnya mata Kehendak Allah juga semata Kudratnya berlaku ke atas beta	97. Siti Rafiah answered his words, While tears streamed from her eyes: "It is all because of Allah's will. What he predestined for me has occurred.
Adapun akan hamba nin tuan Sultan Barbari empunya perempuan Negerinya dialahkan Raja Hindustan Suami hamba sudah tertawan	For your servant, sir, Is the wife of Sultan Barbari. His country defeated by Raja Hindustan, My husband has been captured."
Kepada tuan syeikh dikhabarkannya Daripada hal perjalanannya Serta pula dengan hamilnya Tuan pun sangat belas dan kasihannya	To the sheikh she related all That had to do with her journey, As well as with her pregnancy. The sheikh was full of pity and compassion.
Seketika duduk berperi-peri Datanglah tuan syeikh empunya isteri Serta bersalaman dengan puteri Berapa makanan dianya memberi	They sat for some time conversing, And the sheikh's wife arrived, Greeted the princess, And gave her many kinds of food.
Sudah makan sempurna tentu Berkatalah anak tuan syeikh itu Marilah tidur hai saudaraku Kepada tempat hamba di situ	Once she had been sated, The sheikh's daughter spoke: "Come and sleep, my sister, There in my chamber."

Rafiah pun bangkit dengan segeranya Tiada bergaya rasa badannya Daripada sangat menahan sakitnya Dibawa anak tuan syeikh masuk ke tempatnya	Rafiah arose at once Her body not at all trembling For she was withstanding her pain, And was brought by the sheikh's daughter to her place.
Telah sampai waktu dinihari Rafiah pun sakit tiada terperi Keluh kesah seorang diri Sebentar duduk sebentar berdiri	Once the dawn had broken, Rafiah was struck by great pain, Sighing, moaning and groaning alone, For a moment sitting, for a moment standing.
Anak tuan syeikh bangunlah segera Berkata dengan perlahan suara Mengapakah beradu tiada cendera Apakah sakit hai saudara	The sheikh's daughter arose at once And spoke in a low voice: "Why do you not sleep soundly? What is your pain, my sister?"
Rafiah menjawab dengan perlahan Sakit perut kakanda nin tuan Anak tuan syeikh ibunya didapatkan Mengatakan Rafiah sangat kesakitan	Rafiah answered in a low voice: "My stomach pains me, dear lady." The sheikh's daughter went to fetch her mother, Saying Rafiah was in great pain.
Isteri tuan syeikh pergi segera Seketika duduk Rafiah pun berputera 98. Seorang laki-laki tiada cedera Parasnya elok tiada bertara	The sheikh's wife went at once. After sitting there a while, Rafiah gave birth. 98. A faultless boy, His appearance lovely beyond rival.
Isteri tuan syeikh mengerat pusatnya Lalu dimandikan serta bondanya Setelah sudah diselimutinya Kepada tuan syeikh dibawakannya	The sheikh's wife cut his cord, Then washed him together with his mother. Once she had wrapped him in a blanket, She brought him to the sheikh.
Syeikh menyambut dengan sukacita Dipeluk dicium tubuhnya rata Mengadap qiblat dibangkannya serta Pada telinga kanan didengarkan nyata	The sheikh took him gladly, Embraced him and kissed him all over. Facing Mecca, he recited the call to prayer, Into the baby's right ear he let it be clearly heard.

Setelah sudah demikian peri	Once that had taken place,
Diunjukkan tuan syeikh kepada isteri	The sheikh held the baby out to his wife.
Mak dayang menyambut muka berseri	His wife accepted him, with radiant countenance,
Dibawa kepada Rafiah puteri	And took him to Princess Rafiah.
Disambut Rafiah lalu diribanya	Rafiah accepted him and cradled him on her lap,
Serta dengan belas kasihannya	With pity and affection.
Tiada dapat ditahan hatinya	She could not hold back her heart,
Lalu terhambur air matanya	And tears spilled from her eyes.
Menentang wajah paduka anakanda	Seeing the face of her noble child,
Hancurlah hati di dalam dada	Her heart was crushed in her chest.
Putera nin elok celanya tiada	The prince was lovely and without flaw,
Habislah menurut paduka ayahanda	In all ways like his royal father.
Kata orang yang menceterakan	The teller of the tale related:
Empat puluh hari juga perhentian	For forty days only was the stay,
Rafiah berfikir hendak berjalan	When Rafiah bethought it time to depart,
Puteranya itu hendak ditinggalkan	Intending to leave behind her son.
Adalah kepada suatu hari	On a certain day,
Kepada tuan syeikh Rafiah berperi	Rafiah spoke to the sheikh,
Beberapa takzim hormat diberi	Giving him various respectful greetings,
Serta sujud mencium jari	Making obeisance and kissing his hand.
Rafiah berkata terlalu hormat	Rafiah said with great respect:
Jikalau ada izin tuan keramat	"If my holy master gives leave,
Hamba nin hendak berjalan bangat	Your servant wishes to depart in haste.
Tuan doakan supaya selamat	Sir, pray for my safety.
Adapun akan anak hamba ini	As for your servant's child,
Biarlah dahulu tinggal di sini	Allow him to remain here for a time,
Terserah kepada Tuhan sebati	Entrusted unto God the One,
Zahir kepada tuan minta kasihani	Indeed, from you sir I ask compassion."
99.	99.
Rafiah berkata pilu lakunya	Rafiah spoke with a sorrowful air,
Sepertikan titik air matanya	While tears dropped from her eyes.
Tujuh tahun sampai umurnya	"When he reaches the age of seven,
Mencari hamba suruh dianya	Tell him to seek out your servant."

Tuan syeikh mendengar khabar begitu Ia pun bangkit daripada berteleku Sambil berkata lakunya mutu Hendak ke mana paduka anakku	The sheikh heard those words, Rose up from the floor, Saying with a dejected air: "Where do you wish to go, my royal child?"
Siti Rafiah menjawab khabar Lakunya manis terlalu sabar Jika disampaikan Tuhan qahhar Hajat hamba terlalu besar	Siti Rafiah answered his words, Her demeanour sweet and patient: "If God the powerful permits me, I have a great ambition.
Kerana suami hamba nin tuan Dialahkan oleh Raja Hindustan Jikalau ada mudah-mudahan Sekarang hendak hamba balaskan	For my husband, sir, Was defeated by Raja Hindustan. If it is permitted me, Your servant wishes to avenge him."
Tuan syeikh tertawa lakunya lela Serta berkata in sha' Allah Berkat Nabi Muhammad rasul Allah Hajatmu itu nescaya sampailah	The sheikh laughed, with a cheerful air, And said: "If Allah wills it, By the blessing of His Messenger the Prophet Muhammad That ambition of yours shall be fulfilled."
Tiadalah panjangkan lagi perkataan Oleh tuan syeikh Rafiah diajarkan Daripada ilmu hikmat pakaian Tipu peperangan hulubalang pahlawan	This speech will not be drawn out— By the sheikh Rafiah was instructed, In magical lore and how to use it, The battle ruses of warriors and fighters.
Barang yang ada dalam dadanya Kepada Rafiah diajarkannya Sekalian adanya diketahuinya Rafiah pun suka rasa hatinya	Whatever store of knowledge he had, That he taught to Rafiah. Once she had learned it all, Rafiah was gladdened at heart.
Datang kepada esok pagi-pagi Rafiah bermohon hendaklah pergi Kepada tuan syeikh 'ulama yang tinggi Khidmat menyembah mencium kaki	The next day, early in the morning, Rafiah took her leave, wishing to depart. To the sheikh, the exalted sage, She did obeisance and kissed his feet.

Oleh tuan syeikh dicium kepala
Beberapa doa ditambahi pula
Pergilah anakku muda terala
Disampaikan Allah hajatmu segala

Setelah sudah berperi-peri
Lalu bermohon Rafiah puteri
100.
Kepada tuan syeikh laki isteri
Dengan anak tuan syeikh berpegang
  jari

Sudah bermohon Siti bangsawan
Memeluk mencium puteranya tuan
Sambil menangis putera disusukan
Tinggallah anakku emas tempawan

Puteranya bonda wajah gemilang
Meninggalkan tuan rasaku walang
Mangkin kutatapi kupandang-pandang
Hanguslah hati bagai direndang

Ayuhai anakku gunung gemala
Qalbuku hancur tiada bercela
Menentangkan tuan sepertikan gila
Hilang tak dapat diganti pula

Setelah sudah anak ditangiskan
Dipeluk dicium lalu diletakkan
Kur semangat puteraku tuan
Inilah penyudahan bondamu
  menyusukan

Putera wei apa dayanya bonda
Sebab kerana paduka ayahanda
Jikalau tidak demikian ada
Tiada tertinggalkan tuan anakanda

The sheikh kissed her head,
Adding various prayers.
"Go, my young noble child,
And may Allah fulfil all your
  ambitions."

Once they had spoken together,
Princess Rafiah took her leave
100.
Of the sheikh and his wife,
And held the hand of his daughter.

Once well-born Siti had taken her leave,
She embraced and kissed her son.
While weeping she nursed him:
"Farewell, my child, my beaten gold.

Prince of your mother, of radiant
  countenance,
To leave you makes me bereft.
The more I look and gaze upon you,
The more my heart is burned as
  though roasted on a flame.

O my child, my mountain of gems,
My heart is crushed completely.
Looking upon you as though I were
  mad—
If you are lost, you cannot be replaced."

Once she had lamented her son,
She embraced and kissed him and set
  him down:
"Come hither, soul of my son,
Your mother nurses you for the last
  time.

My son, o, what can your mother do?
This is because of your royal father.
Were it not for him
I would not leave you, child."

Diputuskan hati kepada puteranya	She severed her heart from her son,
Turun berjalan seorang dirinya	Descended from the house and departed alone,
Sambil menyapu air matanya	While wiping away her tears,
Tiadalah tentu tempat ditujunya	Uncertain of her destination.
Ke dalam hutan membawa diri	Into the forest she set off,
Sedikit tidak takut dan ngeri	Not at all afraid or terrified,
Sangat tawakkal hatinya puteri	The princess' heart submissive to God,
Kepada Allah menyerahkan diri	Having given herself up to Allah.
Kata orang yang empunya cerita	Said the teller of the tale:
Tersebut perkataan Rafiah yang pokta	To speak of the matchless Rafiah,
Di dalam hutan terlata-lata	Crawling about in the forest,
Kulit yang permai menjadi lata	Her pretty complexion becoming base.
Berapa lamanya wajah gemilang	For a certain time she of radiant countenance
Beberapa melalui hutan dan padang	Travelled through various forests and plains,
Bertemulah ia tujuh orang hulubalang	Until she met with seven warriors,
Tidur di bawah kayu yang rendang	Asleep beneath a shady tree.

101.
Adapun akan mereka sekalian	As for these men,
Orang sesat mengejar perburuan	They were hunters who had lost their way.
Berapa hari sudah tiada makan	For several days they had not eaten
Tidurlah ia dengan kelemahan	And now slept out of weakness.
Oleh Rafiah dihampirinya	Rafiah drew near,
Serta dilihat diamat-amatinya	Watched and examined them.
Yang seorang itu hebat lakunya	One was of formidable appearance,
Seperti hulubalang rupa pakaiannya	His look and clothes those of a warrior.
Setelah sudah dilihat nyata-nyata	Once she had clearly viewed them,
Mengunus pedang tatah permata	She unsheathed her jewel-studded sword,
Ditindasnya leher hulubalang yang pokta	Slashed at the neck of the matchless warrior,
Taulannya yang keenam dibunuhnya serta	Killing his six companions as well.

Matilah mereka sekalian	Thus they all perished.
Pakaian hulubalang dipakaikan	The warrior's clothes she put on.
Setelah sudah diambilnya	Once she had taken them,
Kuda hulubalang dikenderainya	She made the warrior's horse her mount.
Rafiah menggertakkan kudanya segera	Rafiah spurred her horse at once,
Parasnya elok tiada bertara	Her appearance lovely beyond rival,
Seperti laki-laki yang perwira	Like a valorous man,
Umurnya hampir remaja putera	Whose age was on the cusp of youth.
Lakunya seperti muda bangsawan	Her demeanour that of a young noble,
Di atas kudanya ia berkenderaan	Mounted upon her horse,
Melalui padang merapah hutan	Traversing fields and wandering in forests:
Demikian itu khabarnya tuan	So it was, as the story goes.

IV. Klinkert 130 *Syair Siti Zubaidah*

IV. *Syair Siti Zubaidah*

Hearing that her husband, Zainal Abidin, has been captured by the Chinese princesses, Zubaidah escapes into the forest.

Ia pun berjalan masuk hutan	She then went into the forest,
Semak samun duri dan rotan	Into the undergrowth, thorns and vines.
Jalan yang tentu tidak kelihatan	No clear road was in sight,
Tambahan pulak dengan keberatan	And she was heavy with child.
Siang dan malam berjalan juga	Day and night she walked,
Menurutkan janji untung celaka	Following her destiny, her unlucky fate,
Hati di dalam bagaikan luka	Her heart within as though wounded,
Terkenangkan suaminya sultan paduka	Remembering her husband the royal sultan.
Zubaidah menangis sepanjang hutan	Zubaidah wept as she traversed the forest,
Air matanya jatuh seperti intan	Her tears falling like diamonds,
Teringatkan kasih baginda sultan	Remembering the love of his highness the sultan,
Suatu pun tidak memberi kejatuhan	That in no respect had failed her.

Sedikit juga syak hatinya Keluar perang tidak setahunya Sebab dilarang oleh bondanya Itu pun sudah hilang rasanya	One thing still disquieted her: That he had gone to war without her knowledge, Because he had been forbidden by his mother. But even that [pain] was now gone.
Lalu meratap sepanjang jalan Aduh tuanku sultan handalan 208. Anakada dikandung sampailah bulan Beranaknya tidak berbetulan	This she lamented as she went, "Oh my lord, renowned sultan, 208. Your child I am carrying to term, But its birth will not be as it should.
Hampirlah mati kakanda nan gerang Kerana sudah ditangkap orang Tinggallah adinda badan seorang Apalah jadi kemudiannya gerang	Perhaps you are almost dead, For you have been captured. I am left all alone, What shall become of me?"
Berbalik fikir Siti dermawan Janjinya sudah dibahagikan Tuhan Sudahlah untung gerangan tuan Hilang berani ditangkap perempuan	Generous Siti thought once again Of the fate God had predestined for the sultan. "Such is your fate, it seems, sir, To lose your valour, captured by women.
Baiklah engkau puteri Cina Ku turut juga barang di mana Biarlah aku serta fana Asal bersama raja yang ghana	As for you, Chinese princesses, I shall follow you wherever you go. I'm ready to die as well, So long as it's together with the mighty raja."
Ia berfikir di dalam hati Baik kucari ilmu sakti Kupuhon akan kepada Rabb al-'Izzati Dengan baginda bersama mati	She thought to herself, "I must go in search of magic lore. I implore from the Lord of Honour, That I may die together with his highness."
Sudah berfikir Siti bangsawan Lalu berjalan tidak ketahuan Rasanya sakit, pilu dan rawan Mendengar segala bunyinya hutan	Having thus thought, noble Siti Continued on her unknown way, Feeling pain, sorrow and melancholy, Listening to all the sounds of the forest.

Perutnya besar sangat keberatan	Her stomach was large and heavy,
Hingga berjalan segenap hutan	As she traversed the entire forest.
Sampailah ke desa 'Iraqan Kastan	She reached the city of 'Iraqan Kastan,
Di bawah gunung di tepi hutan	Beneath the mountain, beside the forest.
Gunung 'Iraq tinggi mengawan	'Iraq mountain towered high,
Mercunya seperti sampai ke awan	Its peak seemingly reaching to the clouds.
Di sanalah berhenti Siti bangsawan	There noble Siti halted,
Hampir di negeri kakanda nan tuan	Almost in the country of her brother.
Tetapi tidak pula diketahuinya	But she did not know
Sampailah sudah ia ke negerinya	That she was almost in his city.
Duduklah ia seorang dirinya	She remained alone,
Dirasanya sangat sakit perutnya	Feeling her stomach in great pain.
Lalu bersandar di pohon beraksa	She leant against a fig tree
Mangkin sangat perutnya besar	Her stomach increasing in size,
Rebah bangun serba rasa	She lay down, got up, tried everything,
Terlalu sangat menanggung seksa	Enduring great torments.
Lalu menangis Siti mengindera	Noble Siti wept,
Tahu akan dirinya hendak berputera	Knowing she was about to give birth.
Sakit rasanya tidak terkira	The pain was incalculable.
Budak tu hendak keluar segera	The child was to be born at once.

209.

Ramai berkokok hayam hutan	Forest fowl crowed loudly,
Kiri dan kanan bersahut-sahutan	Left and right, answering one another,
Matahari pun redup tiada kelihatan	The sun went behind a cloud, unseen,
Sepertikan belasnya puteranya sultan	As though it pitied the sultan's child.
Turunlah angin dari angkasa	A wind came down from the heavens,
Bayu berpuput sepoi bahasa	A gentle zephyr blew,
Berkembangan bunga di pohon beraksa	The flowers of the fig tree blossomed,
Seperti mengalukan raja berbangsa	As though welcoming the well-born raja.

Setelah dhohor waktu nan nyata
Berputeralah Zubaidah siti yang pokta
Seorang laki-laki bagai dipeta
Habis menurut ayahanda mahkota
	Once the time of the midday prayer
	  had come,
	Peerless Siti Zubaidah gave birth
	To a son, lovely as a picture,
	In all respects taking after his royal
	  father.

Cahaya wajahnya gemilang warna Tubuh seperti emas kencana Putih kuning syahdu perdana Terus seperti kaca warna	His face shone with glorious sheen, His body was like gold, Yellow and white, lovely, As if seen through coloured glass
Zubaidah terpandang paras anakada Teringatlah ia akan kakanda Habis menurut paras ayahanda Terlalu gundah siti yang syahda	Zubaidah gazed at her child's appearance, Remembering her husband. In all respects he took after his father. Lovely Siti was greatly sorrowful,
Bangunlah ia digagahkannya Disambut anakada dikerat pusatnya Diambilnya air dimandikannya Serta dipangku diberi susunya	She rose up and fortified herself, Took up her child and cut his cord, Took water and bathed him, Held him in her lap and nursed him.

Terlalu suka siti dermawan
Melihat paras putera bangsawan
Kasih dan sayang bercampur rawan
Terkenangkan baginda tidak ketahuan
	Generous Siti was delighted
	At the good looks of the noble prince
	Love and affection mingled with
	  sorrow,
	Thinking of his highness she knew
	  not where.

Menangislah Zubaidah seraya berkata Aduh puteraku gemala mahkota Sudahlah takdir Tuhan semata Di dalam hutan duduk melata	Zubaidah wept and said: "Alas, my son, jewel of the crown, Such is the decree of the Lord of all. In the forest we live humbly.

Bagaimana gerangan kelakuan
  ayahanda
Jikalau melihat paras anakada
Kasih dan sayang di dalam dada
Apa kehendak semuanya ada
	What, perchance, would be your
	  father's response
	If he saw your good looks, my son?
	Love and affection in his heart,
	Whatever you desired would be there."

Duduklah Zubaidah memeliharakan	Zubaidah remained caring for him.
Sudah mandi disusukan	Once he had bathed she nursed him.
Tujuh hari sudah diperanakkan	Seven days after she had given birth,
Zubaidah pun susah memikirkan	Zubaidah was troubled by her thoughts.
Terkenangkan suaminya belum bertentu	Remembering her husband, his fate yet unknown,
Khabar pun tidak barang suatu	Not a word being heard from him.
210.	210.
Mati hidup tidaklah tentu	Dead or alive, even that uncertain,
Terlalu susah hatinya itu	Her heart was greatly distressed.
Ia berfikir serta terpegun	She thought and mused:
Budak ini baik aku tinggalkan	"This child I ought to leave behind.
Hendak dibawak rasanya segan	To bring him I am unwilling,
Menjadi menambahi pulak menyusahkan	For he will add to my troubles.
Aku serahkan kepada Malik al-Bahari	I will entrust him to the Glorious King,
Masakan bodoh Tuhan yang Kahari	For God the All Powerful is no fool.
Hutan pun sama dengan negeri	The forest is to Him the same as the city,
Semuanya perintah Tuhan yang Bahari	All are under the dominion of God the Creator.
Jikalau ada untung tuahku	If I am granted good fortune,
Dipertemukan Allah dengan puteraku	Allah will reunite me with my son.
Hendak dibawak betapa halku	I wish to bring him with me but can I do it?
Kerana berfikir jalannya aku	For I must think of my journey."
Setelah sudah difikirkannya	Once she had thought this,
Disambut anakada disusukannya	She took up her child and nursed him,
Serta dipeluk ciumnya	Embraced him and kissed him,
Berbagai-bagai pulak ratapnya	And many were her lamentations.
Katanya aduh intan mestika	She said: "Alas, talisman, diamond,
Bonda mencari ayahmu juga	Your mother goes in search of your father.
Pergi mengadu untung celaka	She goes to challenge her fortune,
Ku serahkan kepada Tuhan semata	And entrusts you entirely to God.

Tinggallah tuan buahnya hati	I leave you, my heart,
Dipeliharakan Tuhan Rabb al-'Izzati	To be cared for by God, Lord of all Honour.
Semoga didapat orang yang bakti	May you be found by virtuous people,
Supaya diambil dengan seperti	And be taken up as you should.
Jikalau ada asal mahkota	If you are of royal origin,
Sebelah menyebelah di atas tahta	On both sides reigning upon thrones,
Kembalilah engkau asal yang nyata	You shall return to your clear origins,
Dilindungkan Allah orang yang leta	Protected by Allah from base people."
Budak itu pun sepertikan erti	The child seemed to understand,
Memandang bondanya tidak berhenti	Gazing at his mother without cease,
Menghisap susu terhenti-henti	Suckling in fits and starts,
Selaku masyghul di dalam hati	As though he were troubled at heart,
Sambil menangis perlahan-lahan	While he cried quietly,
Suaranya manis tertahan-tahan	His voice sweet and held back.
211.	211.
Zubaidah melihat belas dan kasihan	Zubaidah watched him with pity and affection,
Memandang anakada hal demikian	Gazing at her child in that condition.
Zubaidah pun mengunus cincin di jari	Zubaidah drew a ring from her finger,
Permata zamrud[2] ayahnya memberi	A gem her father had given her,
Bersurat nama sultan yang bahari	Inscribed with the name of the glorious king,
Pendita Ulama turus negeri	Pendita Ulama, pillar of the state.
Dimasukkan kepada jari puteranya	She placed it on her son's finger,
Diselimutkan kain dari suaminya	Wrapped him in a cloth of her husband's,
Antelas emas dipakaikannya	Dressed him in gold velvet,
Terlalu mahal konon harganya	Of great price, or so it is said.
Setelah sudah dipakaikan	Once she had dressed him,
Dipeluk dicium diratapkan	She embraced him, kissed him, lamented over him,
Serta dipangku ditidurkan	Held him in her lap and put him to sleep,
Kerana hendak ditinggalkan	For she wished to leave him.

---

[2] Dh a b-r-j-t

Lalu beradu raja putera	Then the raja's son fell asleep,
Rupanya itu terlalu cendera	It seemed very soundly.
Zubaidah pun belas tidak terkira	Zubaidah was full of great pity
Diputuskan hatinya berjalan segera	But made up her mind to leave at once.
Berjalan menuntut janjinya juga	She set off to discover her fate,
Tawakkalnya tidak lagi terhingga	Her submission to God now limitless,
Terlalu sabar menahan dahaga	Stoical in withstanding thirst,
Lapar pun tidak menjadi duka	Feeling no sorrow at her hunger.
Hanyalah yang ingat kepada hatinya	All that she thought of in her heart
Jalan hendak mencari suaminya	Was how to find her husband.
Putera pun tidak diamatinya	She did not even dwell on her son,
Berserah tanggung kepada Tuhannya	Having given him up to the care of God.
....	Meanwhile, Zubaidah's brother Muhammad Tahir, ruler of 'Iraqan Kastan, travels to Pulau Peringgi and learns of her marriage. Then, together with four royal companions, he goes on a hunting expedition.
216.	216.
Tidaklah lagi dipanjangkan madah	The telling will not be drawn out,
Kerana hati terlalu gundah	For my heart is too distressed.
Sultan 'Iraq kembali sudah	Sultan 'Iraq had then returned,
Segala lasykar semuanya dikerah	And summoned all of his troops.
Alat perburuan semuanya hadir	Hunting equipment was all made ready,
Berhimpun segala menteri wazir	The courtiers and advisers were gathered,
Serta anjing pandai mengusir	As well as dogs good at flushing out game,
Alat senjata tidaklah taksir	And weapons incalculable.
Setelah sudah demikian peri	Once that had been done,
Sampailah waktu dinihari	Dawn now broke.
Berangkatlah baginda keluar negeri	His highness departed from the city,
Diiringkan segala wazir menteri	Accompanied by all advisers and courtiers.

Serta dengan raja keempat	Together with the four rajas,
Memacu kuda terlalu cepat	They spurred their horses on quickly.
Baris berjalan terlalu rapat	The lines marched in close order,
Anjing perburuan terlompat-lompat	The hunting dogs leapt and jumped.
Gemuruhlah bunyi sorak lasykar segala	Deafening were the cries of the soldiers,
Ramai mengiringkan sultan terala	Many accompanying the exalted sultan.
Jaring pukat dibawak pula	Nets and snares were brought along,
Serta melepaskan anjing serigala	And the dogs and jackals were let loose.
217.	217.
Setelah sampai ke dalam hutan	Once they had arrived in the forest,
Lalu berburu paduka sultan	The royal sultan began the hunt.
Anjing menyalak berlompatan	The dogs barked and leapt,
Suatu binatang tiada kelihatan	But not a single animal could be seen.
Terlalu ramai orang berburu	So many people were in the hunt
Di dalam hutan sorak menderu	That the forest rang with shouts,
Anjing menyalak seru-menyeru	The dogs barked and belled,
Tiadalah tentu hendak diluru	Not knowing where to attack.
Seekor binatang haram tiada	There was not a single animal anywhere,
Penatlah sahaja melarikan kuda	The hunters tired themselves riding.
Terlalu hairan sultan syuhada	The great sultan was astonished
Mengapa demikian lakunya ada	At why this was the case.
218.	218.
Lalu bertitah baginda sultan	Then his highness the sultan spoke,
Sambil memandang Raja Hindustan	While gazing at Raja Hindustan,
Penatnya sahaja kita ke hutan	"We have tired ourselves in the forest,
Seekor binatang tiada kelihatan	But not a single animal is to be seen."
Lalu disahut Raja Parsi	Then Raja Parsi answered:
Hutan ini tidak berisi	"This forest is empty.
Anjing melompat salak melangsi	The dogs leap and their barks are shrill,
Suatu pun tidak menggarisi	But not a thing crosses our path."
Suka tertawa Raja Handalan	Raja Handalan laughed with pleasure,
Bergurau senda lima bertaulan	The five friends laughed and teased
Lalu bermadah Raja Handalan	one another.
Marilah kita berjalan-jalan	Then Raja Handalan said:
	"Let us go for a wander.

Hari sudah hampir kan petang	It is almost evening.
Tiada melihat seekor binatang	We have seen no animals.
Penatlah sahaja pergi datang	Tired ourselves with toing and froing,
Membawak tombak beratus batang	And carrying with us hundreds of spears.
Kita berburu baik berhenti	Better that we halt the hunt
Ke lembah gunung kita lihati	And go to look at the mountain valley.
Pergi berjalan bersuka hati	Travel about to amuse ourselves,
Rakyat sekalian suruh berhenti	Leaving the people all here."
Mendengar madah Raja Handalan	Hearing the words of Raja Handalan,
Tersenyum manis sultan handalan	The famed sultan smiled sweetly.
Kelimanya itu sama berjalan	The five of them travelled together,
Berlarikan kuda berbetulan	Riding their horses straight to the mountain.
Di kaki gunung sampailah sudah	They arrived at the foot of the mountain,
Tempat putera Puteri Zubaidah	Where Princess Zubaidah's son was,
Didengar baginda nyatalah sudah	His highness heard distinctly
Budak menangis terlalu indah	A child weeping, very lovely.
Suaranya merdu mendayu-dayu	His voice was sweet and murmuring,
Seperti orang cinta merayu	Like someone sad and plaintive.
Baginda mendengar hatinya sayu	Heartsore, his highness heard
Memandang ke bawah pohon kayu	And looked beneath a tree.
Didengar baginda di sanalah nyata	His highness had heard it distinctly there.
Segera berjalan raja yang pokta	Quickly the peerless raja went,
Diiringkan raja keempatnya serta	Accompanied by the four rajas,
Lalulah sampai duli mahkota	And then the sovereign king arrived there.
Kepada kanak itu baginda terpandang	His highness gazed at the child
Cahayanya persih terlalu terang	Of a brilliant lustrous radiance,
Eloknya bukan sebarang-barang	His beauty of no ordinary kind,
Seperti intan sudah dikarang	Like a diamond in a setting.

219.
Baring di bawah pohon beraksa
Mengisap tangan senentiasa
Beralas kain antelas berselimut kasa
Segera didapatkan raja berbangsa

Kelima raja samalah menerpa
Katanya ini anak siapa
Terlalu elok paras dan rupa
Seperti emas baharu ditempa

Terlalu hairan kelima raja
Melihat budak baharu tersanja
Cahayanya mejelis gemilang durja
Seperti gambar baharu dipuja

Segera disambut oleh baginda
Suka dan cita di dalam dada
Kasih dan sayang belasnya ada
Melihat budak demikian ada

Baginda bertitah manis berseri
Sambil mencium kanan dan kiri
Anak siapa demikian peri
Orang yang mana jatuh ke mari

Apa mula dibuangkannya
Budak nin sangat elok parasnya
Sampainya hati ayah bondanya
Ke dalam hutan membuang puteranya

Dipeluk dicium duli mahkota
Wahai tuan cahaya mata
Tuan ku diambil putera yang nyata
Bolehlah tuan gantikan tahta

219.
Lying beneath the fig tree
Sucking his hand continually,
Lying on a velvet cloth, blanketed in muslin,
The noble king hurried towards him.

The five rajas leapt forward together,
Saying: "Whose child is this,
So lovely in looks and aspect,
Like newly worked gold?"

The five rajas were astonished
To see the child they had just come upon,
His light lovely, his countenance radiant,
Like a newly worshipped image.

At once he was taken up by his highness,
Who became happy and joyous in his heart,
Full of love and affection, pity too,
Seeing such a child.

His highness spoke, sweetly radiant,
While kissing him right and left:
"Whose child is this with such features?
What person has chanced here?

Wherefore was he abandoned,
A child so lovely in appearance?
His mother and father had the heart
To abandon their son in the forest."

The sovereign king embraced and kissed him:
"O, light of my eyes,
I shall take you as my son.
You may be my heir."

Keempat raja sama sukanya Dekat semayam sekaliannya Masing-masing hendak meribanya Terlalu suka memandang parasnya	The four rajas were equally pleased, Sitting all nearby. Each wished to hold the child in his lap, Delighted to gaze on his face.
Lalu bermadah Raja Hindustan Tuah adinda bukan buatan Mendapat anak di dalam hutan Jadi gemala 'Iraqan Kastan	Then Raja Hindustan said: "You are uncommonly fortunate To find a child in the forest, Who will become the jewel of 'Iraqan Kastan.
Tidaklah payah diperanakkan Kita sekadar meliharakan Bondanya sudah disediakan Alangkah suka jikalau dibawakan	For there's no need to be troubled with the birth, We need only care for him. He already has a mother, How pleased she'll be if we bring him to her.
220. Siapa gerangan empunya putera Parasnya elok tiada bertara Apa gerangan kedatangan mara Anakada dibuangkan di tempat yang dura	220. Whose son can this be? His appearance is lovely beyond compare. What disaster can have come, Such that a child was abandoned so far away?"
Raja Parsi menjawab sabda Benarlah sangat titah adinda Di dalam fikiran sangkanya kanda Terlalu masyghul bicara yang ada	Raja Parsi answered his words: "Your words are too true. In my thoughts and surmises, The conclusions are worrying.
Kepadanya tilik nazarnya beta Budak nin bukan orang yang leta Entahkan anak raja bertahta Ditakdirkan Tuhan alam semata	To my intent study, This child is not humble person, But perhaps the son of a reigning raja, Enduring a fate decreed by the Lord of the world.
Inilah tanda orang yang mulia Kain antelas dipakaikan dia Jikalau bukan raja yang kaya Siapa yang ada menaruh dia	This is the sign of one high-born: He is dressed in velvet cloth. If not for mighty raja, Who would own such a thing?"

Sultan 'Irak bertitah pula	Sultan 'Iraq then spoke:
Sungguh kata kanda segala	"All you have said is true.
Bukannya anak orang yang cela	This is not the child of an ignoble person.
Jatuh ke mari apakah mula	Wherefore has he come hither?"
Ramailah ia berkata-kata	Excitedly he spoke,
Terlalu suka di dalam cita	So pleased at heart was he.
Raja keempat bermadah serta	The four rajas joined in:
Budak ini pintaklah beta	"Give me this child.
Beta nin tidak menaruh putera	We too have no sons.
Ingin rasanya tidak terkira	We want him incalculably,
Adinda baik tulus dan mesra	The child, being good, sincere and friendly,
Tanda muafakat lima saudara	Are the sign of agreement between five brothers."
Tersenyum manis sultan yang syuhda	The glorious sultan smiled sweetly.
Jangan begitu kanda adinda	"Do not be so, brothers,
Beta pun sama putera tiada	For I too lack a son.
Samalah kita mengasihi anakada	Together let us care for this child.
Kerana kita sama mendapatnya	Because we found him together,
Samalah kita meliharakannya	Together shall we care for him.
Jikalau besar panjang umurnya	If long life is granted him,
Berbahagi kasih kepadanya	We shall apportion our love to him."
Raja keempat suka tertawa	The four rajas laughed with pleasure,
Mendengarkan madah manis sebahwa	Hearing the sweet words in accordance.
Putera seorang timbangan jiwa	A prince, the apple of their eyes,
Ke dalam negeri baik dibawa	They ought to bring home to the city.

221.
Berganti-ganti anakada dipangku
Terlalu gemar memandang laku
Budak pun menangis hendak bersusu
Suaranya manis terlalu merdu

221.
One after another they held the child,
Greatly pleased to see his ways.
The boy cried wanting milk,
His voice sweet and melodious.

Segera diambil Raja Handalan	At once Raja Handalan took him,
Dibawak bersiar berjalan-jalan	Brought him to walk about,
Rasanya sangat belas kasihan	Feeling great pity and affection,
Melihat anakada hal demikian	Seeing the child in that state,
Sambil bernyanyi cara menggala	While singing in a cheerful manner,
Suaranya merdu seperti biola	His voice as melodious as a violin,
Berbagai bunyi pantunnya pula	Many were his *pantun*,
Mendiamkan anakada mercu gemala	To quiet the child, that pinnacle of jewels.
Sambil berpantun demikian peri	While crooning *pantun* thus,
Anakada dipangku sambil berdiri	Standing and cradling the child.
Bunyinya elok tidak terperi	The sound was unspeakably lovely,
Seperti bunyi kumbang menyeri	Like a bee visiting flowers.
Anak merpati terbang sekawan	"Young pigeons fly in a flock,
Hinggap di puncak balai rong seri	Alighting on the apex of the royal pavilion.
Buahlah hati diamlah tuan	My beloved, hush,
Bondamu ada di dalam negeri	Your mother is there in the city.
Marga Wilis[3] menjala ikan	Marga Wilis is netting fish,
Ikan permainan Berma Sakti	Fish that are the toys of Berma Sakti.
Apalah juga tuan tangiskan	What is there to cry about?
Bonda kelima ada menanti	Your five mothers await you."
Setelah didengar raja keempatnya	Once the four rajas had heard,
Suka tertawa sekaliannya	They all laughed together,
Sambil bertitah dengan sukanya	While saying with pleasure:
Adinda ini sangat pandainya	"You are too skilled."
Budak pun dinyanyikan ayahanda	The child was sung to by his 'father',
Tangan terletak di atas dada	And put his hand on his chest.
Lalu terpandang kepada baginda	Then his highness caught sight
Di jari anakada cincin nan ada	Of the ring upon his finger.
Diambil Raja 'Iraqan Kastan	Raja 'Iraqan Kastan took it:
Cincin zamrud berpita intan	An emerald ring surrounded by diamonds,
Di dalamnya ada tanda suratan	Within it an inscription,
Tersebut nama paduka sultan	With the name of the royal sultan.

---

[3] Assuming this is a proper noun.

Sultan 'Iraq Pandita Ulama
Di dalam cincin tersebut nama
Terlalu hairan raja kelima
Cincin dari mana gerangan menjelma

222.
Cincin ini terlalu nyata
Yang empunya ayahanda beta
Berbalik hairan rasanya cita
Kebesaran Tuhan alam semata

Sultan 'Iraq bermadah pula
Silakan kembali kanda segala
Membawak anakada mercu gemala
Supaya jangan mendapat cela

Lalu berangkat raja jauhari
Membawak anakada putera bestari
Diiringkan segala hulubalang menteri
Sampailah konon ke dalam negeri

Setelah sampai ke dalam kota
Naik mengadap ayahanda pendita
Anakada dibawak jugalah serta
Bersama naik di atas tahta

Kepada ayahanda dipersembahkannya
Mendapat budak sangat eloknya
Suatu cincin kepada jarinya
Nama ayahanda tersurat di dalamnya

Sangat terkejut raja ulama
Melihat cincin tersebut nama
Baginda terpegun sekalian lama
Anak siapa gerangan menjelma

Sultan 'Iraq Pandita Ulama,
In that ring was named.
The five rajas were astonished.
"From whence has this ring
    appeared?

222.
This ring, it is clear,
Belongs to my father.
My thoughts are truly astonished
At the greatness of the Lord of the
    world."

Sultan 'Iraq then spoke:
"Let us at once return,
Bringing the child, summit of jewels,
So that he comes to no harm."

Then the noble king departed,
Taking with him the child, the well-
    born prince,
Accompanied by soldiers and
    courtiers,
And arrived, it is said, in the city.

Once they had reached the town,
He sought audience with his sage
    father.
The child he brought with him,
Together they ascended to the throne.

To his father he explained
That he had found a lovely child,
A ring upon his finger,
With his father's name inscribed.

The wise king was astonished
To see the ring with his name.
He mused a long time.
"Whose child, perchance, has
    appeared?

Cincin ini nyatalah sudah Ayahanda berikan kepada Zubaidah Sekarang mengapa pulak berpindah Ada dipakai budak yang indah	This ring, it is certain, I gave to Zubaidah. Now why has it gone to another, To be worn by a beautiful child?"
Baginda berkata lakunya rawan Budak ini peliharalah tuan Siapa tahu ada pertemuan Dengan adikmu siti dermawan	His highness spoke with a sorrowful demeanour. "Look after this child, sir. Who knows if perhaps you will meet With your sister, generous Siti."
Sultan 'Iraq terlalu sukanya Dipelihara seperti anak dijadikannya Disuruh pelihara kepada isterinya Keempat raja serta membelanya	Sultan 'Iraq was greatly pleased, Looked after him as his own child, Commanded his wife to care for him. The four rajas also raised him.
Dipungutkan segala anak menteri Akan pengasuh putera sendiri Akan raja empat buah negeri Inang pengasuh semua diberi	All the courtiers' children were chosen As guardians for the prince. As for the rajas of the four kingdoms, They provided nannies and nursemaids.
223. Tidak kembali keempatnya Sama meliharakan puteranya Serta berbuat akan pakaiannya Diberi inang menyusukannya	223. The four did not return But cared for the child together. As well as providing his clothing, They gave him a wet nurse to give him suck.
Diberinya pulak nama anakada Raja Ahmad Syah bangsawan muda Terlalu kasih ayahanda bonda Bercerai sehari haram tiada	Then, too, they named the child: Raja Ahmad Syah the young noble. His foster mother and father loved him And would not part from him for a day.
Cerdiklah sudah raja putera Parasnya elok tidak bertara Terlalu kasih sultan mengindera Keempat raja samalah mesra	The prince's wits quickened, His appearance was lovely beyond compare. The royal sultan loved him much, The four rajas together in affection.

Hilang perkataan paduka sultan	Passing from the royal sultan,
Tersebut Zubaidah di dalam hutan	To speak of Zubaidah in the forest,
Pilu dan rawan bukan buatan	Truly sorrowful and distressed,
Berjalan segenap kayu dan rotan	Travelling through trees and vines.
Dengan takdir Tuhan semata	By the decree of God,
Sampailah Zubaidah puteri yang pokta	The peerless princess Zubaidah arrived
Ke sebuah bukit tanahnya rata	At a hill in the midst of level ground,
Di atasnya ada seorang pendita	Upon which dwelled a sage.
Zubaidah berjalan dengan segeranya	Zubaidah went at once,
Di kaki bukit tinggi yang dura	To the foot of the high, distant hill,
Pilu dan rawan tidak terkira	Incalculably sorrowful and distressed,
Bertemu seorang muda perwira	There she met with a young hero.
Seorang puteri di atas batu	A princess was sitting upon a rock,
Parasnya elok sifatnya tentu	Her appearance lovely, her features clear.
Segeralah dekat Zubaidah itu	At once Zubaidah approached
Puteri pun malu bukan suatu	And the princess was truly abashed.
Zubaidah bertanya sambil berperi	Zubaidah asked, speaking:
Tuan nin dengar hamba berperi	"Lady, listen to your servant's words.
Bukit apa nama gerangan peri	What, perchance, is the name of this hill?
Ataunya bukit ataunya negeri	Is it a hill or is it a city?"
Puteri pun tunduk lakunya rawan	The princess bent her head in sorrow,
Sertanya pulak malu-maluan	Listening in embarrassment,
Mendengar kata laki-laki pahlawan	Hearing the words of a valiant man.
Zubaidah tersenyum manis kelakuan	Zubaidah smiled, her ways sweet.
Kata Zubaidah muda bangsawan	Young noble Zubaidah said:
Wahai adinda emas tempawan	"O, sister, beaten gold,
Janganlah tuan malu-maluan	Do not be embarrassed.
Kanda pun sama juga perempuan	For I too am a woman."

224.

Lalu diceterakan olehnya Siti	Then Siti related to her,
Daripada awal mula pekerti	All from the very beginning.
Puteri pun suka rasanya hati	The princess was pleased at heart,
Baharu berkata dengan seperti	And only then spoke as she should.

Puteri bermadah dengan manis warta	The princess spoke with sweet words:
Rukiah kanda namanya beta	"Rukiah is my name.
Anak raja Parsi mahkota	The daughter of the Parsi[17] king.
Ayahanda bonda hilanglah serta	My father and mother both dead."
Rukiah berkhabar sekalian cetera	Rukiah related all her story,
Peri diperbuat oleh saudara	How she had been duped by her brother,
Sampai kepada keluar negara	So that she had left the kingdom,
Diam kepada syeikh mengindera	And lived with the royal syeikh.
Zubaidah pun belas bukan suatu	Zubaidah was greatly moved.
Samalah tuan kanda begitu	"I, lady, am in a like state.
Marilah kita gerangan ke situ	Let us perchance go thither
Mendapat tuan syeikh biar tentu	And meet with the syeikh."
Tidaklah hamba berbanyak peri	I shall not speak much of this.
Sudahlah pergi kedua puteri	Once the two princesses had gone
Diamlah bersama tuan qari	They lived with the holy man,
Belajar ilmu sehari-hari	Obtaining knowledge daily.
Berapa ilmu gagah berani	Several sciences of bravery and valour,
Ism menyebut Tuhan subhani	Spells speaking the highest name of God,
Diajar tuan syeikh dengan sekaliani	Were taught by the syeikh in their entirety,
Terlalu suka usul yang seni	Greatly pleasing the lovely ones.
Ada kepada hari suatu	On a certain day,
Duduk di balai paras yang tentu	The resolute beauties were seated in the pavilion,
Hati Rukiah terlalu mutu	Rukiah's heart was too distressed,
Terkenangkan buatan saudaranya itu	Thinking of her brother's treatment of her.
Kepada Zubaidah ia berkata	To Zubaidah she said:
Wahai kanda muda yang pokta	"O, sister, peerless youth,
Maukah kanda menolong beta	Do you wish to help me?
Pekerjaan besar kepada cita	I have a great deed in mind.

---

[17] Most other MSS give Rukiah as the daughter of the king of Yunan, which makes better sense in terms of the story. See Abdul Rahman al-Ahmadi, p. 338 fn. 101.

Jikalau sampai seperti rencana Dapat membunuh Mahran teruna Adindalah jadi hamba yang hina Perintah barang titah rencana	If my plans are fulfilled, Young Mahran will be killed. I will then become your slave, Command me whatever you will."
Zubaidah tersenyum manis berseri Jangan begitu adinda berperi 225. Jikalau ditolong Tuhan yang kahari Dapatlah melawan raja jauhari	Zubaidah smiled, radiantly sweet, "Do not speak so. 225. If God the powerful helps us, We shall combat the noble raja."
Katanya orang empunya madah Kepada tuan qari bermohon sudah Serta memakai puteri yang indah Cara laki pakaian berpindah	The teller of the tale relates: They took their leave of the holy man, And dressed themselves, the lovely princesses, Changing into the clothes of men.

V. Klinkert 157 *Syair Siti Dhawiyyah*   **V. Excerpt from** *Syair Siti Dhawiyyah*

Tersebut pulak Haris putera Di dalam rumah Siti mengindera Majlis pun sunyi sudah ketara Ia pun sudah berkira-kira	Now to speak of Prince Haris In royal Siti's house The party had died down, that was clear, And he began to consider what to do.
Isteri tidak juga dipeka Kerana hatinya tiada suka Daripada takut ayahnya juga Hendak melalui takut derhaka	His wife he did not heed For he liked her not at all, It was only from fear of his father, Wishing to disobey but fearing disloyalty.
Isterinya belum dipandang nyata Kerana hatinya lagi bercinta Siti kedua dipandang mata Tidaklah lupa di dalam cita	He'd not even taken a good look at his wife For his heart was still entangled With the two Sitis, in his mind's eye, Never forgotten in his thoughts.
Duduk ia di dalam peraduan Laku seperti kepilu-piluan Hatinya tidak berketahuan Teringatkan Hafsah muda cumbuan	He sat in the bedchamber, His demeanour morose, His heart uncertain, Thinking of winsome young Hafsah.

Siti Dhawiyyah sudah mengerti
Akan suaminya bersusah hati
Khabar sepatah belumlah pasti
Memandang dia tidak diamati

Siti Dhawiyyah had understood
That her husband was uneasy,
He had not spoken a single clear word,
Had not looked directly at her.

36.
Teringatlah Siti seperti petua
Ilmu diajarkan nenek yang tua
Di sinilah gerangan ilmu ku bawa
Anak raja ini memberi kecewa

36.
Siti recollected the advice
The lore taught by the old granny.
"Here perhaps will I apply this lore.
For this prince brings regret.

Jikalau tidak laku begini
Tiadalah memakainya ilmunya ini
Hatiku baik aku tahani
Lihatkan pesan orang yang fani

If he did not act this way,
I would not resort to this lore.
My heart I ought to restrain,
And think of the admonitions of those now departed.

Patutlah ayahku sangat berpesan
Kerana sudah ada perasan
Raja yang besar dilawan berbesan
Anaknya kelak memberi bosan

It's fitting that my father was so insistent,
For he already had an inkling
That if a great raja became an in-law,
His son would eventually grow tiresome."

Demikianlah fikir Siti sempurna
Sedikit tidak gundah gulana
Sampailah ia orang bijaksana
Memandang laku ertikan makna

Thus spoke perfect Siti,
Not at all dejected or downcast,
For she was wise,
Deducing meaning from her husband's behaviour.

Siti pun beradu seorangnya
Di dalam rumah sangat sunyinya
Orang pun tidur semuanya
Bekas berjaga sangat letihnya

Siti then went to sleep alone,
In her silent house.
Everyone else was asleep,
Exhausted from their vigil.

Adapun akan Haris teruna
Dilihatnya sunyi di dalam istana
Sudah beradu Siti sempurna
Mangkin bertambah bimbang gulana

As for youthful Haris,
When he saw that the palace was silent,
That Siti was soundly asleep,
His anxiety only increased.

Keluh kesah seorang diri Tidak berpaling kanan dan kiri Hatinya rawan tidak terperi Teringatkan Hafsah lela jauhari	He sighed and stirred alone, Turning neither left nor right, His heart in great turmoil, Thinking of gem-like Hafsah.
Tiadalah dapat ditahankannya Lalulah bangun seorang dirinya Perlahan-lahan mengangkat kakinya Seperti pencuri pulak lakunya	He could not restrain himself, And got up alone, Slowly stealing his way, His actions like those of a thief.
Serta datang ke pintu gedung Sekalian pintu semua bertudung Anak menteri di situ berkampung Berkapar tidur berpegang-pegang	He arrived at the building's gate, All of the gates were closed The sons of the courtiers gathered there Lying about asleep, embracing one another.
37. Haris pun datang membangunkannya Diajaknya pulang sekaliannya Seorang budak daripadanya Mengunci pintu sekaliannya	37. Haris then went to wake them, Asked them all to return with him. One of the lads Unlocked all the doors.
Lalulah ia berjalan pulang Menuju gedung tempat berulang Hari pun senja pancar cemerlang Membuka jendela Siti terbilang	Then he went home Heading for the building that was his haunt, Brilliant dawn then broke, Famed Siti opened the window.
Siti Hafsah membuka jendela Dilihatnya datang raja terala Diiringkan anak menteri segala Lakunya seperti orang yang gila	Siti Hafsah opened the window Saw the exalted raja approaching Accompanied by all the courtiers' sons, Behaving like a madman.
Haris melihat jendela terbuka Hatinya Haris sangatlah suka Berjalan masuk dengan seketika Mendapatkan Siti Hafsah juga	Haris saw the open window And his heart was greatly pleased. He entered at once And went to Siti Hafsah.

Hafsah tertawa seraya bermadah	Hafsah laughed and spoke:
Pengantin baharu sangatlah indah	"The new bridegroom is truly lovely.
Kawin semalam berjalan sudah	After only a night of nuptials,
Muafakatkah sudah Siti yang indah	He has already 'come to an agreement' with lovely Siti.
Muafakatkah sudah dengan isteri	Having reached an agreement with his wife,
Segera sangat berangkat ke mari	How quickly he comes hither.
Pengantin apa demikian peri	What manner of bridegroom is this?
Tiada pernah sehari-hari	Never in all my days have I heard of such."
Raja Haris mendengar kata	Raja Haris heard those words
Ia tersenyum dengan sukacita	And smiled with pleasure.
Lalu bermadah raja yang pokta	Then the matchless raja spoke:
Hamba nin rindu akan juita	"Your servant longed for you, o beauty."
Siti disambut masuk ke peraduan	He embraced Siti and they entered the bedroom,
Serta bergurau senda gurauan	Then they teased and cajoled one another.
Demikianlah konon ceteranya tuan	That, it seems, was the tale, sir,
Haris Fadhilah sangatlah hewan	Haris Fadhilah greatly engrossed in lust.
Tiadalah pulang ia nin lagi	He returned no more,
Kepada isterinya tidaklah pergi	To his wife he did not go.
Duduk bermain petang dan pagi	He disported himself day and night,
Siti kedua giliran dibagi	Giving the two Sitis their turns.
38.	38.
Mangkin bertambah pulak lakunya	His behaviour went from bad to worse:
Siti keempat semua diambilnya	All four Sitis were taken by him.
Bermain muda sangat sukanya	He disported himself with glee,
Tiada perdulikan isterinya	With not a thought of his wife.
Jika siang sudahlah hari	When morning had become full day,
Bermainlah ia ke sana ke mari	He took himself off himself here and there,
Dengan segala anak menteri	With all the courtiers' sons,
Ke darat ke laut setiap hari	On land and sea, every day.

Melayarkan sebawa berlumba	Racing sailing boats together,
Bertaruhkan wang teman dan hamba	Staking money with friends and servants,
Segala permainan semua dicuba	All manner of entertainments he sampled,
Lakunya seperti terkena guna	Behaving as though bewitched.
Sehari-hari itulah kerjanya	Daily such were his activities,
Bermain kuda menyukakan hatinya	Riding horses to amuse himself,
Tiada perduli akan isterinya	With not a thought for his wife,
Malam beradu di rumah mukahnya	Spending the nights with his mistresses.
Perempuan keempat yang digemari	The four women were what he enjoyed,
Seperti orang laki isteri	They lived as man and wives,
Segala kehendak semua diberi	Whatever they wished for he gave them,
Mana yang kurang disuruh cari	Whatever they lacked he ordered be found.
Terlebih pulak dari dahulu	It was even worse than previously,
Mendapat Siti hilanglah malu	Going to the Sitis without shame,
Dibawa bermain ke hilir ke hulu	Taking them on jaunts upstream and down,
Harta diberi banyak terlalu	Giving them vast quantities of wealth.
Siti keempat terlalu suka	The four Sitis were greatly pleased,
Menghias dirinya kerjanya juga	Adorning themselves their only task,
Manjanya tidak lagi terhingga	Their fawning now knowing no bounds,
Barang kehendak dapat belaka	Whatever they wished for they obtained.
Mangkin dikasihannya Haris nin gila	So that mad Haris would love them yet more,
Guna hikmat ditambah pula	Their love charms and spells increased,
Segenap persantapan dibubuh segala	All his food was laced with potions:
Di dalam hikmatnya Haris terala	Noble Haris was ensnared in magic.
Haris Fadhilah bertambah sayang	Haris Fadhilah's love increased,
Tiada bercerai malam dan siang	He left them neither night nor day,
Seperti orang mabuk kepayang	Like someone drunk on *kepayang*[18] fruits,
Fikir sempurna habis melayang	Wholesome thoughts flying from him.

---

[18] A tree, *pangium edule*, that bears intoxicating fruits. See Wilkinson, *Dictionary*, p. 522.

39.
Hilanglah sudah takut malunya
Ayahanda dan bonda tiada
 diperdulikannya
Asyik menurut hawa nafsunya
Hilanglah sudah bicara akalnya

Adat laki-laki sahaja begitu
Terkena hikmat menjadi mutu
Akal dan budi tiada bertentu
Tiadalah ingat barang suatu

Perkataan Haris hamba rantaikan
Siti Dhawiyyah pulak disebutkan
Setelah Haris sudah meninggalkan
Ada seketika ia terpegan

Habislah fikir Siti utama
Hairan ta'jub berapa lama
Bersuami apakah nama
Bangsanya raja bilakan sama

Sampai siang Siti berjaga
Memikirkan suaminya tiada peka
Malu kepada saudara belaka
Pasti ditanya adik dan kaka

Siti berfikir memeluk lutut
Apakah pula menjadiku takut
Kerana ilmu sudahku tuntut
Petuaku sebaik kuikut

Kerana ilmu kupelajari
Diajarkan oleh nenek yang bahari
Lagi ayahku menyuruh mencari
Baik diturut demikian peri

39.
His fear and shame had vanished,
He gave no thought to father or
 mother,
But avidly obeyed his lusts
His discernment and intelligence quite
 gone.

The custom of men is ever thus:
Spell-struck they grow melancholy,
Wits and intelligence are disordered,
They give no thought to anything.

This account of Haris I shall tie up,
And turn to Siti Dhawiyyah.
Once Haris had left her,
She was for a moment stunned.

Excellent Siti thought it through,
Astonished and astounded for some
 time.
What manner of husband was this?
How could she match the lineage of
 a raja?

Siti kept vigil until dawn,
Thinking of her heedless husband,
Ashamed before all her relations,
Sure to be questioned by her siblings.

Siti thought, hugging her knees:
"What indeed should I fear?
For I have asked for knowledge,
The advice given me I ought now
 follow.

For I have studied knowledge
Taught by that venerable granny,
And my father told me to seek it,
I ought to follow that counsel.

Baik juga aku khabarkan	I ought to let it be known.
Petua guruku hendak cubakan	My teacher's tips I shall test.
Jikalau Allah kurniakan	If Allah grants it,
Kemudian aku dapat kebajikan	I will then obtain virtuous results.
Jikalau terjanji dari azali	If it has been predestined,
Pertemuan aku umpama tali	My marriage is like an unseverable bond.
Suamiku itu tentu kembali	My husband will certainly return.
Tidaklah mungkin sekali-kali	It cannot be otherwise at all.
40.	40.
Setelah sudah difikirkan	Once she had considered the matter,
Segala sahayanya dihimpunkan	She gathered all her servants,
Segala rahsia dikatakan	Told them her secret intentions,
Dua puluh dinar seorang diberikan	And gave them twenty dinars apiece.
Diupahnya jangan berkhabar suatu	She bribed them not to speak a word
Mengatakan hal suami begitu	Of what her husband had done,
Dikatakan datang juga ke situ	But to say that he did visit her.
Sekalian sahayanya menurut begitu	All of her servants obeyed.
Setelah sudah berteguh rahsia	Once she had sworn to secrecy
Dengan segala hamba dan sahaya	All her slaves and servants,
Sekalian hambanya disuruh bersedia	Her slaves were ordered to ready
Persantapan Haris raja yang mulia	The meal of Haris, exalted raja.
Segala nikmat yang cita rasa	All delicious delights
Diaturkan di dalam pahar gangsa	Were arranged on brass trays,
Piring dan mangkuk perak suasa	Plates and bowls of silver and gold,
Hadir tersaji senentiasa	Served up and ready always.
Kahwa dan sarbat hadirlah sudah	Coffee and sherbet were already served,
Dengan segala nikmat juadah	With all manner of delectable cakes,
Nasi Kabuli gulai merah[4]	Kabuli rice with red sauce,
Mana yang nikmat kepada lidah	All that delights the tongue.

---

[4] MS: Nasi dan gulai k-w-l-y m-y-d-h. The better reading is taken from SOAS MS 36559.

Betapa adat orang bersuami	According to the custom of married women,
Dapur penanggah tidaklah sunyi	The hearth and the cooking-hut were never quiet.
Itulah pengajaran ibu dan umi	That is the teaching of mothers and aunts,
Siti Dhawiyyah empunya rasmi	Which Siti Dhawiyyah had learnt in the proper way.
Segala pakaian suaminya itu	All her husband's clothes
Hadir tersedia sudahlah tentu	Were certainly ready and waiting.
Sarban dan jubah semua di situ	His turban and robe all were there,
Kasutnya hadir di muka pintu	His shoes set out at the door.
Tempat sembahyangnya dihiaskan	His prayer-place was decorated,
Segala perhiasan disediakan	All ornaments kept ready,
Tirai dewangga digantungkan	Tapestry draperies hung up,
Segala perhiasan disediakan	All ornaments kept ready.
Tempat semayan Haris bertahta	The cloth on which Haris was to sit in state
Hadir terbentang di atas geta	Was ready and spread out on the dais.
Sakhlat beledu indah semata	Embroidered velvet, lovely indeed,
Diletakkan jorong tatah permata	On which was placed a sireh vessel studded in gems.
41.	41.
Tempat perludahan hadirlah sedia	A spittoon was set out
Betapa adat raja yang mulia	According to the custom of exalted kings.
Diadap segala hamba dan sahaya	The dais was faced by all the slaves and servants,
Tempat berhias emas bercahaya	The place adorned with gleaming gold.
Jangan dikata di dalam peraduan	To say nothing of the bedchamber,
Terlalu harum bahu-bahuan	Fragrant with perfumes,
Digantungkan kandil gemilang berawan	Hung with radiant lanterns patterned with clouds,
Warnanya kuning kilau-kilauan	Their colour shining yellow.

Tirai terlabuh tiada terbuka	The drapes were loose and unopened,
Siti nin duduk di getanya juga	Siti remained seated on her dais,
Diadap hamba sahaya belaka	Faced by all her slaves and servants,
Sehari-hari bersuka-suka	Enjoying herself daily.
Ada kepada suatu hari	There came a day
Datanglah Khoja laki isteri	When the Khoja and his wife came
Hendak mengadap Haris bestari	To see noble Haris
Serta anakanda Siti jauhari	And their daughter lovely Siti.
Serta datang duduk tersila	They arrived and sat down crossing their legs,
Laki isteri sama setala	Man and wife in harmony,
Segera menegur Siti terala	At once exalted Siti greeted them,
Menyorongkan puan tatah gemala	And offered the sireh set studded in gems.
Sangat dipermuliakan mamanya itu	She did great honour to her uncle,
Di atas hamparan duduknya itu	Seated there upon the carpet,
Hatinya suka bukan suatu	His heart was greatly pleased,
Melihatkan laku anaknya itu	Seeing the demeanour of that child of his.
Khoja berkata wahai tuan	The Khoja said: "O lady,
Sekarang di mana yang dipertuan	Where now is his highness?
Sungguh menjadi suami bangsawan	Has he in fact become your husband?
Rupanya belumlah bonda [sic] ketahuan	His appearance your father does not know."
Siti mendengar kata mamanya	Siti heard her uncle's words,
Tunduk tersenyum manis lakunya	Bent her head, smiled, her actions sweet,
Berkata dengan halus manisnya	And said, quietly and sweetly,
Perkataan mamaku benar semuanya	"What my uncle says is true.
Sangat inginnya ayahanda serta	My uncle's wish is so great
Hendak mengadap duli mahkota	To meet with the royal monarch,
Supaya berkenalan sekalian rata	So that all may know one another,
Terujuk[5] menjadi tuannya kita	To greet the one who becomes our master.

---

[5] Translation reads this as *terunjuk*.

42.
Anak raja itu lain kelakuan
Sangat pemalu bagai perempuan
Duduk bersembunyi di dalam
  peraduan
Malu dilihat teman dan kawan

Tujuh hari sudah ia bersama
Tiada keluar sekian lama
Malu konon bertemu mama
Diam di sini belumlah lama

Akan sekarang ia tiada
Pergi konon mengadap ayahanda
Petang sekarang baharulah ada
Awal pagi pergi baginda

Jikalau mamaku hendak berjumpa
Pagi-pagi benar janganlah lupa
Datang segala ibu dan bapa
Jikalau petang jadilah hampa

Baharu juga turunnya itu
Kasutnya lupa tinggal di pintu
Berjalan sekadar memakai sepatu
Baharu sampai gerangan di situ

Khoja Ishaq mendengar kata
Terlalu suka di dalam cita
Percayakan khabar Siti yang pokta
Disangkakan sungguh datang mahkota

Dilihat sungguh kasutnya ada
Segala kelengkapan persantap baginda
Hadir disediakan oleh anakanda
Terlalu suka di dalam dada

42.
Yet that prince behaves unusually,
He is as shy as a woman,
Hiding within the bedchamber,
Ashamed of being seen by friends and
  companions.

Seven days have we been together
And not once has he come out
He's shy, it seems, to meet my uncle,
Since he has not lived here long.

As for now, he is not here,
But has gone to his father, it seems.
This afternoon he will be here.
His highness left early in the morning.

If my uncle wishes to meet him
At the crack of dawn, don't forget,
Come with all your relatives,
For in the afternoon he will not be
  here.

He's only just departed,
His shoes forgotten at the door,
Walking only in his sandals,
He's probably just arrived there."

Khoja Ishaq heard these words,
And was greatly pleased at heart,
Believing the tale of matchless Siti,
Assuming it was true about the
  prince's arrival.

He saw that the shoes were indeed
  there,
And all of his highness' eating
  paraphernalia,
There made ready by Siti,
And he was greatly pleased.

Siti pun berjamu kedua mamanya	Siti then served her aunt and uncle
Makan nikmat berbagai rupanya	Food and delicacies of all kinds.
Sudah makan ia sekaliannya	Once they had all eaten,
Lalu bermohon kepada anakandanya	They took their leave from her.
Setelah sampai keesokkan hari	When the next day came,
Kepada waktu pagi hari	In the morning,
Datanglah Khoja laki isteri	The Khoja and his wife arrived,
Serta membawa anak sendiri	Bringing their own children.

43.

Laki-laki perempuan ada belaka	Men and women were both there,
Serta dengan adik dan kaka	Together with siblings old and young,
Membawa sembahan berbagai neka	Bringing offerings of many kinds,
Hendak mengadap Haris paduka	Wanting an audience with royal Haris.
Serta datang ke rumah Siti	Having come to Siti's house,
Orang bermasuk belum berhenti	The people entered in an endless stream,
Memasak kopi membakar roti	Making coffee and baking bread,
Hidangan beratur dengan seperti	The dishes arranged appropriately.
Khoja pun masuk dengan segera	The Khoja entered at once,
Membawa segala sanak saudara	Bringing all his relations,
Ramainya tidak terkira-kira	Their number was incalculable,
Laki-laki perempuan janda dan dara	Men, women, widows and maids.
Siti Dhawiyyah hadir bertahta	Siti Dhawiyyah was there on her throne
Diadap dayang sekaliannya rata	Faced by all her handmaids
Kepada mamanya terpandang mata	She looked her uncle in the eye,
Segera ditegur Siti yang pokta	And at once matchless Siti greeted him.
Suka bercampur belas dan kasihan	Pleasure mixed with pity and compassion
Melihat saudaranya datang sekalian	At seeing all her relations arrive,
Anak beranak beramai-ramaian	With children in tow, en masse,
Membawa persembahan berbagai kian	Bringing gifts of various kinds.

Siti menegur manis suara	Siti greeted them sweetly:
Wahai ibuku silakan segera	"Dear mothers, come at once,
Adik dan kakak sanak saudara	Siblings young and old, relations,
Marilah duduk di hamparan sutera	Come and sit on silken carpets."
Disorongkan Siti puan baiduri	Siti offered them the opal sireh set,
Wajahnya manis amat berseri	Her face sweet and resplendent.
Makanlah Khoja laki isteri	The Khoja and his wife partook of it,
Hatinya suka tidak terperi	Their hearts greatly pleased.
Makanlah sireh segala mereka	All of them partook of sireh
Memandang Siti hatinya suka	Pleased to gaze on Siti,
Terlalu manis dipandang muka	Her face too sweet to the eye,
Seperti gambar baharu direka	Like a picture just painted.
Khoja berkata perlahan-lahan	The Khoja said softly:
Wahai anakku Siti pilihan	"O my child, choice Siti,
Adapun mama datang sekalian	The reason your uncle and all have come
Hendak mengadap yang dipertuan	Is for an audience with his highness.

44.

Serta membawa saudaramu ini	And we've brought all these relations
Supaya dikenal raja yang ghani	That the mighty raja may know them.
Hamba sedia banyak ini	These many slaves are ready,
Boleh bersama hidup dan fani	To live and die with him.
Anakku ramai menaruh saudara	My child has many relations—
Kepada baginda supaya ketara	Let this be known to his highness,
Misalnya ada gempar dan mara	Should danger approach,
Orang inilah dahulu cedera	These people will be first wounded in his defence."
Setelah Siti mendengar sabda	When Siti heard those words,
Terlalu belas di dalam dada	She felt great compassion,
Segala saudaranya mana yang ada	All those relations of hers there
Sangatlah hendak mengadap baginda	Greatly wished for an audience with his highness.
Siti tersenyum seraya menoleh	Siti smiled and turned away
Kepada seorang khadam terpilih	To one of her chosen servants,
Dayang tu sangat pandai berdalih	A handmaid skilled at subterfuge,
Barang khabarnya semuanya boleh	Whatever she was told she was able to do.

Wahai dayang Indera Nuradi[6]	"O handmaid, Indera Nuradi,
Ke mana berangkat baginda tadi	Where did his highness go just now?
Bukan ia pergi mandi	Did he not go to bathe
Kepada kolam batu bersendi	In the pool fringed in stones?"
Dayang tertawa seraya berkata	The handmaid laughed and answered:
Sudah bersiram duli mahkota	"His highness has already bathed.
Membuang air ke jamban bata	He's now at toilet in the stone outhouse,
Si Bandan Kecil mengiringkan serta	Si Bandan Kecil accompanying him."
Khoja mendengar khabarnya itu	Khoja heard that account
Perasan hatinya nyatalah tentu	And believed it utterly.
Menantilah ia sekalian di situ	They all waited there,
Berkata dengan Siti yang tentu	Conversing with unshakeable Siti.
Kata Siti nantilah mama	Siti said: "Wait a while, uncle,
Sanak saudaraku sekalian sama	And all my relations altogether,
Menanti anak raja utama	Wait for the excellent prince,
Datangnya tidak berapa lama	He will come not long from now."
Duduklah pulak Khoja menanti	The Khoja sat waiting,
Sangat percaya kepada hati	Complete belief in his heart,
Minum sarbat dijamu Siti	Drinking sherbert served up by Siti,
Minum kahwa bertambul roti	Drinking coffee and eating bread.

45.
Seketika duduk sekaliannya di situ	They had not been long sitting there
Menanti Haris muda yang tentu	Waiting for young Haris, the indupitable,
Si Bandan Kecil datang ke situ	When Si Bandan Kecil arrived there
Lalu duduk di bawah pintu	And sat below the doorway.
Tersenyum manis Siti yang syahda	Lovely Siti smiled sweetly,
Kepada Si Bandan memberi sabda	To Si Bandan she spoke:
Mengapa engkau ke mari ada	"Why are you here?
Di mana engkau tinggalkan baginda	Where have you left his highness?"

---

[6] n-w r d y.

Si Bandan kecil budak yang cura Sudah sepakat bagai bicara Semu tuannya jangan ketara Memberi takzim dengan segera	Si Bandan Kecil, a joker of a kid, Was in on the pact as had been agreed, That the ruse of his mistress not be revealed, And gave salutation at once.
Kepala tunduk seraya berkata Baginda berangkat ke dalam kota Disambut ayah bondanya serta Bertemu baginda di jamban bata	He bent his head and said: "His highness has left for the city, Greeted by his father and mother, Having met his highness at the stone outhouse.
Baginda tak sempat naik ke mari Titah baginda disuruh berperi Utusan datang dari sebuah negeri Orangnya banyak tidak terperi	His highness had no time to come hither. The king ordered him to go and converse With messengers come from abroad, Many people together with them."
Siti tersenyum seraya memandang Penatlah mamaku sekaliannya datang Jika boleh menanti petang Hampiri gerangan boleh bertentang	Siti smiled and looked: "Uncle and all, how tiring for you to have come. If you can wait until the evening, It seems that you'll be able to meet him.
Kerana semalam hamba khabari Mamaku hendak mengadap sendiri Esok hari ia ke mari Jangan dahulu ke sana ke mari	For yesterday I told him That my uncle himself would come to meet him. Tomorrow he will come, Do not go here or there.
Hari nin datang 'awiz kendala Utusan dari mana datangnya pula Baiklah nanti saudaraku segala Bertemu dengan raja terala	Now the day brings an unexpected obstacle. From whence came this messenger? Better that my relations all wait To meet with the exalted raja.
Anak raja itu baik sekali Semua orang sangat diperduli Sedikit tidak dihalai-balai Patutlah asal sultan terjali	That prince is truly good Paying heed to everyone Nothing at all amiss How right that he's of manifestly royal origin.

Appendix III

46.
Bertuah mamaku dapat menantu
Budinya baik bukan suatu
Pekerjaan hamba semua dibantu
Tidaklah lupa barang sewaktu

Banyaklah hamba berinya harta
Kurnia ayahnya pulak serta
Segala pakaian indah semata
Sekaliannya itu diberikan beta

Itulah sahaja hajatnya ada
Sangatlah suka bermain kuda
Segala permainan semua dipada
Dengan orang muda-muda

Adat orang muda belia
Lagi pun putera sultan yang kaya
Awal siang berjalanlah dia
Pergi bermain bersuka ria

Khoja mendengar madahnya Siti
Terlalu suka rasanya hati
Menantunya baik budi pekerti
Bela pelihara dengan seperti

Kepada hati sangat percaya
Tiada tahu akan rahsia
Dikatakan sungguh katanya dia
Mendengar khabar hatinya ria

Seraya berkata al-hamdu liLlah
Syukurlah tuan pemberian Allah
Fasal bermain jangan disalah
Adat raja sudah terjumlah

46.
My uncle is lucky to have such an
  in-law,
His behaviour is uncommonly virtuous,
He helps me in all my activities,
Never forgetting anything.

He's given me much wealth,
Even things given by his father,
All sorts of lovely clothes,
All of this he's given us.

There is one hankering of his:
He adores horse riding,
Fulfilling his wish for all games,
With young men.

That's the custom of young men,
What more the son of a powerful
  sultan,
Early in the morning he sets off,
To sport and enjoy himself."

The Khoja heard Siti's words,
And was very pleased at heart.
His son-in-law had good manners and
  morals,
And looked after his wife as he should.

He was utterly convinced,
And did not suspect the secret,
He believed she spoke the truth.
Hearing of that story, his heart was
  gleeful.

While saying: "Praise be to Allah,
Give thanks for the blessings of Allah.
As for his sports, don't put him in the
  wrong,
They are considered among the
  customs of rajas.

Anak raja besar sahaja begitu	Great princes behave in just that way
Permainan dia bukannya satu	His sports are more than one.
Jangan ditegur lakunya itu	Do not fault him for that.
Adat raja telah tertentu	It is the fixed custom of rajas.
Asalkan baik budi dan bahasa	As long as his character and comportment are good
Tegur sapanya mengumbut rasa	His words and greetings draw out the heart
Seribu banyak raja berbangsa	A thousand noble rajas
Kita pelihara dengan sentosa	We would care for peacefully.[19]
47.	47.
Akan sekarang mohonlah ayah	As for now, your father takes his leave,
Hendak dinanti terlalu payah	For it is too difficult to wait."
Tersenyum manis Siti Dhawiyyah	Siti Dhawiyyah smiled sweetly,
Serta membalas segala hadiah	And reciprocated all of their gifts.
Mana persembahan saudaranya	Whatever her relations had brought
Diambilnya dengan manis mukanya	She took with a sweet demeanour,
Banyak pulak lagi membalasnya	And a great many gifts she reciprocated,
Lalu bermohon sekaliannya	And then all of them took their leave.
Demikianlah konon caranya itu	That was how she managed it,
Siti Dhawiyyah usul yang tentu	Siti Dhawiyyah, of certain lineage,
Apabila datang saudaranya ke situ	When her relations came there,
Dalihnya banyak bukan suatu	Her subterfuges were many.

VI. Klinkert 164 *Syair Saudagar Bodoh*

VI. *Syair Saudagar Bodoh*

16.	16.
Tersebut perkataan Siti bestari	Turning now to noble Siti,
Saudagar Muda punya isteri	Saudagar Muda's wife,
Menantikan suaminya sehari-hari	Awaiting her husband day after day,
Khabar pun tidak lagi didengari	Hearing no news from him.

---

[19] Provisional translation.

Sudah dikatakan sekalian teman	All his companions had informed her
Suaminya tinggal di negeri Yaman	That he had remained behind in Yemen.
Rasa hati tiadalah nyaman	Her heart was not at all at ease,
Terlalu masyghul Siti budiman	Wise Siti was anxious indeed.
Ia berfikir seorang diri	She thought to herself:
Suamiku itu betapalah peri	What has become of my husband?
Entah ke mana membawa diri	Who knows where he has betaken himself,
Makanya tidak pulang ke mari	That he does not return hither.
Budi bapaknya terlalu banyak	His father's boons were very great
Kepada ayahku anak-beranak	To my father and his progeny.
Dipeliharanya ayahku seperti anak	He cared for my father like a son,
Diberinya modal terlalu banyak	Providing him with much capital.
Sebab ayahku menjadi kaya	The reason my father became rich
Oleh kerana ayahnya dia	Was because of his father.
Sekarang inilah halnya dia	Now this is his condition:
Di negeri orang kena perdaya	Duped in a foreign land.
Jikalau tidak aku mencari	If I do not go in search of him,
Jahatlah namaku tidak terperi	My reputation will be completely ruined.
Kerana aku jadi isteri	For I have become his wife.
Hinalah namaku segenap negeri	My reputation will be base throughout the land.
Setelah sudah difikirkannya	Once she had thought it over,
Lalu menangis seorang dirinya	And wept to herself,
Lalu masuk ke dalam biliknya	She entered her room
Lalu memakai dengan selengkapnya	And dressed herself completely.
Pakai seperti laki yang nyata	She dressed like a true man,
Memakai seperti alim pendita	Dressing like a wise holy man.
Jubah dan serban lengkap semata	Complete with robe and turban,
Kitab dan tafsir dibungkusnya serta	Qur'an and commentary in a bundle.
Setelah sudah demikian peri	Once she had done that,
Berjalanlah ia seorang diri	She went alone,
Berjalan berkuda ke luar negeri	On horseback out of the city,
Menuju jalan di sebelah kiri	Heading for the road on the left.

Negeri Yaman yang ditujunya
Hendak mencari konon suaminya
Berjalan itu dengan masyghulnya
Sampailah ia dengan segeranya

Lalulah masuk ke dalam negeri
Masjid konon yang dicari
Bertemu dengan qadi yang bahari
Memberi salam sambil berdiri

Qadi pun menyahut akan salamnya
Berjabat salam sambil bertanya
Tuan hamba ini dari mana datangnya
Mendapatkan hamba apa hajatnya

Siti tersenyum seraya bersabda
Hamba bernama Khatib Muda
Dari Muskat datangnya anakanda
Sahaja hendak mengadap ayahanda

Lalulah duduk dibawa sertanya
Dibawaknya naik ke suraunya
Dibentangkan hamparan dengan
    mulianya
Makan dan minum diperjamunya

Terlalu suka qadi berida
Melihatkan paras Khatib Muda
Parasnya elok usulnya shuhada
Memberi gemar di dalam dada[7]

17.
Duduklah ia berperi-peri
Bersuratkan kitab sehari-hari
Lidahnya fasih mengeluarkan peri
Lakunya alim sangat bestari

The land of Yemen was her intention,
In search, it seemed, of her husband.
She travelled beset by anxiety,
And reached there speedily.

Then she went into the city,
Looking, it seemed, for the mosque.
Met with the famed qadi,
And greeted him while standing.

The qadi answered 'his' greeting,
Shook 'his' hand and asked:
"Good sir, from whence have you come?
What is your wish in meeting with me?"

Siti smiled and said:
"Your servant's name is Khatib Muda.[20]
Your child has come from Muskat,
Simply to meet with you, father."

Then they sat together,
Brought up into the prayer house.
He laid out a carpet as a mark of
    respect,
Served 'him' with food and drink.

The old qadi was exceedingly pleased
To see Khatib Muda's appearance
    countenance:
'His' visage lovely, 'his' origins exalted,
Giving rise to admiration.

17.
They sat in conversation,
Copying texts day after day.
'His' tongue was fluent in speaking,
'His' demeanour wise and exceedingly
    noble.

---

[7] MS: di dalam di dalam.

[20] I.e., the young *khatib*, or giver of the sermon in the mosque.

Berupa-rupa mengadu ma sha' Allah	They discussed diverse matters,
Semuanya benar tiada yang salah	exclaiming "As Allah wills!"
Dengan qadi sudah samalah	All of it correct, nothing amiss.
Perkataan itu tiada lain alah	To the qadi 'he' was an equal,
	'His' words never going wrong.[21]
Di rumah qadi dia berhenti	'He' stayed at the qadi's house,
Suaminya itu hendak dinanti	In order to wait for her husband.
Diam di surau berbuat bakti	Remaining in the prayer house,
Dipeliharakan qadi dengan seperti	performing devotions,
	Suitably cared for by the qadi.
Ada kepada suatu hari	On a certain day,
Khatib Muda duduk berperi	Khatib Muda sat in conversation
Bersama dengan qadi jauhari	With the noble qadi,
Muridnya banyak kanan dan kiri	Many students to left and right.
Adapun akan Saudagar Muda	As for Saudagar Muda,
Lalu membawak makanan kuda	He passed by carrying horse fodder,
Rumput[8] dipangku di atas dada	Grass carried on his chest,
Lalu dilihat Khatib Muda	And was spied by Khatib Muda.
Khatib Muda lalu berkata	Khatib Muda then said
Kepada orang yang duduk serta	To someone seated with 'him':
Orang itu panggilkan beta	"Summon that man to us.
Terlalu kasihan rasanya cita	I feel such pity for him."
Orang itu pergi dengan segera	The man went at once
Mendapatkan saudagar di pagar pasara	To find the merchant at the market
Lalu berseru nyaring suara	fence,
Bapak miskin ke mari segera	Then he called in a loud voice:
	"Poor father, come at once.
Diri dipanggil tuan Khatib Muda	You are summoned by Khatib Muda,
Di surau itu ianya ada	There in the prayer house."
Lalu disahut saudagar muda	Then Saudagar Muda answered:
Tuan jangan berbuat senda	"Sir, do not make fun.

---

[8] MS: rambut.

[21] Provisional translation.

Apa pula kehendaknya itu Memanggil hamba miskin piatu Malulah hamba bukan suatu Kain dan baju tidak bertentu	What could be his wish, Summoning a miserable pauper such as myself? My shame is great, With disorderly dress and sarung.
Lagipun hamba hendak segera Mengambil upahan orang pasara Dikatanya hamba berjalan dura Dipalunya hamba tidak berkira	And I am in a hurry Working for wages from the marketfolk. They'll say I went the long way, And will beat me severely."
Orang itu berkata pula Sekarang tuan kembali semula Diambilnya tangan lalu dihela Rumput dibawaknya bercela-cela	The man then said: "Now at once return with me, sir." Took his hand and dragged him off, The grass he was carrying spilled.
Serta datang surau itu Dipandang khatib rupanya itu Orang miskin tidak bertentu Kainnya buruk bukan suatu	Having reached the prayer house, The khatib gazed at his form— A pauper, all unkempt, His sarung utterly dishevelled.
Lalu dipandang diamat-amati Dilihatnya tingkah laku pekerti Saudagar Muda nyatalah pasti Dilihatnya ada tanda bukti	'He' gazed at him carefully, Studied his ways and disposition. This was certainly Saudagar Muda, For 'he' saw the signs of proof.
Terlalu belas rasanya hatinya Melihatkan hal suaminya Daripada sebab kurang akalnya Itulah sebab demikian jadinya	Too pitying was 'his' heart Seeing 'his' husband's condition, All because of his deficient wits. That was the reason for this outcome.
Perlahan-lahan ianya berkata Sambil berlinang airnya mata Bapak miskin kenalkan beta Dagang yang arif baharulah nyata	Softly 'he' said, As 'his' tears flowed: "Poor father, let me introduce myself: A wise stranger just now arrived."
18. Demi didengar saudagar muda Segala perkataan Khatib Muda Memberi hormat sambil bersabda Tuan jangan berbuat senda	18. Saudagar Muda, hearing this, The words of Khatib Muda, Made reverence and spoke: "Sir, do not mock me.

Diperhamba ini miskin yang papa Terlebih lagi hendak bersapa Tuan pun sudah sudi menyapa Orang yang hina beginilah rupa	Your servant is a penniless pauper, It is too much already that you address me. Sir, you are good enough to address me, A humble man in this condition:
Duduk mengambil upahan orang Mengambil kerja sebarang-barang Lambat sedikit dimaki orang Mohonlah dahulu hamba nan gerang	I live from the wages of others, Taking whatever work I can. When a little late I am sworn at. Perhaps you will excuse your servant now."
Khatib Muda tersenyum seraya berkata Terlalu belas di dalam cita Nantilah kakanda kita berkata Biarlah hamba memberi harta	Khatib Muda smiled and said, Too pitying in 'his' heart, "Tarry, brother, let us speak. Let me give you some money.
Bapak miskin nyatalah gerang Maka mengerjakan perintah orang Adakah bapak berbuat sembahyang Adakah berutang kepada orang	You are poor, that much is clear, And so you carry out the orders of others. But do you pray? Do you owe debts?"
Ia pun tunduk mendengar kata Sambil berlinang airnya mata Malu rasanya hendak berkata Melihat dirinya terlalu leta	He bent his head at these words, Tears flowing from his eyes, Feeling ashamed to speak, Seeing himself so base.
Sambil berkata perlahan-lahan Tidak sembahyang hambamu tuan Sebab kehendak tidak ketahuan Berkain pun tidak lagi keruan	He answered in a low voice: "Your servant does not pray, sir, For my needs are uncertain, And even my sarung is in a bad state.
Berhutang haram hamba tiada Orang miskin pencarian tiada Mengambil upahan makanan kuda Mencari rezeki jangan tiada	Your servant abhors debts, As a pauper without income. I earn wages in horse fodder, Looking for earnings, let it not be neglected.
Bagaimana hamba hendak sembahyang Kerana kain pasuk berlubang Tambahan hati terlalu bimbang Ke sana ke mari duduk mengimbang	How then can your servant pray For my sarung is riddled with holes, And my heart full of worries. Hither and yon, I live beset by anxiety."

Lalu tersenyum khatib terbilang	The famed khatib smiled,
Katanya bapak janganlah pulang	And said: "Father, do not go back.
Meskipun susah bukan kepalang	Though it may be terribly difficult,
Baik dibawak berdiri sembahyang	Let me bring you to prayer.
Ayuhai bapak hamba bertanya	Father, your servant asks
Diri ini orang mana asalnya	From whence came you?
Di mana negeri mula diamnya	What country did you inhabit?
Berkata benar dengan sungguhnya	Speak truly and sincerely.
Baiklah bapa berkhabar rahsia	It's best for you to reveal your secrets.
Jangan sekali sembunyikan dia	Do not at all conceal them.
Barang kata hamba percaya	Whatever you say your servant will credit.
Khabarkan bapak kepadanya sahaya	Tell me about yourself, father."
Saudagar menyahut suaranya seni	The merchant answered in a fine tone:
Hendak berkata tidak berani	"I wish to speak but do not dare,
Kerana hamba sudah begini	For your servant is in this condition
Masakan percaya orang di sini	And will not be believed by those here."
Khatib berkata al-hamdu liLlah	The khatib said: "Allah be praised!
Khabarkan bapak apakan salah	Tell me, father, for what is the harm?
Berkhabarlah tuan hamba percayalah	Tell me, sir, and your servant will believe it,
Jikalau tiada menjadi salah	If there is no wrong in it."
Saudagar Muda mendengarkan peri	Saudagar Muda heard those words
Berkatalah ia mula dan peri	And so told of the reasons and circumstances,
Zaman tatkala orang yang bahari	Of how in the time of his forebears,
Bapanya kaya di dalam negeri	His father had been a wealthy man in a certain land.

19.

Sampai masanya di negeri Muskat	Up to his time in the land of Muskat,
Dipeliharakan oleh bapak angkat	Where he had been looked after by his adoptive father,
Diberinya isteri jadilah dekat	Given a wife to be made close to him,
Tetapi tidak pulak muafakat	But they had not managed to live in agreement.

Appendix III

Isterinya hamba lalu menyuruhkan
Segala harta suruh panjangkan
Itulah hamba pergi membawakkan
Saudagar Yaman pulak mendayakan

Itulah maka jadi begini
Hendak kembali tiada berani
Takut dimarahkan mentua dan bini
Jadilah tinggal di negeri ini

Setelah didengar khatib bestari
Belas dan kasihan tidak terperi
Suaminya bodoh tidak terperi
Jadilah rosak badan sendiri

Ia berkata manis suara
Maulah tuan menurut bicara
Biarlah hamba ajar berkira
Harta tuan hamba pulang segera

Pergilah tuan hamba ke rumahnya
Mendapatkan saudagar yang dustanya
Pura-pura hendak membeli cincinnya
Mana yang hadir tengah dipakainya

Serta duduk tuan hamba hampiri
Pegang cincinnya serta jarinya
Tanyakan harganya demikian peri
Berapa harga semuanya jari

Jikalau diberinya harga tentu
Tuan hamba keratlah jari suatu
Hamba membeli cincinnya itu
Dengan jarinya harganya tentu

Jikalau ada suatu bicara
Bawaklah pulang ke mari segera
Biarlah hamba berkira-kira
Pulanglah harta tuan hamba segera

"Your servant's wife then instructed me
To extend our wealth.
That was why your servant came hither,
But Saudagar Yaman duped me.

That is the reason for this state.
I want to return but do not dare,
For fear of scolding by my in-laws
    and wife,
And so I remain in this country.

Once the noble khatib had heard,
'His' pity and compassion was great.
Her husband was extremely foolish
And so had destroyed himself.

'He' said in a sweet voice:
"Sir, will you take my advice?
Allow your servant to teach you a
    stratagem
So that your wealth will return at once.

Go, sir, to the house
Of that deceitful merchant.
Pretend that you wish to buy his rings—
Whichever he is wearing at the time.

Sit and go close to him,
Take hold of his ring and his finger both.
Ask the price, in the following way:
'What is the price of the fingers all?'

If he gives you a fixed price
Sir, cut off one of his fingers
'I am buying his ring
With its finger for a fixed price.'

Should there be a dispute
Bring him hither at once
Allow your servant to calculate
How to return your wealth to you
    without delay."

Saudagar Muda mendengar kata
Diajar oleh khatib yang pokta
Terlalu suka rasanya cita
Sujud di kaki dengan sukacita

Saudagar Muda heard these words
Uttered by the peerless khatib.
He felt greatly pleased,
Prostrated himself at his feet in delight.

Katanya itulah sempurna bicara
Tuan mengajar hamba berkira
Dipegangkan khatib kepalanya segera
Janganlah sujud wahai saudara

Saying: "That is excellent counsel.
Sir, you teach me to calculate."
The khatib at once took hold of his head:
"Do not prostrate yourself, brother."

Saudagar Muda suruh mandikan
Serta dibedak dilangirkan
Pakaian yang indah pula dipakaikan
Antelas mashrik yang dikenakan

'He' ordered Saudagar Muda be bathed,
Powdered and salved,
Given lovely clothes to wear,
Eastern satin was what he put on.

Sudah kena pakaian segala
Pulanglah rupanya sedia kala
Parasnya elok muda terala
Sedikit tidak dapat dicela

Once he had completely dressed,
His appearance of old returned:
His looks were fine, young, noble,
Not a bit could be faulted.

Kerana tampan orang yang kaya
Kena pakaian persih amat bercahaya
Terlalu sikap sifat dan gaya
Mukanya persih pulanglah daya

To be handsome like a wealthy man,
He put on lustrous and luminous clothes.
His deportment was elegant and impressive,
His face shone and energy returned.

Setelah sudah terkena pakaian
Disuruhnya ikut orang sekalian
Ke rumah saudagar lalu berjalan
Lenggang dan langkah sangat handalan

Having put on his clothes,
He instructed the people to accompany him.
To the merchant's house they went,
His gait and step were graceful.

20.
Setelah sampai ke rumahnya itu
Saudagar Yaman ada di situ
Sahabat handai datang ke situ
Makan dan minum di kedainya itu

20.
Having reached that house,
Where the Yemeni merchant abided,
Where his friends and companions gathered,
Eating and drinking in the shop,

Saudagar Muda lalulah masuk	Saudagar Muda then entered
Dekat saudagar ianya duduk	Sat down beside the merchant
Sambil mengiri kerisnya dirusuk	While he moved his keris to his left,
Berkilat-kilat rupanya pendok	Its sheath glinting.
Saudagar melihat terlalu ria	The merchant saw this with glee:
Indah pakaian orang yang kaya	The lovely clothes of a wealthy man.
Berjabat tangan hormat mulia	They shook hands in reverential greeting,
Tidaklah lagi dikenalnya dia	For he no longer recognised him.
Berkata sambil tertawa suka	He said, laughing with pleasure:
Saudagarku apa hajatnya juga	"Merchant, what is your wish?
Banyak dagangan berjenis neka	There are many goods of many kinds,
Belilah tuan hamba mana yang suka	Buy of them, sir, whichever you please."
Terkata sambil mengetekkan jari	He spoke thus while wriggling his fingers,
Menunjukkan cincin batu baiduri	Displaying his rings set with opals,
Fairuz di kanan zamburat di kiri	A turquoise on the right, an emerald on the left;
Lakunya bijak tidak terperi	His gestures were clever beyond compare.
Lalulah dekat Saudagar Muda	Then Saudagar Muda came near,
Dipegangnya jari sambil bersabda	Took hold of a finger and said:
Berapa harganya semuanya kakanda	"What is the price of all this, dear brother?
Cincin dan jari mana yang ada	The ring and the finger, whatever is there.
Kerana hendak hamba membelinya	For your servant wishes to buy it.
Khabarkan harga itu semuanya	Tell me the price of it all.
Segeralah kakanda beri harganya	Brother, give me a price at once,
Khabarkan apa dengan sungguhnya	Tell me sincerely what it is."
Saudagar Yaman lalu berkata	Saudagar Yaman then said:
Harga seratus cincinnya beta	"One hundred for my rings
Jikalau perkenan di dalam cita	If that takes your fancy,
Belilah tuan semuanya serta	Sir, buy it all together."

Saudagar Muda sangat sukanya	Saudagar Muda was greatly pleased,
Dicabutnya keris hendak dikeratnya	Pulled out his keris to cut it off.
Saudagar Yaman terkejut hatinya	Saudagar Yaman was alarmed,
Ditangkapnya keris dipegangkannya	Caught hold of the keris and held it.
Tuan hamba ini gilakah gerang	"Sir, are you mad, perchance?
Hendak mengerat jarinya orang	Wanting to cut off someone's finger!
Bukannya jari dijual orang	It's not the finger that people sell,
Cincin juga dibeli sekarang	But the rings alone that are to be bought."
Saudagar Muda lalu berkata	Saudagar Muda then said:
Tadi hamba sudah berkata	"Just now your servant asked
Berapa harganya semuanya serta	For the price of everything all together,
Cincin dan jari semuanya rata	Rings and fingers all in.
Jari ini tidak hamba lepaskan	This finger I will not relinquish.
Harga sudah kakanda putuskan	Brother, you have agreed the price
Semua sekali hamba katakan	For everything together, as your servant said.
Sekarang mengapa pula dilarangkan	Now why do you forbid it?"
Saudagar Yaman terlalu marah	Saudagar Yaman was enraged:
Tidaklah reda barang sezarah	"I don't agree in the least!
Perbuatan apa tidak ketahuan arah	What sort of confused act is this?"
Tubuhnya gemetar mukanya merah	His body shook and his face was red.
Adat apa itulah gerang	"What custom is this, perchance?
Cincin dibeli dikerat tangan	Rings bought and hands cut!
Seperti orang mabuk warangan	Like someone intoxicated by arsenic
Berjual tidak berangan-angan	Selling that which has never been thought of.
Astaghfir Allah khairan bermula	Allah preserve us, what wonder is this,
Kelakuan seperti orang yang gila	The behaviour of a lunatic.
Tidak demikian adat segala	No custom at all is thus.
Barang bicara hamba pun rela	I willingly submit to whatever adjudication."

21.
Lalu berkata Saudagar Muda
Barang ke mana adatnya ada
Marilah kita berbicara kakanda
Mendapat tuan Khatib Muda

Mana orang duduk serta
Semuanya hairan tidak terkata
Seraya berfirkir di dalam cita
Orang ini gilalah nyata

Saudagar kedua berjalan segera
Ke rumah qadi berbicara
Berpegang jari dua setara
Dipegangnya tidak terkira

Tiada dilepaskan lagi tangannya
Sepanjang jalan dengan tengkarnya
Terlalu kecoh bunyi mulutnya
Semuanya orang pergi sertanya

Sampai ke rumah qadi berida
Lalulah naik Saudagar Muda
Sedialah duduk Khatib Muda
Orang sekalian semuanya ada

Lalulah duduk saudagar kedua
Serta mengadap qadi yang tua
Khatib Muda suka tertawa
Apa kehendak saudagar kedua

Saudagar Yaman lalu berkata
Tuan qadi bicarakan beta
Saudagar ini terlalu dusta
Hendak membeli cincinnya kita

Semuanya habis dikatakan
Cincinnya sahaja yang dijualkan
Jari hamba pulak dikeratkan
Bilakan pulak hamba berikan

21.
Then Saudagar Muda said:
"Wherever is customary,
Let us seek adjudication, brother,
By the person of Khatib Muda."

Those people with them
Were all unspeakably astonished,
While thinking to themselves:
"This man is clearly mad."

The two merchants left at once
For the house of the qadi to adjudicate,
The two holding hands,
Holding them tight as could be.

Neither one let go of the other's hand
Along the way, as they disputed,
Their arguments causing an uproar,
While all the people accompanied them.

Arriving at the house of the old qadi
Saudagar Muda went in.
Khatib Muda was already seated,
In the presence of others.

Then the two merchants sat down,
Facing the old qadi.
Khatib Muda laughed with pleasure:
"What is your wish, merchants?"

Saudagar Yaman then spoke:
"Qadi, sir, adjudicate for us.
This merchant is greatly deceitful
In attempting to buy our rings."

He related all:
"The rings alone were what I sold.
But your servant's finger he would
    have severed,
Had I allowed him to."

Qadi pun hairan di dalam hati	The qadi was astonished at heart.
Saudagar ini apalah pekerti	"What can be the intentions of this
Cincin dibeli tangan dikerati	merchant?
Harta orang hendak dikuati	Buying rings and severing hands.
	He wishes to rob others by force."
Kata qadi mengapa begitu	The qadi said: "Why is it thus?
Tiada adat orang yang tentu	This is not the custom of proper folk.
Sekadar dijual cincinnya itu	The rings alone are sold.
Mengapa hendak dikerat jarinya itu	Why did you wish to cut off his finger?"
Lalu berkata khatib bangsawan	Then well-born khatib spoke:
Ayahanda bicarakan dengan setiawan	"Father, judge rightfully,
Jangan bicara tidak ketahuan	Do not judge erratically.
Orang muda ini benarlah tuan	Sir, this young man is in the right.
Dari mulanya ia bertanya	From the start he asked,
Dipegangnya tentu sudah jarinya	Holding the finger, that is certain:
Cincin dan jari berapa harganya	"How much for the ring and the finger?"
Saudagar Yaman memberi harganya	Saudagar Yaman named his price.
Ia pun kecoh dengan bicara	It was he who deceived by his speech."
Di surau pun riuh bunyi suara	The prayer house rang with voices.
Qadi pun khairan tidak terkira	The qadi was incalculably amazed
Khatib Muda di sebelah ketara	That Khatib Muda had taken a clear position.
Adapun akan qadi berida	For the old qadi,
Saudagar Yaman dibenarkan ada	Saudagar Yaman was in the right.
Adapun akan Khatib Muda	For Khatib Muda,
Ia membenarkan Saudagar Muda	Saudagar Muda was in the right.
Qadi berkata salah jalannya	The qadi said: "That is the wrong path.
Bukan begitu di sini adatnya	The custom here is not thus.
Khatib Muda salah fikirnya	Khatib Muda, your thinking is wrong
Di dalam kitab di hukum kanunnya	By the books and by the legal canons.
22.	22.
Ayahanda hukumkan sebenarnya	Your father has judged correctly,
Ayahanda dahulu kiranya	Your father has already considered it.
Tanyalah ayahanda oleh perinya	Ask your father about the matter,
Apakah sebab demikian adanya	For the reason why it is this way."

Lalu berkata khatib bangsawan Yang salah saudagar nan tuan Seekor unta harganya ketahuan Dikatakan semuanya harganya sekalian	Then the well-born khatib said: "The one in the wrong is the merchant, sir. Knowing the price of one camel, He claimed that was the price of all of them.
Lalu berkata Saudagar Muda Mengapa begitu wahai kakanda Harganya satu juga yang ada Yang lain itu mengapa tiada	Then Saudagar Muda said: 'Why thus, dear brother? The price was for merely one. Why not account for the others?'
Berkata pulak Saudagar Yaman Saudagar Muda mengapa demikian Dari mulanya hamba katakan Itulah harganya hamba bayarkan	Then Saudagar Yaman said: 'Saudagar Muda, why is it so? From the beginning your servant said this. That is the price your servant will pay.'
Saudagar Muda hilang kira-kira Tiadalah dapat tipu bicara Duduklah ia dengan sengsara Rasa hatinya sangat cedera	Saudagar Muda lost his discernment, Having neither ruses nor stratagems. He remained, suffering, His feelings greatly wounded."
Setelah didengar Khatib Muda Benarlah itu Saudagar Muda Melepaskan Saudagar Muda Sama berbalas perbuatan yang ada	Having heard Khatib Muda That Saudagar Muda was in the right. Saudagar Muda was let off For paying the merchant back in the same coin.
Berkata pulak qadi yang pokta Itulah bicara yang amat nyata Baiklah pulangkan sekalian unta Jikalau diketahui duli mahkota	The peerless qadi said: "That is a very clear judgement. You'd better return all the camels, Lest it be known by the royal king."
Ia fikir di dalam hatinya Terlalu takut rasa hatinya Lalulah balik ke rumahnya Sekaliannya unta dihantarkannya	Saudagar Yaman considered the matter, Greatly afraid in his heart, Then returned to his home, And sent back all the camels.

Sekalian pulang sudah untanya	Once the camels had all been returned,
Baharulah suka rasa hatinya	Only then did his heart feel glad.
Khatib Muda fikir hatinya	Khatib Muda thought to 'himself':
Sangatlah bodoh rupa suaminya	"How foolish is my husband."
Setelah selesai sudah sekalian	Once all had been concluded,
Khatib Muda hendak berjalan	Khatib Muda wished to depart.
Bermohon kepada qadi nan tuan	Took 'his' leave of the qadi
Serta Saudagar Muda handalan	And of the famed Saudagar Muda.
Lalu berjalan ke luar negeri	Then she travelled out of the city
Menuju jalan ke negeri sendiri	On the road to her own land,
Berjalan tidak berapa hari	Travelling for not many days
Lalulah sampai ke dalam negeri	Before she reached her own land.
Siti pun sampai ke rumahnya	Siti arrived at her house,
Bersalin pakaian dengan segeranya	Quickly changed her clothes,
Di tengah rumahnya duduk dianya	Sat in the midst of her house,
Menantikan datang suaminya	And awaited the arrival of her husband.
Setelah sampai ke dalam negeri	Once he had arrived in the city,
Lantas lalu ke dalam puri	He went at once into his house,
Serta duduk dekat isteri	Sat down beside his wife,
Lalu berkhabar hal dan peri	And told her all that had happened.
Menyahut madah kakanda nan tuan	Answering the speech of her husband,
Seraya berkata perlahan-lahan	She said in a low voice:
Khatib Muda itu membicarakan	"Khatib Muda who ruled on your behalf,
Itulah hamba yang mendapatkan	That was your servant come in search of you."
Saudagar mendengar kata isterinya	The merchant heard his wife's words,
Disambut dipangku diciumnya	Embraced her, took her on his lap and kissed her.
Kasih sungguh tuan rupanya	"It seems you truly love me."
Kepada dianya dimuliakannya	To her he did honour.

23.

Setelah hari hampirkan malam	Once the day was almost night
Saudagar membawak Siti puhalam	The merchant brought alabaster Siti,
Rasanya hati sangatlah dendam	His heart full of passion,
Lalulah baring di atas tilam	To lie upon the bed.

Setelah kasih sudah berjodo	Once love has been matched,
Baharulah puas rasanya kalbu	Only then was his heart satisfied.
Pangku dan belai di dalam kelambu	Embraces and caresses within the bed-draperies,
Kumbang menyeri airnya madu	The beetle drawing out nectar.
Hari pun hampirkan siang	It was then almost day,
Bangunlah Siti paras gemilang[9]	When Siti of radiant appearance arose.
Saudagar Muda kasih bukan kepalang	Saudagar Muda loved her greatly.
Sudah mandi lalu sembahyang	They bathed and then prayed.
Ayahanda bondanya sangat sukanya	Her father and mother were greatly pleased
Melihat anaknya baik dengan suaminya	To see their daughter at peace with her husband.
Berkasih-kasihan keduanya	The two loved one another,
Selamat sempurna semuanya	And lived happily ever after.

---

[9] MS reads "Siti bangunlah Siti paras gemilang".

Notes

Introduction: Romantic *Syair* in 19th-Century Riau

1. This description is indebted to that of Kratz, "Running a Lending Library in Palembang in 1886 A.D", p. 4. Other sources are discussed in Chapter 1.
2. Proudfoot, *Early Malay Printed Books*, p. 29. Proudfoot lists *Syair Siti Dhawiyyah* under the name of its hero, as *Syair Haris Fadhilah*. There are also other *syair* that may belong in this subgenre, including *Syair Raja Nur Peri* and *Syair Kahar Masyhur*, but these lie beyond the remit of this study.
3. Klinkert, *Notulen van de Algemeene en Bestuurs-Vergaderingen van het Bataviaasch Genootschap*, vol. 4, p. 191; Abu Hassan Sham, *Puisi-Puisi Raja Ali Haji*, pp. 77–8.
4. Frye, *The Secular Scripture: A Study of the Structure of Romance*, p. 23.
5. Here and throughout this book, the term "readers" in the context of 19th-century Malay literary culture denotes not only the readers or reciters of the text but also those who listened to that recitation.
6. Written romantic *syair* could of course enter oral tradition. *Syair Sultan Abdul Muluk* forms the basis of a Sumatran theatrical form, *teater dul Muluk*. See Robert Martin Dumas, *'Teater Abdulmuluk' in Zuid-Sumatra*, p. 297.
7. Andaya, ed., *Other Pasts: Women, Gender and History in Early Modern Southeast Asia*, p. 9.
8. Creese, *Women of the Kakawin World*, p. 247.
9. Watt, *The Rise of the Novel: Studies in Defoe, Richardson and Fielding*, pp. 153–4.
10. Contributors to this debate include Voorhoeve, Teeuw, Al-Attas, Sweeney and Braginsky. See Braginsky, *Heritage*, pp. 301–14.
11. Hooykaas cited in Braginsky, *Heritage*, p. 312. Cf. Wieringa, "A Last Admonition to P.P. Roorda van Eysinga in 1823".
12. Braginsky, *Heritage*, pp. 301–14. Braginsky draws on *Hikyat Banjar* to show that sung poems with continuous rhyming were known, and on *Hikyat*

Patani to show that these could include long as well as short compositions. The erotic or suggestive content of these poems, which is related to their performance by palace women, is suggested by a usage in *Hikyat Hang Tuah* and by Hamzah Fansuri's polemics on the subject. Kassim Ahmad, ed., *Hikyat Hang Tuah*, p. 184.

13. "Segala burung di dalam taman itu pun berbunyi, pelbagai bunyinya, ada yang seperti orang bersiul, ada yang seperti orang berbangsi, ada yang seperti orang bersyair, ada yang seperti orang berbait, ada yang seperti orang berseloka, ada yang seperti orang bergurindam, limau mengkar pun bersorak, anggerek pun mengilai, delima tersenyum, dan bunga air mawar berpantun". Shellabear, 27.13. Cited in Teeuw, "The Malay Sha'ir: Problems of Origin and Tradition", p. 441.
14. Cf. Sweeney, *Authors and Audiences in Traditional Malay Literature*; Sweeney, *A Full Hearing: Orality and Literacy in the Malay World*; Proudfoot, "From Recital to Sight-Reading: the Silencing of Texts in Malaysia".
15. Collins, *The Guritan of Radin Suane*; Derks, *The Feast of Storytelling*. On Batak *guritan* and its transition to print, see Rodgers, *Print, Poetics and Politics*.
16. Den Hamer, "De Sair Madi Kentjana", p. 531.
17. Braginsky, *Heritage*, p. 507.
18. Roorda van Eysinga, trans., *Radin Mantri*; Van Hoëvell, ed., "Sjair Bidasari; Een oorspronkelijk Maleisch gedicht"; Hollander, "Sjair Ken Tambuhan; Een oorspronkelijk Maleische gedicht"; Klinkert, "Twee maleische handschriften".
19. For Sweeney's critique of the literary tastes of Winstedt and other European scholars, see *Authors and Audiences in Traditional Malay Literature*, pp. 1–12.
20. Winstedt, *A History of Classical Malay Literature*, p. 134. In contrast, Overbeck was one of the few philologists with an interest in secular *syair*. Cf. "Shaer Burong Punggok"; "Malay Animal and Flower Shaers"; "Shaïr Dandan Setia".
21. Winstedt, *History*, pp. v–vi.
22. For the likeness to Gilbert and Sullivan I am indebted to Ian Proudfoot. Personal communication, July 2007.
23. Teeuw, *et al.*, *A Merry Senhor in the Malay World: Four Texts of the Syair Sinyor Kosta*; Millie, *Bidasari: Jewel of Malay Muslim Culture*; Koster, *Roaming Through Seductive Gardens: Readings in Malay Narrative*, 1997.
24. Vickers, *Journeys of Desire*, p. vii.
25. Teeuw, *et al.*, p. 338.
26. Koster, p. 2.
27. Koster, p. 86.
28. Koster, p. 54.

29. Koster, pp. 3–5.
30. Millie, pp. 243–4, 249, 290.
31. The cover art anachronistically juxtaposes photographs of the lead actress of the film version, clad in a low-cut *kebaya*, and a dour 19th-century (male) court official. The blurb on the back of the book claims that romantic *syair* were characterised by "silky eroticism", and that *Bidasari* is the "sexiest of the romantic syair". By the time the "inquiry into the poem's virtues" is announced, the reader can be in no doubt about the gender of the *syair*. Of course, Millie is not to be held responsible for this "sexing up" (and feminisation) of Malay literature in an attempt to sell it to a Western market.
32. Braginsky, *Erti Keindahan dan Keindahan Erti dalam Kesustasteraan Melayu Klasik*.
33. Braginsky, *Heritage*, pp. 544, 546.
34. Braginsky, *Heritage*, pp. 301, 313.
35. See Kern, "Aantekeningen", p. 628; Salmon, *Literature in Malay by the Chinese of Indonesia*, pp. 19–21; Zaini-Lajoubert, "Le Syair Cerita Siti Akbari de Lie Kim Hok (1884)", pp. 103–4.
36. Quoted in McDonald, "A Polemical Introduction". In *Pulp Fictions of Medieval England: Essays in Popular Romance*, ed. McDonald, p. 3.
37. Putter and Gilbert, eds., *The Spirit of Medieval English Popular Romance*, p. 15.
38. In al-Azhar and Van der Putten, eds., *Di Dalam Berkekalan Persahabatan*, p. 98.
39. Ruthven, *Feminist Literary Studies: An Introduction*, pp. 117–8.
40. McDonald, p. 1.
41. Witcombe, "Images of Women in Classical Malay Fiction", p. 176.
42. Witcombe, p. 176.
43. For instance, in Gullick, *Malay Society in the Late Nineteenth Century*, pp. 218–22.
44. See, for instance, Maier's discussion of Low's attempts to write the history of Kedah from the *Hikayat Merong Mahawangsa*. Maier, *In the Center of Authority: the Malay Hikayat Merong Mahawangsa*. See also Abdul Rahman al-Ahmadi, *Syair Siti Zubaidah Perang China: Perspektif Sejarah*, and Witcombe, "Images of Women in Classical Malay Fiction", p. 174.
45. Sarra, *Fictions of Femininity*, p. 7.
46. Modleski, *Loving With a Vengeance: Mass-Produced Fantasies for Women*, pp. 27–8.
47. Modleski, p. 113.
48. Radway, *Reading the Romance: Women, Patriarchy and Popular Literature*, p. 217.
49. Van der Putten, *His Word is the Truth*, p. 61.

50. De Bruyn Kops, "Sketch of the Rhio-Lingga Archipelago", p. 98.
51. To use the term coined by Carey, *The Cultural Ecology of Early Nineteenth Century Java*.
52. "Domes, pointed arches and other surface embellishments did not appear in Indonesia until the nineteenth century, when ironically they were introduced through Dutch influence over local rulers. Indonesian scholars gradually became familiar with these alien forms as they began to visit Islamic centres in Egypt and India". Tjahjono, ed., *Indonesian Heritage: Architecture*, p. 97.
53. Thomson, "A Glance at Rhio", p. 73.
54. Al-Azhar and Van der Putten, *Di Dalam Berkekalan Persahabatan*, p. 17.
55. Thomson, p. 71.
56. Matheson, "Questions Arising from a Nineteenth-Century Riau Syair", p. 43. The *syair* is said to be by a Malay from Penyengat.
57. Li, *Cross-Dressing in Chinese Opera*, p. 88.
58. Li, p. 4.
59. Li, p. 89.
60. See, for instance, the picture of a "warrior woman" in Liu and Phillips, eds., *Wayang: A History of Chinese Opera in Singapore*, p. 75.
61. *Syair Sultan Yahya* (henceforth *SSY*), p. 26.
62. Klinkert 138, *Syair Sultan Mahmud*, p. 36. Descriptions of Chinese theatrical performances in the Indies may also be found in German language accounts, for which see Kratz, "The Journey to the East", p. 67.
63. Thomson, p. 72.
64. Matheson, "Questions Arising", p. 4.
65. Matheson, "Mahmud, Sultan of Riau and Lingga (1823–1864)", p. 123.
66. Milner, "Islam and the Muslim State", p. 39, n. 124.
67. Matheson, "Mahmud", p. 121.
68. Milner, "Islam and the Muslim State", p. 45.
69. Following Hodgson's definition of *syariah*-mindedness as a particular cultural orientation within Islam, with the agenda set by the ulama, based on strict interpretations of Qur'an, *hadith* and *sunna*. *The Venture of Islam*, vol. 1, p. 238.
70. Matheson, "Strategies of Survival: The Malay Royal Line of Lingga-Riau", pp. 6–38.
71. Barnard, "*Taman Penghiburan*: Entertainment and the Riau Elite in the Late Nineteenth Century", p. 25.
72. Barnard, p. 33.
73. As a widow in Singapore, Raja Aisyah composed several *hikayat*, drawing on the disguised heroine motif, and making her perhaps the first named woman author of prose texts. Cf. Ding Choo Ming, *Raja Aisyah Sulaiman: Pengarang Ulung Wanita Melayu*, pp. 89–101.

74. Matheson, "Questions", p. 6.
75. Vredenbregt, "The Haddj: Some of its Features and Functions in Indonesia", pp. 93, 148.
76. Riddell, *Islam and the Malay-Indonesian World: Transmission and Response*, p. 192.
77. Andaya and Matheson, eds., *Tuhfat*, p. 283.
78. Riddell, p. 192.
79. Dulaurier, "Chronique du Royaume d'Atcheh," pp. 37–8.
80. Cited in Andaya and Matheson, "Islamic Thought and Malay Tradition: The Writings of Raja Ali Haji or Riau (ca. 1809–ca. 1870)", p. 113.
81. Andaya and Matheson, "Islamic Thought", pp. 112–3.
82. Nizami, "Naqshbandiyya", p. 938.
83. Riddell, p. 191.
84. Andaya and Matheson, "Islamic Thought", p. 114.
85. Al-Azhar and Van der Putten, *Di Dalam Berkekalan Persahabatan*, p. viii.
86. Al-Azhar and Van der Putten, pp. 51, 54, 115.
87. Peskes, "Wahhabiyya", p. 40.
88. Dobbin, "Islamic Revivalism in Minangkabau at the Turn of the Nineteenth Century", p. 332.
89. Dobbin, *Islamic Revivalism in a Changing Peasant Economy: Central Sumatra, 1784–1847*, p. 131.
90. Andaya and Matheson, eds., *Tuhfat*, pp. 283–4.
91. Cited in Matheson, "Questions", p. 5.
92. Klinkert 138, *Syair Sultan Mahmud*, p. 20.
93. Matheson, "Suasana Budaya Riau dalam Abad ke-19: Latar Belakang dan Pengaruh", pp. 115–6.
94. Klinkert 139, *Syair Sultan Yahya*, p. 5.
95. Kaptein, intr., *The Muhimmat al-Nafa'is: A Bilingual Meccan Fatwa Collection for Indonesian Muslims from the End of the Nineteenth Century*, pp. 156, 167.
96. Proudfoot, "An Expedition", p. 31.
97. Matheson, "Strategies", pp. 7–8.
98. Van der Putten, *His Word is the Truth*, p. 211. At least 14 of the Malay manuscripts in the Leiden University Library may be traced to Elout and Walbeehm.
99. This is discussed by Kratz, "The Editing of Malay Manuscripts and Textual Criticism", pp. 236–7, and Proudfoot, "An Expedition", p. 3.
100. See, for instance, Ruzy Hashim, *Out of the Shadows: Women in Malay Court Narratives*, p. 13.
101. Gullick, *Malay Society in the Late Nineteenth Century*, pp. 218–22.
102. Thomson, pp. 71–2.
103. Klinkert 138, *Syair Sultan Mahmud*, p. 36.

104. Andaya and Matheson, eds., *Tuhfat*, p. 180.
105. Andaya, "Gender, Islam and the Bugis Diaspora in Nineteenth- and Twentieth-Century Riau", p. 13.
106. Andaya, "Gender, Islam and the Bugis Diaspora", p. 14.
107. Begbie, *The Malayan Peninsula*, pp. 79–81.
108. Begbie, p. 81. *Tuhfat*, p. 237.
109. Matheson, "Strategies", p. 15.
110. Andaya, "Gender, Islam and the Bugis Diaspora", p. 19 n72.
111. Matheson, "Strategies", p. 15.
112. Andaya, "Gender, Islam and the Bugis Diaspora", p. 18.
113. Andaya, "The Changing Role of Women in Premodern South East Asia", pp. 106–14.
114. Klinkert 138, *Syair Sultan Mahmud*, p. 20.
115. *Syair Sultan Mahmud*, pp. 21–2.
116. Abu Hassan Sham, ed., *Puisi-Puisi Raja Ali Haji*, p. 399.
117. See Stivens, "The Hope of the Nation", p. 188.

Chapter 1: Not Just Fryers of Bananas and Sweet Potatoes: Women in the Malay Literary Community

1. "Tambahan pula pada tatkala ia membaca adalah suara yang didengarnya pada balik pagar pada pihak dalam rumah yang memanggil baca hikayat itu adalah bergerak. Pada hati yang lagi membaca si bebal itu: 'Inilah gerangan perempuan juga yang berahi akan suaraku ini mengintai pada balik pagar, daripada seperti berahi pada suaraku akan akan pekerjaannya memasak kopi dan menggoreng pisang dan ubi ditinggalkannya'. Demikianlah pada hatinya si bebal yang tiada punya malu itu!" Braginsky, "Malay Scribes on their Craft and Audience", pp. 45, 53.
2. "... menunjukkan kaum wanita di Penyengat pada abad ke-19 dan awal abad ke-20 telah dapat melepasi imej sebagai gadis pingitan atau suri rumahtangga semata-mata dan telah melangkah ke arah melahirkan karya-karya sama ada kreatif atau bentuk nasihat". Abu Hassan Sham, *Syair-Syair Melayu Riau*, p. 70.
3. "Ini dimaksudkan bahawa kaum Hawa tidak semestinya berperanan di dapur sahaja". Abdul Mutalib Abdul Ghani, ed., *Syair Siti Zubaidah Perang Cina*, p. xix.
4. "Pada ketika itu kebolehan literasi secara umumnya hanya dimiliki oleh kaum lelaki". Jelani Harun, "Sifat-Sifat Perempuan Menurut Syeikh Nuruddin ar-Raniri", p. 37.
5. Andaya, "Introduction", p. 5.
6. Stevenson and Ho, eds., *Crossing the Bridge*; Dejean, *Tender Geographies: Women and the Origins of the Novel in France*; Chang and Saussy, eds.,

Women Writers of Traditional China: An Anthology of Poetry and Criticism.
7. Woolf, *A Room of One's Own*, pp. 50–1.
8. Kratz, "Running a Lending Library in Palembang in 1886 A.D", p. 4.
9. "Ayoai sekalian ibu bestari". Kratz, "Lending Library", p. 7.
10. Kratz, "Lending Library", p. 6 fn. 7.
11. "Perempuan sekalian suka hikayat / membaca syair segala riwayat / tiap-tiap waktu setiap saat". *Antologi*, p. 38.
12. "… puteri itu mualim, tahu ia pada ilmu syair, dan baik khatnya pada menyurat, dan paham ia pada ilmu falak". Winstedt, ed., *Hikayat Bayan Budiman*, p. 146.
13. BL B.5 (IO 2608) *Hikayat Putra Jaya Pati*, f. 26. I am indebted to Vladimir Braginsky for this reference, and for correcting Winstedt's claim that this text is a version of *Hikayat Indraputra*. Cf. Winstedt, *History of Classical Malay Literature*, pp. 52, 57.
14. Klinkert 139, *Syair Sultan Yahya*, p. 4.
15. Klinkert 164, *Syair Saudagar Bodoh*, p. 8.
16. On the Islamisation of these *syair*, see Koster, "Making it New in 1884: Lie Kim Hok's *Syair Siti Akbari*", p. 99, and Chapter 2.
17. Wife of Tunku Raja Muda Selangor to Francis Light, SOAS MS 40320/1, f. 4. In Gallop, *Legacy of the Malay Letter/Warisan Warkah Melayu*, p. 201. Siti Sabariah Cahaya Alam of Kedah to Light, SOAS MS 40320/10, f. 7.7; William Farquhar to Tengku Puteri Riau, British Library Add. 12398, f. 15r; Sultanah Siti Fatimah of Pamanah to Farquhar, Library of Congress MS Jawi 12, f. 40, in Gallop, pp. 201, 220, 223; C.P. Elout to Tengku Puteri, Wieringa, *Catalogue*, p. 427.
18. BL Malay Mss B3. "Kertas Olanda dilayang angin". Folio 44 recto. For a discussion of the formulaic nature of Malay love letters, see Wieringa, *Catalogue*, p. 427.
19. KITLV Or. 171 I, J, K, L, O, P, Q, R. Kratz, "Like a Fish Gasping for Water: The Letters of a Temporary Spouse from Bengkulu", p. 255.
20. Reid, *Southeast Asia in the Age of Commerce, 1450–1680, vol. 1*, pp. 215–25.
21. Reid, p. 218.
22. Cf. Reid, p. 217.
23. Unfortunately, the report does not detail how the data was collected, but see *Volkstelling*, vol. 8, p. 36.
24. "In all the towns of the Federated Malay States, however, except Kampar, the number of females returned as literate is so large compared with the figures for Singapore, Penang and Malacca that considerable doubt must be felt as to the accuracy of the returns. The percentage of literates in the female population of Ceylon towns was 35.2 in 1921, but Ceylon is far in

advance of Malaya in the matter of female education". Nathan, *Census of British Malaya 1921*, pp. 107, 109.
25. Reid, p. 217.
26. Jones, "The origins of the Malay manuscript tradition", p. 139. Cf. Kozok, "A 14th Century Malay Manuscript from Kerinci", p. 44.
27. Siti Hawa Haji Salleh, *Kesusasteraan Melayu Abad Kesembilan Belas*, pp. 10–1.
28. Baron, *The Women's Awakening in Egypt*, pp. 80–1.
29. Tucker, *Women in Nineteenth-Century Egypt*, p. 124.
30. Baron, p. 81.
31. Baron, p. 82.
32. Tucker, p. 124.
33. Abu Hassan Sham, *Puisi-Puisi Raja Ali Haji*, p. 433. This verse is marginalia on the earliest surviving manuscript, dated to 1914, so it may relate to a slightly later era. However, the manuscript did belong to a Penyengat woman, Raja Halimah Abdullah. Abu Hassan Sham, pp. 145–6, 363.
34. Vaughan, "Notes on the Malays of Pinang and Province Wellesley", p. 122. There were also several girls' schools set up by missionary societies, but these would hardly have educated significant numbers. See Bryson, "The Education of Girls in the Nineteenth Century".
35. My translation. Roolvink and Dateok Besar, eds., *Hikajat Abdullah*, pp. 15, 18.
36. Or, indeed, by mothers. The renowned Indonesian Muslim intellectual HAMKA (Haji Abdul Mailk Karim Amrullah) recounts that he received his earliest education from his mother. Cited in Ulrich Kratz, "Islamic Attitudes toward Modern Indonesian Literature", p. 65.
37. Mohamad Said, *Memoirs of a Menteri Besar*, p. 52.
38. Mohamad Said, pp. 46, 52.
39. Mohamad Said, p. 78.
40. Mohamad Said, pp. 79–81.
41. Gullick, *Malay Society*, p. 25.
42. Mohamad Said, p. 78.
43. Mohamad Said, p. 79.
44. Reid cites the memoirs of a Sumatran writer who noted that "girls were not allowed to go to school, lest their ability to write was used to send love letters to some youth". Muhamad Radjab, *Semasa Ketjil di Kampung (1913–1928)*, in Reid, vol. 1, p. 220.
45. Based on Van den Berg's report on Islamic education in the Netherlands Indies in 1885, Dhofier writes that female students were enrolled in the two basic levels of schooling, but "only male students were permitted" to attend *pesantren*, the highest level. Dhofier, *The Pesantren Tradition*, pp. 14–5.
46. Mohamad Said, p. 52.

47. The single female copyist of a Malay work in Ricklef and Voorhoeve's catalogue of Indonesian manuscripts in Great Britain is Rukiah binti Muhammad Ali, who copied Nuruddin al-Raniri's *Akhbar al-Akhira*, in Klang, Selangor, in 1874. Ricklefs and Voorhoeve, *Indonesian Manuscripts in Great Britain*, p. 127. Compendia of religious tales also belonged to Nyonya Sawang, Nyonya Halimah, Nyonya Tasnim and Nyonya Haji Da'ima: Cod. Or. 7324 Iskandar, *Catalogue*, p. 417; Cod. Or. 1953, p. 53; Cod. Or. 7325, p. 418; Cod. Or. 7305, p. 408.
48. Miller, *Subject to Change: Reading Feminist Writing*, p. 75.
49. "Van de meeste HSS. heb ik noch de naam des schrijvers, noch den tijd van vervaardiging, noch de plaats van afkomst kunnen vermelden, omdat die niet bekend zijn", *Notulen*, vol. 4, p. 191.
50. As Bruns wrote with regard to medieval Europe, the manuscript is always "tacitly unfinished: it is never fully present but is always available for a later hand to bring it more completely into the open". "The Originality of Texts in a Manuscript Culture", p. 126.
51. Voorhoeve, "A Malay Scriptorium", p. 262.
52. Klinkert 139, *Syair Sultan Yahya*, p. 2.
53. Klinkert also noted that his copy of *Syair Selindung Delima* was "copied by a woman at Penyengat", but did not provide a name. See Iskandar, *Catalogue*, p. 733.
54. Drewes, *Directions for Travellers on the Mystic Path*, p. 198.
55. For a fuller discussion of how Dutch philologists' predelictions shaped the surviving Riau manuscript corpus, see Mulaika Hijjas, "Victorious Princesses and Virtuous Wives", pp. 40–6.
56. See <http://www.sabda.org/sejarah/artikel/dicari_penerjemah_alkitab.htm>
57. "Klinkert (Hillebrandus Cornelius)", p. 244.
58. Van Ronkel, "Catalogus der Maleische Handschriften", p. 321. Unfortunately, Van Ronkel does not date the MS, and his note is now lost.
59. "Hikayat Sultan Abdul Muluk yang sudah kita nazimkan sendiri dengan bahasa Melayu Johor yang terpakai pada masa ini". Roorda van Eysinga, p. 291.
60. "Syahdan itu surat [i.e., *Surat Kurais Raja Alam*] bahasa Melayu yang halus, akan tetapi khatnya sudah banyak rusak dan perkataannya pun banyak rusak, karena itu suratan perempuan". In *Di Dalam Berkekalan Persahabatan*, eds. Van der Putten and Al-Azhar, p. 40.
61. See Van der Putten, *His Word is the Truth*, p. 212.
62. Teeuw, "The Malay Sha'ir: Problems of Origin and Tradition".
63. Abu Hassan Sham, *Puisi-Puisi Raja Ali Haji*, p. 374.
64. Proudfoot, "An Expedition into the Politics of Malay Philology", p. 31.
65. Braginsky, *Heritage*, p. 542.
66. Abu Hassan Sham, *Syair-Syair Melayu Riau*, p. 67.

67. Matthes, 1856, quoted in Reid, *Southeast Asia, vol. 1*, p. 219.
68. *Syair* commemorating voyages go back at least to Raja Chulan's 1761 *syair* on a trip taken by Sultan Iskandar of Perak. See Braginsky, *Heritage*, p. 567.
69. On Engku Puteri's influence, see Andaya and Matheson, eds., *Tuhfat*, pp. 211, 222, 237, 245, 254. On the texts, see Wieringa, *Catalogue*, pp. 77, 127–9. Or is *Syair Perang Johor* composed by her? The beginning reads: "inilah syair dari Engku Puteri (this is a *syair* from Engku Puteri)".
70. Tengku or Engku Selangor is probably Engku Puteri's younger half-sister, Engku Tengah, who was Tengku Ampuan of Selangor.
71. Wieringa, *Catalogue*, facsimile on p. 76.
72. Cod. Or. 1761. Wieringa, *Catalogue*, pp. 127–9.
73. Begbie, *Malayan Peninsula*, p. 285.
74. Iskandar, p. 17.
75. Ricklefs, *The Seen and Unseen Worlds in Java, 1726–1749: History, Literature and Islam in the Court of Pakubuwana II*, p. 28.
76. Riddell, *Transferring a Tradition: 'Abd al-Ra'uf al-Singkili's Rendering into Malay of the Jalalayn Commentary*, pp. 13–4.
77. *Katalog Manuskrip Melayu Koleksi Perpustakaan Negara Malaysia: Tambahan Pertama*, pp. 36, 42, 49.
78. Cf. the mid-19th century Javanese princess Sekhar Kedhaton, daughter of Pakubuwono VII, who refused to marry and "ascended to a legendary status of unrivaled spiritual prowess". She is also said to be the author of a number of literary works. In Florida, "Sex Wars: Writing Gender Relations in Nineteenth-Century Java", pp. 215–6.
79. Den Hamer, "De Sair Madi Kentjana", p. 531.
80. See Proudfoot on how Penyengat has come to occupy a "peculiar position in the history of Malay philology", "An Expedition into the Politics of Malay Philology", p. 31. Similarly, Kratz points out how European intervention may have distorted the manuscript record, in "The Editing of Malay Manuscripts and Textual Criticism", pp. 236–7.
81. Siti Hawa Haji Salleh, *Kesusasteraan Melayu Abad Kesembilan-Belas*, p. 24.
82. Kamarulzaman bin Abdul Halim *et al.*, eds., *Bunga Rampai Sastera Lama II*, p. 57. However, the two manuscripts of *Hikayat Koris Mengindera* listed in Dewan Bahasa's catalogue are said to have belonged to Sharifah Mastura binti Syed Shahabudin and Che' Manja Lara, wife of Sultan Abdul Hamid Halim Syah. *Katalog Manuskrip Koleksi Perpustakaan Dewan Bahasa*, pp. 28–9.
83. *Katalog Manuskrip Koleksi Perpustakaan Dewan Bahasa*, pp. 40, 48, 50.
84. *Katalog Manuskrip Melayu Koleksi Perpustakaan Negara Malaysia Tambahan Kedua*, pp. 61, 154. *Tambahan Ketiga*, p. 34.

85. Iskandar, pp. 53, 417–8.
86. Iskandar, pp. 728, 733. Iskandar has Encik Seni as a man, but may be a female name.
87. "Hikayat Tuan Puteri Nur Lelah dipinjam oleh Rasyimah pada empat / hari bulan Rabi'a al-awwal tahun Belanda 1863 iaitu sudah dibaca dua malam / hampir ke tiga serta dipulangkan kepada yang empunya itupun kami mintak / terima kasih yang amat banyak sebab terlalu sekali kesukaan kami mendengarkannya / beberapa cumbu2an Syah Firman dua bersaudara dengan isterinya Tuan Puteri Indera Seloka [?] serta Tuan Puteri Nur Lela Cahaya adanya". The owner of the manuscript has the non-gender specific name Encik Sulung, "cucu kepada Encik Ribut orang Tanjung Pinang". Klinkert 32, *Hikayat Syah Firman*, final page. Cf. Van der Putten, *His Word is the Truth*, p. 226.
88. Ding, *Raja Aisyah Sulaiman*, pp. 175–86.
89. "Inilah terkarang oleh Raja Aisyah binti Raja Haji Sulaiman, Raja Pulau Penyengat. Dan telah disalin pula oleh hamba yang karib pada 14hb Ogos, 1917, bersamaan dengan 1hb Syawal, 1325. Dan telah disalin pula oleh hamba ini hikayat di dalam bandar negeri Kedah, Alor Setar, dan telah tamatlah menyalin pada jam pukul 12.30 hari Jumaat, pada 18hb Zulhijjah 1531 Hijrah". Possibly "hamba yang karib" is a misreading of the more usual "hamba yang gharib". Ding, p. 179.
90. Personal communication from Annabel Gallop, 24 March 2004. For Tengku Ampuan Mariam's book on dance, see Siti Zainon Ismail and Harun Mat Piah, *Lambang Sari: Tari Gamelan Terengganu*.
91. Though *Hikayat Syams al-Anwar* seems never to have been lithographed, three other works by Raja Aisyah were published in the 1920s.
92. Klinkert, "Twee Maleische Handschriften", p. 512.
93. Ding, p. 181.
94. Ding, pp. 182–3.
95. Proudfoot, "From Recital to Sight-Reading: the Silencing of Texts in Malaysia", p. 120.
96. That genres are gendered is suggested by Braginsky, *Heritage*, p. 544: "in the framework of Malay love epics as a whole, the romantic *syair* proves to be a kind of female counterpart of the 'more masculine' *hikayat*. It goes without saying that this is a tendency rather than the rule".
97. Creese, *Women of the Kakawin World*, p. 39.

Chapter 2: The Best Ones Make You Cry: Genre, Gender and Catharsis

1. Matheson, "*Kisah Pelayaran ke Riau*: Journey to Riau, 1984", p. 9.
2. Jackson, *Literature, Psychoanalysis and the New Sciences of Mind*, p. 4.
3. On this hierarchy of genres, see Braginsky, *Heritage*, p. 301.

4. Poerbatjaraka, *Tjeritera Pandji Dalam Perbandingan*, pp. 406–8. The standard works on Panji are Poerbatjaraka and Rassers, *De Panji Roman* (PhD thesis, Leiden University, 1922), but see Vickers, *Journeys of Desire*, pp. 5–7, for why these may be less than helpful, even in the Javanese and Balinese contexts.
5. Kumar, "Sailing Up the Map: A Re-examination of Constructs of Javaneseness in the Light of New Evidence", p. 34.
6. Braginsky, *Heritage*, p. 158.
7. Iskandar, pp. 702, 705. Van Ronkel, pp. 33–42, 69–72, 61–6.
8. Klinkert 138, *Syair Sultan Mahmud*, pp. 15, 54, 62, 79, 82.
9. *Syair Sultan Mahmud*, pp. 33, 64 and 80.
10. On 20th-century manuscripts (*Hikayat Jinatur Jayeng Kusuma, Hikayat Misa Prabu Jaya, Hikayat Misa Susupan*), see Abdul Rahman Kaeh, *Hikayat Misa Taman Jayeng Kusuma: Sebuah Kajian Kritis*, pp. 22–3.
11. Harun Mat Piah, *Cerita-Cerita Panji Melayu*, pp. 80, 86. For details of the content of *Panji Jayeng Tilam*, see the introduction in *Hikayat Panji Semirang*, ed. Noriah Mohamed, p. xvii.
12. Nilprapassorn, "A Study of the Dramatic Poems of the Panji Cycle in Thailand", p. 1.
13. Nilprapassorn, p. 78.
14. P. 2.
15. Poerbatjaraka p. 409, cited by Harun Mat Piah, p. 29. Cf. Robson, "Java in Malay Literature", p. 40: "The Thai version of the Panji story, known as the *Inao*, found its way up the Peninsula to Ayudhya, where according to tradition a princess took it from the oral information of her maids who were probably Malays ... The *basa Jawa* words found in the Thai court language and theatrical idiom, while they look like Javanese, are in fact taken from Malay literary works heavily influenced by Javanese, namely the Panji stories which were once popular in the Malay world and were perhaps passed via Kelantan and Patani into Thailand and thus to Ayudhya".
16. Harun Mat Piah, p. 86.
17. Braginsky, *Heritage*, p. 161.
18. Harun Mat Piah, pp. 6, 76.
19. Nik Maimunah binti Yahya and Zaharah Mohd. Khalid, *Bunga Rampai Sastera Lama V: Panji Semirang & Ken Tambohan*. The manuscript is Leiden Cod. Or. 1765, but the editors have also incorporated a *syair* version. Another manuscript of *Panji Kuda Semirang*, in the Cohen Stuart collection, is described by Poerbatjaraka, pp. 4 ff.
20. Noriah Mohamed, ed., *Hikayat Panji Semirang*. This may be based on an earlier Pustaka Antara edition but no information is given about the source.

21. Klinkert 12 and 13 (two copies), *Hikayat Mesa Perabu Jaya*. Iskandar, pp. 705–6.
22. Harun Mat Piah, pp. 73–6.
23. "Membuang diri hendak pergi mengembara", ed. Noriah Mohamed, p. 37.
24. "Meski ia kecil dan belum berakal, ia sudah mengetahui akan martabat dirinya", ed, Noriah Mohamed, p. 6.
25. For this episode in detail, see Appendix II.
26. Pp. 73–4.
27. Klinkert 132, p. 128.
28. "Anak panah yang dipegangnya seolah-olah hendak gugur ke bumi dari sebab hatinya amat rawan melihat Raden Inu itu", ed. Noriah Mohamed, p. 64.
29. Koster, "Making it New in 1884: Lie Kim Hok's *Syair Siti Akbari*", p. 99. See Braginsky for the suggestion that "being a 'new' genre form, *syair* was Islamized more quickly and more deeply than *hikayat*", *Heritage*, p. 314.
30. Noriah Mohamed ed., *Hikayat Panji Semirang*, p. 1.
31. Abu Hassan Sham, ed., *Puisi-Puisi Raja Ali Haji*, p. 375.
32. Abu Hassan Sham, ed., *Puisi-Puisi Raja Ali Haji*, p. 383.
33. Al-Azhar and Van der Putten, *Di Dalam Berkekalan Persahabatan*, p. 40.
34. For the Klinkert manuscript (Klinkert 39), see Iskandar, *Catalogue*, p. 716. For the Perak manuscript, see *Katalog Manuskrip Koleksi Perpustakaan Dewan Bahasa*, pp. 28–9, and *Bunga Rampai Sastera Lama II*, eds. Kamarulzaman bin Abdul Halim *et al.*, p. 57.
35. Quoted in Siti Hawa Haji Salleh, *Kesusasteraan Melayu Abad Kesembilan Belas*, p. 271.
36. The episode is summarised by Muhammad Khatib bin Abdul Hamid, "Hikayat Koris Mengindera". In *Bunga Rampai Sastera Lama II*, eds. Kamarulzaman bin Abdul Halim *et al.*, pp. 76–7.
37. "Yang boleh menyerahkan diri". In *Puisi-Puisi*, ed. Abu Hassan Sham, p. 280.
38. Abu Hassan Sham, ed., *Puisi-Puisi*, p. 325.
39. "Adab al-zawjah 'ala al-zawj iaitu adab isteri atas suami". In *Puisi-Puisi*, ed. Abu Hassan Sham, pp. 331, 435–43.
40. For one of the few articles on this topic, see Mukherjee, "Fatimah in Nusantara".
41. Russell Jones, ed., trans., *Hikayat Sultan Ibrahim ibn Adham*, p. 173.
42. "Barang siapa perempuan disuruh oleh suaminya maka tiada dikerjakan maka dimurkai Allah Ta'ala perempuan itu dan jikalau ia sembahyang dan puasa sekalipun tiada diterima Allah Ta'ala segala amalnya itu di dalam neraka akan tempatnya". Klinkert 33, *Hikayat Nabi Mengajar Anaknya Fatimah*, p. 26.
43. PNRI Ml. 42 B, *Hikayat Darma Ta'siah*, pp. 17–34.

44. "Il suffit de dire ici que le mariage est une sorte d'esclavage: la femme devient donc l'esclave de son mari, elle a à lui obéir sans restriction pour tout ce qu'il réclame d'elle, si cela ne constitue pas une désobéissance vis-à-vis de Dieu". In *Ghazâlî: Le Livre de Bons Usages en Matière de Mariage*, trans. Bousquet and Bercher, p. 104. However, the section of the *Ihya* dealing with marriage is rather little known, and there is no evidence that it was included in the early Malay translations. The translation of al-Palimbani, for instance, is of an abridged version of the *Ihya* and does not include it. Though Raja Ali Haji was much influenced by al-Ghazali, it is not possible to state with certainty that he was familiar with the book on marriage.
45. *Syair Burung*, in *Antologi Syair Simbolik*, p. 111. See also the Malay Concordance Project, at <http://www.anu.edu.au/asianstudies/proudfoot/MCP/N/Ungg_bib.html>.
46. Proudfoot, *Early Malay Printed Books*, p. 29.
47. "Lalailah ia serta dengan malasnya hendak tidur, serta hairanlah ia akan dirinya dengan tercengang-cengang ke sana ke mari". Abdullah bin Abdul Qadir Munsyi, *Hikayat Panca Tanderan*, p. v.
48. "Kerana segala hamba Allah yang berakal itu jikalau menengar suatu riwayat, atau hikayat, atau nasihat, maka adalah diambil pada hatinya seolah-olah orang yang masuk ke dalam suatu kebun yang banyak buah-buahan dan bunga-bungaan dan yang aneka-aneka perbagai warnanya. Maka lalu dipilihnyalah daripada segala buah-buahan dan bunga-bungaan itu, serta mana yang baik rasacita daripada buah-buahan maka diambilnyalah dan dimakannyalah, dan mana-mana juga yang menjadi mabuk dan lalai dimakannya, buah-buahan itu dibuangkannyalah kerana takut menjadu mudharat atas hati". My translation. In Braginsky, "Malay scribes on their craft and audiences", p. 52.
49. Braginsky, "Malay Scribes", p. 46.
50. See Raja Ali Haji on "suratan perempuan" in Van der Putten and Al-Azhar, p. 40.
51. For the Malay case, see Peletz, *Reason and Passion: Representations of Gender in a Malay Society*, pp. 234–5.
52. Murasaki Shikibu, *The Tale of Genji*, p. 461.
53. Chaucer, "The Nun's Priest's Tale". In Carey and Fowler, eds., *The Canterbury Tales*, fragment 7, lines 3210–3.
54. My translation. "Maka segala laki-laki dan perempuan jikalau menengar hikayat yang baik ceriteranya menjadi rindu dan jadi berahi hatinya pada hikayat itu. Adalah setengahnya yang berahi kepada yang membaca, istimewa yang baik suaranya dan lagunya, maka bertambahlah berahi hati yang menengar itu. Jangankan perempuan tiada menjadi gemirang hatinya, sedang laki-laki kebanyakan menjadi berdebar hatinya menengar ceritera

hikayat itu berpatutan dengan suara yang membaca". Braginsky, "Malay Scribes", pp. 52–3.
55. For further information on the family, see Chambert-Loir, "Malay Literature in the Nineteenth Century: the Fadli Connection".
56. "Barang yang menengar rusak di hati", "Syair Buah-Buahan", *Antologi Syair Simbolik*, p. 38.
57. *Antologi*, p. 42.
58. "Perempuan sekalian suka hikayat / membaca syair segala riwayat / tiap-tiap waktu setiap saat", *Antologi*, p. 38.
59. Letter of 26 June 1858, Al-Azhar and Van der Putten, eds., p. 39.
60. This is a bamboo Aeolian harp.
61. "Maka segala gundik raja pun berahilah akan Hang Jebat. Maka raja pun terlalu sukacita mendengarkan Hang Jebat membaca hikayat itu, suaranya terlaku manis seperti buluh perindu, kerana Hang Jebat pandai mengadakan suara memberi sekalian mendengar dia pilu dan rawan; barang siapa mendengar dia menjadi kasih hatinya. Maka raja pun beradulah diribanya Hang Jebat. Maka Hang Jebat pun berhenti daripada membaca itu lalu bernyanyi pula mengulit raja beradu itu, terlalu sekali merdu suaranya. Maka raja pun tidurlah diriba Hang Jebat terlalu nyedar". In *Hikayat Hang Tuah*, ed. Kassim Ahmad, pp. 291–2.
62. Quoted in Braginsky, *Heritage*, p. 116. For Malay text, see A. Samad Ahmad, ed., *Sulalatus Salatin (Sejarah Melayu)*, p. 253.
63. Quoted in Sarra, *Fictions of Femininity: Literary Inventions of Gender in Japanese Court Women's Memoirs*, p. 129. For identification in romance novels, see Radway, *Reading the Romance: Women, Patriarchy, and Popular Literature*, p. 84.
64. Brownstein, *Becoming a Heroine: Reading about Women in Novels*, p. xxi. For further application of Brownstein's definition of the heroine, see Chapter 5.
65. Modleski, *Loving with a Vengeance: Mass-Produced Fantasies for Women*, p. 41.
66. "Cuma urusan perempuan sesama perempuan sahaja". In *Syair Siti Zubaidah Perang Cina*, ed. Abdul Mutalib Abdul Ghani, p. xxiv.
67. Modleski, p. 45.
68. Modleski associates different popular forms with particular life stages (courtship is associated with Harlequin romance novels, marriage with the Gothic romance, motherhood and family with the television soap opera), p. 61.
69. Modleski, p. 111.
70. Radway, p. 14.
71. For Plato, poetry is "a crippling of the mind", from which the citizens of the Republic should be protected. Eric Havelock, *Preface to Plato* (Cambridge:

Belknap Press, 1982 [1963]), pp. 4–5. Cf. McDonald, "Romance, so its censors insist, perverts the mind; it incites illicit thought, obscene behaviour and a propensity for violent action", p. 3.
72. Arazi, "Shi'r". In *Encyclopedia of Islam*, p. 459.
73. Quoted and translated in Braginsky, *Heritage*, p. 325.
74. "Hikayat yang tiada berfaedah adanya, karena dalam hikayat itu terbanyak juga dustanya kepada memberi mudarat". Quoted in *Hikayat Indraputra: A Malay Romance*, ed. S.W.R. Mulyadi, p. 23.
75. Sunarti *et al.*, *Sastra Lisan Banjar*, p. 191.
76. Wilken, "Het Shamanisme bij de Volken van den Indischen Archipel", p. 348. On the *biduan*, see Braginsky, *Heritage*, p. 544.
77. Maxwell, "Shamanism in Perak", p. 225.
78. Den Hamer, "De Sair Madi Kentjana", p. 531.
79. For Lombok, see Ecklund quoted in Sweeney, *Authors and Audiences in Traditional Malay Literature*, p. 75.
80. Robson, "The Power of Poetry", p. 76. See also Ben Arps, "Singing the Life of Joseph: An All-Night Reading of the *Lontar Yusup* in Banyuwangi, East Java".
81. Wilkinson, *Papers on Malay Subjects. Part I: Malay Literature*, p. 42; Muhammad Haji Salleh, "Duka Sengsara yang Indah: Estetika Melayu dari Duka Alam", pp. 212–4, 222; Matheson, "Questions Arising from a Nineteenth-Century Riau *Syair*", pp. 24–6.
82. Braginsky, *Heritage*, pp. 331–2.
83. Overbeck, "Malay Animal and Flower Shaers", p. 111.
84. Wilkinson, *Papers*, p. 42.
85. Given the unpleasant associations some readers may have with beetles, a more congenial translation of *kumbang* could be "bees" (which would also suit the English notion of "the birds and the bees"). However, Wilkinson is clear that the default meaning of *kumbang* is the carpenter beetle (although *kumbang madu* can be used instead of the more common *lebah madu* for "bee"), *Malay-English Dictionary*, p. 623. The translation of *kumbang* as beetle is therefore retained here, for the sake of cultural specificity.
86. Klinkert 132, *Syair Siti Zuhrah*, p. 1.
87. *Syair Siti Zuhrah*, p. 273.
88. See further Chapter 3.
89. See note 60.
90. Abdul Mutalib Abdul Ghani, p. 71.
91. *Antologi*, p. 42.
92. Wikan, *Managing Turbulent Hearts: A Balinese Formula for Living*, pp. 49, 80.
93. Laderman, *Taming the Wind of Desire: Psychology, Medicine, and Aesthetics in Malay Shamanistic Performance*, pp. 56, 82.

94. Klinkert 139, *Syair Sultan Yahya*, p. 8.
95. "Rasanya tidak tertahan sabar / lalulah pengsan rebah terkapar", *Syair Sultan Yahya*, p. 30.
96. P. 86.
97. Wilkinson gives "cinta" as "[d]evoting much thought to. Of care, longing, regret, love, mourning and solicitude generally ... Menchinta: to love or regret". *Malay-English Dictionary*, p. 228.
98. "Supaya janganlah memberi mudharat pada tubuh masing-masing jikalau diam jadi penyakit kesudahannya itu". British Library Add. 12387, *Hikayat Mesa Taman Sira Panji Jayeng Kusuma*, p. 4.
99. "Akan jadi penghibur hati yang dendam"; "hendak pun dikeluarkannya yang ada dalam hatinya itu, tiada datang kebajikan padanya; oleh kerana itulah maka dikarang hikayat ini bernama Cekel Wanengpati"; Royal Asiatic Society Raffles 23, *Hikayat Cekel Waneng Pati*. I am grateful to Professor Braginksy for providing me with this reference.
100. Laderman, p. 87.
101. Jackson, p. 4.
102. Jackson, p. 72.
103. Modleski, p. 57.

Chapter 3: Ruling Passions: The Control of Emotion in *Syair Siti Zuhrah* and *Syair Sultan Yahya*

1. This summary is based on Klinkert 132.
2. This summary is based on Klinkert 139.
3. Setan? Sunan? Sutan? The 1898 romanized edition gives the name as Encik Santan!
4. Winstedt, ed., *Hikayat Anggun Che Tunggal* (Singapore: Methodist Publishing House, 1914).
5. For the list of manuscripts, see Appendix II.
6. Klinkert 132, *Syair Siti Zuhrah*, p. 272. Henceforth referred to as *SSZuh*.
7. Klinkert 139, *Syair Sultan Yahya*, p. 2. Henceforth referred to as *SSY*. Although "saudara dagang" might be the expected formulation, the Jawi here reads "d-g-y-ng", whereas "dagang" is consistently spelt "d-a-g-ng".
8. Braginsky, "Evolution of the Verse Structure of the Malay *Syair*", pp. 148–9.
9. "Duduknya itu sama perempuan", *SSZuh*, p. 272.
10. Cf. Mulaika Hijjas, "The Nursemaid's Tale", p. 274.
11. Braginsky, "Malay Scribes on their Craft and Audience", pp. 40–1.
12. Klinkert 142, *Syair Sultan Marit*, p. 6.
13. Braginsky, "Malay Scribes", p. 38.
14. *SSY*, p. 140.
15. "Sakitnya tuan tiada berbapa", "harapkan kasih sanak saudara / diam seperti di dalam bara". *SSZuh*, p. 271.

16. "Sampailah sehari miskin yang hina / diperbuat seperti berhala Cina". *SSZuh*, p. 273.
17. "Saudara daging tiadalah sayang", "saudara daging janganlah jinak". *SSY*, pp. 2, 31.
18. Brownstein, *Becoming a Heroine: Reading about Women in Novels*, p. xxi.
19. For the (lack of) characterisation of Tun Kudu, see Ruzy Hashim, "Bringing Tun Kudu Out of the Shadows"; on the characterisation of Lela Mayang, see Teeuw, Dumas, *et al., A Merry Senhor in the Malay World*, p. 89.
20. *SSY*, p. 22.
21. *SSZuh*, p. 81.
22. "Tingkah dan laku bagai perempuan". In *SSZuh*, p. 111. Cf. Wahyunah Abd. Ghani, ed., *Hikayat Nakhoda Muda*, which thematises the contrast between "natural", biological markers of femininity and cultural, behavioural markers even further.
23. *SSZuh*, p. 227.
24. "Perkasa sungguh jiwanya bonda / dapat menaklukkan kanda adinda". *SSZuh*, p. 109.
25. *SSY*, p. 109.
26. *SSY*, p. 30.
27. *SSY*, p. 31–2.
28. "Puteri Nurkiyah belum mengerti / belum tahu menaruh hati". *SSZuh*, p. 8.
29. *SSZuh*, p. 26.
30. "Seperti anjing mengeluarkan hawa". *SSZuh*, p. 40.
31. *SSZuh*, p. 53.
32. *SSZuh*, p. 53.
33. *SSY*, p. 23.
34. *SSY*, pp. 41–2.
35. "Hilanglah aib, malu dan sopan". *SSY*, p. 42.
36. "Gila menangis tersedu-sedu / kepada juragan hatinya rindu". *SSY*, p. 78.
37. A kind of coconut tree.
38. *SSY*, p. 86.
39. "Sehari-hari bersuka ria / lepaslah sudah mara bahaya". *SSY*, p. 90.
40. "Lepaslah sudah daripada bahaya", "seperti saudara sendiri". *SSY*, p. 138.
41. "Datanglah rawan kepada hatinya / lalu menangis di dalam selubungnya". *SSZuh*, p. 206.
42. *SSZuh*, p. 208.
43. *SSZuh*, p. 209. While the implied homoeroticism strikes the contemporary reader, it is not commented upon at all in the text. The absence of heteronormativity in this and other *syair*, but especially in earlier *hikayat*, would be worthy of a study in itself!
44. I.e., Klinkert 164, *Syair Saudagar Bodoh*, p. 4, and Klinkert 157, *Syair Siti Dhawiyyah*, p. 38.

45. *SSZuh*, pp. 209–10.
46. *SSY*, p. 70.
47. H.C. Klinkert, *Nieuw Maleisch-Nederlandsch Woordenboek* (Leiden: E. J. Brill, 1930). Defines "*tidoer memoenggoeng*, met her achterste in iem. schoot liggen te slapen, Sj. Sult. Jah", p. 694.
48. *SSY*, p. 70.
49. "Terlalu gundah di dalam qalbu / diam termenung termangu-mangu". *SSY*, p. 74.
50. "Lepas daripada bencana" and "lepas daripada malapetaka". *SSZuh*, pp. 225, 234.
51. Creese, *Women of the Kakawin World*, p. 175; Vickers, *Journeys of Desire*, p. 190.
52. Noriah Mohamed, ed., *Hikayat Panji Semirang*, p. 76.
53. "Muafakatlah ia laki isteri". *SSZuh*, p. 238.
54. *Syair Saudagar Bodoh*, p. 19.
55. *SSY*, p. 107.
56. See Teeuw ed., *Shair Ken Tambuhan*, pp. 27–36, and Robson, ed., *Hikajat Andaken Penurat*, p. 32. For further discussion of Creese and Vickers on this type-scene, see Chapter 4, Section IV.
57. "Hairan terlalai". *SSY*, p. 28.
58. The text reads: b-y-d-w-r-y, *baiduri*.
59. *SSY*, p. 130.
60. *SSY*, pp. 26–7.
61. "Seperti emas ditempa", "Inu di benua Jawa". *SSZuh*, pp. 106, 111.
62. "Seperti laki-laki yang jati". *SSZuh*, p. 83.
63. *SSY*, pp. 66–7.
64. *SSZuh*, p. 84.
65. Creese, p. 27.
66. I.e., *Heritage*, pp. 243–58.
67. Creese, p. 28.

Chapter 4: From Battlefield to Bedroom: War and Marriage in *Syair Siti Zubaidah* and *Syair Sultan Abdul Muluk*

1. Though the Javanese term *jayeng*, "victorious over", requires an object, in these Malay *syair*, it is used as an adjective, simply meaning "victorious".
2. Abu Hassan Sham, *Syair-Syair Melayu Riau*, pp. 68–9.
3. Above, p. 40.
4. Van der Putten, "Printing in Riau", p. 725.
5. This summary is based on Abu Hassam Sham's edition, itself based on the 1847 *Tijdschrift* version. However, the story does not differ in the various manuscripts.

6. This summary is based on Klinkert 130, which is not significantly different from the published editions of Abdul Mutalib Abdul Ghani and Abdul Rahman al-Ahmadi.
7. Following Rose, *Gender and Heroism in Early Modern English Literature*, p. xv.
8. "Sempurna bernama perempuan". *Syair Sultan Abdul Muluk* (henceforth referred to as *SSAM*), p. 592.
9. "Mati yang baik terlalu bina / nama laki-laki dengan sempurna". Klinkert 132, *Syair Siti Zuhrah* (henceforth *SSZuh*), p. 167.
10. "Kita perempuan apakan daya / mana perintah Tuhan yang kaya / tiadalah dapat mengelakkan dia". *SSAM*, p. 584.
11. "Rabb al-'Alamayn empunya perintah", "alamat laki-laki tidak begitu". *SSAM*, pp. 613–4.
12. For the dating of the text, see Braginsky, *Heritage of Traditional Malay Literature*, p. 323.
13. "Ada pun tuan puteri itu suka menjadi pahlawan. Sentiasa hari seratus adi dan johan yang gagah berani dilawannya berganti-ganti dan beberapa raja-raja yang sakti dilawannya mengadu kesaktiannya. Habislah alah olehnya. Umurnya baharu dua belas tahun. Maka apabila tiada diberi oleh ayahanda dan bonda berperang dan mengadu kesaktian, maka ia pun menangis berguling-guling hingga pengsan bagaikan mati, tiada khabarkan dirinya". In *Bunga Rampai Sastera Lama II*, eds. Kamarulzaman bin Abdul Halim et al., p. 36.
14. "Seperti orang yang mati berhadapan dengan orang yang memandikan dia maka sekali-kali tiada ia mempunyai tadbir dan ikhtiyar dan inilah yang terlebih tinggi daripada segala tawakal itu". 'Abd al-Samad al-Palimbani, *Siyar al-Salikin*, pp. 106–7.
15. *SSAM*, p. 595.
16. Corruption of "Tawakkal 'ala al-hayy alazhi la yamut ila akhir al-ayat". Qur'an 25:58. Cf. *Siyar al-Salikin*, p. 101.
17. Klinkert 130, *Syair Siti Zubaidah* (henceforth *SSZub*), p. 207.
18. "Hutan pun sama dengan negeri / semuanya perintah Tuhan yang bahari". *SSZub*, p. 210.
19. "Tiada berketahuan tempatnya pergi / menurut mana sekehendak kaki". *SSAM*, p. 596.
20. "Hajat … terlalu besar". *SSAM*, p. 601.
21. "Perintah Tuhan yang Qahhari". *SSAM*, p. 566.
22. "Rabb al-Alamin empunya perintah / daripada azal dijalani sudah / tiadalah dapat lagi dibantah". *SSAM*, p. 614.
23. *SSZub*, p. 197.
24. "Hari ini bercarilah beta". *SSZub*, p. 206.

25. "Malu kepada isi negeri / lalulah patik membuangkan diri", "bukannya mencari anakada itu". *SSZub*, p. 351.
26. *SSAM*, p. 584.
27. "Seperti laki-laki yang perwira". *SSAM*, p. 604.
28. For instance, Paduka Liku in *Hikayat Panji Semirang* poisons the heroines' mother with *tapai*, p. 20.
29. *SSAM*, p. 566.
30. Similarly, Javanese *kakawin* rarely "consider women as mothers". Creese, *Women of the Kakawin World*, p. 71.
31. "Demikianlah fardhu di atas perempuan / tegah suaminya jangan dilawan", PNRI W. 260 *Syair Raja Damsyik*, 673b. From the Malay Concordance Project, available at <http://www.anu.edu.au/asianstudies/ahcen/proudfoot/mmp/mmp.html>.
32. This line is given as it appears in Klinkert 130, p. 178. Abdul Mutalib Abdul Ghani's edition, *Syair Siti Zubaidah Perang Cina*, has "duduk berpingit seperti perempuan", p. 201.
33. *SSZub*, p. 201.
34. "Sudahlah untung gerangan tuan / hilang berani ditangkap perempuan". *SSZub*, p. 188.
35. "Banyaklah mati pahlawan terutama / alangkah masyur warta dan nama". *SSZub*, p. 178,
36. "Nama laki-laki dengan sempurna", "nama laki-laki yang jati". *SSZuh*, pp. 157, 168.
37. "Mana yang berani lalu melawan / mana yang penakut habis ditawan". *SSZub*, p. 153.
38. "Membalas malu". *SSZub*, p. 255.
39. *SSAM*, p. 601.
40. *SSZub*, p. 243.
41. *SSZub*, p. 244.
42. "Barang perkataan memberi faedah", "baik budi sultan mahkota", "melanggar Cina maulah serta". *SSZub*, pp. 243–4.
43. "Perang nan bukan [ke]rja perempuan". *SSZub*, p. 168.
44. *SSZub*, p. 182.
45. *SSAM*, p. 651.
46. "Carilah bela bersungguh hati". *SSZub*, p. 148.
47. *SSZub*, p. 211.
48. "Lalu berperang bertusok-tusokan dan bertikam-tikaman serta berpalu-paluan, tetapi Kuda Perwira dan Kuda Perancha, di dalam berperang itu, keduanya berlaku seperti kelakuan orang perempuan, iaitu tangannya tiada terlepas daripada memegang baju tentang dadanya seperti takut terbuka rupanya dan takut kelihatan, bahawa ia orang perempuan; jika kelihatan itu nescaya akan terbukalah rahsianya dan ia akan mendapat malu; jadi

seboleh-boleh ditutupinya akan kedua buah rahsia yang ada di dadanya, supaya jangan nyata dilihat orang". *Hikayat Panji Semirang*, p. 62.
49. Cf. Wilkinson's definition of *bela*: "Blood-offering in the way of self-immolation, propitiation or vengeance; atonement by blood. In the old literature, specifically, of suttee ...". *Malay-English Dictionary*, p. 102.
50. "Ada juga orang yang membela kematianmu. Tiada engkau mati seorang". In *Bunga Rampai Sastera Lama VIII: Hikayat Chekel Waneng Pati*, ed. Baharuddin Zainal, p. 221.
51. *SSAM*, p. 587.
52. See, for instance, the didactic texts discussed in Chapter 2.
53. "Paradise Lost" (IV.298).
54. *SSAM*, p. 588.
55. *SSZub*, p. 154.
56. "Kematian yang indah". *SSZub*, p. 70.
57. Vickers, *Journeys of Desire*, pp. 161, 190. Cf. *prang-prang*, "the fight of love" and *amrang*, *pinrang*, "to stab" in Zoetmulder, *Old Javanese-English Dictionary*, p. 1398.
58. *SSZub*, p. 193.
59. "Buah hati cahayanya mata / janganlah tuan sangatlah menta"; "mana yang ada segala senjata", "mana suka tikamlah beta". *SSZub*, p. 196.
60. *SSZub*, p. 307.
61. For *Hikayat Syah Kobat*, see Kamarulzaman bin Abdul Halim, *et al.*, *Bunga Rampai Sastera Lama II*.
62. *SSZub*, p. 200.
63. "Terlalu hairan puteri semua / terbang melayang rasanya jiwa". *SSZub*, pp. 229–30.
64. *SSZub*, p. 232.
65. "Tiada dipanjangkan lagi ceteranya / payah sangat mencari sajaknya". *SSAM*, p. 636. "Damai" seems to be used in these *syair* to mean the consummation of marriage. Cf. Wilkinson on the "nasi damai", "a ceremonial meal shared by bride and bridegroom in token of bridal harmony after consummation".
66. "Puteri-puteri Sang Nata Wirasab Raden Cendera Kesu'ma dan Raden Anglang Mendira dibawa bersama-sama dengannya [i.e., Raden Galuh as Panji Semirang]. Kedua-dua puteri itu hairan melihat Panji Semirang yang sama sekali tiada menganggu mereka. Fikir mereka, "Kedi" gerangan rupanya, maka tiada ia gemar akan perempuan. Sayang sekali laki-laki bagus begini tiada empunya nafsu". Mereka pun tersenyumlah sama sendirinya". In *Bunga Rampai Sastera Lama V*, eds. Nik Maimunah binti Yahya and Zaharah Mohd. Khalid, p. 46. Cf. the Pustaka Antara edition, *Hikayat Panji Semirang*, in which the two princesses are amazed that Panji Semirang does no more than "berpeluk-pelukan dan bercium-ciuman serta bercubit-

cubitan dan bersenda gurau sahaja", "merely embracing, kissing, giving love-pinches, and teasing", p. 76.
67. "Sepuluh-puluh isteri sultan paduka / iparlah juga kepada kita". *SSAM*, p. 687.
68. *SSZub*, p. 307.
69. "Pengantin baharu adatnya begitu / jika sehari belumlah tentu". *SSZub*, p. 315.
70. "Memberikan suaminya terlalu rela", "terlalu besar beroleh pahala". *SSZub*, p. 309.
71. "Ma'lumlah orang menaruh dendam / bertemu kehendak hati di dalam / kalbu berahi bilakan padam". *SSZub*, p. 363.
72. *SSZub*, p. 130.
73. "Dosa tuanku diampunkan sudah", "jangan berbahasa patik tuanku". *SSZub*, p. 303.
74. "Negeri Barbaham persembahan adinda / kakandalah memiliki barang yang ada". *SSAM*, p. 701.
75. *SSZub*, p. 323.
76. "Punya negara itu isterinya". *SSZub*, p. 323.
77. *SSZub*, pp. 354–5.
78. *SSZub*, p. 355.
79. *SSZub*, pp. 377–8.
80. "Turut kehendak suami". *SSZub*, p. 320.
81. *SSZub*, p. 346.
82. "Kasih dan sayang bertambah pula / seperti mendapat gunung gemala". *SSZub*, p. 697.
83. "Laki-laki terbilang". *SSAM*, p. 660.
84. "Nipis-nipis baju di dalam, *SSAM*, p. 697; "baju yang satu", *SSZub*, p. 289.
85. "Hendak ditegur rasanya ngeri". *SSAM*, p. 670.
86. *SSZub*, pp. 289–90.
87. *SSAM*, p. 697.
88. Andaya, "Gender, Islam and the Bugis Diaspora", p. 27.

Chapter 5: Calculating Women, Foolish Men: Reason in *Syair Siti Dhawiyyah* and *Syair Saudagar Bodoh*

1. See, for example, Peletz, "Neither Reasonable nor Responsible", pp. 88–93.
2. For further details on possible Arabic influences on these *syair*, see Hijjas, "Victorious Princesses", pp. 89–94.
3. The summary is based on Klinkert 164, the only extant manuscript of the text.
4. The summary is based on Klinkert 157. The text is also known as *Syair Haris Fadhilah*.

5. "Sjair Haris / opgesteld door / Toewan Bilal Aboe / priesten aan de Moskee op het / eiland Penjingat, [illegible] 1864 [illegible] / 30 jaren dood / afgeschreven door / eene Maleische vrouw van / Penjingat of Mars". Klinkert 157, *Syair Siti Dhawiyyah*, p. 1. Henceforth referred to as *SSDh*.
6. "Di belakang masjid Encik Fatimah Riau", BN Mal.Pol. 278; "faqir al-Husain ibn Ismail orang Bugis T-w-b-y-l-a-[ng-m]", SOAS MS 36559, last page. For the complete list of manuscripts, see Appendix I.
7. Proudfoot, *Early Malay Printed Books*, pp. 29, 250–2.
8. Proudfoot, *Early Malay Printed Books*, p. 463. The following discussion refers to the manuscript version rather than the lithographs, unless otherwise noted.
9. "Opgesteld door Radja Kalzoum dochter van Radja Ali Hadji te Penjengat, ongeveerd [?] 4 jaren geleden dus in 1861". Klinkert 164, *Syair Saudagar Bodoh*, p. 1. Henceforth referred to as *SSB*.
10. Proudfoot, *Early Malay Printed Books*, p. 49.
11. For Syair Puteri Akal, see Braginsky, *Heritage of Traditional Malay Literature*, pp. 539–41. For two different texts going under the name *Hikayat Nakhoda Muda*, which nevertheless deal with similar themes, see Mohd. Yusof Md. Nor, *Antologi Enam Hikayat*, pp. 106–31; and Wahyunah Abdul Ghani, ed., *Hikayat Nakhoda Muda*.
12. *SSDh*, p. 1.
13. I.e., inside the front cover of SOAS MS 36559: "a romantic poem on the love of a prince of Basrah and a merchant's daughter". This evaluation is repeated by Voorhoeve and Ricklefs, p. 161.
14. For *Hikayat Derma Ta'siah* see *Antologi Enam Hikayat*, pp. 74–82. For *hikayat* about Fatimah, see Mukherjee, "Fatimah in Nusantara". For *Syair Sultan Mansur*, see Van Ronkel, *Catalogus*, pp. 337–8.
15. "Dengarkan tuan suatu peri / ceritanya konon orang yang bahari". *SSB*, p. 2.
16. "Ceteranya bodoh", Raja Kalsum, *Syair Saudagar Bodoh*, lithograph, Singapore 1297 AH, p. 51.
17. Rahman, "'Aql", pp. 341–2.
18. See Jumsari Jusuf, ed., *Tajussalatin*; Marre, ed., *Makota Radja-Radja ou la Couronne des Rois*.
19. Jusuf, p. 98.
20. "Akal yang terang", "ilmu perempuan". *SSDh*, p. 4.
21. "Akhirnya kelak tiada sempurna / beroleh malu nama pun hina". *SSDh*, p. 6.
22. For details of a handbook of practical magic by a woman from Penyengat, *Perhimpunan Gunawan Bagi Laki-Laki dan Perempuan*, see Andaya, "Gender, Islam and the Bugis Diaspora", p. 99.
23. *SSDh*, p. 100.

24. *SSDh*, p. 88.
25. "Ada yang mulia ada yang hina". *SSDh*, p. 76.
26. "Kikalau perempuan banyak akalnya / harta kita juga disukanya". *SSDh*, p. 77.
27. *SSDh*, p. 16.
28. "Asyik menurut hawa nafsunya / hilanglah sudah bicara akalnya". *SSDh*, pp. 14, 39.
29. "Akalnya sempurna lagi berani / bakti kepada Tuhan Rabbani". *SSB*, p. 2.
30. *SSB*, p. 10.
31. Following the meaning of "toeleoes" given in von de Wall, *Wordenboek* ("zeker; vast; ongeveinsd; oprecht"), p. 427.
32. *SSB*, p. 12.
33. "Akal anaknya terlalu nyata / terlalu suka di dalam cita". *SBB*, p. 13.
34. "Hendak pulang tidak berani / takut dimarahkan mentua dan bini". *SBB*, p. 19.
35. "Suaminya bodoh tidak terperi / jadilah rosak badan sendiri". *SBB*, p. 19.
36. "Saudagar kasih bukan keraja / anaknya seorang terlalu manja". *SBB*, p. 2.
37. "Suatu pun tidak tahunya / sehingga bermain juga kerjanya". *SSDh*, p. 14.
38. "Adat bersuami", "ilmu laki-laki menaruh bini". *SSDh*, pp. 11, 76.
39. "Neneklah ganti ibu dan bapa / mengajarkan akal begini rupa". *SSDh*, p. 80.
40. *SSDh*, p. 58.
41. "Sekalian ditegur saudagar budiman / semuanya hairan memandang rawan", "tambahan asyik dengan penciuman / semuanya hairan memandang roman". *SSDh*, pp. 68–9.
42. "Untung dan rugi semua ditahunya". *SSB*, p. 13.
43. "Khatib Muda fikir hatinya / sangatlah bodoh rupa suaminya". *SSDh*, p. 22.
44. "Anakanda baik beri isteri / dapatlah ia akal yang bahari". *SSDh*, p. 24; "adat laki-laki akal sempurna / cari perempuan yang bijaksana". *SSB*, p. 9.
45. *SSDh*, p. 39.
46. *SSDh*, p. 56.
47. Abu Hassan Sham, ed., pp. 330–1.
48. *Orang semenda dengan tempat semenda / Bag[a]i mentimun dengan durian / Menggolek pun luka / Kena golek pun luka*. Quoted in Peletz, *Reason and Passion*, p. 65.
49. Abu Hassan Sham, ed., pp. 369–70.
50. In Chapter 4, sections 2–3.
51. Cf. Abdullah bin Abdul Qadir Munsyi, *Hikayat Panca Tanderan*, pp. iv–vi.
52. "Menghasilkan kepada segala orang yang berakal dan memberi kecelaan kepada segala orang yang bodoh". Braginsky, "Malay Scribes on their Craft and Audience", p. 52.
53. Abu Hassan Sham, ed., "Syair Siti Sianah". In *Puisi-Puisi Raja Ali Haji*, p. 379.

54. Braginsky, *Heritage*, pp. 340, 478.
55. Bakhtin, *Rabelais and His World*, pp. 73, 474.
56. In a testament to the text's subtlety, the real didactic import of *Hikayat Hang Tuah* has been much debated. See, for example, Kassim Ahmad, *Characterisation in Hikayat Hang Tuah*; Braginsky, *Heritage*, pp. 475–8.
57. Bakhtin, p. 3.
58. Shaiful Bahri bin Mohd. Radzi, "Malay Humorous Tales", p. 323–4.
59. "Yang berpesan entah siapa / alim pendita gerangan menyerupa". *SSDh*, p. 72.
60. "Nyarisnya mati kita sekawan / lupakan pesan keramat perempuan". *SSDh*, p. 73.
61. "Kebal sangat doanya itu / kepada Allah Tuhan yang satu". *SSDh*, pp. 72–3.
62. A similar recipe for gaining spiritual authority through complete submission may be found in *Hikayat Darmata'siah*. See Mohd. Yusof Md. Nor, ed., *Antologi Enam Hikayat*, pp. 74–82. On anthropological discussions of the Javanese belief that women have more difficulty acquiring spiritual power because they have less self-control, see Brenner, "Why Women Rule the Roost: Rethinking Javanese Ideologies of Gender and Self-Control", p. 29.
63. "Ngilu kepala hati pun rawan". *SSDh*, p. 26.
64. *SSDh*, p. 26.
65. *SSDh*, p. 42.
66. Maier, "The Laughter of Kemala al-Arifin: The Tale of the Bearded Civet Cat", p. 53.
67. Wilkinson, *Dictionary*, p. 441.
68. *SSB*, p. 22.
69. *SSB*, p. 49.
70. *SSDh*, p. 49.
71. *SSDh*, p. 74.
72. Burton, trans., *The Book of the Thousand Nights and a Night*, vol. VI, p. 179.
73. Bakhtin, *Rabelais and His World*, p. 474.
74. See especially, Peletz, *Reason and Passion*, p. 257.
75. Brenner, p. 41.

Conclusion: The Heritage of the Disguised Heroine *Syair*

1. Peletz, *Reason and Passion*, p. 257.
2. Mohd. Taib Osman, *An Introduction to the Development of Modern Malay Language and Literature*, pp. 21–2.
3. For modern editions, see Rodgers, trans., *Sitti Djaoerah: A Novel of Colonial Indonesia*; Pramoedya Ananta Toer, ed., *Hikayat Siti Mariah*.
4. Ungku Maimunah Mohd. Tahir, *Modern Malay Literature: A Historical Perspective*, pp. 20, 35–6.

5. Hooker, *Writing a New Society: Social Change Through the Novel in Malay*, pp. 126–9.
6. "Cerita yang boleh jadi pengajaran dan tauladan dan ikhtibar dan sebagainya. Bukan dongeng atau cerita-cerita ajaib yang tiada terupa pada akal zaman ini". Ungku Maimunah's translation, pp. 26–7.
7. Ungku Maimunah, p. 52.
8. Ungku Maimunah, p. 36.
9. Zaini-Lajoubert, *L'Image de la Femme dans les Litteratures Modernes Indonesienne et Malaise*, pp. 38–9.
10. Das, "Musa Seeks Forgiveness", p. 10.
11. Speech given by Datuk Seri Mohd. Najib bin Tun Abdul Razak, December 24, 2004, at the prize-giving ceremony for Hadiah Sastera Perdana 2002/2003. Available at <www.pmo.gov.my> [accessed 16 February 2006].
12. See Tan, *Bangsawan: A Social and Stylistic History of Popular Malay Opera*, especially Chapter 2, "The Development of Urban Entertainment and Commercial Theatre, c. 1880–c. 1930", pp. 8–34.
13. "Diagnostic Survey and Master Plan for Singapore", 1954, cited in Harper, *The End of Empire and the Making of Malaya*, p. 283.
14. See Sharifah Zinjuaher H.M. Ariffin and Hang Tuah Arshad, *Sejarah Filem Melayu*.
15. Hicks, *Syair Selindung Delima*, pp. 212–5.
16. "…serta sha'er2 Siti Zabidah, Panji Semerang dan sebagainya". Adibah Amin, *Seroja Masih di Kolam*, p. 128.
17. "Perlahan2 kata2, susunan ayat dan ungkapan2 lama itu menjadi mesra dengannya, dan terasa pula manis disebut2". Adibah, p. 128.
18. Dzirina Mahadzir, "Telling Tales in Malay".
19. Amir Muhammad, "Raising a Stink: Shahnon Ahmad's Satire Outrages the Malaysian Establishment".
20. "Ini bertentangan dengan karya sastera serius yang diterbitkan oleh DBP sendiri yang "tidak laku" dijual dan tidak diminati, kecuali jika dipilih untuk dijadikan buku teks". Mohd. Affandi Hassan, "Apa itu novel popular?"
21. "Bengkel ini membuktikan bahawa karya popular mengandungi nilai-nilai sastera yang boleh diangkat dan jika diasuh serta digilap bakat penulisannya mampu melahirkan karya sastera serius yang bersifat intelektual. Karya mereka bukan sekadar cerita cinta semata-mata tetapi sarat dengan maklumat yang dapat menambah pengetahuan pembaca, meskipun terdapat segelintir penulis yang menulis sekadar ingin mengaut keuntungan semata-mata tanpa memikirkan langsung nilai sastera". Mohd. Taib Nordin, "Novel Popular: Antara Komersialisme dan Intelektualisme".
22. Lipscombe, "Chick Lit Becomes Hip Lit in Indonesia".
23. Naparstek, "Escaping the Censor".

24. The cautionary tales in Nur al-Din al-Raniri's chapter on women are, according to one scholar, "suitable to be taken as models by all women, including Malay women, especially when connected with Islamic values"; "sesuai dijadikan iktibar oleh semua wanita, termasuk wanita-wanita Melayu, khususnya apabila dikaitkan dengan nilai-nilai keislaman". Jelani Harun, "Sifat-Sifat Perempuan", p. 34.
25. Nagata, "Heritage as a Site of Resistance: From Architecture to Political Activism in Urban Penang", p. 181.
26. *Writing a New Society*, p. xv.
27. This was included in the controversial "Joint Memorandum on National Culture by the Major Chinese Organisations in Malaysia, 1983" issued by various Chinese Assembly Halls and Chambers of Commerce, cited in *Malaysian Cultural Policy and Democracy*, ed. Kua, p. 246.
28. Bestor quoted in Kessler, "Archaism and Modernity: Contemporary Malay Political Culture", p. 133.
29. Proudfoot, "An Expedition into the Politics of Malay Philology", p. 1.
30. I.e., "Masyarakat lama bangsa Melayu terdiri daripada kehidupan kampung yang aman tenteram, dikuasai oleh kekuatan adat, agama, dan kepercayaan-kepercayaan karut kepada hantu polong dan arwah-arwah". "The old society of the Malay race was made up of peaceful village life, controlled by the strength of custom, religion and nonsensical beliefs in the *polong* ghost and spirits". In *Citra Wanita dalam Sastera Melayu, 1930–1990*, eds. Ahmad Kamal Abdullah and Siti Aisah Murad, p. xi. There is a certain wistfulness in contrast to Jelani Harun's assertion that in the 16th and 17th centuries, "the fathers were the kings of the household with true charisma. It was they who determined all aspects of the management of family life while the wives only remained at home and obeyed the guidance of their husbands", "kaum bapa merupakan raja rumahtangga yang benar-benar berwibawa. Merekalah yang menentukan segala urusan hidup berkeluarga sementara pihak isteri hanya tinggal di rumah dan menurut patuh segala pimpinan suami", "Sifat-Sifat Perempuan", p. 36.

Bibliography

Manuscripts

BL Add. 12387 *Hikayat Mesa Taman Sira Panji Jayeng Kusuma*.
BL B.5 (IO 2608) *Hikayat Putra Jaya Pati*.
BL Malay Mss. B3 *Surat Kirim Kepada Perempuan*.
BN Mal.-Pol. 278 *Syair Haris Fadhilah*.
PNRI Ml. 42 B *Hikayat Derma Ta'siah*.
PNRI W. 257 *Syair Sultan Abdul Muluk*.
Royal Asiatic Society Raffles 23 *Hikayat Cekel Waneng Pati*.
SOAS MS 36559 *Syair Haris Fadhilah*.
UBL Cod. Or. 7342 *Syair Sultan Abdul Muluk*.
UBL Klinkert 130 *Syair Siti Zubaidah*.
UBL Klinkert 132 *Syair Siti Zuhrah*.
UBL Klinkert 138 *Syair Sultan Mahmud*.
UBL Klinkert 139 *Syair Sultan Yahya*.
UBL Klinkert 142 *Syair Sultan Marit*.
UBL Klinkert 157 *Syair Siti Dhawiyyah*.
UBL Klinkert 164 *Syair Saudagar Bodoh*.
UBL Klinkert 33 *Hikayat Nabi Mengajar Anaknya Fatimah*.
UBL Klinkert 32 *Hikayat Syah Firman*.

Books and Articles

A. Samad Ahmad, ed. *Sulalatus Salatin (Sejarah Melayu)*. Kuala Lumpur: Dewan Bahasa dan Pustaka, 1979.

Abd al-Samad al-Palimbani. *Siyar al-Salikin*. Singapore: Pustaka Nasional, 198–.

Abdul Mutalib Abdul Ghani. *Syair Siti Zubaidah Perang Cina*. Kuala Lumpur: Dewan Bahasa dan Pustaka, 1983.

Abdul Rahman al-Ahmadi. *Syair Siti Zubaidah Perang China: Perspektif Sejarah*. Kuala Lumpur: Perpustakaan Negara Malaysia, 1994.
Abdul Rahman Kaeh. *Hikayat Misa Taman Jayeng Kusuma: Sebuah Kajian Kritis*. Kuala Lumpur: Utusan Publications, 1977.
Abdullah bin Abdul Qadir Munsyi. *Hikayat Panca Tanderan*. Petaling Jaya: Fajar Bakti, 1985.
Abu Hassan Sham, ed. *Puisi-Puisi Raja Ali Haji*. Kuala Lumpur: Dewan Bahasa dan Pustaka, 1993.
———, ed. *Syair-Syair Melayu Riau*. Kuala Lumpur: Perpustakaan Negara Malaysia, 1995.
Adibah Amin. *Seroja Masih di Kolam*. Kuala Lumpur: Pustaka Melayu Baru, 1968.
Ahmad Kamal Abdullah and Siti Aisah Murad, eds. *Citra Wanita dalam Sastera Melayu, 1930–1990*. Kuala Lumpur: DBP, 2000.
al-Azhar and Jan van der Putten. *Di Dalam Berkekalan Persahabatan: 'In Everlasting Friendship'. Letters from Raja Ali Haji*. Leiden: Semaian, 1995.
Amir Muhammad. "Raising a Stink: Shahnon Ahmad's Satire Outrages the Malaysian Establishment". *Asiaweek*, 7 May 1999.
Andaya, Barbara Watson. "The Changing Role of Women in Premodern South East Asia". *South East Asia Research* 2, 2 (1994): 99–116.
———. "Gender, Islam and the Bugis Diaspora in Nineteenth- and Twentieth-Century Riau". Paper presented to "The Bugis Diaspora and Islamic Dissemination in the 20th Century Malay-Indonesian Archipelago". Makassar, Indonesia, 6–8 June 2003 (also published in *Sari* 21 (2003): 77–108).
———. "Introduction". In *Other Pasts: Women, Gender and History in Early Modern Southeast Asia*, ed. Andaya. Honolulu: Center for Southeast Asian Studies, 2000.
Andaya, Barbara and Virginia Matheson. "Islamic Thought and Malay Tradition: The Writings of Raja Ali Haji or Riau (ca. 1809–ca. 1870)". In *Perceptions of the Past in Southeast Asia*, eds. A. Reid and D. Marr. Singapore: Heinemann, 1979, pp. 108–28.
———, eds., trans. *The Precious Gift (Tuhfat al-Nafis)*. Kuala Lumpur: Oxford University Press, 1982.
Antologi Syair Simbolik dalam Sastera Indonesia Lama. Jakarta: Departemen Pendidikan dan Kebudayaan, n.d.
Arazi, A. "Sh'ir". *Encyclopaedia of Islam*, 2nd ed, vol. IX, pp. 448–62.
Arps, Ben. "Singing the Life of Joseph: An All-Night Reading of the *Lontar Yusup* in Banyuwangi, East Java". *Indonesia Circle* 53 (1990): 35–58.
Baharuddin Zainal, ed. *Bunga Rampai Sastera Lama VIII: Hikayat Chekel Waneng Pati*. Kuala Lumpur: Dewan Bahasa dan Pustaka, 1965.

Bakhtin, Mikhail. *Rabelais and His World*, trans. Hélène Iswolsky. Bloomington: Indiana University Press, 1984.

Barnard, Timothy P. "*Taman Penghiburan*: Entertainment and the Riau Elite in the Late Nineteenth Century". *JMBRAS* 67, 2 (1994): 17–46.

Baron, Beth. *The Women's Awakening in Egypt*. New Haven: Yale University Press, 1994.

Begbie, P.J. *The Malayan Peninsula*. Kuala Lumpur: Oxford University Press, 1967 (1834).

Behrend, T.E. *Perpustakaan Nasional Republik Indonesia*. Jakarta: Yayasan Obor Indonesia, 1998.

Bousquet. G.-H. and L. Bercher, trans., *Ghazâlî: Le Livre de Bons Usages en Matière de Mariage*. Paris: Maisonneuve, 1989.

Braginsky, Vladimir. "Evolution of the Verse Structure of the Malay *Syair*". *Archipel* 42 (1991): 133–54.

———. *Erti Keindahan dan Keindahan Erti dalam Kesusasteraan Melayu Klasik*. Kuala Lumpur: Dewan Bahasa dan Pustaka, 1994.

———. "Malay Scribes on their Craft and Audience (with special reference to the description of the reading assembly by Safirin bin Usman Fadli)". *IMW* 86 (2002): 37–61.

———. *The Heritage of Traditional Malay Literature*. Leiden: KITLV Press, 2004.

Brenner, Suzanne A. "Why Women Rule the Roost: Rethinking Javanese Ideologies of Gender and Self-Control". In *Bewitching Women, Pious Men: Gender and Body Politics in Southeast Asia*, eds. Aihwa Ong and Michael Peletz. Berkeley: University of California Press, 1995, pp. 19–50.

Brownstein, Rachel M. *Becoming a Heroine: Reading about Women in Novels*. Harmondsworth: Penguin Books, 1984.

Bruns, Gerald L. "The Originality of Texts in a Manuscript Culture". *Comparative Literature* 32, 2 (1980): 113–29.

Bryson, Hugh. "The Education of Girls in the Nineteenth Century". *Malaysia* (November 1970): 11–14.

Burton, Richard F. *The Book of the Thousand Nights and a Night*, vol. 4. London: Burton Club, 1885.

Carey, John and Alastair Fowler, eds. *The Poems of John Milton*. London: Longman, 1980.

Carey, P.B.R. *The Cultural Ecology of Early Nineteenth Century Java*. Singapore: Occasional Paper No. 24, 1974.

Chambert-Loir, Henri. "Malay Literature in the Nineteenth Century: the Fadli Connection". In *Variation, Transformation and Meaning*, eds. J.J. Ras and S.O. Robson. Leiden: KITLV Press, 1991.

Chang Kang-i Sun and Haun Saussy, eds. *Women Writers of Traditional China: An Anthology of Poetry and Criticism*. Stanford: Stanford University Press, 1999.

Collins, William A. *The Guritan of Radin Suane*. Leiden: KITLV Press, 1998.
Creese, Helen. *Women of the Kakawin World: Marriage and Sexuality in the Indic Courts of Java and Bali*. New York and London: M.E. Sharpe, 2004.
Das, K. "Musa Seeks Forgiveness". *Far Eastern Economic Review*, 12 July 1984.
De Bruyn Kops, G.F. "Sketch of the Riau Lingga Archipelago". *Journal of the Indian Archipelago and Eastern Asia* 9 (1855): 96–108.
DeJean, Joan. *Tender Geographies: Women and the Origins of the Novel in France*. New York: Columbia University Press, 1991.
Den Hamer, C. "De Sair Madi Kentjana". *Tijdschrift voor Indische Taal-, Land- en Volkenkunde* 33 (1890): 531–64.
Derks, Will. *The Feast of Storytelling*. Jakarta: RUL, 1994.
Dhofier, Zamakhsyari. *The Pesantren Tradition: The Role of the Kyai in the Maintenance of Traditional Islam in Java*. Arizona: Program for Southeast Asian Studies Monograph Series, 1999.
Ding Choo Ming. *Raja Aisyah Sulaiman: Pengarang Ulung Wanita Melayu*. Bangi: Penerbit Universiti Kebangsaan Malaysia, 1999.
Dobbin, Christine. "Islamic Revivalism in Minangkabau at the Turn of the Nineteenth Century". *Modern Asian Studies* 8, 3 (1974): 319–45.
———. *Islamic Revivalism in a Changing Peasant Economy: Central Sumatra, 1784–1847*. London: Curzon Press, 1983.
Drewes, G.W.J. *Directions for Travellers on the Mystic Path*. The Hague: Martinus Nijhoff, 1977.
Dumas, Robert Martin. *'Teater Abdulmuluk' in Zuid-Sumatra*. Leiden: CNWS, 2000.
Dzirina Mahadzir. "Telling Tales in Malay". *The Star*, 26 February 2006.
Florida, Nancy K. "Sex Wars: Writing Gender Relations in Nineteenth-Century Java". In *Fantasizing the Feminine in Indonesia*, ed. Laurie J. Sears. Durham: Duke University Press, 1996, pp. 207–24.
Frye, Northrop. *The Secular Scripture: A Study of the Structure of Romance*. Cambridge: Harvard University Press, 1976.
Gallop, Annabel Teh. *The Legacy of the Malay Letter/Warisan Warkah Melayu*. London: The British Library for the National Archives of Malaysia, 1994.
Gullick, J.M. *Malay Society in the Late Nineteenth Century*. Singapore: Oxford University Press, 1987.
Harper, T.N. *The End of Empire and the Making of Malaya*. Cambridge: Cambridge University Press, 1999.
Harun Mat Piah. *Cerita-Cerita Panji Melayu*. Kuala Lumpur: DBP, 1980.
Havelock, Eric. *Preface to Plato*. Cambridge: Belknap Press, 1982 (1963).
Hicks, Sarah E. "*Syair Selindung Delima*: A Literary and Philological Study". PhD thesis, SOAS, University of London, 2006.
Hikayat Panji Semirang. Kuala Lumpur: Pustaka Antara, 1963.

Hodgson, Marshall G.S. *The Venture of Islam: Conscience and History in a World Civilization. Vol. 1: The Classical Age of Islam.* Chicago: University of Chicago Press, 1974.

Hoëvell, W.R. van, ed. "Sjair Bidasari". *Verhandelingen can het Koninklijk Bataviaasch Genootschap van Kunsten en Wetenschappen* 19 (1843): 1–486.

Hollander, J.J. de. "Sjair Ken Tambuhan". Leiden: Brill, 1856.

Hooker, Virginia Matheson. *Writing a New Society: Social Change Through the Novel in Malay.* Honolulu: University of Hawai'i Press, 2000.

Iskandar, Teuku. *Catalogue of Malay, Minangkabau and South Sumatran Manuscripts in the Netherlands.* Leiden: Documentatiebureau Islam-Christendom, 1999.

Jackson, Leonard. *Literature, Psychoanalysis and the New Sciences of Mind.* Harlow: Pearson Education Ltd., 2000.

Jelani Harun. "Sifat-Sifat Perempuan Menurut Syeikh Nuruddin ar-Raniri Dalam *Kitab Bustanus Salatin*". *Dewan Sastera* 26 (October 1996): 33–9.

Jones, Russell, ed., trans. *Hikayat Sultan Ibrahim ibn Adham.* Berkeley: CSEAS, 1985.

Jumsari Jusuf, ed. *Tajussalatin.* Jakarta: Departemen Pendidikan dan Kebudayaan, 1979.

Kamarulzaman bin Abdul Halim *et al.*, eds. *Bunga Rampai Sastera Lama II.* Kuala Lumpur: Dewan Bahasa dan Pustaka, 1962.

Kaptein, Nico. *The Muhimmat al-Nafa'is: A Bilingual Meccan Fatwa Collection for Indonesian Muslims from the End of the Nineteenth Century.* Jakarta: INIS, 1997.

Kassim Ahmad, ed. *Hikayat Hang Tuah.* Kuala Lumpur: Dewan Bahasa dan Pustaka, 1966.

———. *Characterisation in Hikayat Hang Tuah.* Kuala Lumpur: Dewan Bahasa dan Pustaka, 1966.

Katalog Induk Manuskrip Melayu di Malaysia. Kuala Lumpur: Perpustakaan Negara Malaysia, 1993.

Katalog Manuskrip Koleksi Perpustakaan Dewan Bahasa. Kuala Lumpur: Dewan Bahasa dan Pustaka, 1983.

Katalog Manuskrip Melayu Koleksi Perpustakaan Negara Malaysia: Tambahan Pertama. Kuala Lumpur: Perpustakaan Negara Malaysia, 2001.

Katalog Manuskrip Melayu Koleksi Perpustakaan Negara Malaysia Tambahan Kedua. Kuala Lumpur: Perpustakaan Negara Malaysia, 2002.

Katalog Manuskrip Melayu Koleksi Perpustakaan Negara Malaysia Tambahan Ketiga. Kuala Lumpur: Perpustakaan Negara Malaysia, 2003.

Katalog Manuskrip Melayu Koleksi Perpustakaan Negara Malaysia Tambahan Keempat. Kuala Lumpur: Perpustakaan Negara Malaysia.

Kern, W. "Aantekeningen op de Sja'ir Hemop". Excerpted and trans. J.J. Ras. *Hikajat Bandjar: A Study in Malay Historiography.* 's-Gravenhage: Bibliotheca Indonesica, 1968, pp. 628–9.

Kessler, Clive S. "Archaism and Modernity: Contemporary Malay Political Culture". In *Fragmented Vision: Culture and Politics in Contemporary Malaysia*, eds. Joel S. Kahn and Francis Loh Kok Wah. Sydney: Asian Studies Association of Australia, 1992, pp. 133–57.

Khomkai Nilprapassorn. "A Study of the Dramatic Poems of the Panji Cycle in Thailand". PhD thesis, SOAS, University of London, 1966.

"Klinkert (Hillebrandus Cornelius)". Vol. 2. *Encyclopaedie van Netherlands Indië.* 's-Gravenhaag-Leiden: Martinus Nijhoff, 1902, p. 244.

Klinkert, H.C. *Nieuw Maleisch-Nederlandsch Woordenboek.* Leiden: E.J. Brill, 1930.

———. "Twee Maleische handschriften". *Bijdragen* 28 (1880): 512–22.

Koster, G.L. "Making it New in 1884: Lie Kim Hok's *Syair Siti Akbari*". *Bijdragen tot de Taal-, Land- en Volkenkunde* 154, 1 (1998): 95–115.

———. *Roaming Through Seductive Gardens: Readings in Malay Narrative.* Leiden: KITLV Press, 1997.

Kratz, E.U. "Running a Lending Library in Palembang in 1886 A.D". *Indonesia Circle* 14 (1977): 3–12.

———. "Islamic Attitudes Toward Modern Indonesian Literature". In *Cultural Contact and Textual Interpretation*, eds. C.D. Grijns and S.O. Robson. Dordrecht: Foris Publications, 1986, pp. 60–93.

———. "The Editing of Malay Manuscripts and Textual Criticism". *Bijdragen* 137 (1988): 229–43.

———. Review of the reprint of R.O. Winstedt's *A History of Malay Literature. JMBRAS* 65, 2 (1992): 103–5.

———. "Like a Fish Gasping for Water: The Letters of a Temporary Spouse from Bengkulu". *Indonesia and the Malay World* 34 (2006): 247–80.

Kua Kia Soong, ed. *Malaysian Cultural Policy and Democracy*, 2nd ed. Kuala Lumpur: Resource and Research Centre, 1990.

Kumar, Ann. "Sailing Up the Map: A Reexamination of Constructs of Javaneseness in the Light of New Evidence". *IMW* 34 (2006): 23–38.

Laderman, Carol. *Taming the Wind of Desire: Psychology, Medicine, and Aesthetics in Malay Shamanistic Performance.* Berkeley: University of California Press, 1991.

Li Siu Leung. *Cross-Dressing in Chinese Opera.* Hong Kong: Hong Kong University Press, 2003.

Lipscombe, Becky. "Chick-lit Becomes Hip Lit in Indonesia". *BBC*, 10 September 2003, at <http://news.bbc.co.uk/1/hi/world/asia-pacific/3093038.stm>.

Maier, H.M.J. "The Laughter of Kemala al-Arifin: The Tale of the Bearded Civet Cat". In *Variation, Transformation and Meaning: Studies in Honour of A. Teeuw*, eds. J.J. Ras and S.O. Robson. Leiden: KITLV Press, 1991, pp. 53–72.

———. *In the Center of Authority: the Malay Hikayat Merong Mahawangsa*. Ithaca: Studies on Southeast Asia, 1988.

Manuskrip Melayu Perpustakaan Negara Malaysia: Satu Katalog Ringkas. Kuala Lumpur: Perpustakaan Negara Malaysia, 1987.

Marre, Aristide, ed. *Makota Radja-Radja ou la Couronne des Rois*. Paris: Maisonneuve, 1881.

Matheson, Virginia. "Mahmud, Sultan of Riau and Lingga (1823–1864)". *Indonesia* 13 (1972): 119–46.

———. "Questions Arising from a Nineteenth-Century Riau Syair". *RIMA* 17 (1983): 1–61.

———. "*Kisah Pelayaran ke Riau*: Journey to Riau, 1984". *Indonesia Circle* 36 (1985): 3–22.

———. "Strategies of Survival: The Malay Royal Line of Lingga-Riau". *Journal of Southeast Asian Studies* 17, 1 (1986): 6–38.

———. "Suasana Budaya Riau dalam Abad ke-19: Latar Belakang dan Pengaruh". In *Tradisi Johor-Riau: Kertas Kerja Hari Sastera 1983*. Kuala Lumpur: DBP, 1987, pp. 103–29.

Maxwell, W.E. "Shamanism in Perak". *JSBRAS* 12 (1883): 222–32.

McDonald, Nicola, ed. *Pulp Fictions of Medieval England: Essays in Popular Romance*. Manchester: Manchester University Press, 2004.

Miller, Nancy K. *Subject to Change: Reading Feminist Writing*. New York: Columbia University Press, 1988.

Millie, Julian, ed. *Bidasari: Jewel of Malay-Muslim Culture*. Leiden: KITLV Press, 2004.

Milner, A.C. "Islam and the Muslim State". In *Islam in Southeast Asia*, ed. M.B. Hooker. Leiden: E.J. Brill, 1988, pp. 23–49.

Modleski, Tanya. *Loving With a Vengeance: Mass-Produced Fantasies for Women*. New York: Routledge, 1990.

Mohamad Said, Tan Sri Datuk. *Memoirs of a Menteri Besar: Early Days*. Singapore: Heinemann Asia, 1982.

Mohd. Affandi Hassan. "Apa itu Novel Popular?" *Utusan Malaysia*, December 2006, at <http://www.utusan.com.my/utusan/content.asp?y=2006&dt=1210&pub=Utusan_Malaysia&sec=Sastera&pg=sa_01.htm> [accessed 29 August 2007].

Mohd. Taib Nordin. "Novel Popular: Antara Komersialisme dengan Intelektualisme". *Berita Harian*, December 2006, at <http://www.bharian.com.my/Misc/DBP/Artikel/Sastera/20061220123017/ArtSastera> [accessed 29 August 2007].

Mohd. Taib Osman. *An Introduction to the Development of Modern Malay Language and Literature*. Singapore: Eastern Universities Press, 1961.

Mohd. Yusof Md. Nor, ed. *Antologi Enam Hikayat*. Petaling Jaya: Fajar Bakti, 1989.
Muhammad Haji Salleh. "Duka Sengsara yang Indah: Estetika Melayu dari Duka Alam". In *Ilmu-Ilmu Humaniora: Persembahan bagi Prof. Dra. Siti Baroroh Baried dan Prof. Dr. Sulastin Sutrisno*. Yogyakarta: Fakultas Sastra Universitas Gadjah Mada, 1991, pp. 209–23.
Mukherjee, Wendy. "Fatimah in Nusantara". *Sari* 23 (2005): 137–52.
Mulaika Hijjas. "Victorious Princesses and Virtuous Wives: Popular *Syair* from Nineteenth-Century Riau". PhD thesis, SOAS, University of London, 2007.
———. "The Nursemaid's Tale: Representations of the *Inang* in *Syair Sultan Mahmud* and *Syair Siti Zuhrah*". *IMW* 97 (2005): 265–79.
Mulyadi, S.W.R. *Hikayat Indraputra: A Malay Romance*. Holland: Foris, 1983.
Murasaki Shikibu. *The Tale of Genji*, trans. Royall Tyler. New York: Penguin, 2001.
Nagata, Judith. "Heritage as a Site of Resistance: From Architecture to Political Activism in Urban Penang". In *Risking Malaysia: Culture, Politics and Identity*, eds. Maznah Mohamad and Wong Soak Koon. Bangi: Penerbit Universiti Kebangsaan Malaysia, 2001.
Naparstek, Ben. "Escaping the Censor". *The Jerusalem Post*, 20 April 2006 (online edition).
Nathan, J.F. *The Census of British Malaya 1921*. London: Waterlow and Sons Ltd., 1922.
Nik Maimunah binti Yahya and Zaharah Mohd. Khalid. *Bunga Rampai Sastera Lama V: Panji Semirang & Ken Tambohan*. Kuala Lumpur: DBP, 1964.
Nizami, K.A. "Naqshbandiyya". *Encyclopedia of Islam*, 2nd ed., pp. 935–93.
Noriah Mohamed, ed. *Hikayat Panji Semirang*. Kuala Lumpur: DBP, 1992.
Notulen van de Algemeene en Bestuurs-Vergaderingen van het Bataviaasch Genootschaap van Kunsten en Wetenschappen 4 (1867).
Overbeck, H. "Malay Animal and Flower Shaers". *JMBRAS* 12 (1934): 108–48.
———. "Shaer Burong Punggok". *JSBRAS* 67 (1914): 193–218.
———. "Shaïr Dandan Setia". *JMBRAS* 10, 1 (1932): 141–58.
Peletz, Michael G. *Reason and Passion: Representations of Gender in a Malay Society*. Berkeley: University of California Press, 1996.
———. "Neither Reasonable nor Responsible: Contrasting Representations of Masculinity in a Malay Society". In *Bewitching Women, Pious Men: Gender and Body Politics in Southeast Asia*, eds. Peletz, Michael G. and Aihwa Ong. Berkeley: University of California Press, 1995, pp. 76–123.
Peskes, Esther. "Wahhabiyya". *Encyclopedia of Islam*, 2nd ed, pp. 39–45.
Poerbatjaraka, R.M.N. *Tjeritera Pandji Dalam Perbandingan*. Jakarta: Gunung Angung, 1968.
Proudfoot, Ian. *Early Malay Printed Books*. Kuala Lumpur: Universiti Malaya, 1993.

———. *The Print Threshold in Malaysia*. Clayton, Vic.: Centre of Southeast Asian Studies, Monash University, 1994.

———. "From Recital to Sight-Reading: the Silencing of Texts in Malaysia". *IMW* 87 (2002): 117–44.

———. "An Expedition into the Politics of Malay Philology". *JMBRAS* 76, 1 (2003): 1–53.

Putten, Jan van der. *His Word is the Truth: Haji Ibrahim's Letters and Other Writings*. Leiden: CNWS, 2001.

———. "Printing in Riau: Two Steps Toward Modernity". *Bijdragen tot de Taal-, Land- en Volkenkunde* 153, 4 (1997): 717–36.

Putter, Ad and Jane Gilbert, eds. *The Spirit of Medieval English Popular Romance*. Harlow: Longman, 2000.

Radway, Janice. *Reading the Romance: Women, Patriarchy and Popular Literature*. London: Verso, 1984.

Rahman, Fazlur. "'Aql". In *Encyclopedia of Islam*, 2nd ed.

Raja Kalsum binti Raja Ali Haji. *Syair Saudagar Bodoh*, Singapore 1297 AH.

Rassers, W.H. *Panji the Culture Hero: A Structural Study of Religion in Java*. The Hague: Nijhoff, 1959.

Reid, Anthony. *Southeast Asia in the Age of Commerce, 1450–1680*, vol. 1. New Haven: Yale University Press, 1988.

Ricklefs, M.C. and Petrus Voorhoeve. *Indonesian Manuscripts in Great Britain*. Oxford: Oxford University Press, 1977.

Ricklefs, M.C. *The Seen and Unseen Worlds in Java, 1726–1749: History, Literature and Islam in the Court of Pakubuwana II*. NSW: ASAA Southeast Asia Publications Series, 1998.

Riddell, Peter. *Islam and the Malay-Indonesian World: Transmission and Response*. Honolulu: University of Hawai'i Press, 2001.

———. *Transferring a Tradition: 'Abd al-Ra'uf al-Singkili's Rendering into Malay of the Jalalayn Commentary*. Berkeley: Monograph Series, Centers for South and Southeast Asian Studies, 1990.

Robson, S.O., ed., trans. *Hikajat Andaken Penurat*. The Hague: Nijhoff, 1969.

———. "The Power of Poetry". *RIMA* 10, 1 (1976): 76–81.

———. "Java in Malay Literature". In *Looking in Odd Mirrors: The Java Sea*, eds. V.J.H. Houben, H.M.J. Maier and W. van der Molen. Leiden: Semaian, 1992, pp. 27–42.

Rodgers, Susan, trans. *Sitti Djaoerah: A Novel of Colonial Indonesia*. Madison: Centre for Southeast Asian Studies, 1997.

———. *Print, Poetics and Politics: A Sumatran Epic in the Colonial Indies and New Order Indonesia*. Leiden: KITLV Press, 2005.

Ronkel, P.S. van. "Catalogus der Maleische Handschriften van het Koninklijk Instituut voor de Taal-, Land- en Volkenkunde van Nederlandsch-Indie".

In *Bijdragen tot de Taal-, Land- en Volkenkunde van Nederlandsch-Indie*. 's-Gravenhage: Martinus Nijhoff, 1908, pp. 181–248.
Roolvink, R. and R.A. Dateok Besar, eds. *Hikajat Abdullah*. Jakarta: Penerbit Djambatan, 1953.
Roorda van Eysinga, P.P. "Abdoel Moeloek, koning van Barbarije". *Tijdschrift voor Nederlandsch Indie* 9, 4 (1847): 285–526.
―――, trans. *Radin Mantri*. Breda: Broese, 1838.
Rose, Mary Beth. *Gender and Heroism in Early Modern English Literature*. Chicago and London: University of Chicago Press, 2002.
Ruthven, K.K. *Feminist Literary Studies: An Introduction*. Cambridge: Cambridge University Press, 1984.
Ruzy Hashim. "Bringing Tun Kudu Out of the Shadows: Interdisciplinary Approaches to Understanding the Female Presence in the *Sejarah Melayu*". In *Other Pasts: Women, Gender and History in Early Modern Southeast Asia*, ed. Barbara Watson Andaya. Hawai'i: Center for Southeast Asian Studies, 2000, pp. 105–24.
―――. *Out of the Shadows: Women in Malay Court Narratives*. Bangi: Penerbit Universiti Kebangsaan Malaysia, 2003.
Salmon, Claudine. *Literature in Malay by the Chinese of Indonesia: A Provisional Annotated Bibliography*. Paris: Editions de la Maison des Sciences de l'Homme, 1981.
Sarra, Edith. *Fictions of Femininity: Literary Inventions of Gender in Japanese Court Women's Memoirs*. Stanford: Stanford University Press, 1999.
Shaiful Bahri bin Mohd. Radzi. "Malay Humorous Tales: Performance, Corpus of Oral Texts and its Study". Unpublished doctoral thesis, University of London, SOAS, 2000.
Sharifah Zinjuaher H.M. Ariffin and Hang Tuah Arshad. *Sejarah Filem Melayu*. Kuala Lumpur: Penerbitan Sri Sharifah, 1980.
Siti Hawa Haji Salleh. *Kesusasteraan Melayu Abad Kesembilan-Belas*. Kuala Lumpur: Dewan Bahasa dan Pustaka, 2002.
Siti Zainon Ismail and Harun Mat Piah. *Lambang Sari: Tari Gamelan Terengganu*. Bangi: UKM, 1986.
Stevenson, Barbara and Cynthia Ho. *Crossing the Bridge: Comparative Essays on Medieval European and Heian Japanese Women Writers*. New York: Palgrave, 2000.
Stivens, Maila. "The Hope of the Nation: State, Religion and Modernity in the Construction of Teenagerhood in Contemporary Malaysia". In *Coming of Age in South and Southeast Asia: Youth, Courtship and Sexuality*, eds. Lenore Manderson and Pranee Liamputtong Rice. London: Curzon, 2002, pp. 188–206.
Sunarti *et al.*, *Sastra Lisan Banjar*. Jakarta: Pusat Pembinaan dan Pengembangan Bahasa, 1978.

Sweeney, Amin. *Authors and Audiences in Traditional Malay Literature*. Berkeley: Center for South and Southeast Asian Studies, 1980.

———. *A Full Hearing: Orality and Literacy in the Malay World*. Berkeley: University of California Press, 1987.

Tan Sooi Beng. *Bangsawan: A Social and Stylistic History of Popular Malay Opera*. Penang: The Asian Centre, 1997.

Teeuw, A. "The Malay Sha'ir: Problems of Origin and Tradition". *BKI* 122 (1966): 429–46.

———. *Shair Ken Tambuhan*. Kuala Lumpur: Oxford University Press, 1966.

Teeuw, A., R. Dumas, Muhammad Haji Salleh, R. Tol and M.J. van Yperen. *A Merry Senhor in the Malay World: Four Texts of the Syair Sinyor Kosta*, 2 vols. Leiden: KITLV Press, 2004.

Thomson, J.T. "A Glance at Rhio". *Journal of the Indian Archipelago and Eastern Asia* 1 (1847): 68–74.

Tjahjono, Gunawan, ed. *Indonesian Heritage: Architecture*. Singapore: Archipelago Press, 1998.

Toer, Pramoedya Ananta, ed. *Hikayat Siti Mariah*. Jakarta: Lentera Dipantara, 2003.

Tucker, Judith E. *Women in Nineteenth-Century Egypt*. Cambridge: Cambridge University Press, 1985.

Ungku Maimunah Mohd. Tahir. *Modern Malay Literature: A Historical Perspective*. Singapore: Institute of Southeast Asian Studies, 1987.

Vaughan, J.D. "Notes on the Malays of Pinang and Province Wellesley". *Journal of the Indian Archipelago and Eastern Asia* 2, 2 (1857): 115–75.

Vickers, Adrian. *Journeys of Desire: A Study of the Balinese Text Malat*. Leiden: KITLV Press, 2005.

Volkstelling 1930. Census of 1930 in the Netherlands Indies, 8 vols. Batavia: Landsdrukkerij, 1933–1935.

Voorhoeve, P. "A Malay Scriptorium". In *Malayan and Indonesian Studies*, eds. John Bastin and R. Roolvink. Oxford: Clarendon, 1964.

Vredenbregt, Jacob. "The Haddj: Some of its Features and Functions in Indonesia". *BKI* 118, 1 (1962): 91–154.

Wahyunah Abd. Gani, ed. *Hikayat Nakhoda Muda*. Kuala Lumpur: Dewan Bahasa dan Pustaka, 2004.

Wall, H. von de. *Maleisch-Nedlerlandsch Woordenboek*. Batavia: Landsdrukkerij, 1877.

Watt, Ian. *The Rise of the Novel: Studies in Defoe, Richardson and Fielding*. London: Chatto & Windus, 1957.

Wieringa, E.P. "A Last Admonition to P.P. Roorda van Eysinga in 1828: Haji Zainal Abidin's *Syair Alif Ba Ta*". *Bijdragen* 154 (1998): 116–28.

———. "Female Emancipation or Literary Convention? The Theme of the Woman who Set Out to Free her Husband in the Malay *Syair Saudagar Bodoh* (ca. 1861) by Raja Kalzum". *RIMA* 31, 2 (1997): 11–27.

———. *Catalogue of Malay and Minangkabau Manuscripts*, vol. 1. Leiden: Legatum Warnerianum, 1998.
Wikan, Unni. *Managing Turbulent Hearts: A Balinese Formula for Living*. Chicago: University of Chicago Press, 1990.
Wilken, G.A. "Het Shamanisme bij de Volken van den Indischen Archipel". *De Verspreide Geschriften*, vol. 3. Semarang/Surabaya/'s-Gravenhage: G.C.T. van Dorp & Co, 1912, pp. 323–97.
Wilkinson, R.J. *Papers on Malay Subjects. Malay Literature, Part I. Romance. History. Poetry*. Kuala Lumpur: F.M.S. Government Press, 1907.
———. *A Malay-English Dictionary (Romanised)*, Parts I and II. Mytilene, Greece: Salavopoulos and Kinderlis, 1932.
Winstedt, R.O., ed. *Hikayat Anggun Che Tunggal*. Singapore: Methodist Publishing House, 1914.
———. *A History of Classical Malay Literature*. Kuala Lumpur: MBRAS, 1996 (1939).
———. *Hikayat Bayan Budiman*. Kuala Lumpur: Oxford University Press, 1966.
Witcombe, Karen. "Images of Women in Classical Malay Fiction". In *Researching the Fragments: Histories of Women in the Asian Context*, eds. Caroline Brewer and Anne-Marie Medcalf. Quezon City: New Day Publishers, 2000, pp. 162–76.
Woolf, Virginia. *A Room of One's Own*. London: Penguin, 2000 (1928).
Za'aba. "Modern Developments". *JMBRAS* 17, 3 (1940).
Zaini-Lajoubert, Monique. *L'Image de la Femme dans les Litteratures Modernes Indonesienne et Malaise*. Paris: Cahier d'Archipel, 1994.
———. "Le Syair Cerita Siti Akbari de Lie Kim Hok (1884), un avatar de Syair Abdul Muluk (1846)". *Archipel* 48 (1994): 103–24.
Zoetmulder, P.J. *Old Javanese-English Dictionary*. 's-Gravenhage: Martinus Nijhoff, 1982.
Zumbroich, Thomas J. "'Teeth as Black as a Bumble Bee's Wings': The Ethnobotany of Teeth Blackening in Southeast Asia". *Ethnobotany Research and Applications* 7 (2009): 381–98.

Websites

http://www.anu.edu.au/asianstudies/ahcen/proudfoot/mmp/mmp.html
http://www.bharian.com.my
http://www.pmo.gov.my
http://www.sabda.org/sejarah/artikel/dicari_penerjemah_alkitab.htm
http://www.utusan.com.my

Index

'Abd al-Samad al-Palimbani, 119, 44
Abdul Mutalib Abdul Ghani, 30, 64
Abdul Rahman al-Ahmadi, 11
Abdul Rauf al-Singkili, 43
Abdullah bin Abdul Qadir Munsyi, 35, 49, 60, 62, 72
Abu Hassan Sham, 2, 30, 40
Aceh, 18, 25–6, 42–3, 67
Adat Aceh, 18
adat, 16
    bersuami, 146, 153
    laki-laki, 134, 159
Adibah Amin, 176, 178
akal, 40, 127, 138–9, 142–3, 147–8, 151–69, 173,
    see also reason
Akhbar al-Akhirat fi Ahwal al-Qiyama, 43
al-Azhar, 19
al-Ghazali, 55, 59, 119
Andaya, Barbara Watson, 3, 24–5, 30, 141
Anggun Che Tunggal, 81–2
Angkatan Sasterawan '50, 175
anonymity, 31, 38
Arabian Nights, 40, 50–1, 168

audiences, 2–3, 6, 9, 12, 50, 70, 75, 84, 102–9, 151, 166, 175–6
    female, 2, 9, 24, 47, 178
authorship, 31, 37–9, 170

Bakhtin, Mikhail, 163, 168–9, 178
bakti
    of men, 96
    of wives, 57, 109–10, 121, 128, 133–7, 148–9, 153, 160, 169, 172
Bali, 11, 47, 71
    literature of, 6, 93, 131
bangsawan theatre, 2, 175–6
Banjar, 5, 34, 43, 68
Baron, Beth, 34
Batavia, 29–30, 39, 49, 60, 171
Batavia Society, *see* Bataviaasch Genootschaap
Bataviaasch Genootschaap, 38
battle
    against in?del enemies, 54, 77, 109, 112, 116
    as gendered activity, 121–6, 172
    as sexual metaphor, 130–8, *see also* wedding night
    between hero and heroine, 54, 76
    between princesses, 52–3, 102

Bayan al-Shirk, 44, 74
beauty, 75, 102–7, 172
   of the hero, 54, 94, 1o2, 124, 133, 157
   of the heroine, 15, 32, 51, 54, 78, 102–3, 127–8, 144, 155
   of the text, 7–10, 105–7
Begbie, Peter, 24–5
bela, 120–1, 129–30, 131
Bengkalis, 68
Bengkulu, 171
biduan, 4, 9, 68
Bintan, 14
birth, 30, 68, 111–2, 115–6, 122
bodoh, 151–2, 157, 162
Braginsky, Vladimir, 9–10, 40, 69, 85, 107, 163
Brownstein, Rachel, 87
buang diri, 53, 121
budi, 82–3, 151, 159
Bugis-Malay
   alliance, 15–6
   aristocracy, 8, 14
Bukhari al-Jauhari, 67, 151

catharsis, 28, 48–50, 72–3, 86, 172
censuses, 33–4
Chaucer, 61
Chinese
   literature, 15, 31, 50, 127
   opera (*wayang Cina*), 15
   people, 10, 14–5, 22, 23
Christianity, 34
Christians, 17, 19, 77, 129, *see also* Serani
Cik Soda, 44
Cik Teh Afiah, 57
cinta berahi, 93, 96, 125
class divisions, 23, 73, 92, 93, 163, 174
   literacy and, 33
   literary taste and, 3
   women's literary production and, 30

co-wives, 53, 65–7, 74, 134, 137–8, 161
conversion to Islam, 15, 77, 129
Creese, Helen, 3, 11–2, 47, 101, 107–8, 130
cultural formula, 3–4

Daeng Wuh, 3, 30–1, 38, 82, 84
dagang persona, 8, 37, 70, 82–7, 93, 101, 120, 137, 150
dalam, 24, 98, 137, 172
De Bruyn Kops, G.F., 14
de-eroticisation, 27, 55, 96, 101, 107–8, 133, 172
Den Hamer, C., 5, 43
dendam, 56–7, 93, 96, 125, *see also nafsu* and *cinta berahi*
desire
   and literature, 12, 49, 61, 65, 69
   feminine, 61–3, 65, 88, 132
   masculine, 52, 57, 65, 93, 100
Dewan Bahasa dan Pustaka, 44–5, 175, 179
didactic
   genre, 58
   texts 2, 47, 49, 57–9, 153, 171–2, *see also* individual titles
didacticism 2, 8–9, 30, 39, 49, 60, 108, 151, 162–3, 173, 178
   and humour, 162–9
disguise,
   cross-dressing or metamorphosis, 50,
   heroine's assumption of, 103–4, 121–2
Doa Kanzil 'Arasy, 44, 74
Dutch Resident, 14, 16
   Angelbeek, 20
   Elout, 22
   Netscher, 14, 19
   Walbeehm, 22, 42

education,
  colonial, 35–6, 174
  female, 31–7
  religious, 34–6
Egypt, 21, 34
Encik Ismail bin Datuk Kerkun, 41
Encik Jamilah, 30, 31, 38
Encik Kamariah, 20, 24, 26, 30–1, 38, 41, 170
Encik Seni, 44
Encik Tipah, 30–1, 38, 44
Encik Wuk, 46
Encik Zainab binti al-Marhum Tuan Haji Abdul Hamid, 44
Engku Puteri (Raja Hamidah binti Raja Haji), 24–5, 27, 41–3, 64, 171
eroticism, 57, 70, 84, 87, 96, 101, 107–8
  and gender ambiguity, 50, 128, 104, 128
  and literature, 4, 29, 36, 70, 104
  of *syair* heroine, 63, 84, 87
exemplar, romance heroine as, 1, 49, 55, 65–6, 84, 87–8, 90, 92, 141, 143, 164

faedah, 63, 162, 174
fantasy (wish fulfilment), 12, 65, 67, 101
fatwa, 18, 21
film, 2, 102, 176
folk
  culture, 3, 53, 163, 169
  tales, 15, 50, 81, 150, 163
  theatre, 9
Frye, Northrop, 2
functional spheres, 9, 74

gender
  images, 4, 12, 30, 169
  stereotypes, 9, 10, 32, 61, 100, 125

genre, 10, 11, 15, 31, 33, 64, 138, 170, 174–5
Gullick, J.M., 23, 36
Gurindam Dua Belas, 57, 173, 175
guritan, 5

Haji Abdul Wahab, 42
Haji Ibrahim, 39
hajj pilgrimage, 18, 20, 41
Hamzah Fansuri, 4
Harun Mat Piah, 51–2, 54
heritage, literary, 7, 174–9
heroics, gendered, 110, 117–30
heroism, 135, 141
Hicks, Sarah, 176
hikayat, 3, 12, 21, 29, 38, 60, *see also* under individual titles
  as men's reading, 47
  as women's reading, 31, 36, 43, 55–7, 62
  dangers of, *see* recitation
  popularity of, 36, 56, 67
Hikayat Anak Pengajian, 9, 60, 162
Hikayat Bayan Budiman, 32
Hikayat Cekel Waneng Pati, 72, 129
Hikayat Darma Ta'siah, 44, 58, 151
Hikayat Fatimah Bersuami, 44, 58, 151
Hikayat Ghulam, 42
Hikayat Hang Tuah, 4, 63, 96, 163
Hikayat Inderaputra, 32
Hikayat Isma Yatim, 32, 45
Hikayat Koris Mengindera, 44, 56–7, 162, *see also Surat Kurais Raja Alam*
Hikayat Musang Berjanggut, 168
Hikayat Nabi Muhammad Mengajar Anaknya, 163, 168
Hikayat Nakhoda Muda, 150
Hikayat Panji Kuda Semirang, 52, 134
Hikayat Panji Semirang, 52–5, 100, 128
Hikayat Putra Jaya Pati, 32
Hikayat Raja Khandak, 44

Hikayat Sultan Abdul Muluk, 39
Hikayat Sultan Bustaman, 36
Hikayat Sultan Ibrahim ibn Ahdam,
 58
Hikayat Sultan Taburat, 62
Hikayat Syah Firman, 44
Hikayat Syah Kobat, 118, 132
Hikayat Syamsul Anwar, 44–5
Hoëvell, W.R. van, 5
Hollander, J.J. de, 5
homoeroticism, 98–100
Hooker, Virginia Matheson, *see*
 Matheson
Hooykaas, C., 4
Husain bin Ismail, 149

identification, with romance heroine,
 63–5, 75, 86–7
Ihya 'Ulum al-Din, *see* al-Ghazali
ilmu, 59, 76, 126, 151
 akhirat, 56–7
 bakti, 153
 hikmat (or *guna* or *pesona*), 152–3,
 159, 161
 perempuan, 146, 152, 153
imaginary, the, 11, 74
inang, 30, *see also* Encik Kamariah
 in *Syair Siti Dhawiyyah*, 146
 in *Syair Siti Zubaidah*, 115
 in *Syair Siti Zuhrah*, 66, 76–7,
 83–4, 88, 92–3, 106
Inayat Shah, 43
Ishak Haji Mohamad, 174
Islam and literacy, 34
Islamic revivalism, 18, 31, *see also*
 syariah-mindedness
Islamisation of *syair*, 6, 53–5, 121,
 129, 134
isteri jayeng, 109

Jackson, Leonard, 49, 73
Japan, 12, 30, 49, 50, 63

Java, *see also* *kakawin*
Jawi, 35–6, 52, 171
Jelani Harun, 30
Johor, 16, 25, 39, 41, 45, 80

Kahle, Louisa Wilhemina, 38
kakawin, 4, 47, 93, 101, 107–8
Kapitan Cina, 15
Kedah, 43, 45, 171
Kelantan, 26, 43
keramat, 104, 164–5
Keringkasan Sejarah Melayu, 25
Kifayat al-Muhtajin, 43
Kisah Engku Puteri, 41–2
kitab, 38, 59–60, *see also* individual
 titles
Kitab Seribu Masa'il, 44
Kitab Tawhid, 44, 74
Klinkert, H.C., 2, 5, 22, 31, 37–9,
 43–4, 46, 50, 53, 56, 82–4, 110,
 149–50, 170
Koster, Gijs, 6–8, 54
Kratz, Ulrich, 31–2
Kumar, Ann, 50

Laderman, Carol, 71–2, 74
Lampung, 33
Leiden, 6, 21, 38, 42
lending library, 31–2
letters, 19, 30, 33, 39, 171
Lingga, 15, 17, 19–20, 22–3, 25–7,
 38, 41–3, 51, 56, 170, *see also*
 Sultan Mahmud
linguistic purity, 22
literacy, 3, 8, 36
 female, 5, 31–7, 47, 171, *see also*
 education
 modernity, 31, 33
literary
 formulae, 64, 84–5
 tropes, 6, 26, 33, 51, 60, 103, 110,
 130, 148, 172

lithograph, 146, 149, 151, 167
lithographic printing, 2–3, 170
Lombok, 68
Low, James, 12

main puteri, 72–4
Malacca, 6, 15, 16, 22, 24, 35, 63, 96
malu, 42, 69, 88–90, 98, 124, 131, 137, 140, 153
   as gender marker, 89, 166–7
   loss of, 88
manuscript
   circulation, 3, 31, 43–7, 149
   collections, 21–2, 42, 43–4, 50
   copying, 17, 37, 45, 85
   copyists, 28, 37–43, 44, 83–5, 108, 172
   tradition, 8, 10, 37–8, 45
Mariam binti Muhammad Amin, 44
marriage, 12, 67, 68, 109, 148, 160, see also wedding, wifehood and polygamy
   as slavery, 59
   as source of social status, 24
   consummation of, 146, 156
   forced, 123
   of syair heroine, 64–6, 77–6, 80–1, 101, 114, 141, 147
   resistance of syair hero to, 132, 166
   resistance of syair heroine to, 76, 94, 146
   status of wife within, 135, 163, 168
Matheson, Virginia, 16–7, 21–2, 25, 48–9, 69, 179
Maxwell, W.E., 68
McDonald, Nicola, 11
Mecca, 14, 18, 20–1, 35, 41
Middle East, 18, 19, 21
   as fictional setting, 27–8, 53, 55, 142–3, 160
   Islam in, 14

Miller, Nancy, 37
Millie, Julian, 6, 8–9
Minangkabau, 20, 53, 69
Mir'at al-Tullab, 43
modernist, 17
modernity, 30–1, 33, 45, 171, 175–9
Modleski, Tanya, 12–3, 64–6, 73
Mohamad Said, Tan Sri Datuk Dr., 35–6
moral panics, 27
motherhood, 122, see also pregnancy, birth
Muhammad Bakir, 32, 61–2, 67, 70,
Muhammad Haji Salleh, 6, 69
Muhammad Said bin Haji Muhammad Saman, 57
Muslim
   characters in syair, 64, 77, 80–1, 89, 109, 124, 129
   hero, 16,
   historiography, 19,
   literary characteristics, 6, 8
   reform movements, 18, 25, 55, 72
   wives, 59, 123

nafsu, 40, 96, 125, 133, 142, 152, 157, 161–2, 173
Nagata, Judith, 179
Naqshbandiyya Sufi order, 19
Negeri Sembilan, 35, 161
Newbold, Thomas, 12
novel, 63, 73, 175, see also romance novel
   English, 4, 10–1, 87–8
   Malay and Indonesian, 174, 176–9
   pornographic, 174
Nyonya Halimah, 44
Nyonya Sawang, 44
Nyonya Tasnim, 44

oral literature, 3, 5, 8–9, 47, 164
Overbeck, H., 69

Paderi uprising, 20
pahala, 55, 153
palace women, 3, 23, 41, 43, 52, 63,
  see also inang
Palembang, 31–2
Panji
  "Islamised," 54–5
  prince, 50, 52, 56, 95, 103
  princess, 54–5, 143
  tales, 28, 32, 50–4, 81, 93, 158, see
    also under individual titles
pantun, 5, 20, 33, 40, 79, 104–8, 142,
  172, 174
patriarchal oppression, 13, 23, 31, 67
Peletz, Michael, 173
Penang, 35, 179
Penyengat, 2, 8, 55
  and Islamic revival, 14, 18–9, 31,
    40, 68, 95, 108
  as literary centre, 21–2
  description of, 14–9
  women in, 23, 24, 27, 56
  women writers of, 30–1, 34, 38,
    40–1, 43–6, 82, 110, 170
Perak, 44, 56, 68, 171
philological collecting, 5, 18, 21–2,
  42–3, see also under individual
  names
philology, 8,
pleasures of the text, 2, 33, 48–9, 57,
  63–7, 73, 93, 150, 174–5
Poerbatjaraka, R.M.N., 51
poetics, 9, 11, 107
poetry, polemics against, 67–8
polygamy, 57, 59, 134, 138, 141, 161,
  see also marriage *and* co-wives
popular culture, 12, 175, 178
popular literature, 3, 4, 11, 12, 49–50,
  171–2, 177–8
pregnancy, 68, 11–2, 116, 122
Proudfoot, Ian, 40, 47, 149, 179
psychoanalytic theories, 12, 73, 84

puteri jayeng, 109, 136, 141
Putten, Jan van der, 19

Qur'an, 16, 119, see also recitation

Radway, Janice, 12–3, 67
Raja Ahmad, 19
Raja Aisyah Sulaiman, 17, 44–5
Raja Ali bin Raja Ja'afar, Yamtuan
  Muda of Penyengat, 19, 20–1,
  26–7, 40
Raja Ali Haji, 9–12, 14, 16, 18–20,
  175, see also under titles of his
  texts
  as author of syair, 39–40, 110, 168,
    178
  female relatives of, 31, 39, 40,
    44, 58, 110, see also under
    individual names
  views on syair and hikayat, 40, 49,
    55–60, 62, 74
  views on women, 26–7, 35, 64,
    171
Raja Haji, Yamtuan Muda of
  Penyengat, 16, 19, 24
Raja Ja'afar, Yamtuan Muda of
  Penyengat, 24
Raja Kalsum, 3, 30–1, 38–9, 149–50
Raja Muhammad Yusuf, Yamtuan
  Muda of Penyengat, 25
Raja Safiah, 30–1, 38
Raja Salihah, 12, 30–1, 39, 110
Ratu Pakubuwana, 42
rawan, 75, 84, 172
  and beauty, 102–8
  and catharsis, 86
  of syair composer, 69, 85–7
  of syair hero, 70, 93–102, 132
  of syair heroine, 87–93
  reason and passion, dichotomy, 28,
    74, 142, 173, see also akal and
    nafsu

recitation
  benefits of, 72–4
  dangers of, 60–1, 70, 73, 176
  hikayat or *syair*, 1–2, 5, 9–10, 21, 29, 47, 50, 68–9, 75, 17
  Qur'an, 32–5, 55, 60, 70, 88, 115, 116
  styles (*lagham*), 21, 62
recognition scene, 1–2, 51, 65, 104, 114, 116–7, 125, 138–41
Reid, Anthony, 33–4, 171
religious texts, 2, 32, 37, 44, 58, 165, *see also kitab and individual titles*
repetition, 6, 66
repression of negative emotions, 71–3, 75, 93, 99, 108, 172
rescue of male relative, 1–2, 53, 60, 64, 111, 114–6, 120, 123–4, 139–40, 143, 148, 155, 170–3
Riau
  aristocracy, 17, 20, 44–5, 48
  as home of all Malay female authors, 31, 40
  as home of Malay language, 22, 38
  history, 16–9, 24–5, 170
  manuscripts, 21–2, 50, 82, 149
Riddell, Peter, 18–9
Risalat Adab Murid Akan Syeikh, 43
ritual, 40, 68–9, 73
Robson, S.O., 68
romance
  *and r*eligion, 37, 44, 57
  as feminine genre, 36–7, 60–1, 67
  European courtly, 10–1, 87–8
  genre, 28, 58–9, 74
  novel in English, 12–3, 64–7
  novel in Malay, 177
  popular, 2, 11, 49–50, 171–2
romantic adventure *syair* genre, 39, 48–52, 58, 171–2
Romanticism, 40
Ronkel, P.S. van, 38

Roorda van Eysinga, P.P., 5, 22, 39, 149
royal regalia, 25, 41–2
Rusydiah Club, 17

sabil, 129–30
Safirin bin Usman Fadli, 9, 29–30, 32, 49, 60–2, 70, 72, 150–1, 161–2, 174
sakti, 109, 126
Sarra, Edith, 12
sastera wangi, 178
Sejarah Melayu, 4–5, 63, 88, 176
Serani, 77
sexual
  attractiveness, *see* eroticism
  relations, 20, 57–8, 98, 100–1, 133–4, 156, 159, 169, 178 and violence, 4, 100–1
Sharh Hadith Arba'in, 43
Sharifah Mastura binti Syed Shahabudin, 44
Siak 38, 43, 110, 171
Siak *selir*, 44
sibling
  relationship, 65, 97
  subplot, 50–2
Singapore, 16–8, 25, 45, 149, 170, 175–6
Siti Hawa Haji Salleh, 43
Siyar al-Salikin, 119
structuralism, 7
Sufism, 4, 19, 21, 68
Sulawesi, 33, 41
Sultan Mahmud of Lingga,
Sumatra, 5, 8, 20, 22, 33, 43, 81
  oral performance genres, 5
Surat Kurais Raja Alam, 39
Sweeney, Amin, 8
syair
  as popular literature, 2, 28, 38, 149–50, 174

genre, 4, 6, 9, 10, 41
verse form, 2
Syair Bidasari, 4–6, 8, 106
Syair Buah-Buahan, 4, 32, 61–2, 67, 69–70, 106
Syair Burung or *Syair Unggas*, 59
Syair Dewa Syah Syarif, 44
Syair Ikan Terubuk, 4, 68
Syair Inggeris Menyerang Kota, 4
Syair Juragan Budiman, see Syair Sultan Yahya
Syair Kahar Masyhur, 5, 66
Syair Kahwin Tan Tik Cu, 15
Syair Kampung Gelam Terbakar, 4
Syair Ken Tambuhan, 5–6, 40, 66, 101
Syair Kumbang Mengindera, 4, 31, 38
Syair Madhi, 44
Syair Perang Johor, 41
Syair Raja Muda Perlis, 44
Syair Raja Nur Peri, 66
Syair Saudagar Bodoh, summary, 143–6
Syair Selindung Delima, 4, 6, 66, 176
Syair Sinyor Kosta, 4, 6, 88
Syair Siti Dhawiyyah, 146–8
Syair Siti Sianah, 26, 35, 40, 55–60, 160–2, 168
Syair Siti Zubaidah, summary, 115–7
Syair Siti Zuhrah, summary, 76–7
Syair Sultan Abdul Muluk, summary, 111–4
Syair Sultan Mahmud, 4, 16, 20, 23, 26, 31, 38, 41
Syair Sultan Mansur Syah Gempita, 5, see also *Syair Sultan Mansur*
Syair Sultan Mansur, 44, 46, 151
Syair Sultan Marit, 31, 38, 44, 85
Syair Sultan Yahya, summary, 77–81
Syair Suluh Pegawai, 39–40, 168
Syair Tengku Selangor, 41

Syair Unggas, see Syair Burung
Syair Yatim Nestapa, 5, 31, 38, 66
syariah-mindedness, 17, 18, 21, 27, 36, 40, 56, 68, 108, 175
Syarifah Hanum binti Syed Hamzah, 44
Syeikh Ahmad Dahlan, 21

Taj al-'Alam of Aceh, 42
Taj al-Salatin, see Bukhari al-Jauhari
Tale of Genji, The, 30, 50, 61, 63
Tanjung Pinang, 14–6, 22
Tarikah 'Alawiyyah, 44
tawakal, 119–21, 138, 172
teater dul Muluk, 8
Teeuw, A., 6, 8
Tengku Abdul Rahman, 24
Tengku Ampuan Mariam, 45, 174
Tengku Bilik binti Raja Abdullah, 110
Tengku Bun, 48
Tengku Fatimah, 25,
Tengku Fatimah Puteri al-Marhum Sultan Abu Bakar, 45
Tengku Husain, 25
Tengku Kalthum binti Sultan Abdul Hamid, 44
Tengku Khalid Hitam, 17
Tengku Sepiah, 48–9
Tengku Zamzam, 44
Terengganu, 16, 43, 45, 71–2, 171, 174
theatre, see *bangsawan* and Chinese opera
Thomson, J.T., 14–5, 23–4
Tibyan fi Ma'rifat al-Adyan, 43
Tijdschrift voor Neerlands Indië, 39
Timmerman Thyssen, 25
trade, 16, 23, 33, 111, 113, 147, 157–8
Tuan Bilal Abu, 46, 149, 150
Tucker, Judith E., 34

Tuhfat al-Nafis, 16–20, 24–5, 41–2, 64

Ungku Maimunah Mohd Tahir, 174

veiling of women, 26–7, 180
Vickers, Adrian, 6, 101, 130
Von de Wall, Hermann, 19–20, 22, 39, 43, 50, 56, 62, 170

Wahhabi movement, 20–1
war, *see* battle
wayang Cina, *see* Chinese opera
wedding
    celebration, 14–5, 23–4, 51, 68
    in *syair*, 80, 111, 115, 147
    night in *syair*, 90, 93, 101, 148, 153
Western influence, 14, 16–7, 176
wifehood, 66, 122, 161
Wikkan, Uni, 71
Wilkinson, R.J., 69
Winstedt, R.O., 6
Witcombe, Karen, 11
wives, women as, 58, 122, *see also* wifehood

women
    manuscript lenders, 44–7
    manuscript owners, 43–6
    manuscript patrons, 41–3,
    readers, 4, 11, 12, 32, 36, 37, 56–9, 61–7, 171, 180, *see also* audiences, female
    rulers, 26, 131, *see also* Aceh, Kelantan
    syair composers, 23, 24, 37–40, 43, 44–5, 149, 170–1
warriors in literature, 126–7
writers, modern Malay and Indonesian, 175, 177–8
writers or authors, 22, 30–1,
Woolf, Virginia, 31

Yamtuan Muda
    of Penyengat, 2, 14, 16, 22, 25, 41, 45 *see also* individual names
    of Siak, 44, 110
Za'aba, 174
Zaini-Lajoubert, Monique, 175